Word for Windows 2
The Visual Learning Guide

Available Now!

Windows 3.1: The Visual Learning Guide
Excel 4 for Windows: The Visual Learning Guide
Word for Windows 2: The Visual Learning Guide

How to Order:

Quantity discounts are available from the publisher, Prima Publishing, P.O. Box 1260BK, Rocklin, CA 95677; telephone (916) 786-0426. On your letterhead include information concerning the intended use of the books and the number of books you wish to purchase.

Word for Windows 2
The Visual Learning Guide

David C. Gardner, Ph.D.

Grace Joely Beatty, Ph.D.

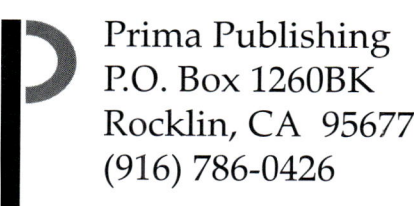

Prima Publishing
P.O. Box 1260BK
Rocklin, CA 95677
(916) 786-0426

Copyright © 1993 by The Gardner Beatty Group

All rights reserved. No part of this book may be reproduced or transmitted in any form or by any means, electronic or mechanical, including photocopying, recording, or by any information storage or retrieval system without written permission from Prima Publishing, except for the inclusion of quotations in a review.

Managing Editor: Roger Stewart
Project Manager: Laurie Stewart
Production: Marian Hartsough Associates
Interior Design: Grace Joely Beatty, S. Linda Beatty, David C. Gardner, Laurie Stewart, and Kim Bartusch
Technical Editing: Harriet Serenkin
Copyediting: Chet Bell
Cover Design: Kirschner-Caroff Design
Color Separations: Ocean Quigley
Index: Katherine Stimson

Prima Publishing
Rocklin, CA 95677-1260

Every effort has been made to supply complete and accurate information. However, neither the publisher nor the authors assume any responsibility for its use, nor for any infringements of patents or other rights of third parties that would result.

> **Library of Congress Cataloging-in-Publication Data**
>
> Gardner, David C.
>   Word for Windows 2 : the visual learning guide / David C. Gardner and Grace Joely Beatty
>   p.   cm.
>   Includes index.
>   ISBN 1-55958-240-5 : $19.95
>   1. Microsoft Word for Windows   2. Word processing—Computer programs.
>   I. Beatty, Grace Joely   II. Title.
> Z52.5.M523B44   1992
> 652.5'5369—dc20   9143913
>   CIP

93 94 95 96 RRD 10 9 8 7 6 5 4 3 2

Printed in the United States of America

Acknowledgments

We are deeply indebted to reviewers around the country who gave generously of their time to test every step in the manuscript. Joseph and Shirley Beatty, David Coburn, Tom and Maura Healy, Jeannie Jones, Bill Nipper, and David Sauer cannot be thanked enough!

Lisa Anderson and Carolyn Holder are our production team, reviewers, proofreaders, screen capturers, and friends. They and Margaret Short keep us functioning.

We are personally and professionally delighted to work with everyone at Prima Publishing especially Roger Stewart, our managing editor, and Laurie Stewart, our project manager.

Harriet Serenkin, our technical editor, Chet Bell, our copy editor, Ocean Quigley, our color separator, and Marian Hartsough, our production manager, contribute immensely to the final product.

Bill Gladstone and Matt Wagner of Waterside Productions created the idea for this series. Their faith in us has never wavered.

Joseph and Shirley Beatty made this series possible. We can never repay them.

Asher Shapiro has always been there when we needed him.

Paula Gardner Capaldo and David Capaldo have been terrific. Thanks, Joshua and Jessica, for being such wonderful kids! Our project humorist, Mike Bumgardner, always came through when we needed a boost!

We could not have met the deadlines without the technical support of Ray Holder our electrical genius, Fred Harper of Dymerc International, and Microsoft's outstanding technical support staff. Thank you all!

Contents at a Glance

	Introduction	xv
Part I	**Entering and Editing Text**	**1**
Chapter 1	Changing Margins and Fonts and Entering Text	3
Chapter 2	Naming and Saving a Document	25
Chapter 3	Closing a File and Opening a Saved File	39
Chapter 4	Using the Grammar Checker, Spelling Checker, and Thesaurus	45
Chapter 5	Editing a Document	55
Chapter 6	Printing a File	77
Part II	**Formatting a Document**	**81**
Chapter 7	Customizing Text	83
Chapter 8	Setting and Applying Tabs	95
Chapter 9	Separating a Document into Sections, and Adding a Header and Footer	111
Chapter 10	Changing the View	119
Part III	**Mailing Lists and Envelopes**	**129**
Chapter 11	Printing and Envelope	131
Chapter 12	Creating a Mailing List	149
Chapter 13	Editing a Mailing List and Printing a Form Letter	159
Chapter 14	Printing Envelopes for a Mailing List	183
Chapter 15	Converting a Mailing List Created in Another Program	187
Part IV	**Additional Topics**	**197**
Chapter 16	Searching for a File	199
Chapter 17	Creating a Glossary	207
Chapter 18	Introducing Styles	215
Part V	**Appendix**	**229**
Appendix	Installing Word for Windows 2	231
Index		**243**

CONTENTS

Introduction xv

Part I: Entering and Editing Text 1

Chapter 1: Changing Margins and Fonts and Entering Text 3
Opening Word for Windows for the First Time 3
Displaying the Toolbar, Ribbon, and Ruler 6
Setting Margins 7
Changing the Font and the Font Size 8
    Changing the Font 8
    Changing Font Size 10
Entering Text 11
    Creating the Letterhead 11
    Displaying Paragraph, Space, and Tab Symbols 13
    Entering the Date, Address, and Salutation 14
    Entering the Body of the Letter 15
Inserting a Symbol and Finishing the Letter 18

Chapter 2: Naming and Saving a Document 25
Creating a Working Directory 25
    Opening File Manager 25
Changing the View of File Manager 27
    Maximizing File Manager 27
    Creating a Directory 28
    Checking the New Directory and Closing File Manager 30
    Changing the Working Directory Statement in Windows 30
    Returning to Word 32

Naming and Saving a File 33
    Filling in the Summary Info 35
Saving Automatically 37

Chapter 3: Closing a File and Opening a Saved File.............................39

Saving and Closing a File 39
    Saving a File 39
    Closing a File 40
Closing Word for Windows 40
Booting Up Word 41
Opening a Saved File 41
    Method #1 41
    Method #2 42

Chapter 4: Using the Grammar Checker, Spelling Checker, and Thesaurus..45

Using the Grammar Checker and Spelling Checker 45
    Adding a Word to the Dictionary..46
    Ignoring a Suggested Change 46
    Making a Correction in the Letter 47
    Continuing the Grammar and Spelling Check......................................48
Using the Thesaurus 51
    Using the Find Command 51
    Replacing a Word with the Thesaurus 52

Chapter 5: Editing a Document 55

Adding Letters and Words 55
Deleting and Replacing Words and Combining Paragraphs 57
    Deleting Words 57
    Undoing an Edit 58

  Combining Paragraphs 59
  Inserting a Soft Return 60
  Using the Replace Command 62
 Drag and Drop Moving 63
 Inserting a Page Break 65
  Changing the Position of a Page Break 67
 Copying and Pasting Text 68
  Copying and Pasting Text with the Edit Menu 68
  Using the Copy Tool 72
  Using the Go To Command 73
  Using the Paste Tool 74
 Typing Over Highlighted Text and Saving the File 75

Chapter 6: Printing a File 77
 Printing with the Print Tool 77
 Printing from the Menu Bar 78
  Printing Selected Pages 79
  Printing the Entire Document 80

Part II: Formatting a Document 81

Chapter 7: Customizing Text 83
 Changing Type Size 83
 Making Text Bold 84
 Making Text Italic 85
 Centering Text 86
 "Reading" the Ribbon 88
 Adding a Border and Shading 89
  Adding a Border 89

Shading the Boxed Text 91

Creating a Bulleted List...93

Chapter 8: Setting and Applying Tabs 95

Setting a Left-Aligned Tab with the Ruler 95

Inserting a Leader with a Right-Aligned Tab 97

Setting a Left-Aligned Tab from the Menu Bar 99

Clearing a Tab..102

Opening a New Document...104

Setting a Right-Aligned Tab with the Mouse 104

Setting a Center-Aligned Tab with the Mouse 105

Setting a Decimal tab with the Mouse 106

Setting a Decimal Tab from the Menu Bar 107

Applying Tabs 108

Closing the Document Without Saving 110

Chapter 9: Separating a Document into Sections and Adding a Header and Footer 111

Separating a Document into Two Sections 111

Deleting the Page Break...114

Creating a Header 114

Creating a Footer...116

Chapter 10: Changing the View..119

Page Layout View 119

Scrolling Through Pages in Page Layout View 120

Print Preview 121

Scrolling Through Pages in Print Preview 122

Displaying Margins in Print Preview 122

Printing in Print Preview...123

Draft View...124
    Returning to Normal View from the Menu Bar 125
Zoom View...126
    Magnifying the View (Zooming In)...126
    Reducing the View (Zooming Out)..127
    Returning to Normal View Using the Zoom 100 Percent Tool 128

Part III: Mailing Lists and Envelopes............................129

Chapter 11: Printing an Envelope 131
Using the Envelope Tool..131
    Printing with a LaserJet Series II or III Printer 132
    Printing with a Dot-Matrix Printer 133
Printing the Return Address 135
    Omitting and Restoring the Standard (Default) Return Address 137
Customizing the Return Address...137
    Attaching the Envelope to the Letter..137
    Opening the Style Dialog Box..138
    Changing the Font and Point Size...139
    Making the First Line of the Address Bold..142
Printing the Letter and the Attached Envelope..143
Printing the Attached Envelope Without the Letter 145
Printing the Letter Without the Attached Envelope 145
Closing Without Saving the Attached Envelope..146

Chapter 12: Creating a Mailing List..149
Setting Up a Data Entry Table 149
    Opening a New Document File...149
    Opening the Print Merge Setup Dialog Box..150

    Entering the Field Names for the Data Entry Table 151

    Entering Names and Addresses into the Data Entry Table 155

    Saving the Mailing List 158

Chapter 13: Editing a Mailing List and Printing a Form Letter 159

    Adding Fields to a Mailing List 159

        Attaching a Mailing List to a Letter 159

        Adding Fields to the Attached Mailing List 161

        Entering More Data in a Mailing List Data File 165

    Setting Up a Form Letter 169

        Attaching a Mailing List to a Letter 169

        Inserting Merge Fields into a Form Letter 171

        Inserting Personalized Information into the Body of the Letter 175

        Inserting Personalized Information into the Header 177

    Printing the Form Letter 178

    Saving Your Form Letter 180

Chapter 14: Printing Envelopes for a Mailing List 183

    Addressing the Envelope 183

    Attaching the Envelope to the Form Letter 184

    Merge Printing the Envelopes 185

    To Save or Not to Save 186

        Saving the Attached Envelope 186

        Exiting Without Saving the Attached Envelope 186

Chapter 15: Converting a Mailing List Created in Another Program 187

    Converting a DOS-Based Mailing List 187

        Saving the Converted File 189

    Attaching the Converted Mailing List to a Form Letter 190

    Adding a Header Record to a Converted Mailing List 193

    Checking the Header Record 194

Exiting Word 195

Part IV: Additional Topics 197

Chapter 16: Searching for a File 199

Opening the Find File Dialog Box 199

Finding a File in Your Current Directory 200

Searching for a File in a Different Directory 201

    Searching with a Keyword 202

Exiting Word 206

Chapter 17: Creating a Glossary 207

Creating a Glossary Item 207

Inserting a Glossary Item in a New File 209

Saving a Glossary Item and Exiting Word 211

Chapter 18: Introducing Styles 215

Creating Two New Styles 215

    Opening a New Document 215

    Setting Up a New Style for a Heading in the Document 216

    Adding the New Style to the Style List 217

    Setting Up a New Style for the Body Text 219

    Viewing the Style List 222

Applying the New Styles to Different Text 223

Permanently Saving the New Styles 224

Copying the New Styles to Another Document 225

    Viewing the Style List 227

Exiting Word 227

Part V: Appendix 229

Appendix: Installing Word for Windows 2 231
Backing Up Your Word Disks 231
Installing Word for Windows 2..232
Moving Word to Your Customized Group Window 240
    Deleting the Word Group Icon 241

Index 243

INTRODUCTION

Customize Your Learning

Prima *Visual Learning Guides* are not like any other computer books you have ever seen. They are based on our years in the classroom, our corporate consulting, and our research at Boston University on the best ways to teach technical information to nontechnical learners. Most important, this series is based on the feedback of a panel of reviewers from across the country who range in computer knowledge from "panicked at the thought" to sophisticated.

This is not an everything-you've-ever-wanted-to-know-about-Word-but-didn't-know-enough-to-ask book. It is designed to give you the information you need to perform basic (and some not-so-basic) functions with confidence and skill. It is a book that our reviewers claim makes it "really easy" for anyone to learn Word quickly.

Each chapter is illustrated with full-color screens to guide you through every task. The combination of screens, step-by-step instructions, and pointers makes it impossible for you to get lost or confused as you follow along on your own computer. You can either work through from beginning to end or skip around to master the skills you need. If you have a specific goal you want to accomplish now, choose it from the following section.

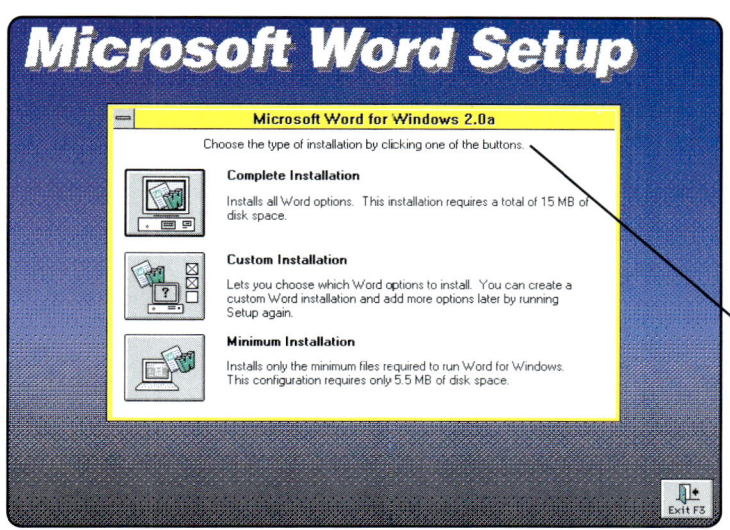

SELECTING YOUR GOALS

From the choices below, select your personal goals so you can start using Word immediately.

❖ I would like help installing Word for Windows 2.

Go to the Appendix, "Installing Word for Windows 2."

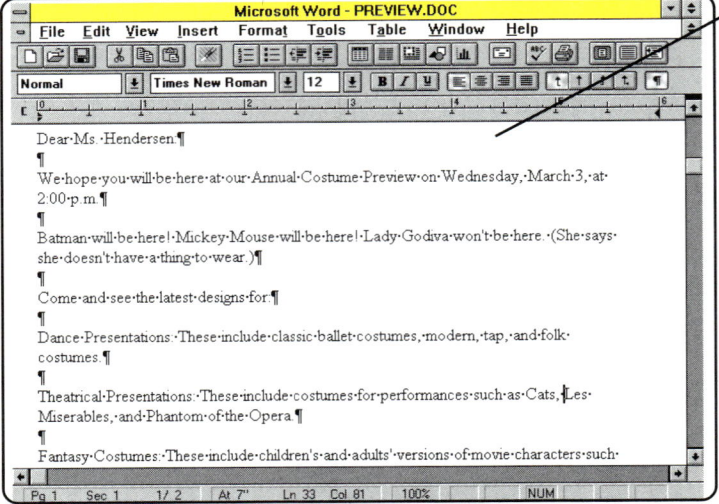

❖ I'm new to Word and I want to learn how to create a letter.

Turn to Part I, "Entering and Editing Text," to set margins, change the font, enter and edit text, save, and print. You will also learn how to set up a special directory for your daily work.

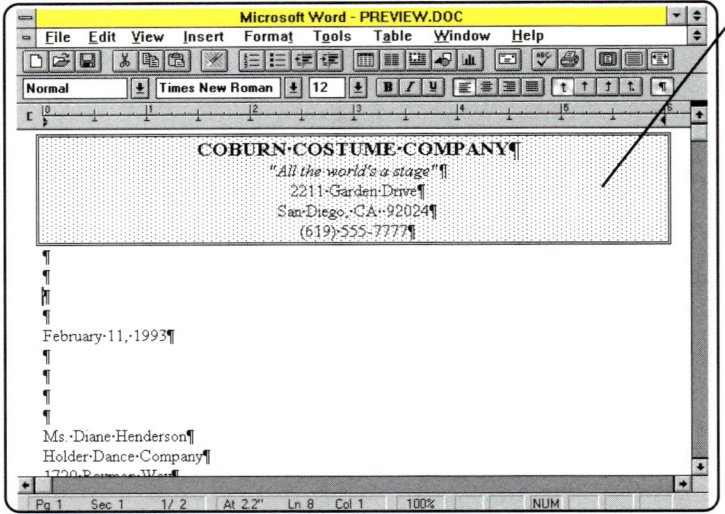

❖ I want to know how to customize a document.

Turn to Part II, "Formatting a Document," to learn how to customize text by changing the type style to bold or italic. You will also learn how to center text and create special effects like shaded borders.

INTRODUCTION: CUSTOMIZE YOUR LEARNING

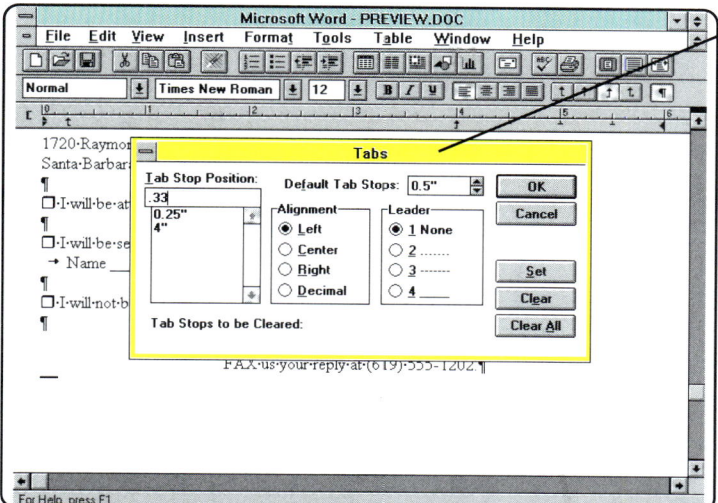

❖ I want to do special functions such as setting tabs and creating headers and footers.

Turn to Chapter 8, "Setting and Applying Tabs," to learn how to set and apply tabs. Refer to Chapter 9, "Separating a Document into Sections, and Adding a Header and a Footer." Also see Chapter 10, "Changing the View," to learn how to view a header and footer on the screen.

❖ I want to know how to use Word's special Envelope tool.

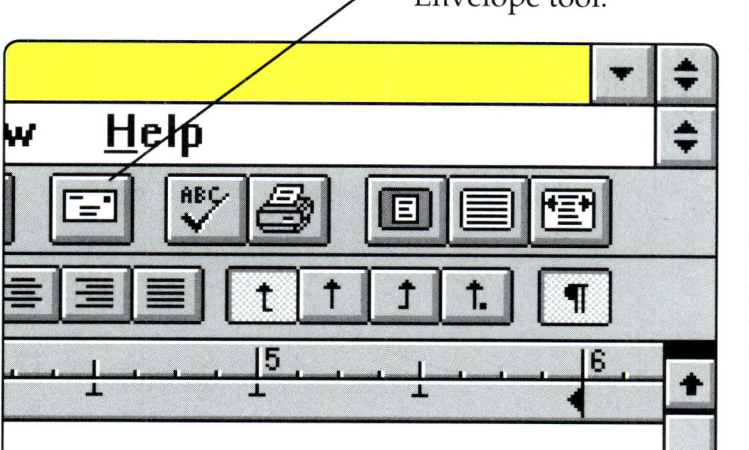

Turn to Chapter 11, "Printing an Envelope," to learn how to print a single envelope.

Chapter 14, "Printing Envelopes for a Mailing List," covers how to print merge envelopes.

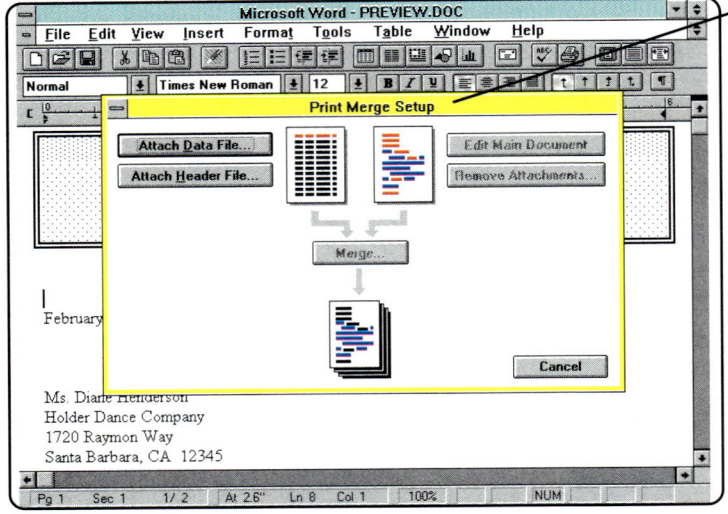

❖ I want to learn how to create and print personalized versions of a form letter using Word's Print Merge feature.

In Chapter 12, you will learn how to create a mailing list. Chapter 13 teaches you how to edit a mailing list and print a personalized version of a form letter. Chapter 14 covers how to print envelopes for your mailing list.

If you are switching to Word from another word processing program such as WordPerfect or WordStar, see Chapter 15 to learn how to convert a mailing list created in another program.

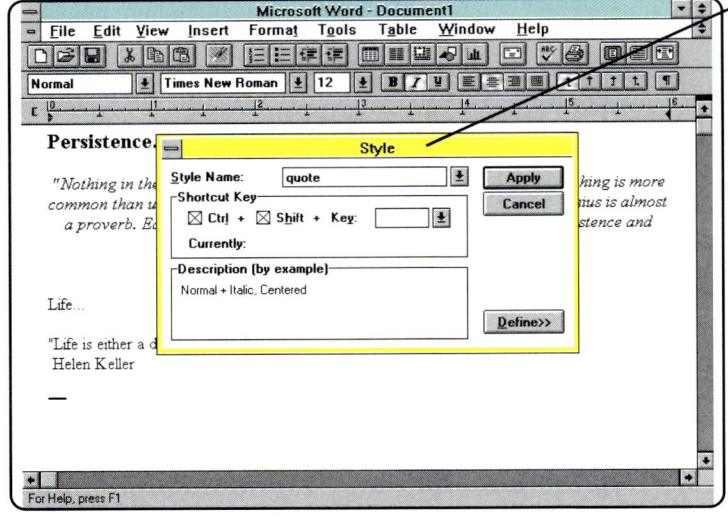

❖ I want to learn more about the use of styles and the Glossary.

Turn to Chapters 17 and 18 in Part IV, "Additional Topics."

You will also learn how to find a file in Chapter 16, "Searching for a File."

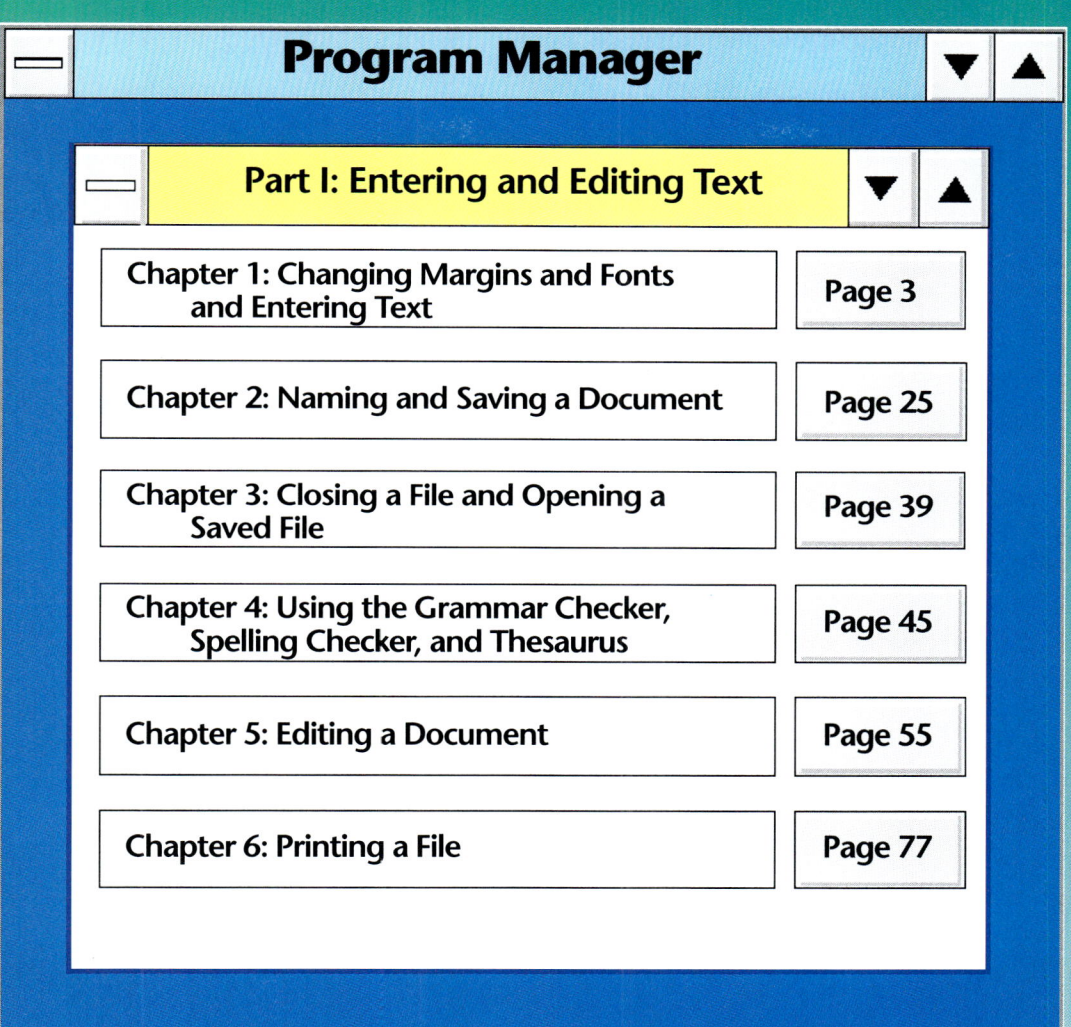

CHAPTER 1

Changing Margins and Fonts and Entering Text

Word for Windows 2 is a powerful word processing program that allows you to not only create documents easily, but also gives you the option to customize your text and add design elements. You can take advantage of its many features to create exciting and attractive documents. In this chapter you will do the following:

- ❖ Open a Word for Windows document
- ❖ Set margins
- ❖ Change the font and the font size
- ❖ Enter text
- ❖ Display paragraph and space symbols
- ❖ Learn to read the status bar
- ❖ Use special fonts to insert symbols into the text

OPENING WORD FOR WINDOWS FOR THE FIRST TIME

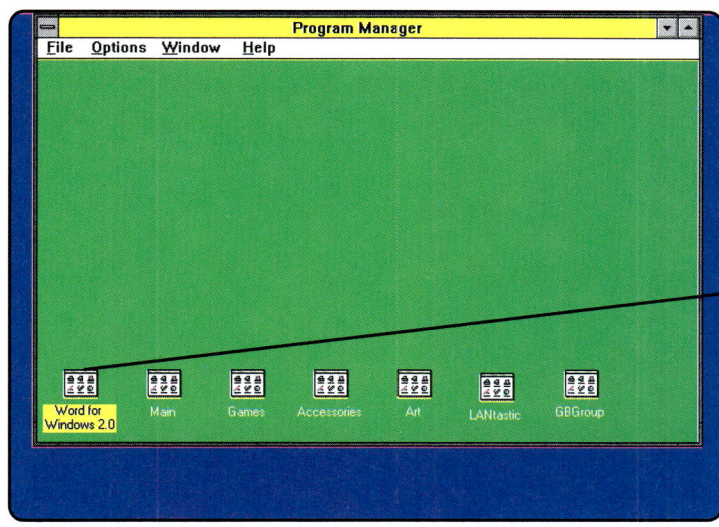

1. **Type win** at the C:\> (C prompt) on your screen to open, or *boot up*, Windows. You will probably have different group icons at the bottom of your screen than you see in this example.

Depending on how Word was installed on your computer, there may be a separate group icon for Word for Windows 2.0 at the bottom of your screen.

In this example, Word was moved to a customized group named GBGroup. (See the Appendix, "Installing Word for Windows 2" for directions on moving the Word icon into a customized group.)

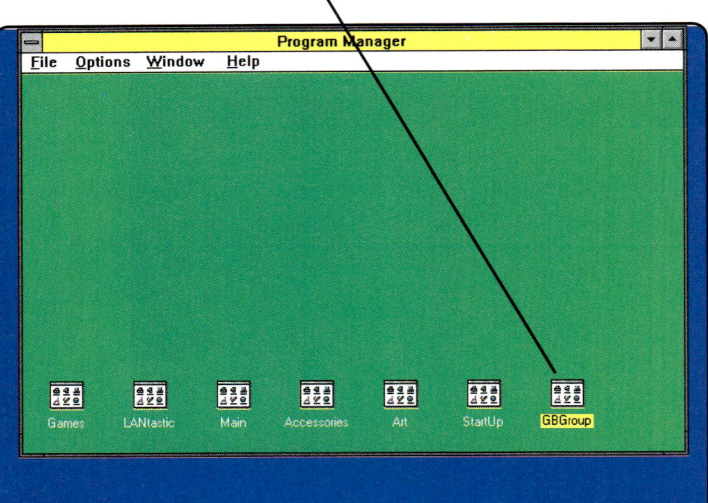

2. Click twice quickly on the **group icon** that contains Word. This will open up a window. If you are new to Windows, it may take a little practice to get the right rhythm on the double-click. Don't worry if the icon jumps around when you click on it.

Your group window will have different icons from those you see in this example. The icon for Microsoft Word will be the same, however.

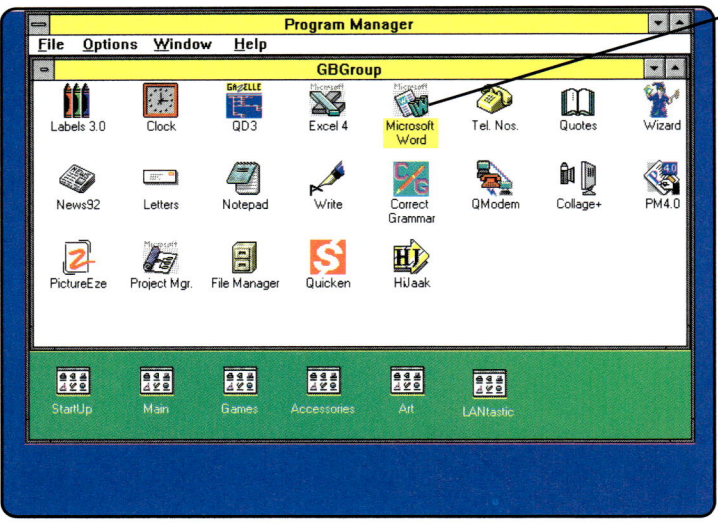

3. Click twice on the **Microsoft Word icon**. You will see an hourglass, then the copyright information for Word. Then you will see one of the views of the opening Word screen shown on the next page.

CHAPTER 1: CHANGING MARGINS AND FONTS AND ENTERING TEXT

This is one view of the opening screen for a new document. Notice the top title bar is labeled "Microsoft Word."

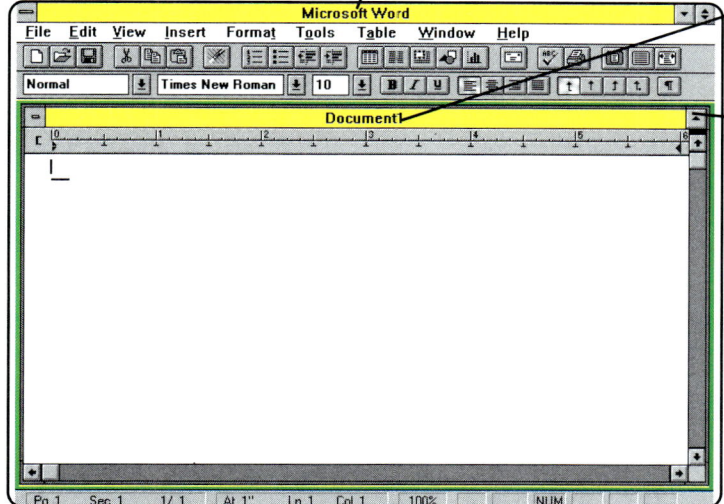

The second title bar is labeled "Document1."

If this is the view you see, **click** on the **Maximize button** (▲) on the right of the Document1 title bar.

This will cause Document1 to fill the screen. Your screen will look like the example below.

This is the other view you may see when Word first appears on your screen. You may prefer this view since it shows more of your workspace.

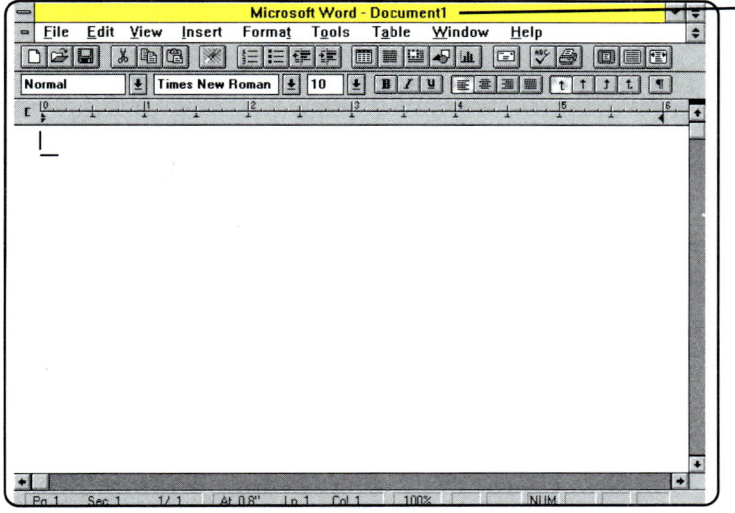

Notice that there is only one title bar and it's labeled "Microsoft Word - Document1."

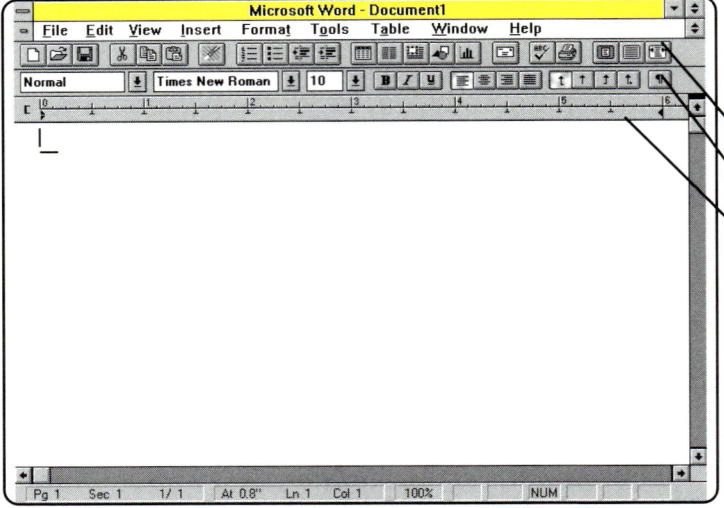

You should see the following items on your screen:

❖ Toolbar
❖ Ribbon
❖ Ruler

If you see all of these items, go to the section "Setting Margins" on page 7. If you do not see the toolbar, ribbon, and ruler, go to the following section.

DISPLAYING THE TOOLBAR, RIBBON, AND RULER

1. Click on **View** in the menu bar. A pull-down menu will appear. Notice that Toolbar, Ribbon, and ruler appear as choices on the pull-down menu.

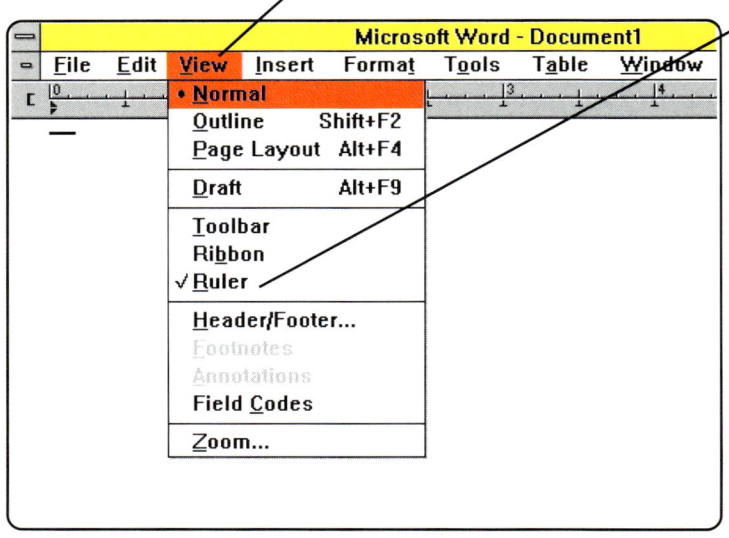

In this example only Ruler is checked. Therefore, only the ruler shows at the top of the screen. If one or more of the elements does not show on your screen, **click** on the **item's name** you are missing. The pull-down menu will disappear and the item will appear on your screen. If you are missing more than one of the items, you will need to repeat the process for each item you are missing.

CHAPTER 1: CHANGING MARGINS AND FONTS AND ENTERING TEXT

SETTING MARGINS

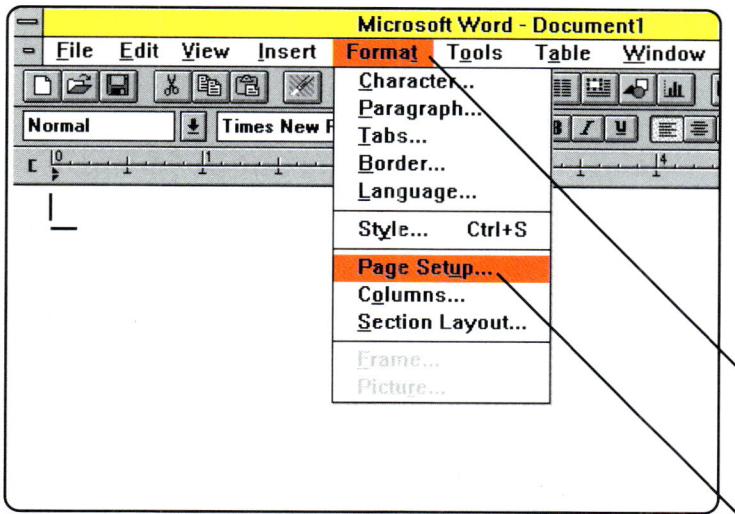

The standard (*default*) margins in Word are pre-set at 1 inch on the top and bottom and 1.25 inches on the left and right. You can change any or all of these settings. In this example you will change the top margin.

1. **Click** on **Format** in the menu bar. A pull-down menu will appear.

2. **Click** on **Page Setup**. The Page Setup dialog box will appear.

3. **Click** on **Margins** to insert a black dot in the circle if one is not already there. (In Windows terminology the circle is called an *option button*.)

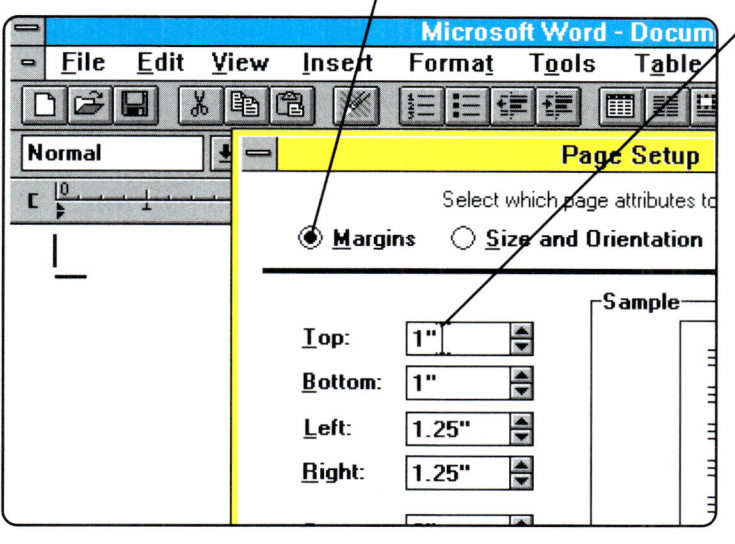

4. **Place** the mouse pointer to the **right of 1"** in the Top box. The pointer will change to an I-beam.

5. **Press and hold** the mouse button and **drag** the I-beam to the left **over 1"**. 1" will be highlighted.

WORD FOR WINDOWS 2: THE VISUAL LEARNING GUIDE

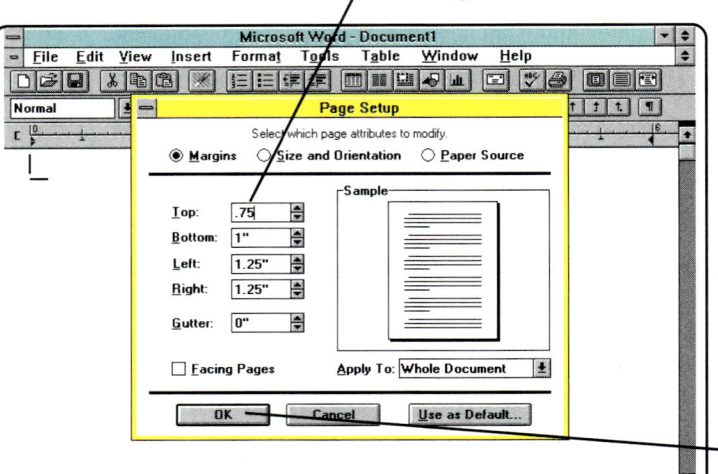

6. Type .75. It will replace 1". (It's not necessary to type " after the number.) this will decrease the top margin to .75 inch. You are making the top margin smaller than standard to give yourself the extra room to create the letterhead in the example in this chapter. (If you are going to print on stationery that already has a letterhead, the top margin for a short-to-medium-length letter should be about 2.5 inches.)

7. Click on **OK**. The Page Setup dialog box will disappear.

CHANGING THE FONT AND THE FONT SIZE

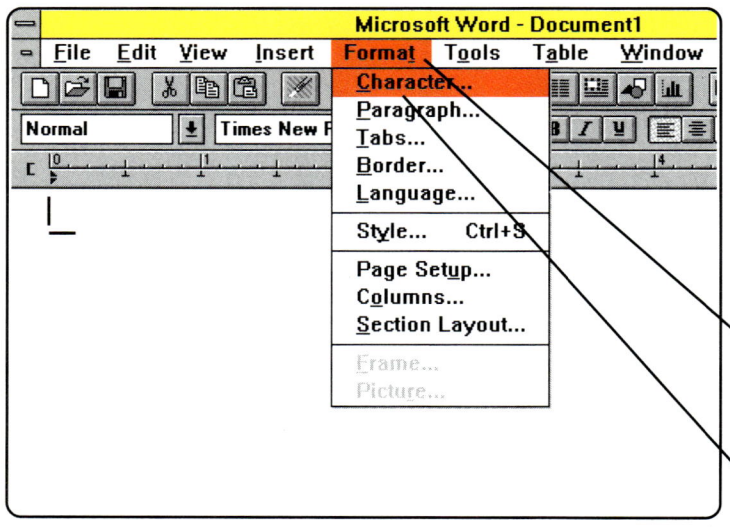

Word is set to print with the Times New Roman *font*, or type style. In this example you will learn how to change the font.

Changing the Font

1. Click on **Format** in the menu bar. A pull-down menu will appear.

2. Click on **Character**. The Character dialog box will appear.

CHAPTER 1: CHANGING MARGINS AND FONTS AND ENTERING TEXT

3. **Click** on ↓ to the right of the Font box. A drop-down list of fonts will appear. Your list may be different from the one you see here, depending on the fonts you have installed on your computer.

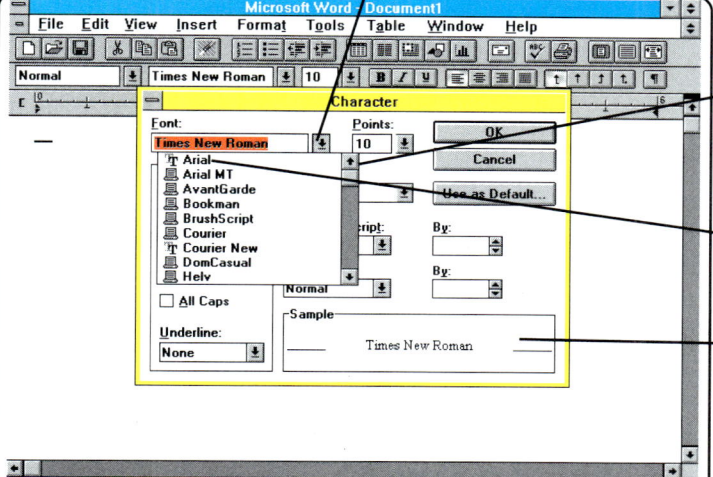

4. **Click repeatedly** on ↑ on the scroll bar to scroll up to the top of the list.

5. **Click** on **Arial**. The drop-down list will disappear.

The Sample box will change (see the sample box in the next example) and show what the Arial font looks like.

6. **Click** on ↓ to the right of the Font box to open up the drop-down list.

7. **Repeat steps 4 through 6** to see other fonts. (**Click** on ↓ on the scroll bar to scroll down the list of fonts.)

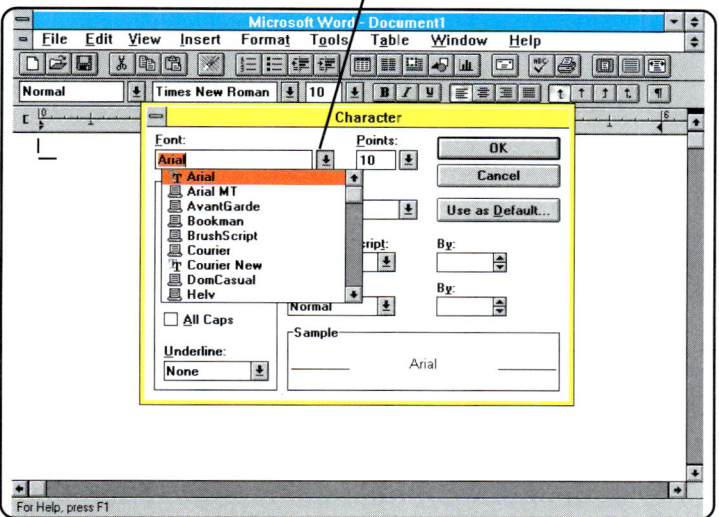

8. **Click** on **Times New Roman** if you would like your letter to look like the sample letter in this chapter. If you prefer to choose another font, your lines may end differently than you see in the following examples. That's okay. Just be aware that you may see differences.

Changing Font Size

Fonts are measured in *points*. Letters are typically written in 10- or 12-point type. In this section you will change the point size of the Times New Roman font from 10 to 12.

1. **Click** on ↓ to the right of the Points box. A drop-down list will appear.

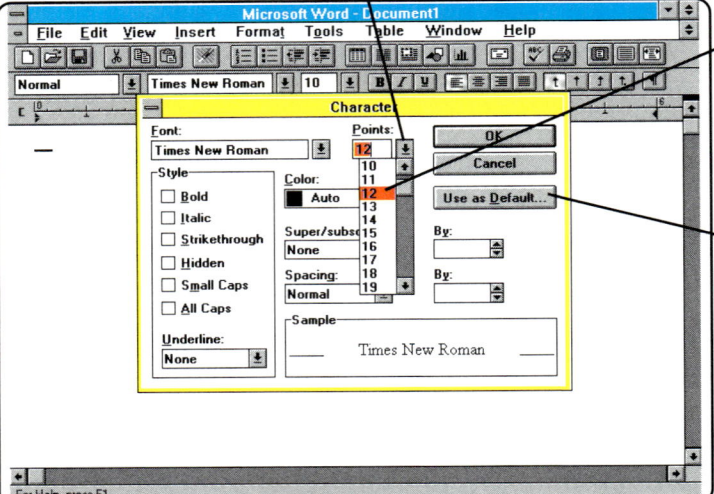

2. **Click** on **12** to make the font larger. The drop-down list will disappear and "12" will appear in the Points box.

3. **Click** on the **Use as Default button** to set Times New Roman with a point size of 12 as the standard settings for all future documents. (These can, of course, be changed or customized at any time.)

The Microsoft Word message box appears, asking you to confirm the change.

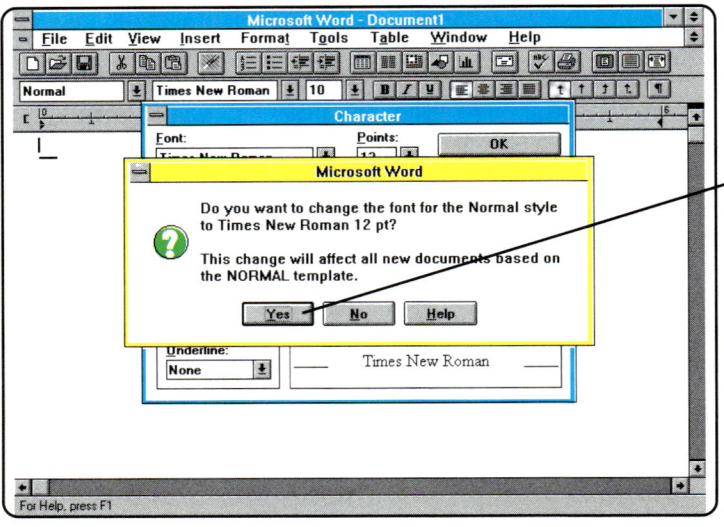

4. **Click** on **Yes**. Both boxes will close and you will be returned to a screen that looks like the one on the next page.

CHAPTER 1: CHANGING MARGINS AND FONTS AND ENTERING TEXT

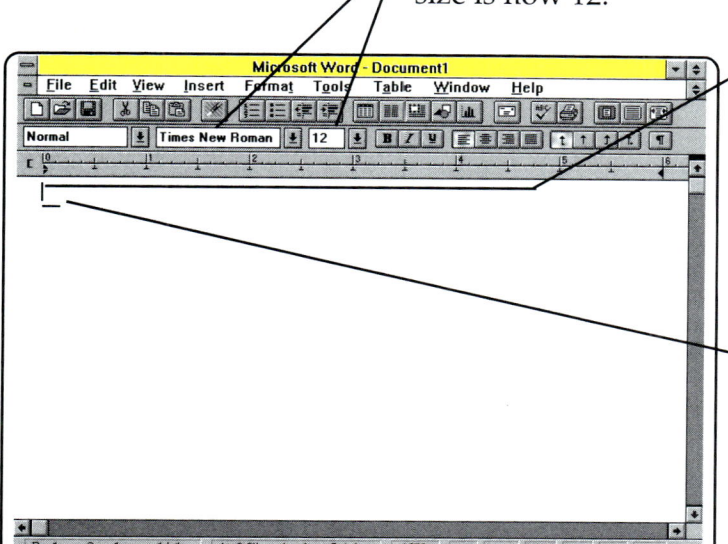

Notice the font is Times New Roman and the point size is now 12.

You will see a flashing vertical bar at the top of the file. This is called the *insertion point*. It shows where the text will be placed, or inserted, when you begin typing.

You will also see a horizontal bar below the insertion point. This is called the *end mark*. It will move down the screen as you start each new line of type. It marks the end of the material in the file. Since you haven't entered any text yet, the end mark is at the top of the file.

ENTERING TEXT

You are now ready to type a letter. In the following examples you will type a letter from the Coburn Costume Company inviting a customer to come to the Annual Costume Preview.

Creating the Letterhead

The first thing you will type is the company name and return address.

Notice that the insertion point is flashing at the beginning of the document. This means you can start typing and the text will begin at the insertion point.

1. Press the **Caps Lock key** to turn on the capital letters feature so that the text you type will appear as capital letters.

2. Type COBURN COSTUME COMPANY.

3. Press Enter.

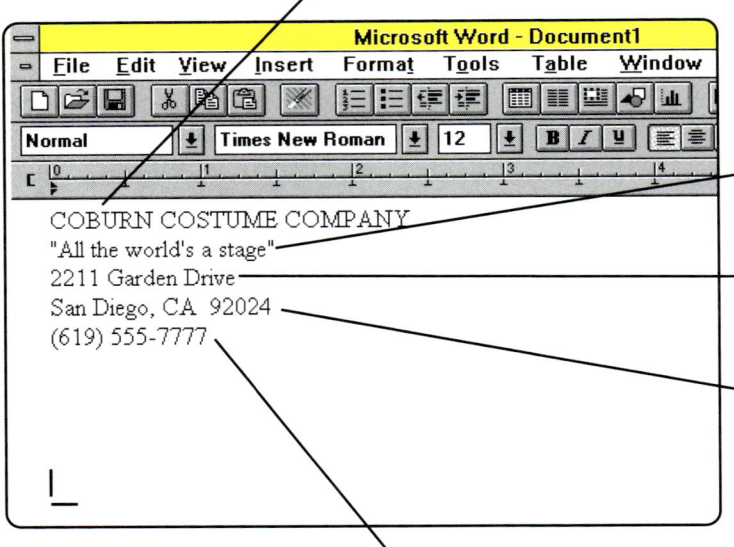

4. Press Caps Lock again to turn off the capital letters feature.

5. Type "All the world's a stage" and **press Enter**.

6. Type 2211 Garden Drive and **press Enter**.

7. Type San Diego, CA 92024. (**Press** the **Spacebar twice** after CA.) **Press Enter**.

8. Type (619) 555-7777.

9. Press Enter five times. Your screen will look like this example.

Displaying Paragraph, Space, and Tab Symbols

Word can display symbols for paragraphs, spaces, and tabs. It is helpful to see these symbols when you are setting up a document. Though you can see them on the document, they will not print.

In this section you will use the Show/Hide ¶ button, which is located on the ribbon, to display paragraph, space, and tab symbols.

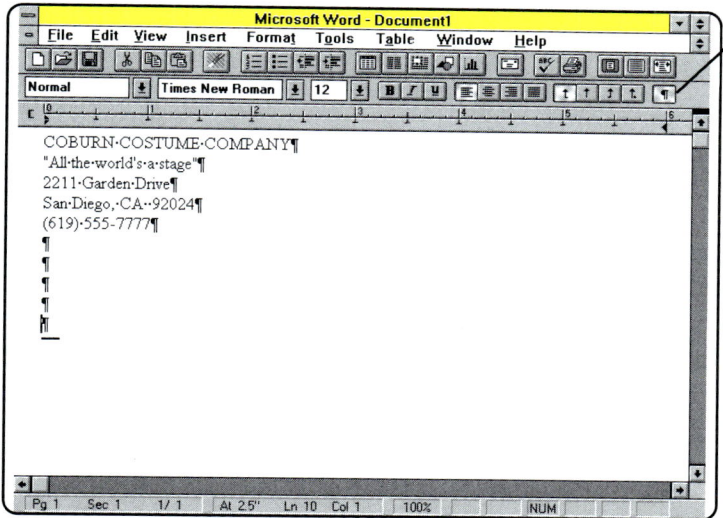

1. **Click** on the **Show/Hide ¶ button** on the right side of the ribbon. When you click on the button it appears to be depressed and slightly lighter in color. Paragraph symbols (¶) will now appear in the text.

Notice the dots between the words. Each dot represents a space you create by pressing the Spacebar.

Also notice the ¶ at the end of each line and the five ¶ symbols at the end of the text. A ¶ appears each time you press the Enter key.

The Show/Hide ¶ button works like a toggle switch. Click it once to turn it on, click it again to turn it off. Click it a third time to turn it on again. Try it for yourself.

Entering the Date, Address, and Salutation

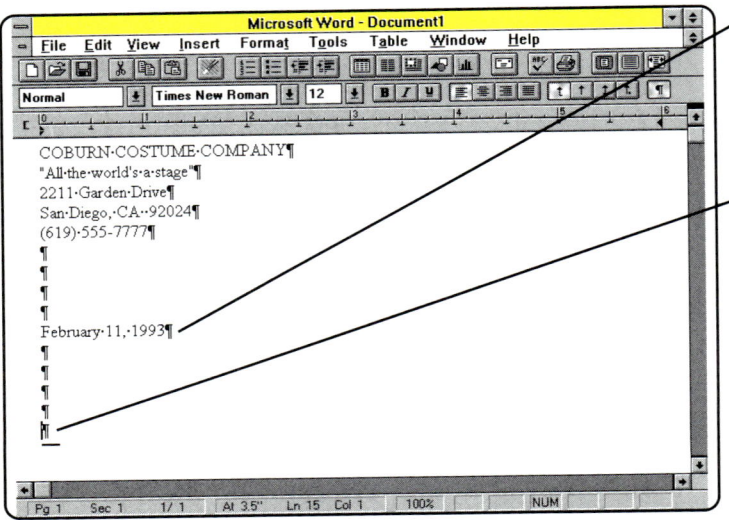

1. **Type** the date. Use today's date instead of the date you see in the example.

2. **Press Enter five times**. Five ¶ symbols will appear.

3. **Type** the following lines. **Press Enter** after each line.

Ms. Diane Hendersen
Holder Dance Company
1720 Raymon Way
Santa Barbara, CA 12345
(**Press** the **Spacebar twice** after CA.)

4. **Press Enter twice** after the last line. The screen will automatically scroll (move up) to make room for the additional lines.

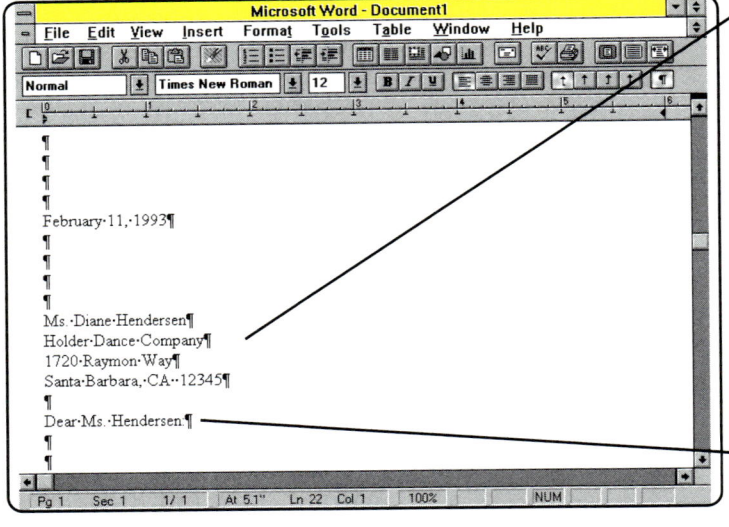

5. **Type Dear Ms. Hendersen:** (don't forget the colon).

6. **Press Enter twice**.

Entering the Body of the Letter

You are now ready to enter the body of the letter. Like all word processing programs, you can type without worrying about your right margin. Word will wrap the text around to the next line automatically. Press the Spacebar only once after the period at the end of a sentence. Press Enter only at the end of a paragraph. Press Enter twice to insert a double line space after a paragraph.

In word processing programs, a paragraph is considered to be any text that is followed by the Enter command. Therefore, each of the single lines you have already typed is considered an individual paragraph.

1. Type the text below. It contains errors (shown in red) that you will correct later, so include them if you want to follow along with these procedures. If you make an unintentional typing error, press Backspace and type the correct letters.

We hope you will be her at our Annual Costume Preview on Wednesday, March 3, at 2 p.m.

Batman will be here! Mickey Mouse will be here!

Lady Godiva won't be here. (She says she doesn't have a thing to wear.)

Come and see the latest designs for:

Dance Presentations: These include classic ballet costumes, modern, tap, and folk costumes.

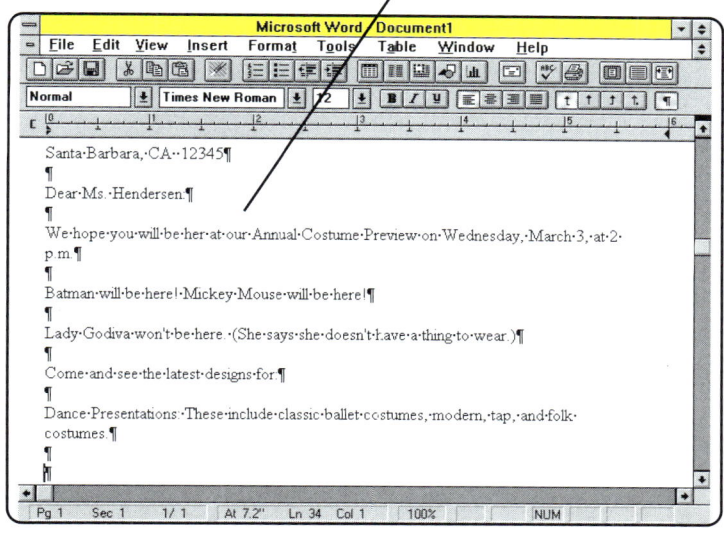

2. Continue typing the following text. Remember, press the Enter key *only* at the end of a paragraph.

Theatrical Presentations: These include costumes for performances such as Cats, Les Miserables, and Phantom of the Opera.

Fantasy Costumes: These include childrens and adults versions of movie characters such as Batman, Catwoman, and Disney characters such as Mickey Mouse.

Historical Characters: These include characters such as Napoleon and Josephine and masks for current political figures.

Because you are a valued customer, Ms. Hendersen, you will recieve a 1 percent discount on any order placed at the Preview.

Please return a copy of the reply form below by Friday, February 19.

3. Press Enter twice after the last line.

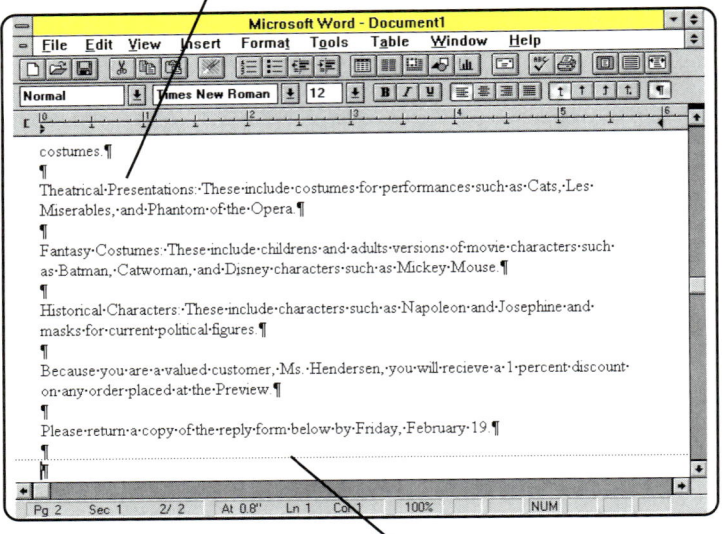

Notice the dotted line that appears. This is the *automatic page break*. It indicates the end of the first page. You will learn how to change the location of the page break in Chapter 5, "Editing a Document."

The exact location of the automatic page break depends on the margins you set and the size of the font.

CHAPTER 1: CHANGING MARGINS AND FONTS AND ENTERING TEXT

17

Notice the *status bar* at the bottom of your screen. The status bar contains information about your document.

① **Pg 2** at the far left of the status bar tells you that the insertion point is on page 2 of the document.

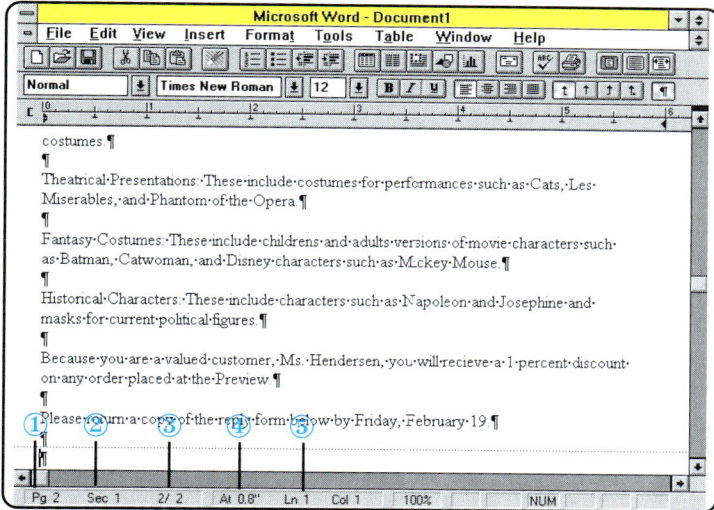

② **Sec 1** means that you haven't divided the document into sections. The entire document is labeled "Sec 1." (Creating sections is covered in Chapter 9.)

③ **2/2** means you are on page 2 of a two-page file (document).

④ **At 0.8"** means that the cursor is 0.8 inch from the top of the page as it will print.

⑤ **Ln 1** means that the cursor is on the first line below the top margin. The exact number of lines on the page depends on the width of the margins and the font size you choose.

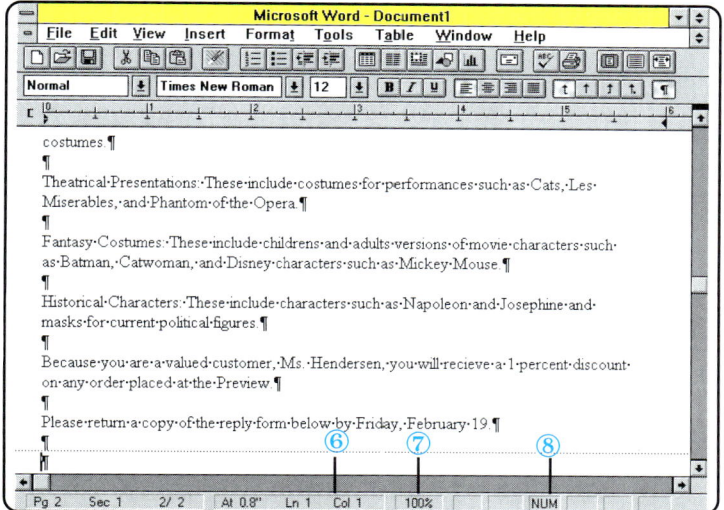

⑥ **Col 1** means the cursor is in the first space next to the left margin. The exact number of columns (or spaces) that will fit across the page depends on the margins and font size.

⑦ **100%** means you are in standard view.

⑧ **NUM** means the Num Lock key is on.

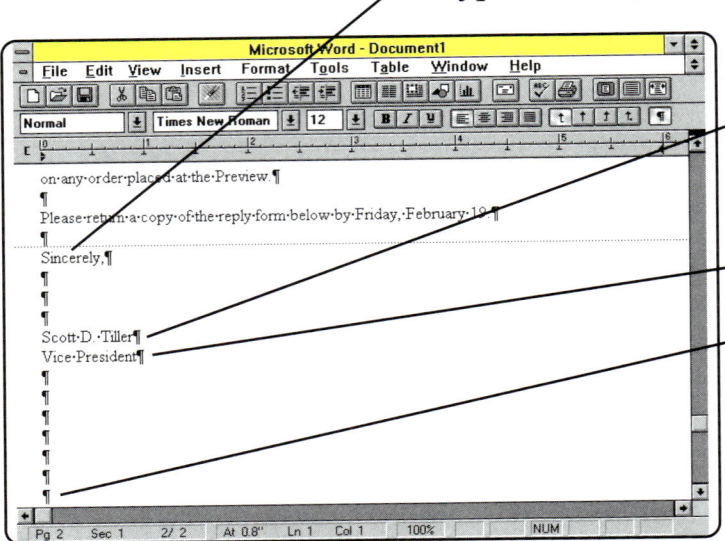

4. **Type Sincerely,** (don't forget the comma).

5. **Press Enter five times.**

6. **Type Scott D. Tiller.**

7. **Press Enter.**

8. **Type Vice President.**

9. **Press Enter seven times.** Your screen will look like this example.

INSERTING A SYMBOL AND FINISHING THE LETTER

Windows 3.1 comes with a number of fonts, one of which is called Wingdings. This font has symbols instead of letters. In this section, you will insert two different symbols into the text.

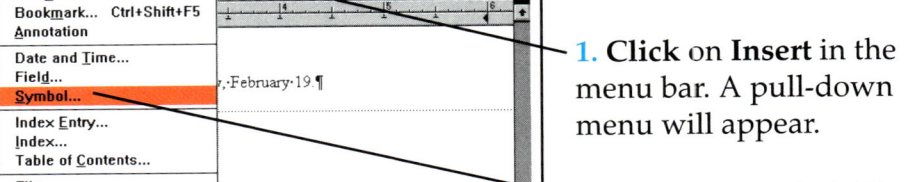

1. **Click** on **Insert** in the menu bar. A pull-down menu will appear.

2. **Click** on **Symbol**. The Symbol dialog box will appear.

CHAPTER 1: CHANGING MARGINS AND FONTS AND ENTERING TEXT

3. Click on ⬇ to the right of the Symbols From box. A drop-down list of fonts will appear. The contents of the list depends on the fonts you have installed on your computer. Your list may be different from the one you see in this example.

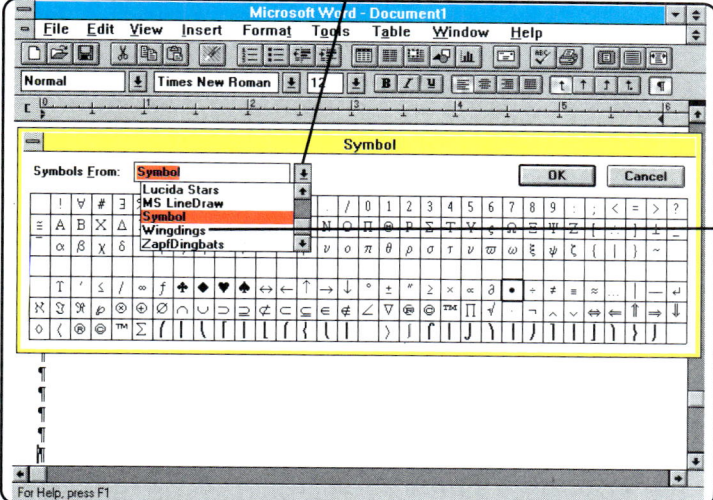

4. Click on ⬆ or ⬇ to scroll up or down the list until you see Wingdings. (It's possible that Wingdings already shows in the box.)

5. Click on **Wingdings**. The drop-down list will disappear and "Wingdings" will appear in the Symbols From list box. The Wingdings symbol set will appear in the Symbol dialog box.

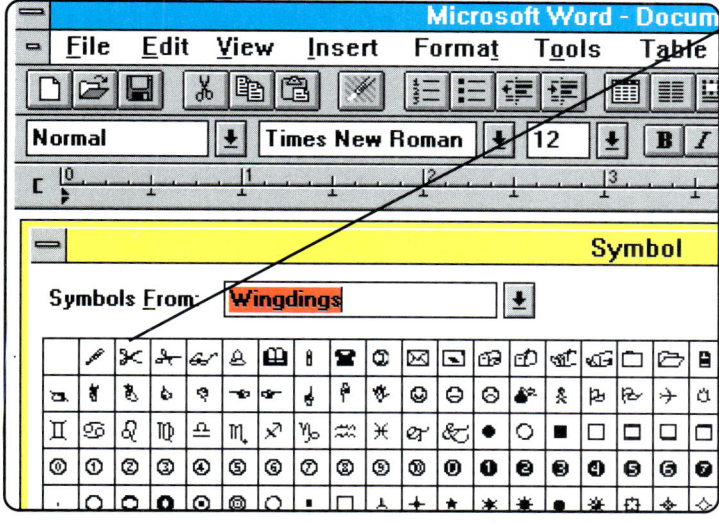

6. Place the mouse pointer on the **scissors symbol**, which is in the third column from the left in the first row. (It's possible that your scissors may be in a different spot.)

7. Press and hold the left mouse button. The symbol will be enlarged so you can see it better.

8. Release the mouse button and the symbol will be reduced in size. It will be surrounded by a selection border.

You can repeat steps 6 through 8 to see other symbols. Make sure to click on the scissors again when you have finished.

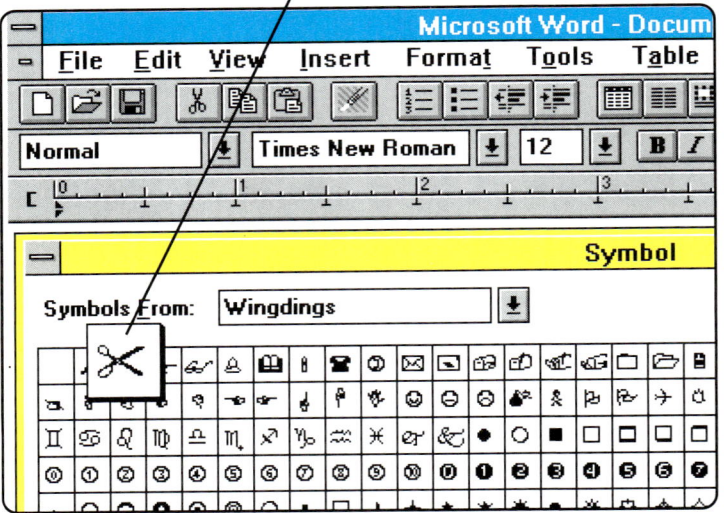

9. Click on **OK**. The Symbol dialog box will disappear and the scissors will appear in the letter document at the insertion point.

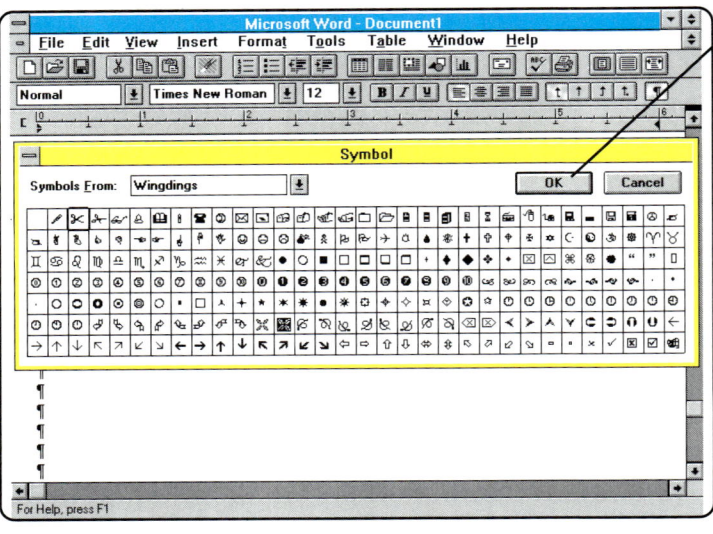

CHAPTER 1: CHANGING MARGINS AND FONTS AND ENTERING TEXT   21

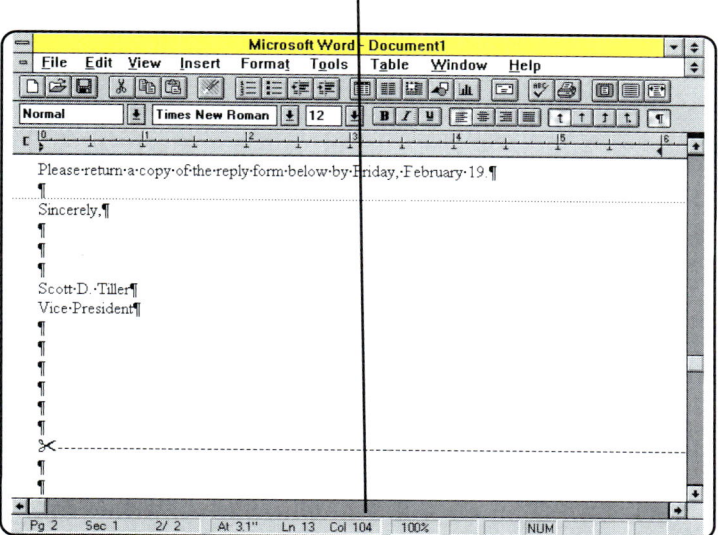

10. **Press and hold** the **Hyphen key** until Col in the status bar at the bottom of the screen reads Col 104. (The number at the bottom of the screen won't change as long as you are holding down the Hyphen key. Release the key occasionally so the new Col number can register.) If you go beyond 104, the extra hyphens will wrap around to the next line. Simply press the Backspace key until the insertion point goes back to the previous line.

11. **Press Enter twice**.

12. **Repeat steps 1 and 2** in this section to open the Symbol dialog box.

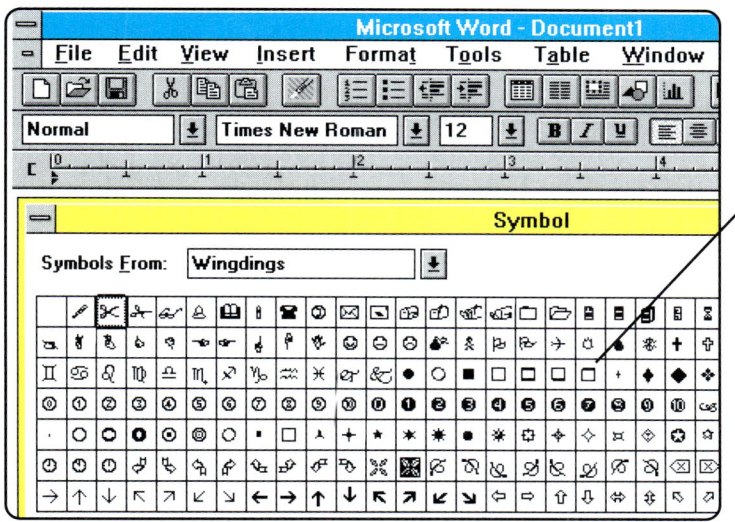

The Wingdings symbol set will show in the Symbol dialog box because it is the last font that you used.

13. **Place** the mouse pointer on the **fourth square shape** in the **third line**. (It may be in a different spot on your screen.)

14. **Press and hold** the left mouse button. The symbol will be enlarged. (You can simply click on the symbol you want, then go to step 16. However, when you press and hold the mouse button it allows you to see the symbol more clearly and confirm that it is the symbol you want.)

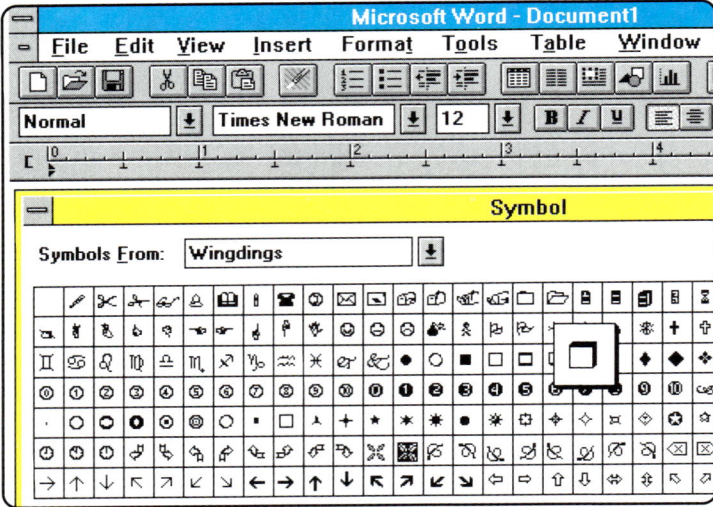

15. **Release** the mouse button. The symbol will be surrounded by a selection border.

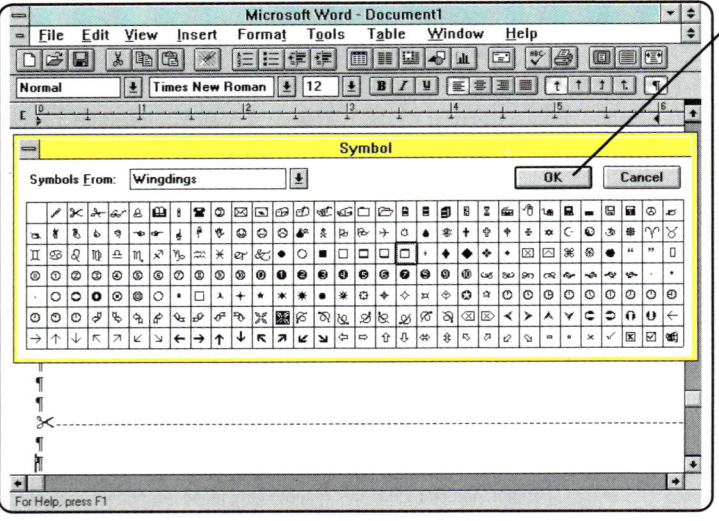

16. **Click** on **OK**. The symbol will be inserted into the letter.

CHAPTER 1: CHANGING MARGINS AND FONTS AND ENTERING TEXT   **23**

17. **Press** the **Spacebar**.

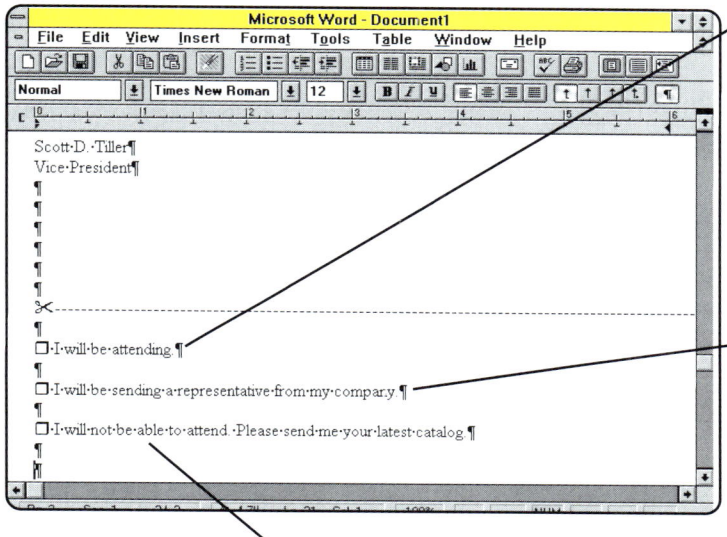

18. **Type** the sentence **I will be attending.** (don't forget the period).

19. **Press Enter twice**.

20. **Repeat steps 12 through 17** to insert the square into the text.

21. **Type** the sentence **I will be sending a representative from my company.** (include the period).

22. **Press Enter twice**.

23. **Repeat steps 12 through 17** to insert the square into the text a third time.

24. **Type** the following sentences (including the periods): **I will not be able to attend. Please send me your latest catalog.**

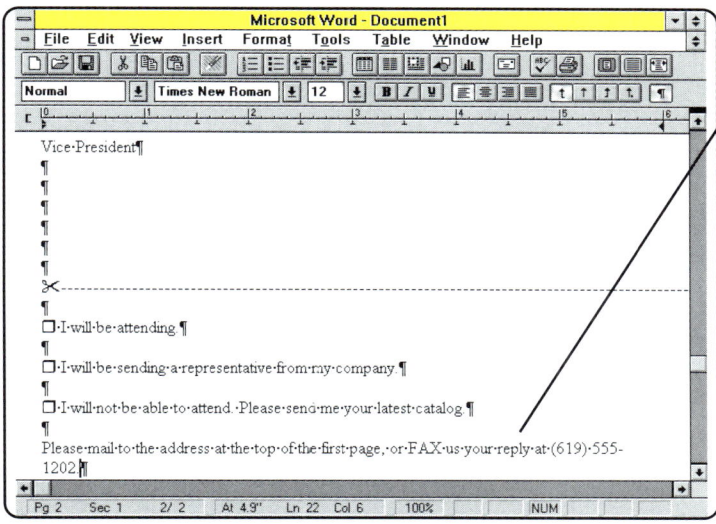

25. **Press Enter twice**.

26. **Type** the sentence **Please mail to the address at the top of the first page, or FAX us your reply at (619) 555-1202.** (include the period).

Congratulations! You just created a letter in Word. In Chapter 2, you will name the letter and save it.

Naming and Saving a Document

CHAPTER 2

Saving a file is as easy as clicking your mouse in Word for Windows 2. There's even an Automatic Save feature that you can use to save your work at specific intervals. Word is set up to save files to the WINWORD directory—the same directory that contains the files that run Word. Therefore, it's a good idea to create another directory, called a *working directory*, and save your daily work to this directory. This way your daily work is not mixed into the WINWORD directory and the files that run Word. You can do this very easily by using File Manager. In this chapter you will do the following:

❖ Create a working directory
❖ Name and save a document to the working directory
❖ Set the Automatic Save feature to save your document every 10 minutes

CREATING A WORKING DIRECTORY

In this section you will use File Manager to create a working directory for your Word documents.

Opening File Manager

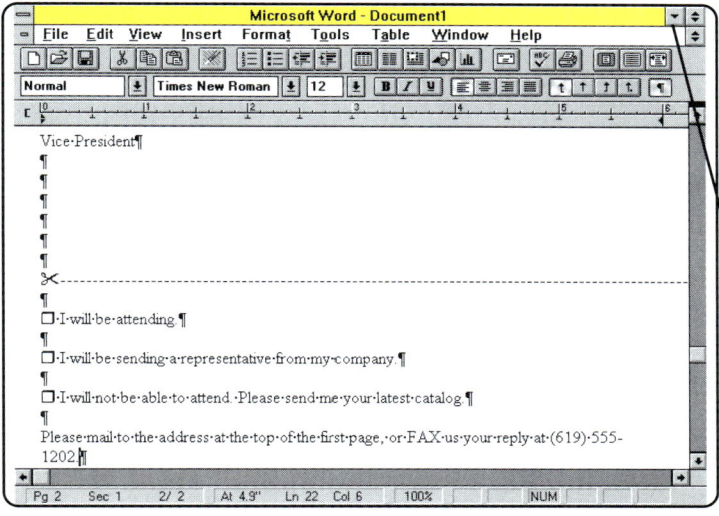

1. Click on the **Minimize button** (▼) on the right of the Microsoft Word title bar. This will minimize Word to an icon at the bottom of your screen.

In this example File Manager is located in the same customized group that holds Word. Your File Manager may be located in the Main group or in another group.

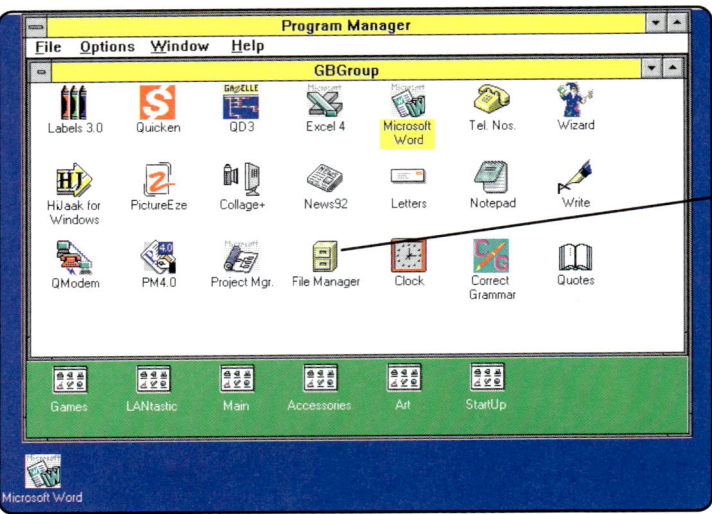

2. **Click twice** on the **group icon** that contains the File Manager. The group will open up to a window.

3. **Click twice** on the **File Manager icon**. The File Manager window will appear on your screen. It may appear in a different location and in a different size than you see in the next example.

In this example the Windows directory is highlighted. On your computer, the C:\ may be highlighted. The contents of File Manager depends on the programs you have installed on your computer. Your list will be different from what you see here.

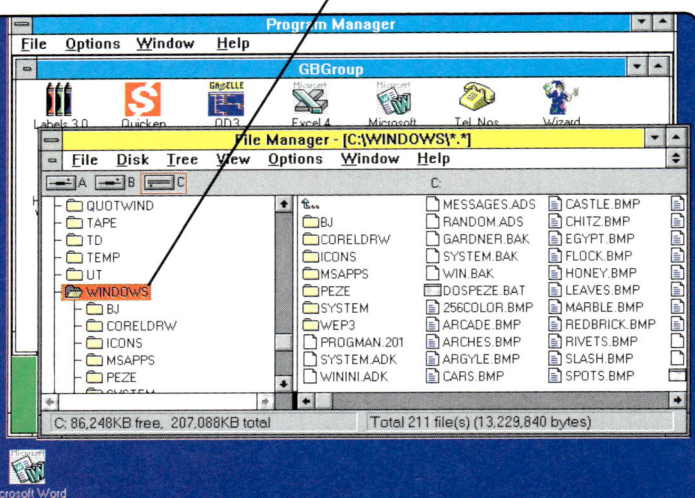

CHANGING THE VIEW OF FILE MANAGER

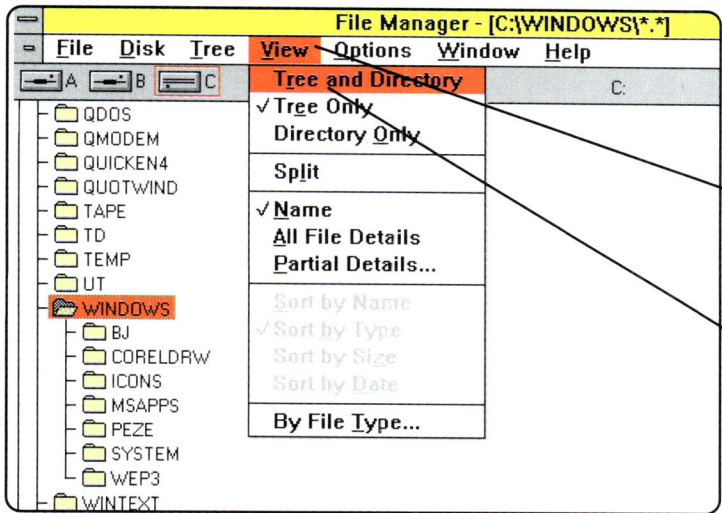

If File Manager does not show a list of files on the right, you can change the view to display the list.

1. **Click** on **View** in the menu bar. A pull-down menu will appear.

2. **Click** on **Tree and Directory**. The list of files in the highlighted directory will appear on the right side of the File Manager window.

Maximizing File Manager

If File Manager already fills the screen, go on to "Creating a Directory." If your File Manager window does not fill the screen, complete the following step.

1. **Click** on the **Maximize button (▲)** on the right side of the File Manager title bar. The File Manager window will be maximized to fill the screen.

Creating a Directory

You are now ready to create a directory you will use to store your Word document files.

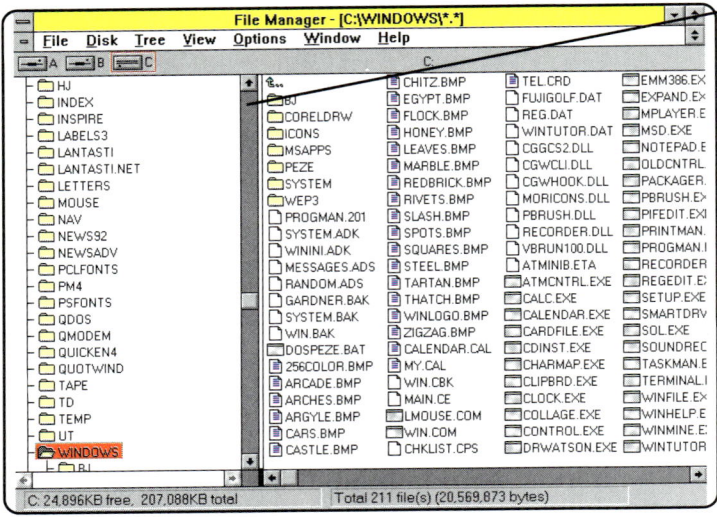

1. **Click repeatedly** on the **top of the scroll bar**. This will move you rapidly up the list until you can see the C:\ at the top.

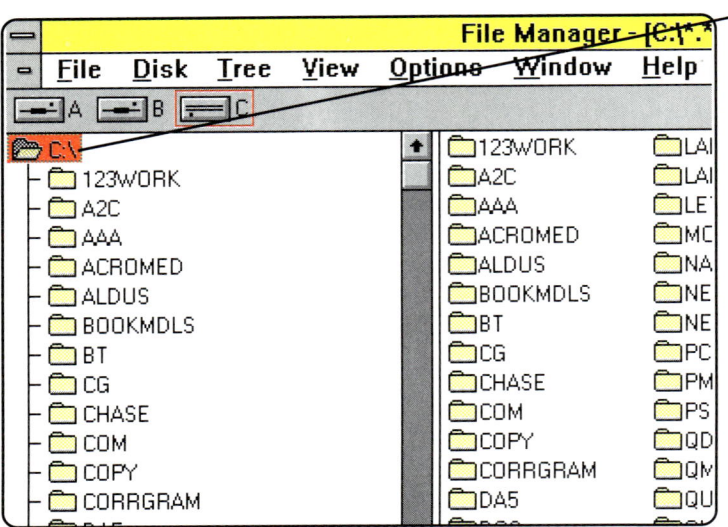

2. **Click** on **C:**. It will be highlighted. A list of the directories on the C drive will be displayed on the right side of the screen. Your list will be different from what you see here.

CHAPTER 2: NAMING AND SAVING A DOCUMENT

3. **Click** on **File** in the menu bar. A pull-down menu will appear.

4. **Click** on **Create Directory**. The Create Directory dialog box will appear.

5. Since the cursor is already flashing in the Name box, **type wwdoc** (which stands for Word for Windows documents). You can give this new directory another name if you prefer, but you must use no more than eight letters in the name.

6. **Click** on **OK**. The dialog box will close.

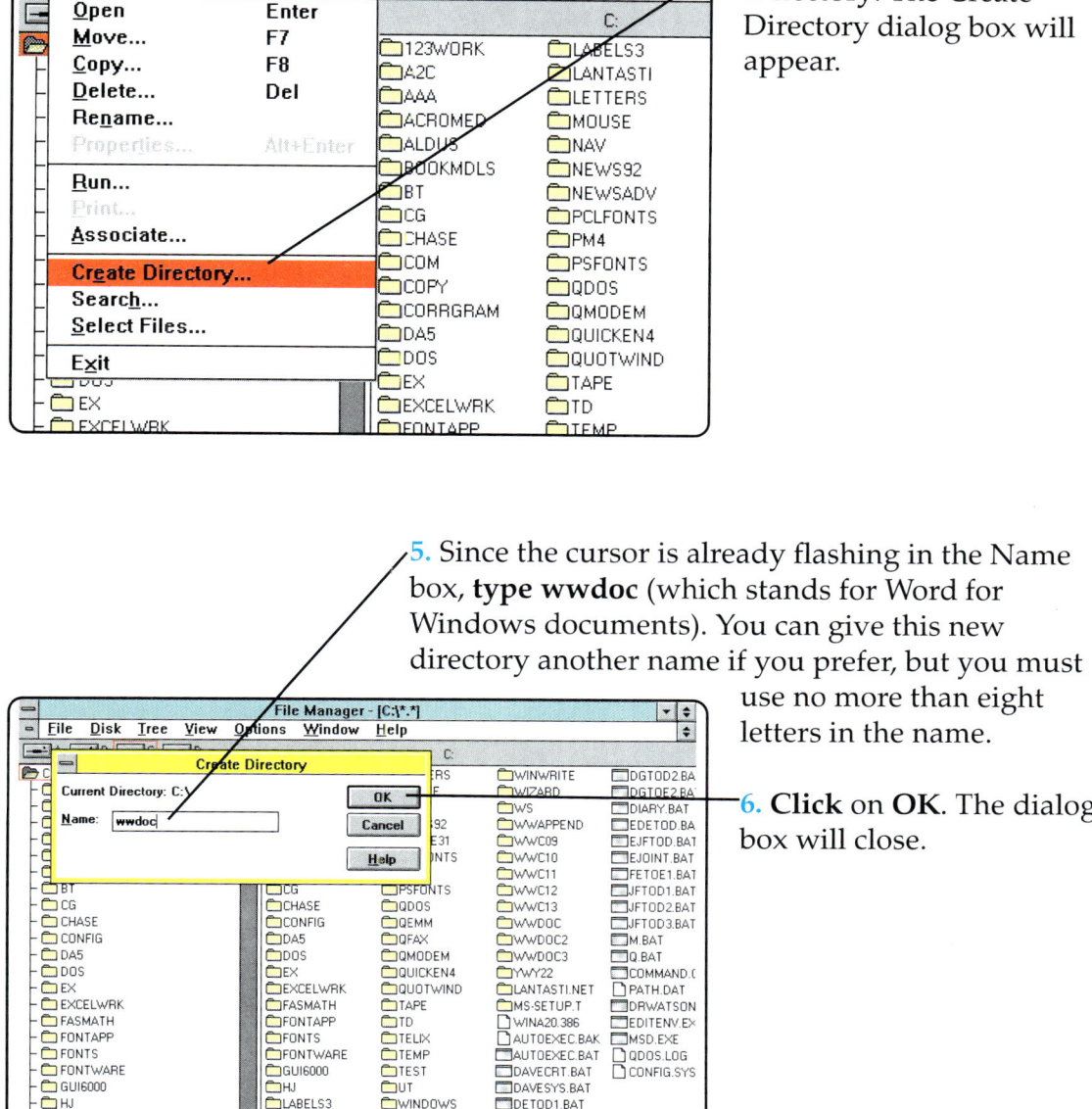

Checking the New Directory and Closing File Manager

1. Press the **End key** to go to the end of the directory list on the left. You will see the WWDOC listing. 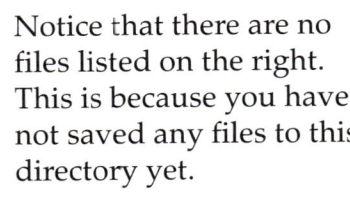 Your list will be different from what you see here.

Notice that there are no files listed on the right. This is because you have not saved any files to this directory yet.

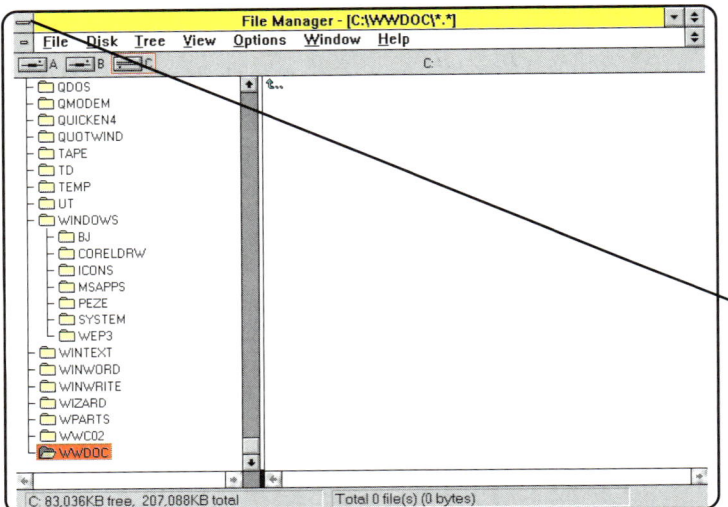

2. Click twice on the **top Control menu box** (□) on the left of the File Manager title bar. This will close File Manager.

Changing the Working Directory Statement in Windows

Although you have created a directory for your work files, Windows doesn't know that it is supposed to use this as the working directory. In this section you will change the working directory statement to reflect the new WWDOC directory.

CHAPTER 2: NAMING AND SAVING A DOCUMENT

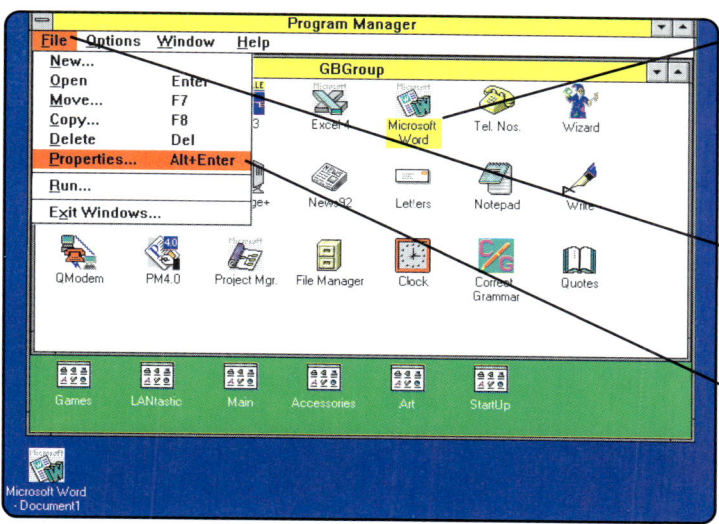

1. **Click** *once* on the **Microsoft Word icon** in whatever group window it appears. The name will be highlighted.

2. **Click** on **File** in the menu bar. A pull-down menu will appear.

3. **Click** on **Properties**. The Program Item Properties dialog box will appear.

4. **Place** the mouse pointer to the **right of WINWORD** in the Working Directory box and **click** to set it in place.

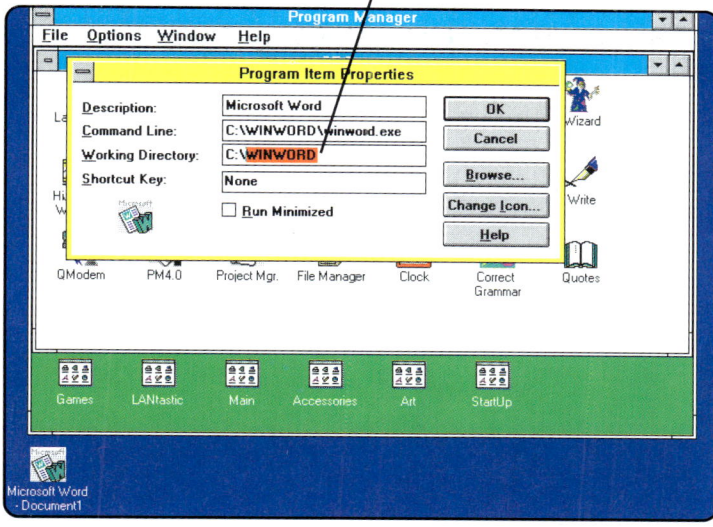

5. **Press and hold** the mouse button and **drag** the pointer to the left **over WINWORD**. It will be highlighted. (Be careful not to highlight C:\.)

6. Type wwdoc. It will replace the highlighted text.

7. Click on **OK**. The dialog box will disappear.

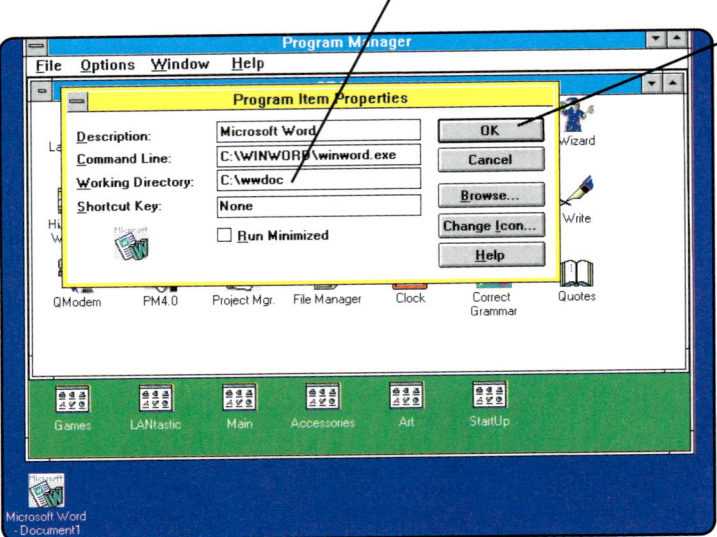

Returning to Word

1. Click twice on the **Microsoft Word icon** at the bottom of your screen. Word will be restored to a window. You will be exactly where you were when you minimized the program.

You are now ready to save the letter.

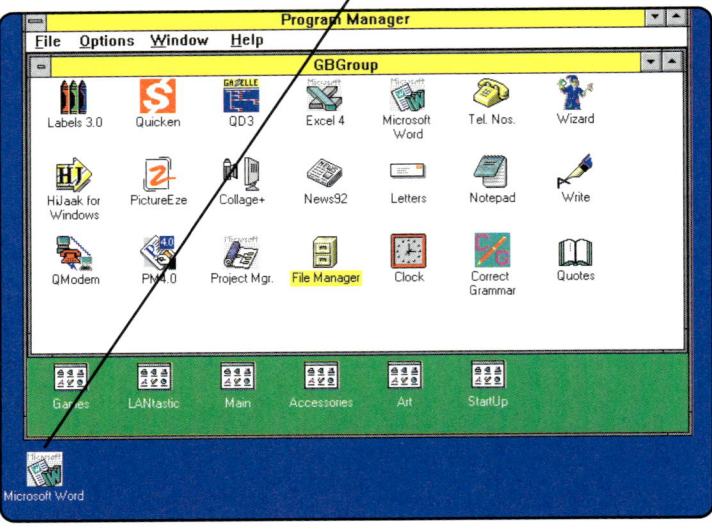

NAMING AND SAVING A FILE

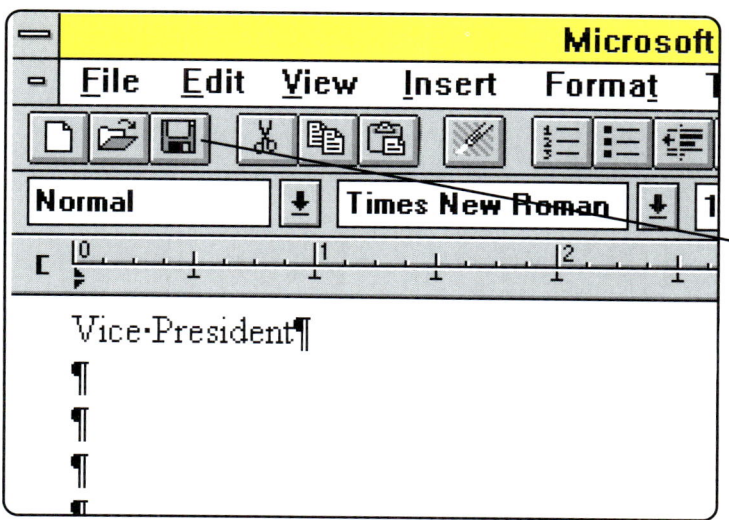

In this section you will name the letter you typed in Chapter 1 and save it to the WWDOC working directory.

1. Click on the **Save tool** in the toolbar. Since you have not named the file yet, the Save As dialog box will appear.

Notice the open folders beside c:\ and winword. These tell you that you are currently working in the WINWORD directory on the C drive. Since you want to save this file to the WWDOC directory, you must bring up the list of all directories on the C drive.

2. Click twice on **c:**. An alphabetical list of directories on the C drive will appear in the Directories list box.

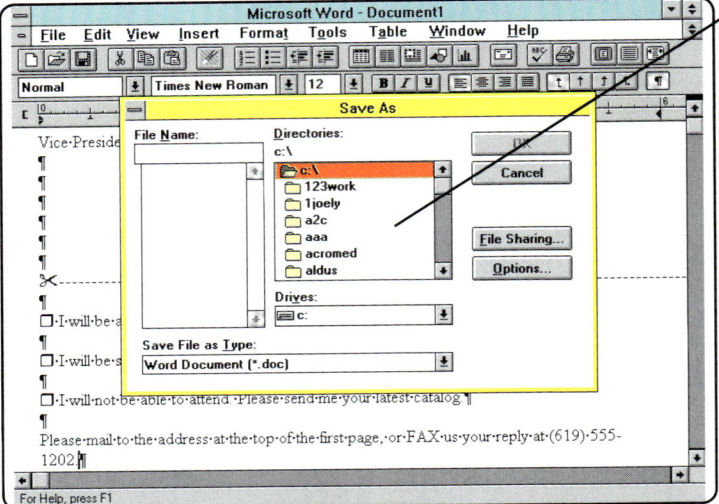

This is the alphabetical list of directories on the computer. Your list will be different from the one you see here.

3. Press the **End key**. You will go to the end of the directories list. (You can also **type w**. This will take you to the first directory beginning with the letter "w." Then scroll down to the WWDOC directory.)

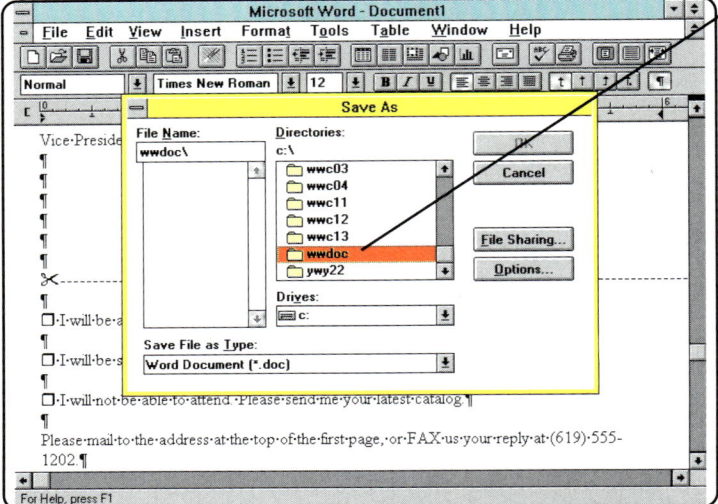

4. Click on **wwdoc** if it is not already highlighted.

From now on all your files will automatically be saved to the WWDOC directory.

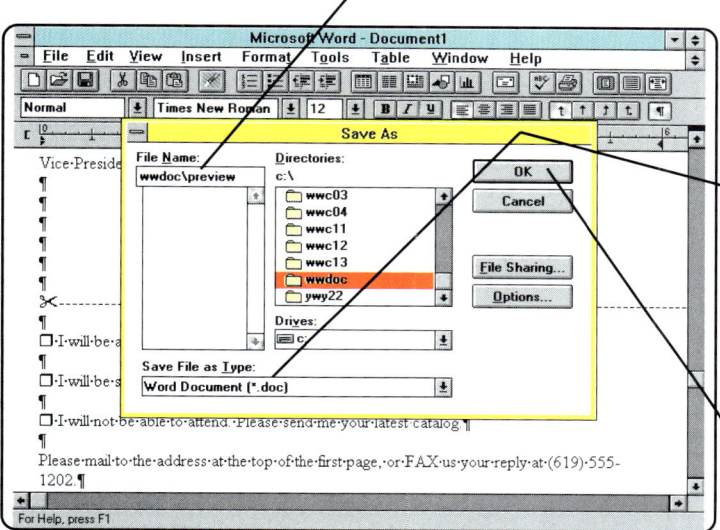

5. Place the mouse pointer to the **right of WWDOC** in the File Name box. **Click** to set it in place. On your screen the box will display only "wwdoc\."

6. Type preview.

7. Confirm that **Word Document (*.doc)** is in the Save File as Type box. This means that the file will be saved as a Word document file.

8. Click on **OK**. The Summary Info dialog box will appear on your screen.

Filling in the Summary Info

When you save a file for the first time, Word displays the Summary Info dialog box. Filling in information in this dialog box is optional. However, the information you add will be useful if you want to search for a file later.

The cursor is flashing in the Title box. On your screen the box will be empty.

1. Type Annual Costume Preview letter. The title can be longer and more descriptive than the filename.

2. **Press** the **Tab key**. The insertion point will move to the Subject box. On your screen it will be empty.

3. **Type Annual Costume Preview**.

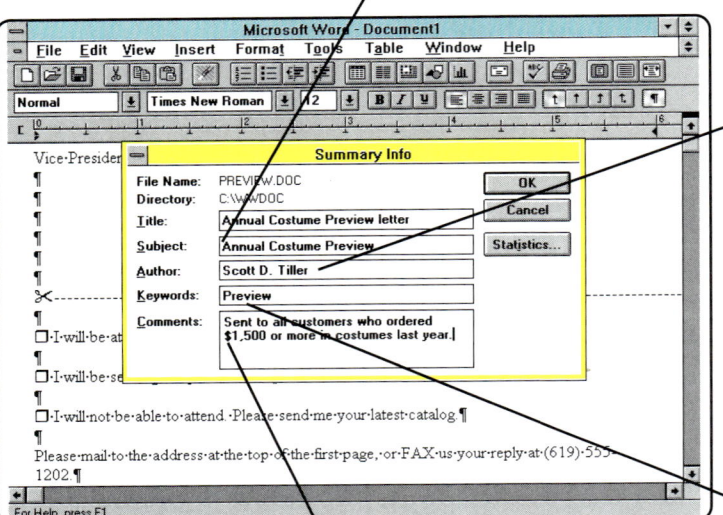

The Author name is the name that was typed in during setup (in this example, Scott D. Tiller). You can change this by dragging the mouse pointer over the name and highlighting it. Then type the name you want. It will replace the highlighted name.

4. **Press Tab**. The insertion point will move to the Keywords box. **Type Preview**. You can include information such as account numbers in this box. Separate key words with spaces.

5. **Press Tab** to move to the Comments box and type the following: **Sent to all customers who ordered $1,500 or more in costumes last year.** (include the period).

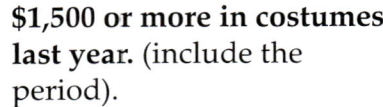

6. **Click** on **OK**. The dialog box will close and the letter will be on your screen.

Directions on how to use this information to search for files is in Chapter 16, "Searching for a File."

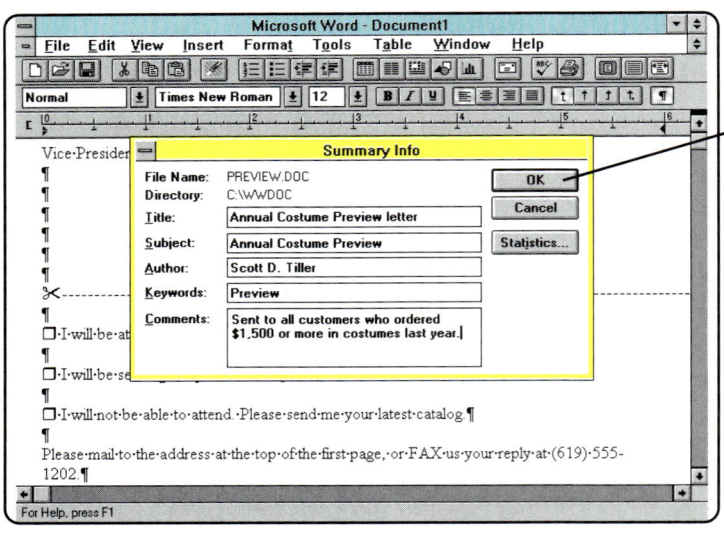

CHAPTER 2: NAMING AND SAVING A DOCUMENT

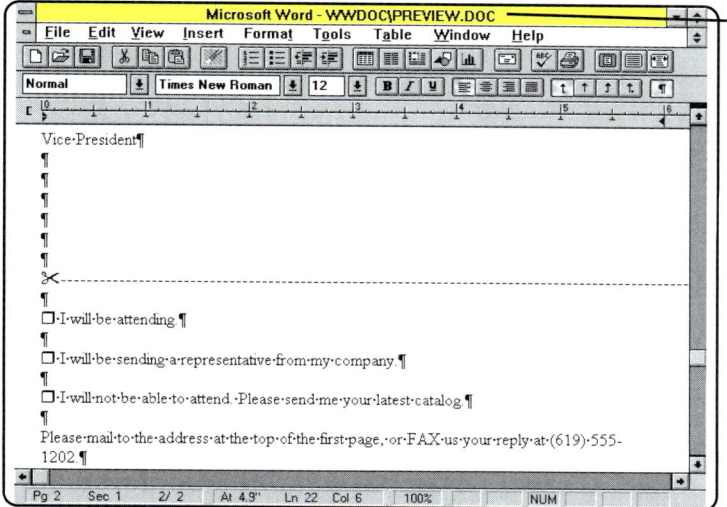

Notice that the filename, WWDOC\PREVIEW.DOC, in the title bar shows the directory as part of the filename.

SAVING AUTOMATICALLY

You can set Word to save your work automatically at specific intervals. This does not take the place of a Save command, but it provides a handy backup in case of a power outage or system failure.

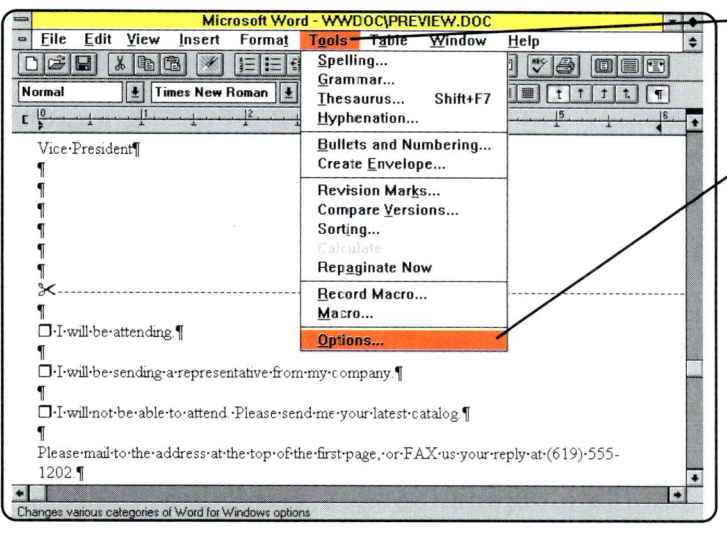

1. **Click** on **Tools** in the menu bar. A pull-down menu will appear.

2. **Click** on **Options**. The Options dialog box will appear.

3. **Click** on the **Save icon** if it is not already highlighted. (In order to see Save, you may have to use the ↓ or ↑ to scroll through the Category list box.)

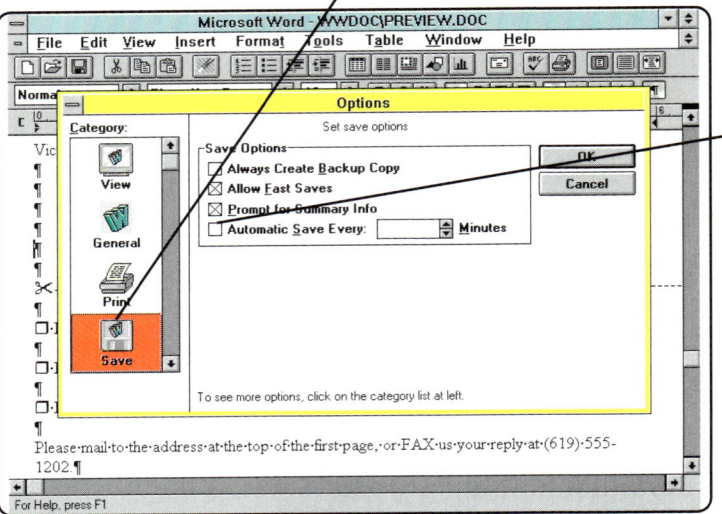

4. **Click** on **Automatic Save Every** to insert an ✕ in the check box.

Notice that "10" appears automatically in the Minutes box.

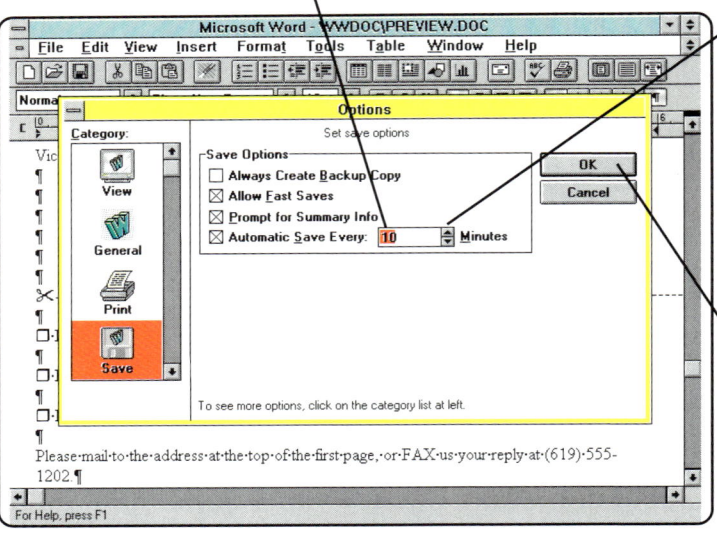

5. **Click** the **up arrow** to increase the time between automatic saves. **Click** the **down arrow** to decrease the time between automatic saves. In this example, the time will be left at 10 minutes.

6. **Click** on **OK**. The Options dialog box will disappear and the letter will be on your screen.

CHAPTER 3

Closing a File and Opening a Saved File

Since Word for Windows 2 is a Windows-based program, it uses standard Windows commands to open and close files. As in all Windows programs, there are several ways to open and close files. In this chapter you will do the following:

❖ Close a file
❖ Close Word for Windows
❖ Learn two ways to open a saved file

SAVING AND CLOSING A FILE

In this section you will close the PREVIEW.DOC file you created in Chapter 1. Even though you saved the file in Chapter 2, these procedures will start with saving the file. Saving often is a good habit to develop.

Saving a File

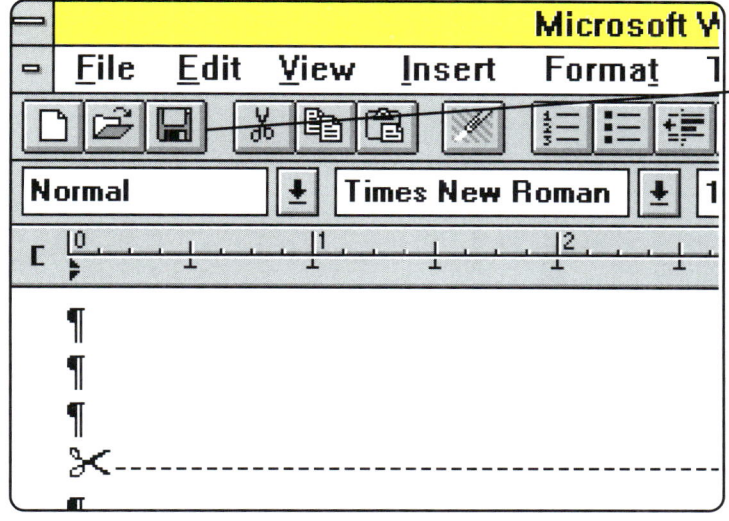

1. Click on the **Save tool** in the toolbar.

The hourglass will appear briefly. You won't see any other difference in your screen, but the file and any changes are now saved. Since you already saved the file, you will not see the Save As dialog box.

Closing a File

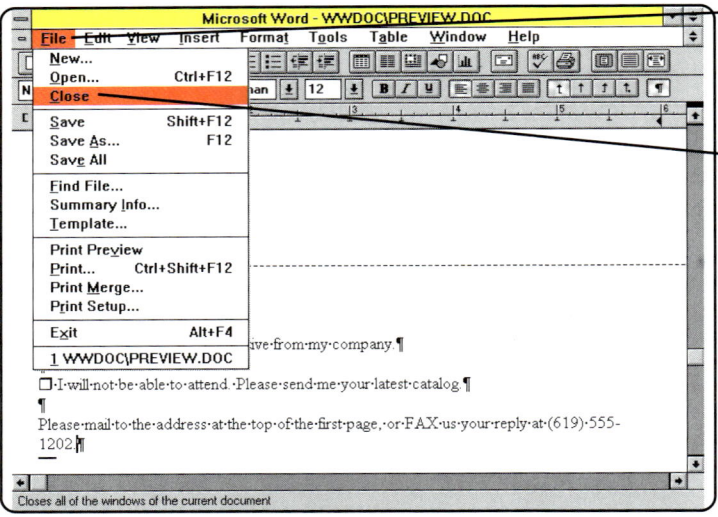

1. **Click** on **File** in the menu bar. A pull-down menu will appear.

2. **Click** on **Close**. The file will close and you will see a blank Word screen.

CLOSING WORD FOR WINDOWS

In this section you will close the Word program.

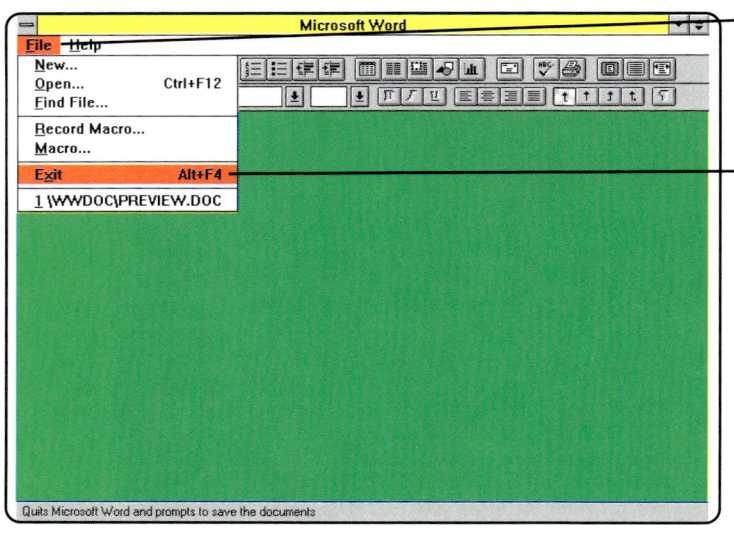

1. **Click** on **File** in the menu bar. A pull-down menu will appear.

2. **Click** on **Exit**. Word will close and you will be back at Program Manager with the group that contains Word.

CHAPTER 3: CLOSING A FILE AND OPENING A SAVED FILE

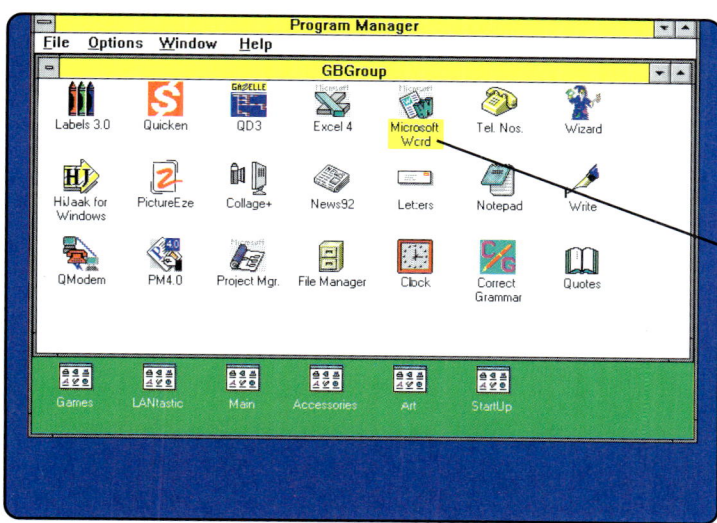

BOOTING UP WORD

Boot up is computer talk for start.

1. Click twice on the **Microsoft Word icon** in whatever group it happens to be.

After a pause, Word will appear on your screen with a blank Document1 file.

OPENING A SAVED FILE

There are several ways to open a saved file. In Method #1, you will use the File pull-down menu.

Method #1

1. Click on **File** in the menu bar. A pull-down menu will appear.

At the bottom of the File pull-down menu, Word lists the four most recent files you have opened. If you have a new Word program, there will be only one file listed. If others have used Word before you, you may see up to four files listed.

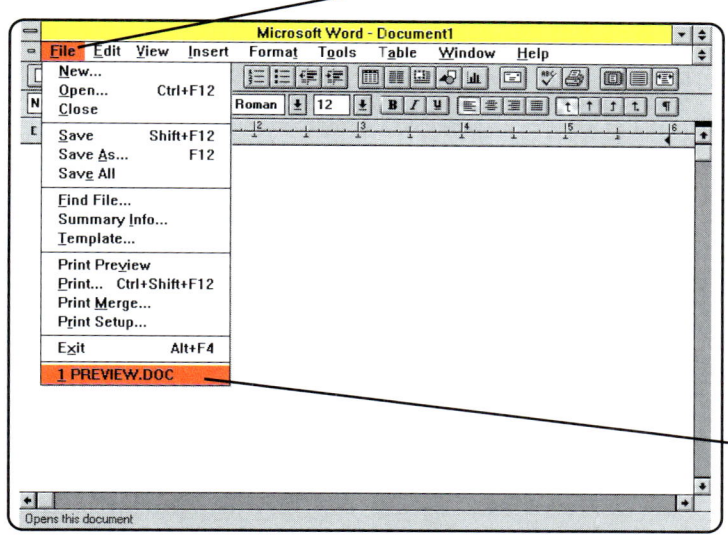

2. Click on **PREVIEW.DOC** in the file list. The file will appear on your screen.

Method #2

Method #2 uses the Open tool in the toolbar. In order to try this method, you will have to close the PREVIEW.DOC file.

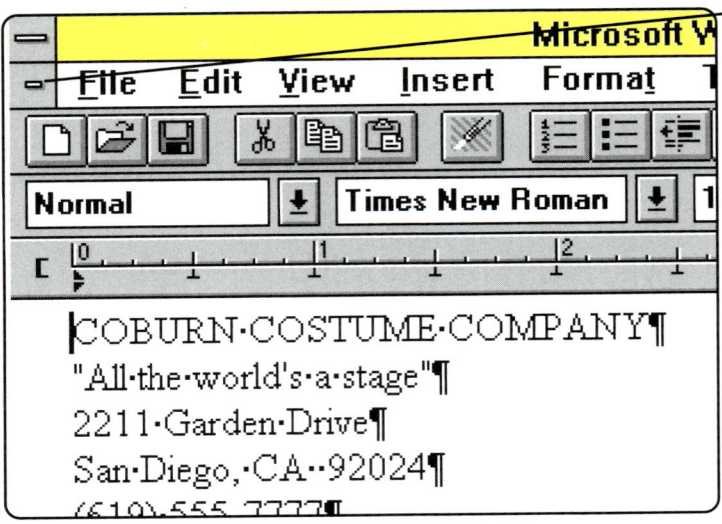

1. Click twice on the **Control menu box** (□) to the left of the menu bar. (Be careful not to click on the Control menu box in the Microsoft Word title bar. That will close the entire program.) The file will close and you will see a blank Word screen.

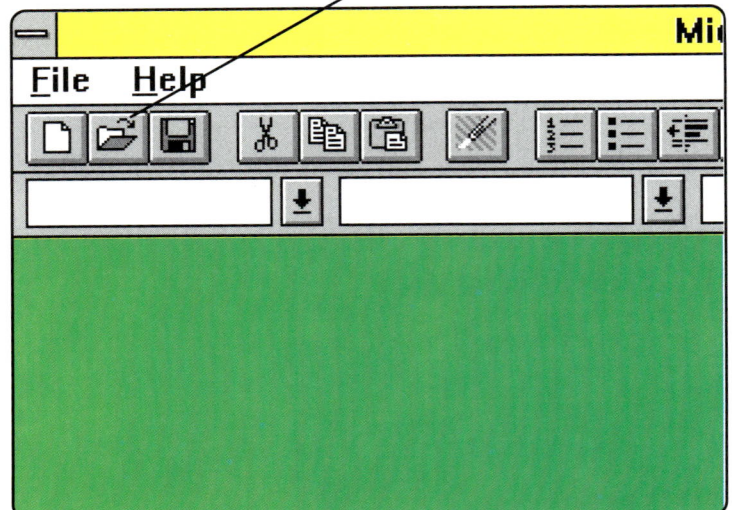

2. Click on the **Open tool** in the toolbar. The Open dialog box will appear.

CHAPTER 3: CLOSING A FILE AND OPENING A SAVED FILE   43

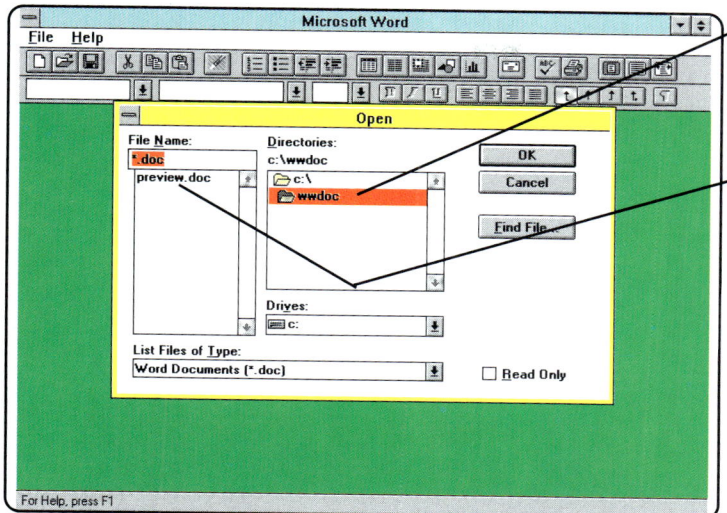

Notice that the WWDOC directory now appears in the Directories list box.

3. Click twice on **preview.doc** in the File Name list box. (You can also click once on preview.doc to highlight it, then click on OK.) The file will appear on your screen.

In the next chapter you will learn how to use the Grammar and Spelling Checker and the Thesaurus that come with Word.

CHAPTER 4

Using the Grammar Checker, Spelling Checker, and Thesaurus

Word for Windows 2 has two handy utilities that will check your grammar and spelling and make suggestions for changes. It also contains a Thesaurus that will offer a list of synonyms. Now, if it would only go out for coffee . . . In this chapter you will do the following:

❖ Use the Grammar Checker and Spelling Checker
❖ Use the Thesaurus

USING THE GRAMMAR CHECKER AND SPELLING CHECKER

You can use the Spelling Checker alone or with the Grammar Checker. When you use the Grammar Checker, however, the Spelling Checker is always included. In order to complete the following procedures, you should be at the beginning of the PREVIEW.DOC file.

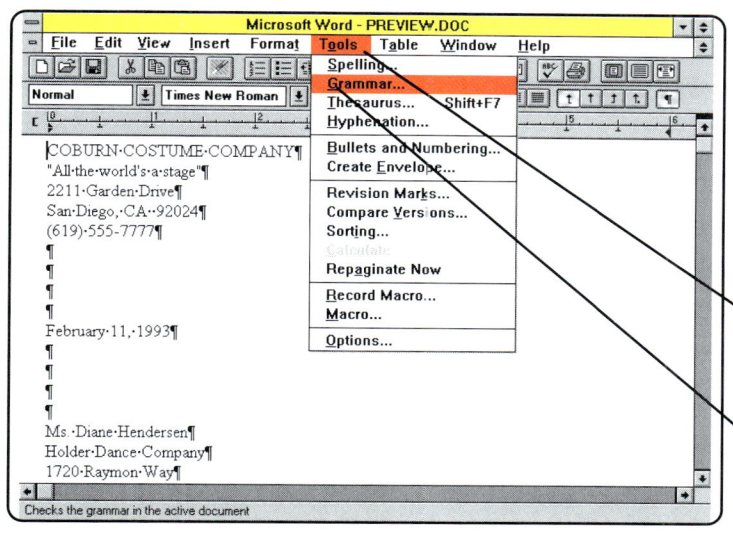

1. Press and hold Ctrl as you **press** the **Home key** (Ctrl + Home). This will move the cursor to the beginning of the file.

2. Click on **Tools** in the menu bar. A pull-down menu will appear.

3. Click on **Grammar**. A dialog box will appear.

45

Notice that "COBURN" is highlighted in the letter and the Spelling dialog box is on your screen.

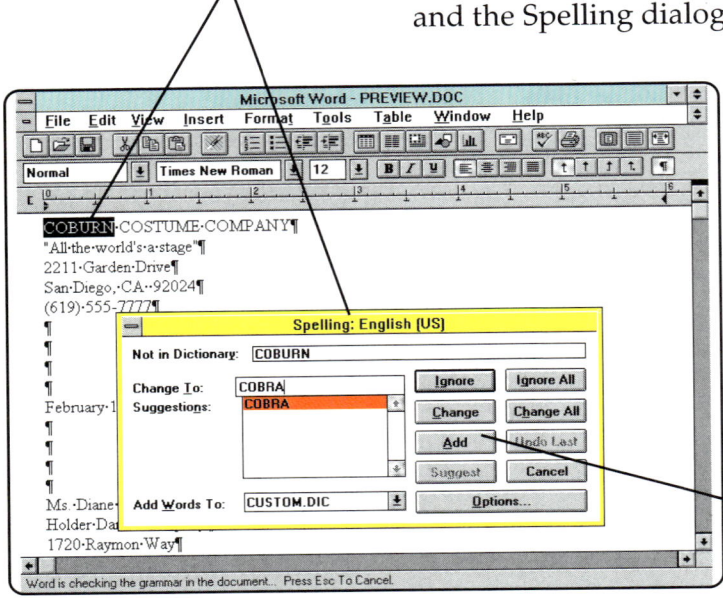

Adding a Word to the Dictionary

Since the company name will be used constantly in your communications, add it to the custom dictionary. This means that Word will recognize the name in the future and not tag it as a misspelled or unrecognized word.

1. **Click** on **Add**. You will see an hourglass as Word goes to the next misspelled word or grammatical error.

Ignoring a Suggested Change

The dictionary is not programmed to recognize most proper names. If the name is one which you will use often, add it to the dictionary as you did above. If you will not use it often, you can choose to ignore Word's identification of it as a misspelled word.

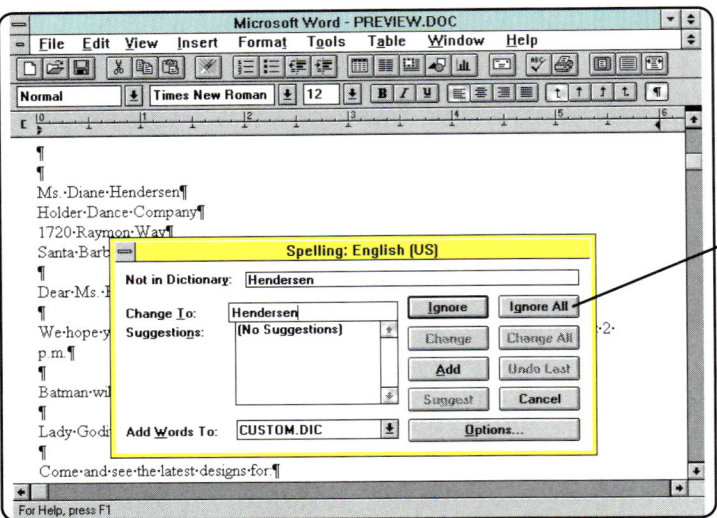

1. **Click** on **Ignore All**. Since "Hendersen" appears more than once in the letter, this will tell Word to ignore all occurrences of it.

CHAPTER 4: GRAMMAR CHECKER, SPELLING CHECKER, AND THESAURUS

47

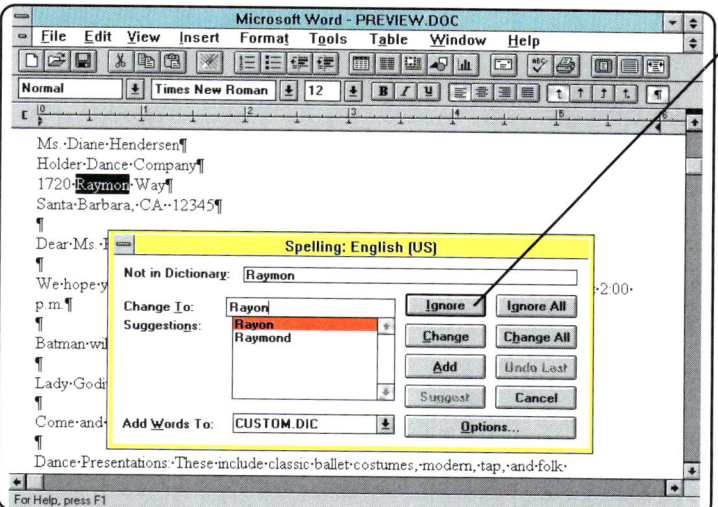

2. Click on **Ignore** since "Raymon" is spelled correctly. Word will go to the next spelling or grammatical error.

Making a Correction in the Letter

Sometimes the Grammar Checker will point out a change that you must make yourself, as in the time change in this example.

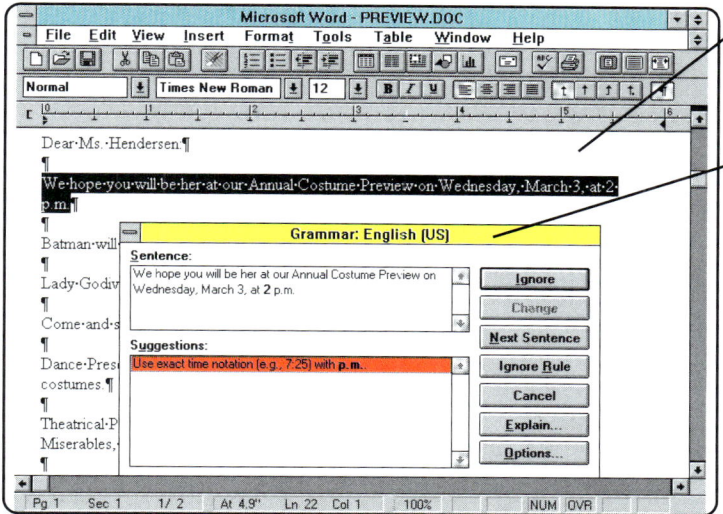

1. Click anywhere on the letter to make it the active window.

Notice that the Grammar dialog box appears on the screen when Word identifies a grammatical error.

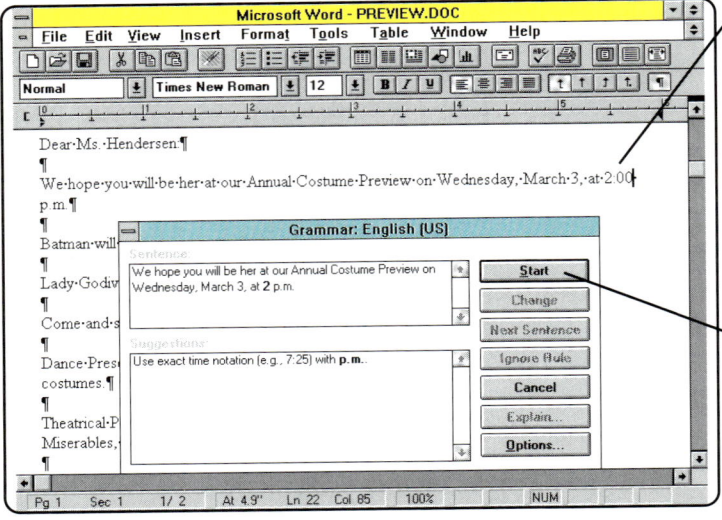

2. Place the mouse pointer **after "2." Click** to set it in place. (On your screen you will see only the number "2.")

3. Type :00. The time now is 2:00.

4. Click on **Start** to resume the grammar and spelling check.

Continuing the Grammar and Spelling Check

Notice the Spelling dialog box has appeared on top of the Grammar dialog box. Word has identified "Batman" as an unrecognized word.

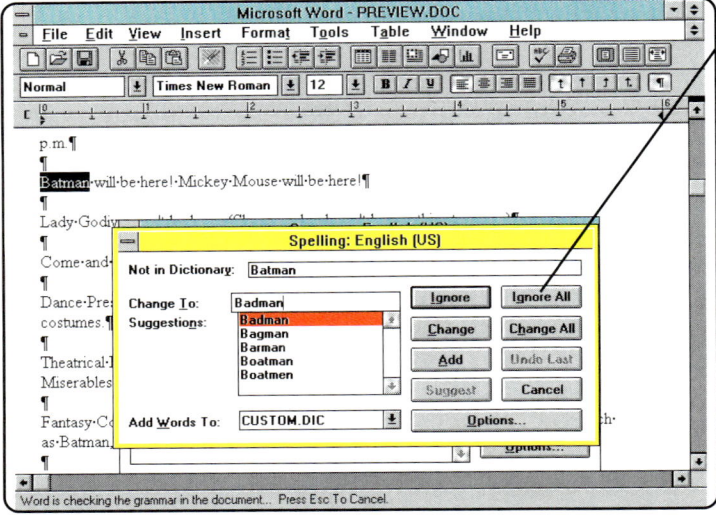

1. Click on **Ignore All**.

Word then identifies "Mickey" as a misspelled word.

2. Click on **Ignore All**.

3. Click on **Ignore** when Word identifies "Godiva," then "Les" and "Miserables" as misspelled words.

CHAPTER 4: GRAMMAR CHECKER, SPELLING CHECKER, AND THESAURUS

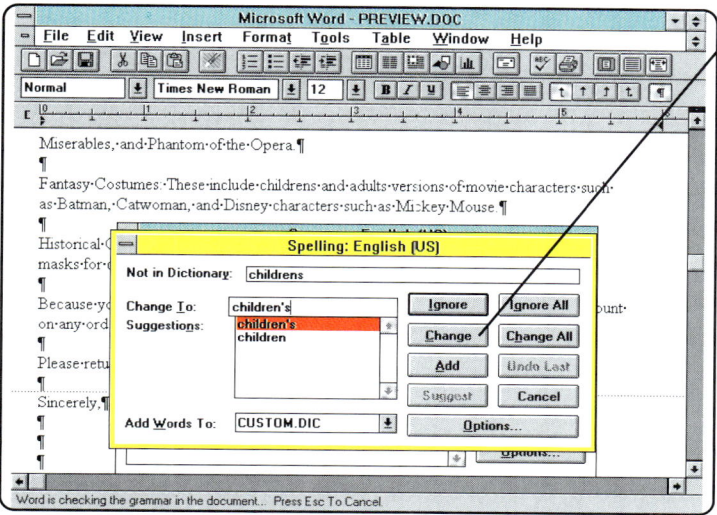

4. Click on **Change** to change "childrens" to "children's."

5. Click on **Ignore** when Word identifies "Catwoman" and "Disney" as misspelled words.

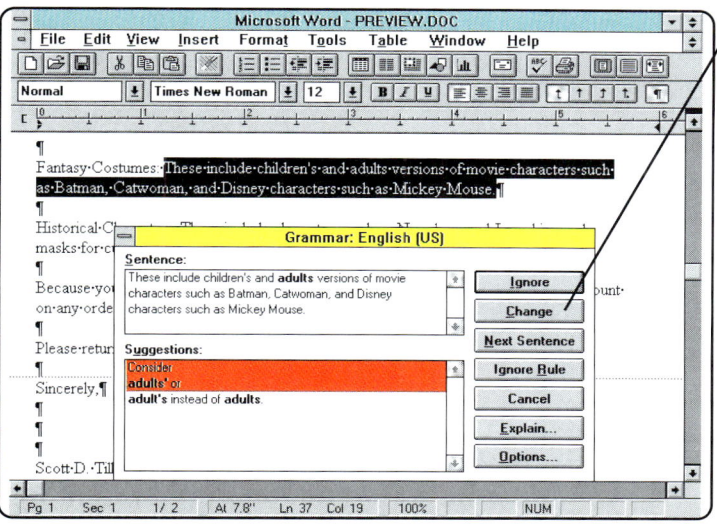

6. Click on **Change** to change "adults" to the possessive "adults'."

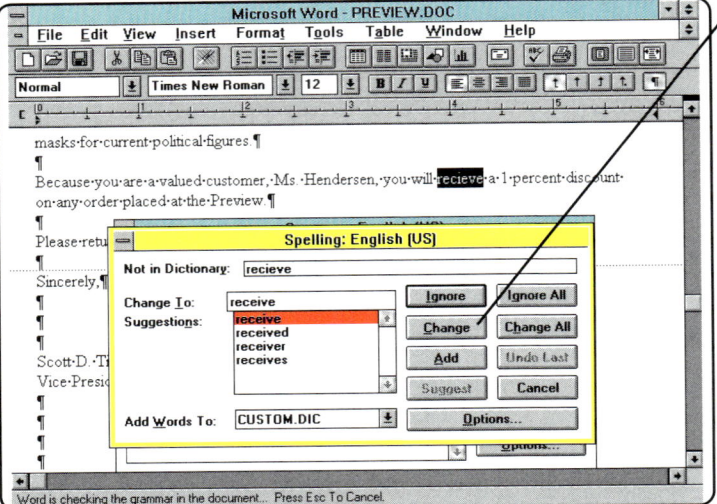

7. **Click** on **Change** to change "recieve" to "receive."

You may see a message asking if you want Word to continue checking at the beginning of the document.

8. **Click** on **No**.

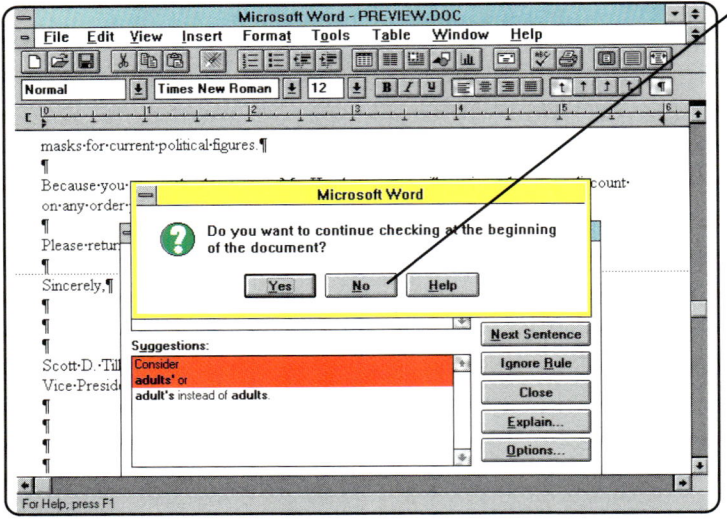

CHAPTER 4: GRAMMAR CHECKER, SPELLING CHECKER, AND THESAURUS

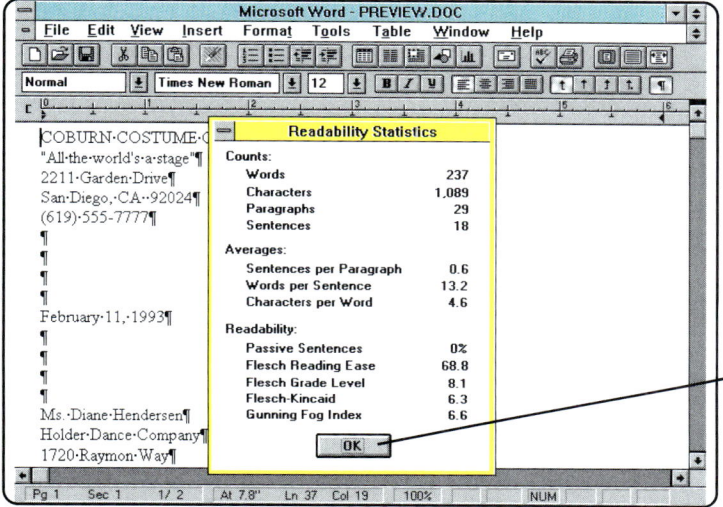

When the grammar check is complete, Word displays statistics about the readability of the document. See the *Microsoft Word for Windows User's Guide* for more information about the readability of a document.

9. Click on **OK**. The dialog box will disappear and you will be returned to the letter.

USING THE THESAURUS

In this section you will use the Thesaurus to view words that can replace "political." First, however, you will use the Find command to locate the word.

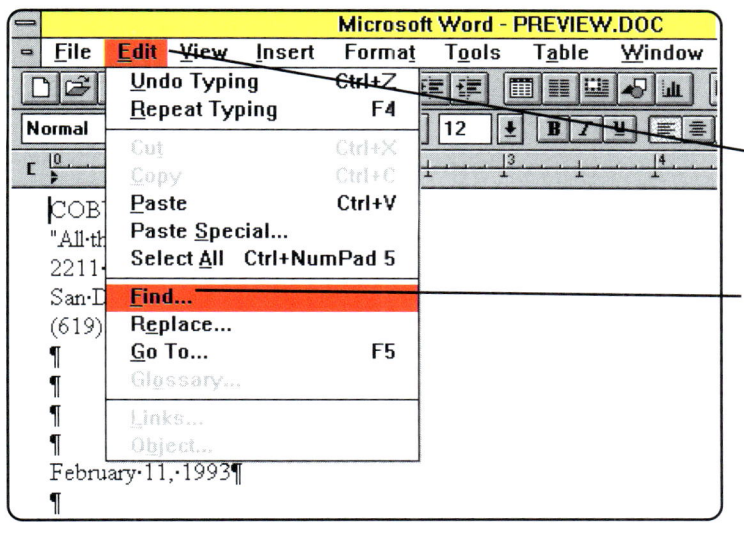

Using the Find Command

1. Click on **Edit** in the menu bar. A pull-down menu will appear.

2. Click on **Find**. The Find dialog box will appear.

52 WORD FOR WINDOWS 2: THE VISUAL LEARNING GUIDE

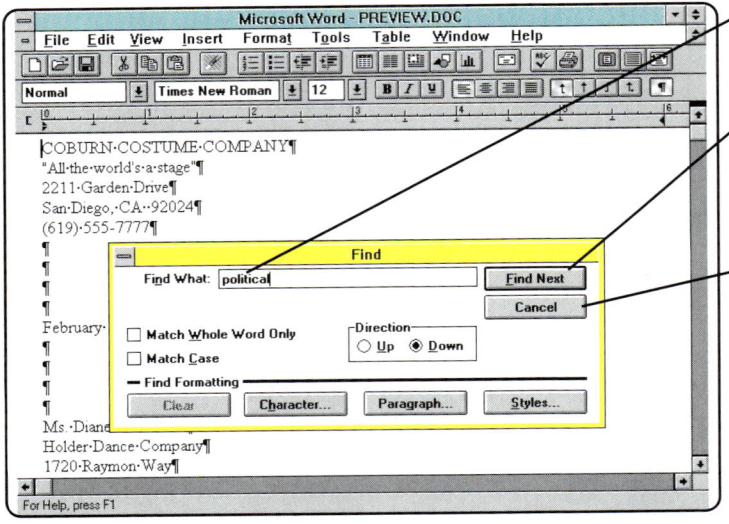

3. **Type** the word **political** in the Find What box.

4. **Click** on **Find Next**. Word will highlight "political" in the letter.

5. **Click** on **Cancel** to close the Find dialog box.

Replacing a Word with the Thesaurus

Normally, the word you want to check with the Thesaurus must be highlighted. If you have been following these procedures, "political" was highlighted by the Find command. Therefore, you can simply continue with the following steps.

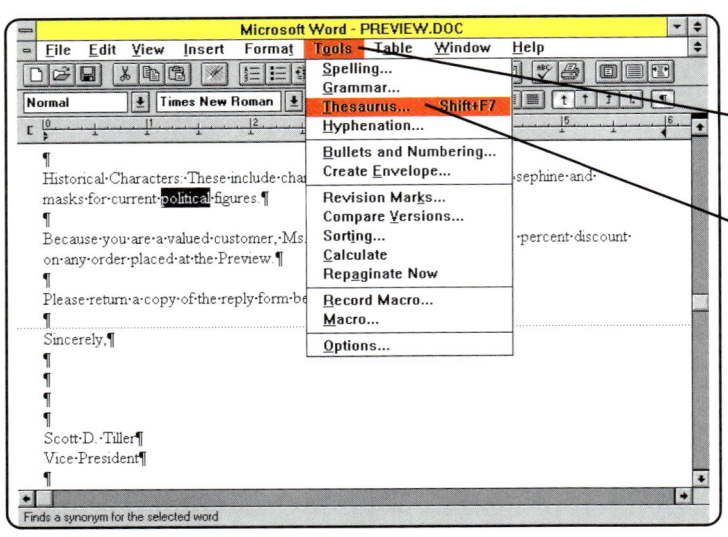

1. **Click** on **Tools**. A pull-down menu will appear.

2. **Click** on **Thesaurus**. The Thesaurus dialog box will appear.

CHAPTER 4: GRAMMAR CHECKER, SPELLING CHECKER, AND THESAURUS

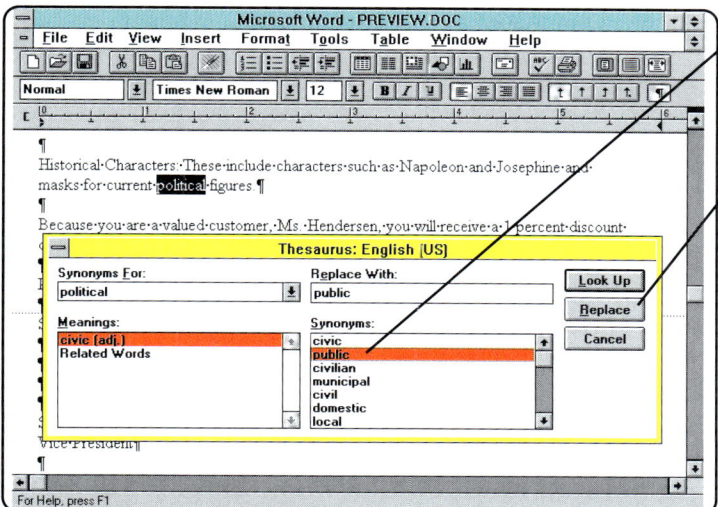

3. **Click** on **"public"** in the Synonyms list box. It will be highlighted.

4. **Click** on **Replace** to make the change. "Political" will be replaced by "public."

5. **Press and hold Ctrl** as you **press Home** (Ctrl + Home). You will be returned to the beginning of the file.

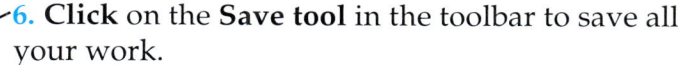

6. **Click** on the **Save tool** in the toolbar to save all your work.

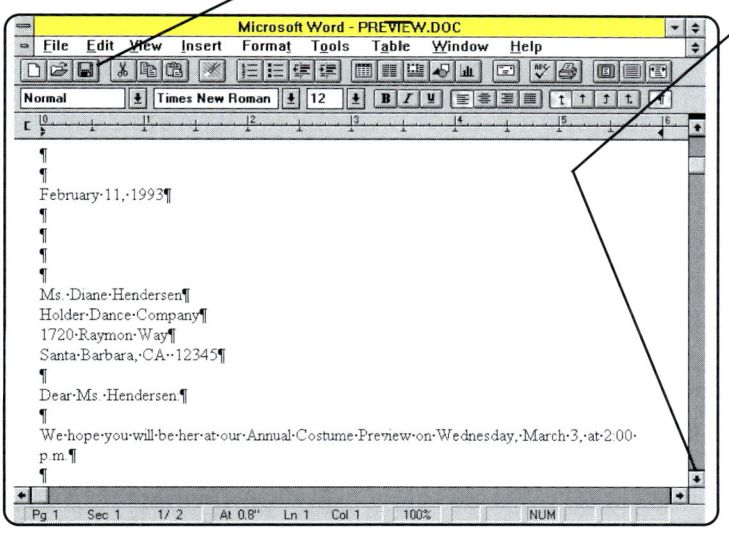

7. **Click** on ↓ to scroll down to the first sentence in the letter.

Notice that Word did not identify "her" in the first sentence as a misspelled word. This is because "her" is a correctly spelled word. It is incorrectly spelled only in the context of this sentence, where it should be "here." Computers are not ready to take over the world just yet.

In Chapter 5, "Editing a Document," you will correct this error and make other changes in the letter.

CHAPTER 5

Editing a Document

If this is the first time you have used a Windows-based word processing program, you will be delighted with the ease with which you can edit a document. Word for Windows 2 has even improved on standard Windows editing commands by adding special features such as drag-and-drop moving and Edit Undo. In this chapter you will do the following:

❖ Add and delete letters and words and combine paragraphs

❖ Use the Edit Undo feature

❖ Use the Replace All command to correct an error that occurs in several places

❖ Move and copy text

❖ Insert and change the position of the page break

ADDING LETTERS AND WORDS

In this section you will make a number of corrections to the letter. The first will be to change "her" to "here."

1. **Place** the mouse pointer at the **end of "her."** Notice that the mouse pointer is in the shape of an I-beam when it is in the letter. **Click** to set it in place.

2. **Type** the letter **e**. The word will become "here." Notice that "2:00" moves to the next line automatically.

55

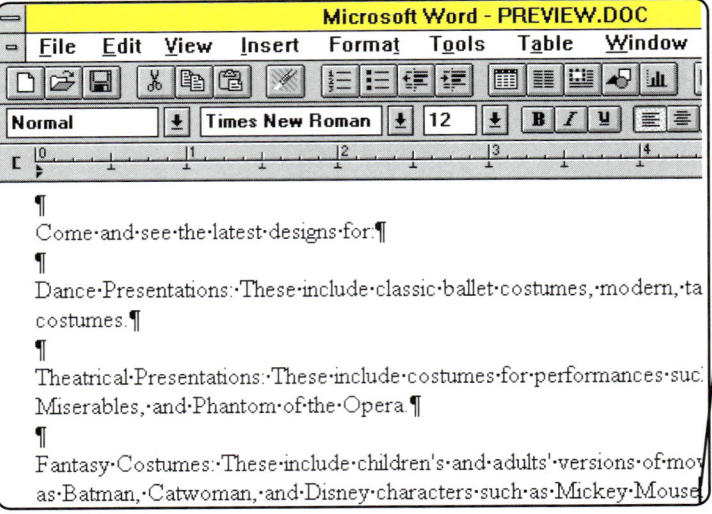

3. Click on ↓ to scroll down to the two lines beginning with "Fantasy Costumes."

4. Place the mouse pointer at the end of the sentence **between "Mouse" and the period**. **Click** the mouse button to set the insertion point in place.

5. Press the **Spacebar** then **type** the words **and Donald Duck**. Notice that the period moves as you add words.

6. Click on ↓ until you can see the sentence that begins "Because you are a valued customer."

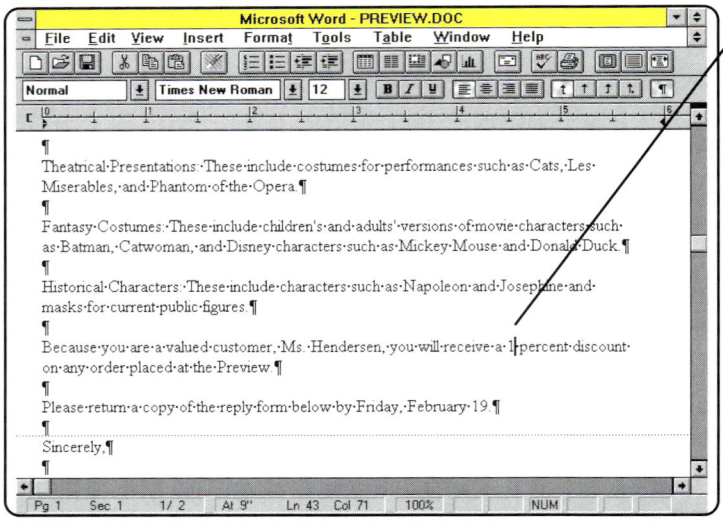

7. Place the mouse pointer **after the number 1**. **Click** to set it in place.

8. Type the number **8**. The number will become "18." Notice that "discount" moves to the next line automatically.

CHAPTER 5: EDITING A DOCUMENT

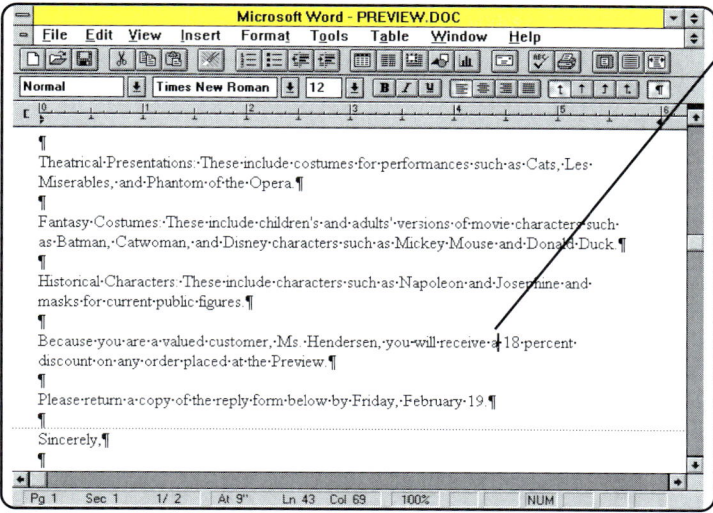

9. Press ← on your keyboard **three times** to move the insertion point to the right of "a." (Make sure your Num Lock key is off if you are using the arrow keys on your numeric keypad.)

10. Type the letter **n** to make the word "an."

DELETING AND REPLACING WORDS AND COMBINING PARAGRAPHS

In this section, you will delete unnecessary words.

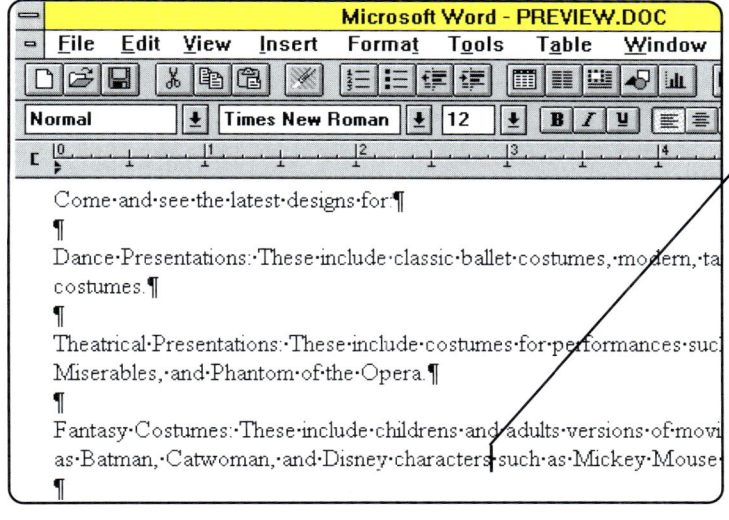

Deleting Words

1. Place the I-beam at the **right of "Disney characters." Click** to set it in place.

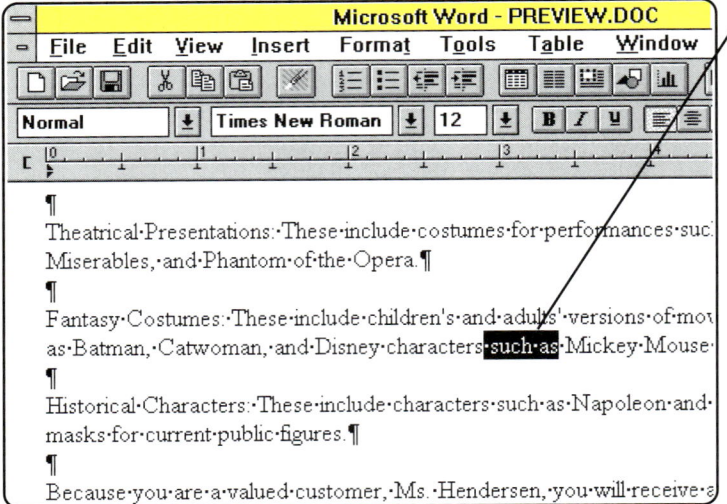

2. Press and hold the mouse button and **drag** the mouse pointer **over "such as."** They will be highlighted. Be sure to highlight the dot before "such," but be careful *not* to highlight the dot after "as," since you don't want to delete the space the second dot represents.

3. Release the mouse button, then **press** the **Del key**. The highlighted words will disappear.

Undoing an Edit

What if you decide you don't want to delete those words? Word has an Undo feature on the Edit menu that makes it easy for you to change your mind as long as you haven't done anything else after deleting the words.

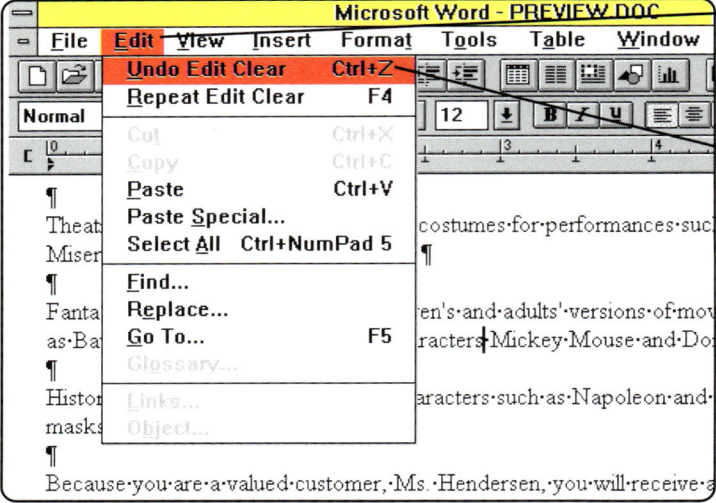

1. Click on **Edit** in the menu bar. A pull-down menu will appear.

2. Click on **Undo Edit Clear**. The deleted words will be restored to the text (but only if you do this step **before** you do anything else).

You can even undo an undo.

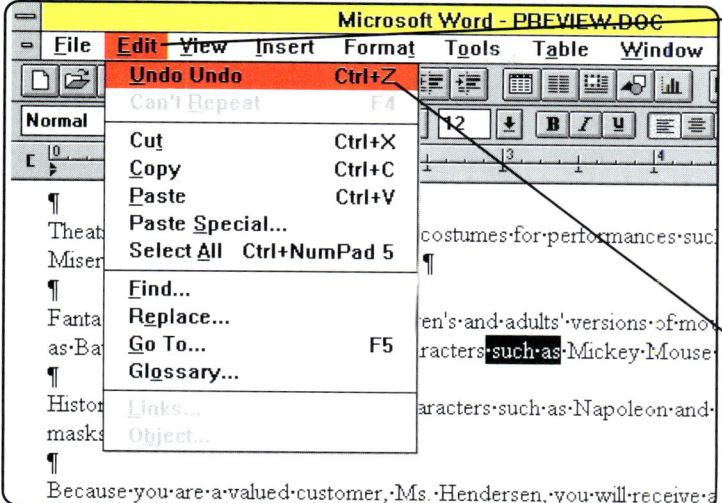

3. Click on **Edit** in the menu bar. A pull-down menu will appear. Notice that now the first option is Undo Undo. The menu choice changes depending on what your last editing change was.

4. Click on **Undo Undo**. The words will be deleted once again.

Combining Paragraphs

In this section you will put the Lady Godiva sentences into the preceding paragraph with Batman and Mickey Mouse.

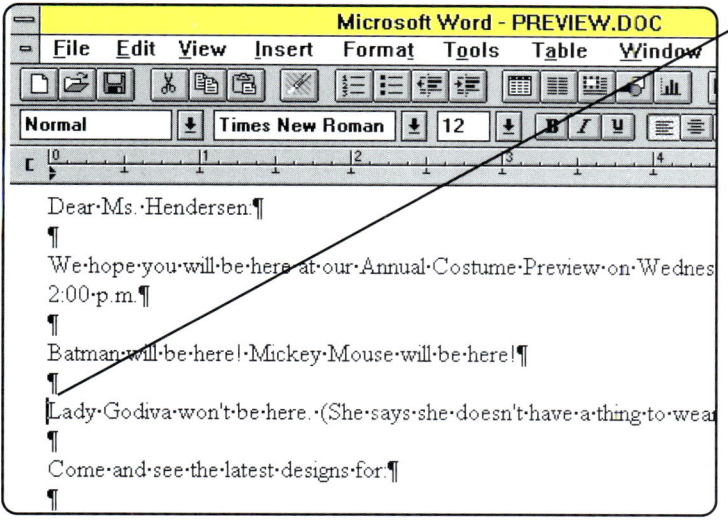

1. Click on ↑ to scroll up to the sentence beginning with "Lady Godiva."

2. Place the mouse pointer at the **beginning** of the **"Lady Godiva" sentence**. Make sure the pointer is in the shape of an I-beam. Place the pointer as close to "Lady" as you can to ensure that it is an I-beam. **Click** to set it in place.

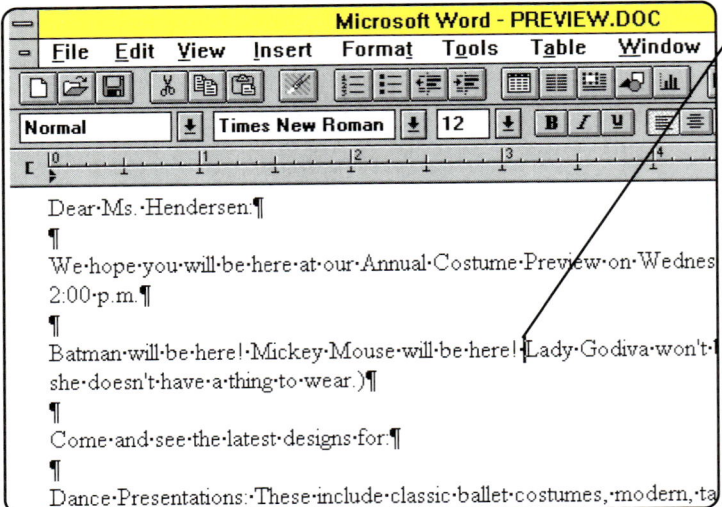

3. Press the **Backspace key twice** then **press** the **Spacebar**. This will bring the entire Lady Godiva paragraph up to the end of the Mickey Mouse sentence and put a space between the sentences.

Inserting a Soft Return

In the example you see here, it would look better if "Les" was on the same line with "Miserables." If you press the Enter key, however, you will insert a paragraph mark (called a *hard return*) and make the second line a separate paragraph. You can, however, move "Les" to the next line with what is called a *soft return*. Unlike hard returns, soft returns are not recognized as paragraph endings in Word. This is an important formatting distinction, which will be discussed in Chapter 7, "Customizing Text."

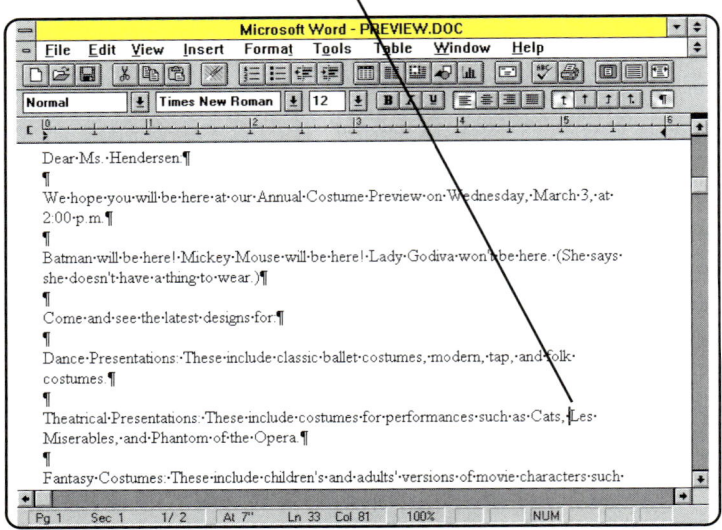

1. Place the mouse pointer to the **left of "Les,"** after the dot. **Click** to set it in place.

CHAPTER 5: EDITING A DOCUMENT

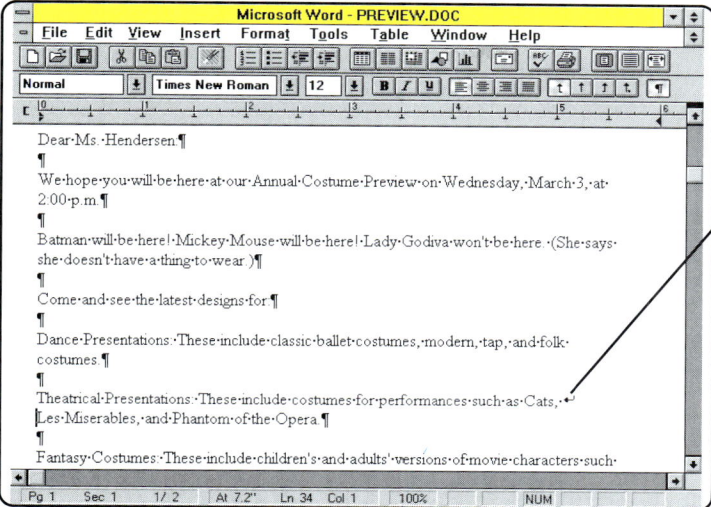

2. Press and hold the **Shift key** as you **press Enter** (Shift + Enter). "Les" will move to the next line.

Notice the symbol indicating a soft return at the end of the line.

3. Press and hold Ctrl as you **press End** (Ctrl + End). This will take you to the end of the file.

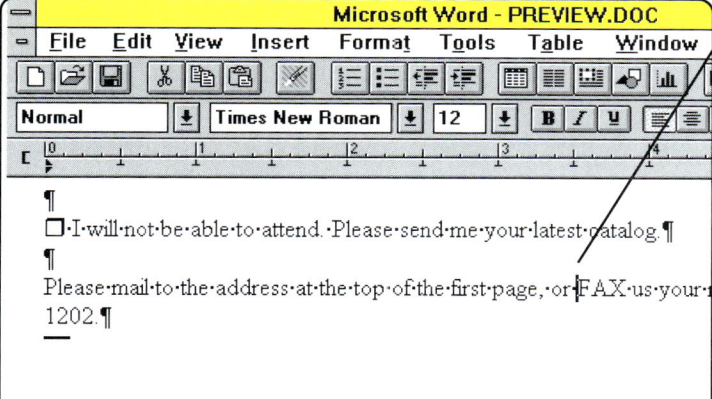

4. Repeat steps 1 and 2 to insert a soft return and put the part of the sentence beginning with "FAX" on the next line.

Using the Replace Command

In this example you will replace "sen" at the end of "Hendersen" with "son." You can replace each "sen" individually or you can use the Replace command to find and replace each occurrence automatically. Since the Replace command starts its search from the insertion point, go to the beginning of the file.

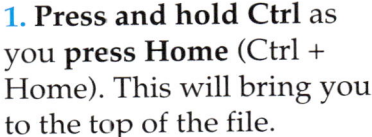

1. **Press and hold Ctrl** as you **press Home** (Ctrl + Home). This will bring you to the top of the file.

2. **Click** on **Edit** in the menu bar. A pull-down menu will appear.

3. **Click** on **Replace**. The Replace dialog box will appear.

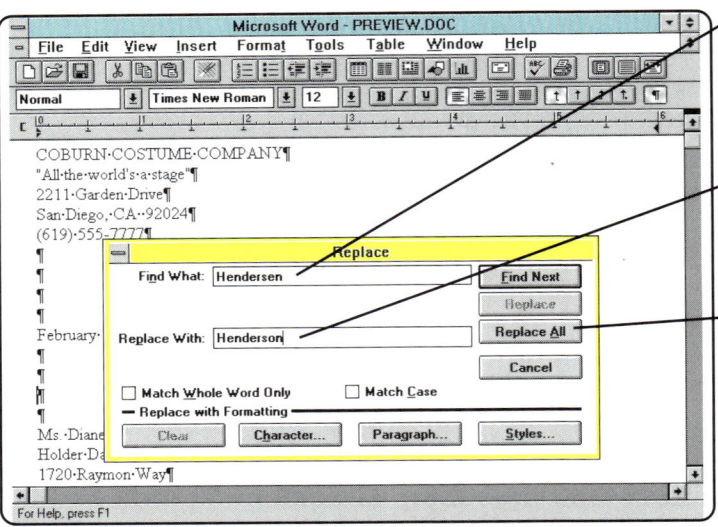

4. Since the insertion point is already flashing in the Find What box, simply **type Hendersen**.

5. **Click** on the **Replace With box** and **type Henderson**.

6. **Click** on **Replace All**. An hourglass will appear briefly as Word makes all the changes. (See the *User's Guide* for more details about the Replace command.)

CHAPTER 5: EDITING A DOCUMENT

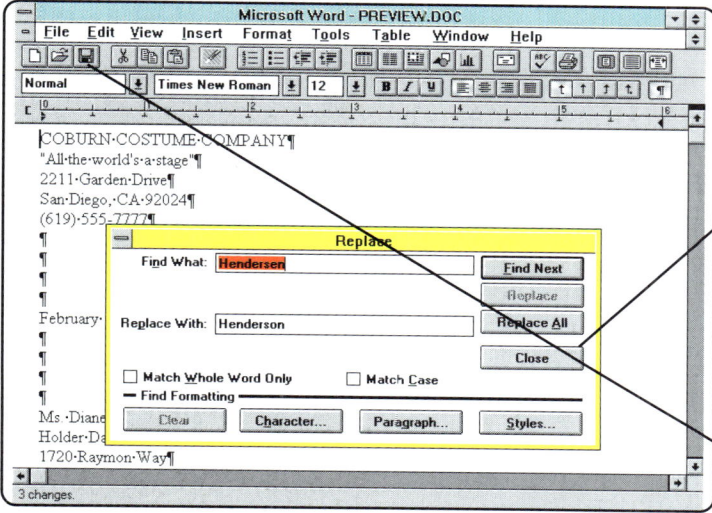

When Word has completed the changes, the Cancel button in the dialog box will change to Close.

7. **Click** on **Close**. The dialog box will disappear and the letter will be on your screen with all corrections made. Pretty neat, don't you think?

8. **Click** on the **Save button** in the ribbon to save all your work.

DRAG-AND-DROP MOVING

In this section you will move the first sentence to a different spot in the letter.

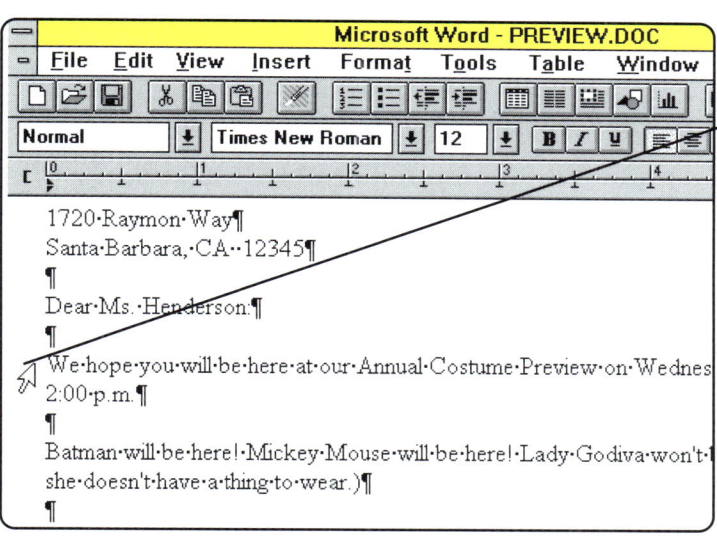

1. **Click** on ↓ to scroll down so that you can see the first three or four paragraphs.

2. **Place** the mouse pointer in the left margin **beside the first paragraph**. It will change to an arrow.

3. **Click twice**. The entire paragraph will be highlighted. (If you click once only the single line beside the arrow will be highlighted.)

4. Place the mouse pointer **on top of** "**We**."

5. Press and hold the mouse button and **drag** the pointer down to the **end of the next paragraph**. You will see a dotted insertion point and a small square being dragged by the arrow.

6. Place the dotted insertion point to the **left of the paragraph symbol** and **release** the mouse button. The paragraph will be moved to that spot.

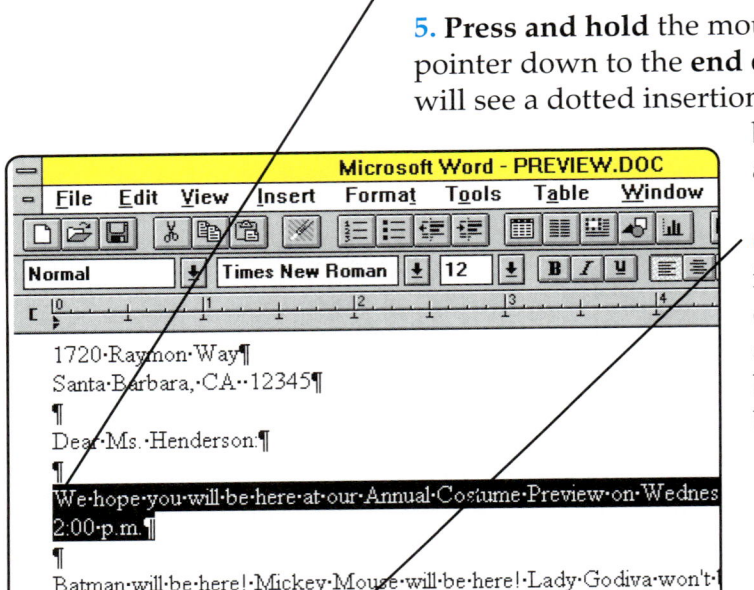

7. Click to the **left of "We hope."** The highlighting will disappear and you will see the flashing insertion point.

8. Press Enter twice to insert a double space between the end of the Batman paragraph and the We hope paragraph.

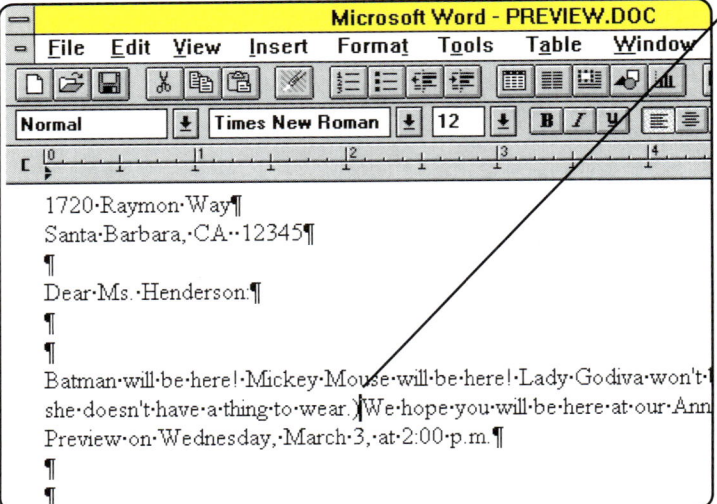

CHAPTER 5: EDITING A DOCUMENT

Notice that there is now an extra paragraph mark (and a blank line) at the beginning of the letter.

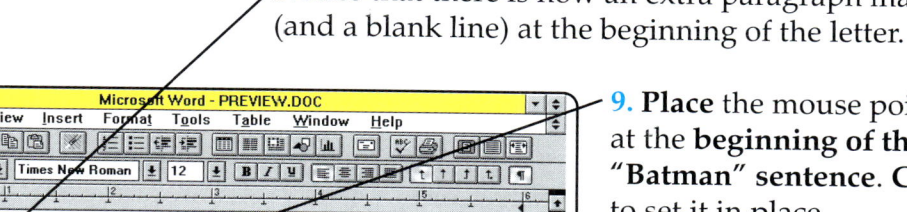

9. Place the mouse pointer at the **beginning of the "Batman" sentence**. **Click** to set it in place.

10. Press Backspace once. The sentence is moved up one line and the blank line is removed.

11. Repeat steps 9 and 10 to remove the blank line above the "Come and see" sentence.

INSERTING A PAGE BREAK

Word does not necessarily insert an automatic page break in a place that makes sense within the context of the document. Fortunately, it's easy to change the position of the page break.

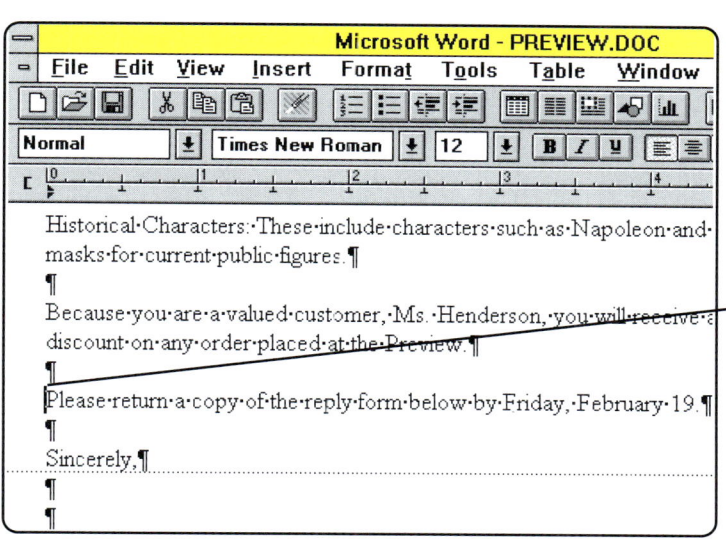

1. Click on ↓ until you can see the dotted line that signifies the automatic page break inserted by Word.

2. Place the mouse pointer at the **beginning of the "Please return" sentence**. **Click** to set it in place.

3. Click on **Insert** in the menu bar. A pull-down menu will appear.

4. Click on **Break**. The Break dialog box will appear.

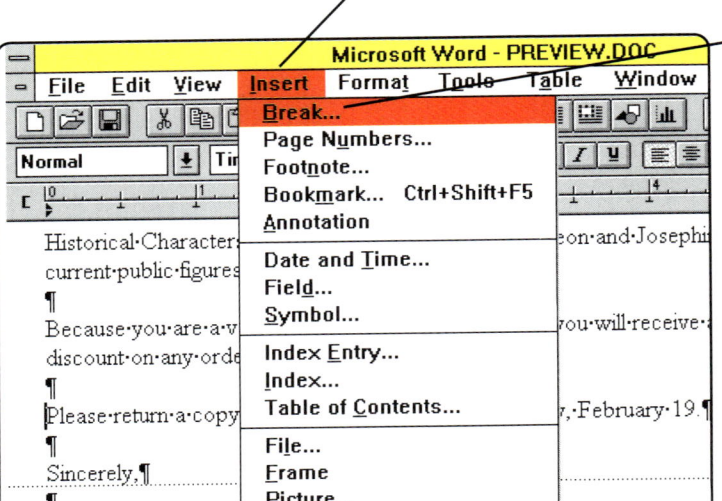

5. Click on **Page Break** to insert a dot in the circle if one is not already there.

6. Click on **OK**. A page break will be inserted into the letter at the insertion point.

When you insert a page break into text, the automatic page break disappears.

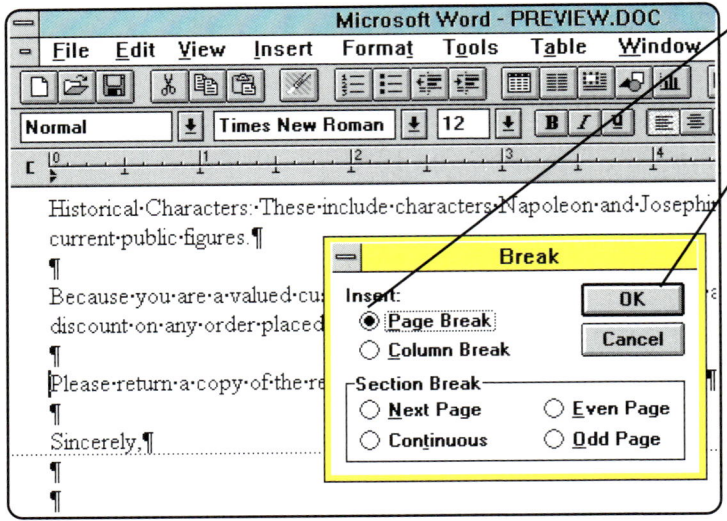

Changing the Position of a Page Break

In this example you will change the position of the page break you just inserted.

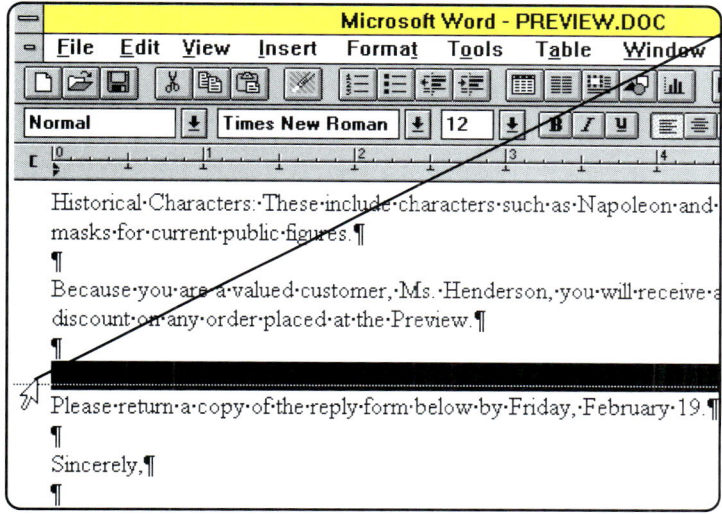

1. **Place** the mouse pointer in the left margin **on the page break** you just inserted. It will change to an arrow.

2. **Click** on the **page break**. It will be highlighted.

3. **Press Del**. The page break will be deleted.

Notice that the automatic page break appears again.

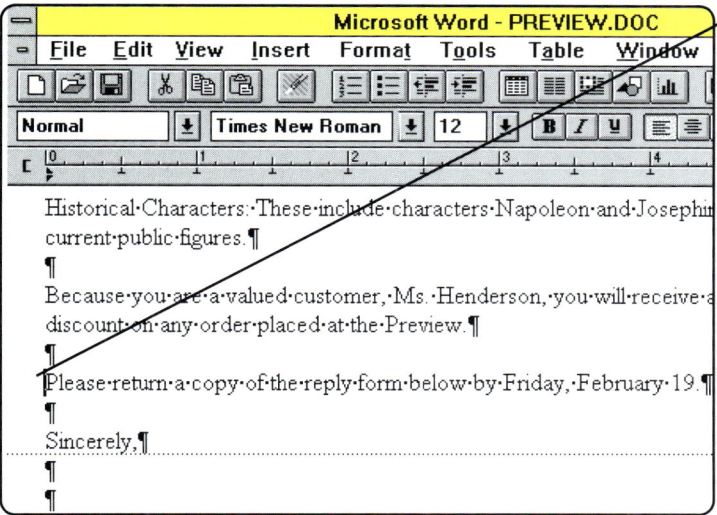

4. **Place** the mouse pointer at the **beginning of the "Please return" sentence** if the insertion point is not already there. **Click** to set it in place.

5. **Press and hold Ctrl**, then **press Enter** (Ctrl + Enter). This is another way to insert a page break.

COPYING AND PASTING TEXT

In this section you will learn two ways to copy text from one section of a document to another.

Copying and Pasting Text with the Edit Menu

In this example you will copy text from page 1 of the letter onto page 2.

1. Click on ⬆ to scroll up to the second paragraph on page 1.

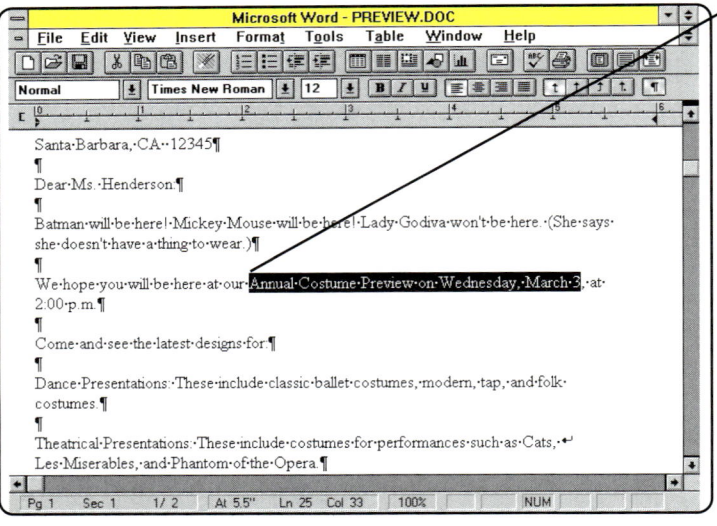

2. Place the mouse pointer to the **left of "Annual Costume Preview." Click** to set it in place.

3. Press and hold the mouse button and **drag** the insertion point **over "Annual Costume Preview on Wednesday, March 3."** They will be highlighted. **Release** the mouse button.

CHAPTER 5: EDITING A DOCUMENT

4. **Click** on **Edit** in the menu bar. A pull-down menu will appear.

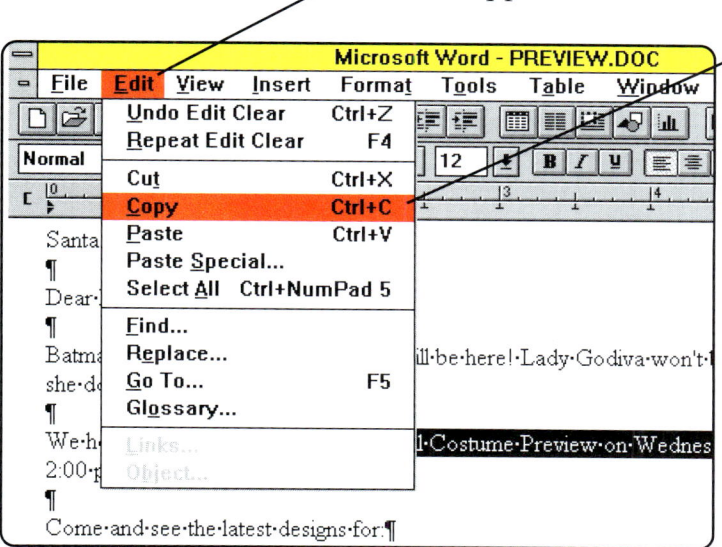

5. **Click** on **Copy**. You will not see any change in your screen, but the highlighted text is now copied to the Clipboard. It will stay there until it is replaced by text from another Copy, Cut, or Delete command.

6. **Press and hold Ctrl**, then **press End** (Ctrl + End). This will take you to the end of the file.

7. **Click** on ↑ until you can see the scissors.

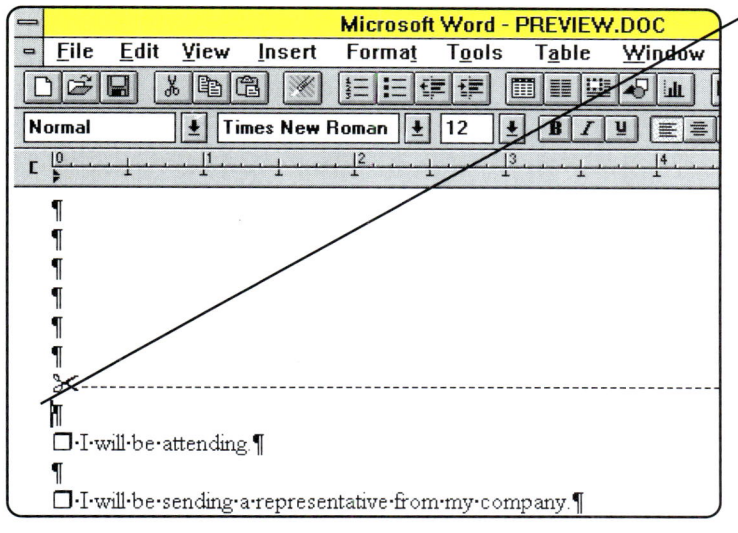

8. **Place** the mouse pointer to the **left of the paragraph symbol** just below the scissors. **Click** to set the pointer in place.

9. **Click** on **Edit** in the menu bar. A pull-down menu will appear.

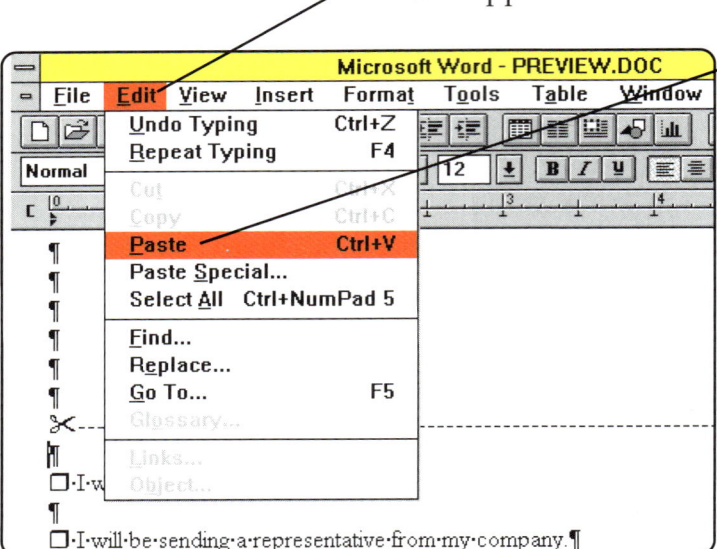

10. **Click** on **Paste**. The text that you copied to the Clipboard will be copied into the document starting at the insertion point.

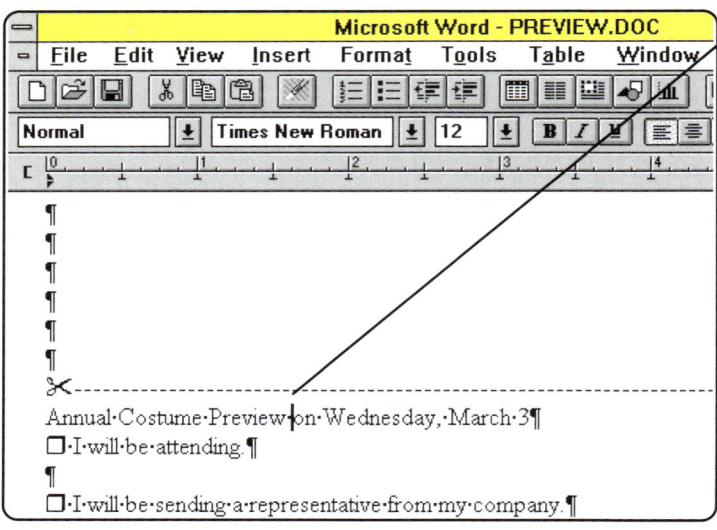

11. **Place** the mouse pointer to the **left of "on." Click** to set it in place.

12. **Press Enter** to move "on Wednesday, March 3" to the next line.

13. **Place** the mouse pointer to the **left of "on."** If you place it close to the word it will change to an I-beam. You may have to fiddle with the position of the pointer to get it to change to the I-beam. (If you place it too far out in the left margin it will change to an arrow and the arrow won't perform the following procedure.)

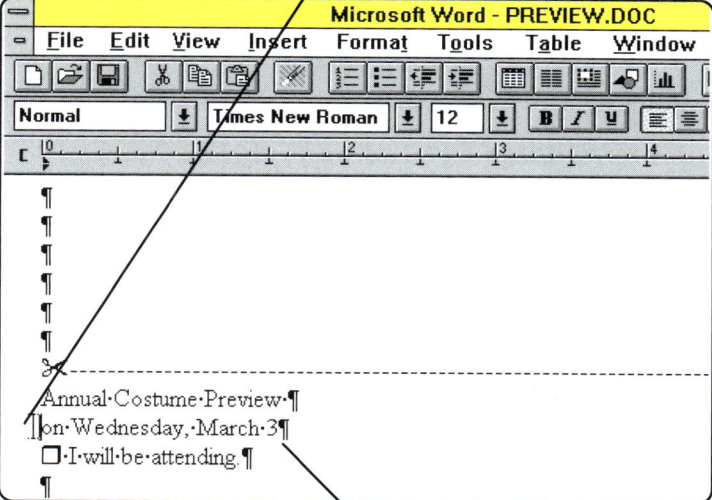

14. **Click twice**. This will highlight the entire word and the space after it. (This is a handy way to highlight a single word.)

15. **Press Del**. The highlighted text will be deleted.

16. **Place** the mouse pointer to the **left of the paragraph symbol** at the end of "March 3." **Click** to set it in place.

17. **Press Enter twice** to insert two blank lines after the date.

Using the Copy Tool

In this three-part example you will use the Copy and Paste tools to copy Ms. Henderson's name and address on the first page and place it on the return form on the second page. First you will copy the text.

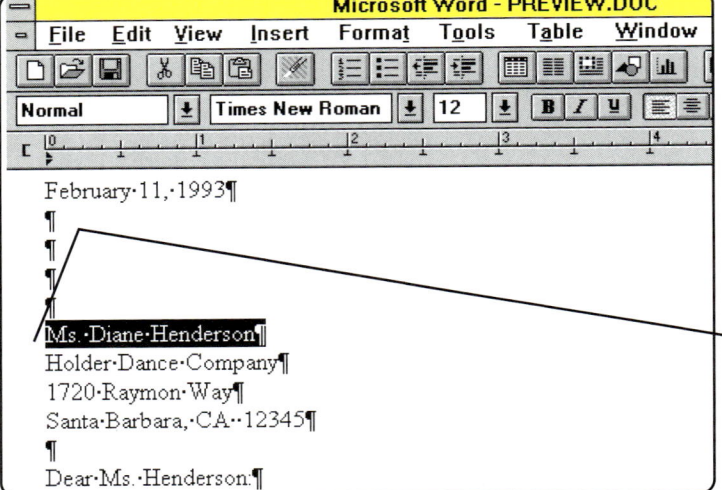

1. **Press and hold Ctrl**, then **press Home** (Ctrl + Home) to go to the top of the file. Then scroll down until you can see Ms. Henderson's name and address.

2. **Click** on the left margin **beside "Ms. Diane Henderson."** The line will be highlighted.

3. **Press and hold Shift** and **click** in the left margin **next to the last line of the address**. All lines between the first and second clicks will be highlighted. (This is a quick way to select a series of paragraphs.)

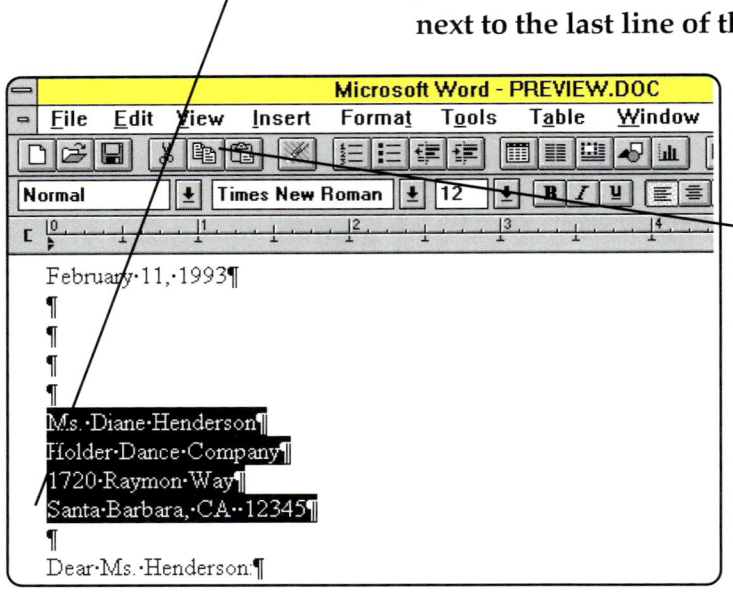

4. **Click** on the **Copy tool** in the toolbar. You won't see any difference in your screen, but the highlighted (selected) text is now copied to the Clipboard.

In the next procedure, you will use the Go To command to get to page 2 quickly.

Using the Go To Command

Using the Go To command is a quick way to move around in multipage documents. In this example you will use it to go to the top of page 2.

1. **Click** on **Edit** in the menu bar. A pull-down menu will appear.

2. **Click** on **Go To**. The Go To dialog box will appear.

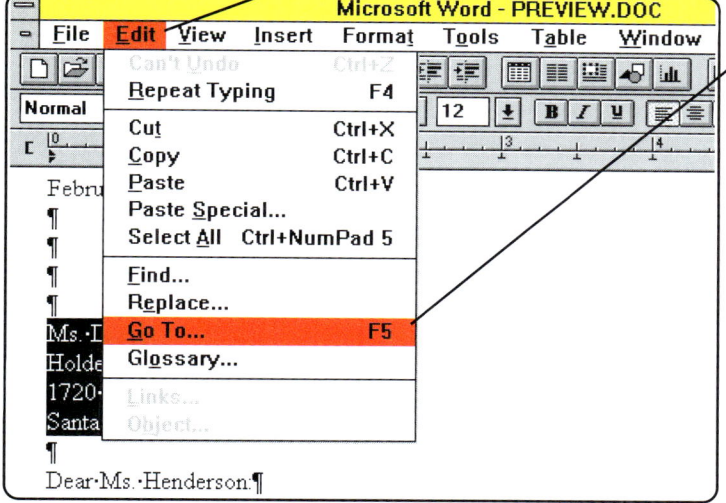

3. **Type** the number **2** in the Go To box.

4. **Click** on **OK**. The insertion point will move to the top of page 2 and page 2 will be displayed on the screen.

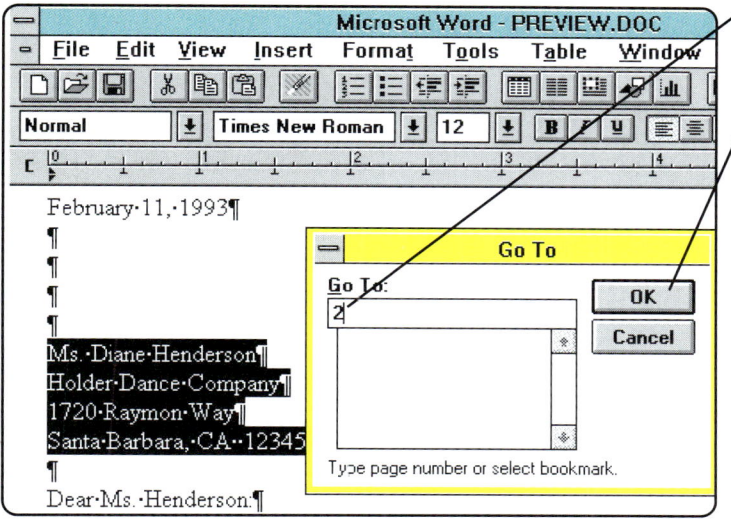

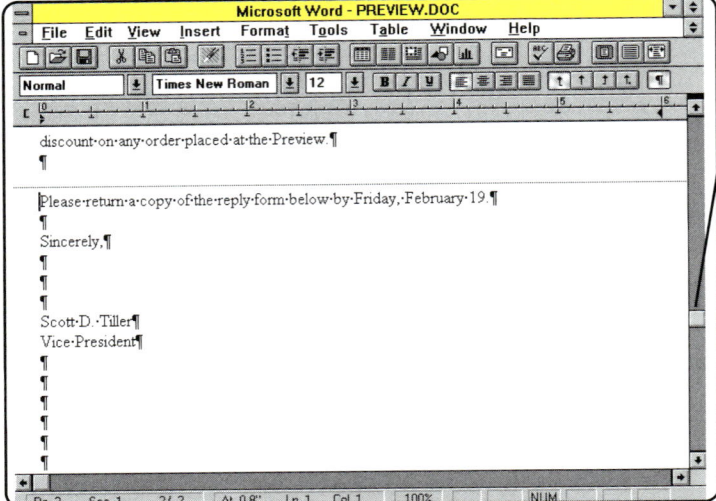

5. **Click** on the **scroll bar** about three quarters of the way down. This will take you three quarters of the way through the file and bring the return form into view.

Using the Paste Tool

1. **Place** the mouse pointer to the **left of the paragraph symbol above "☐ I will be attending."** **Click** to set it in place.

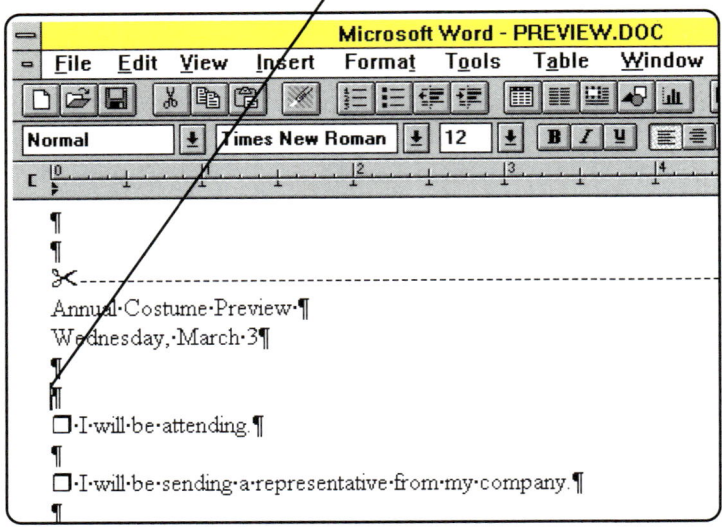

2. **Press Enter** to insert another blank line in the text. You will see three paragraph symbols.

CHAPTER 5: EDITING A DOCUMENT

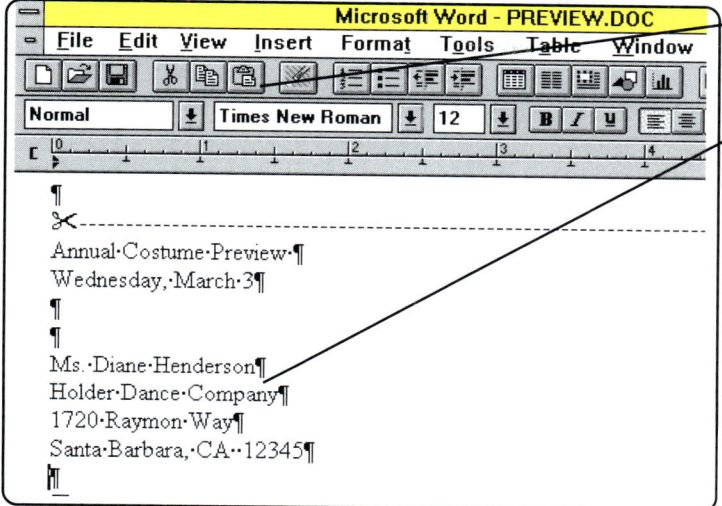

3. Click on the **Paste tool** in the toolbar.

The text you copied to the Clipboard with the Copy tool is now pasted in the letter at the insertion point.

TYPING OVER HIGHLIGHTED TEXT AND SAVING THE FILE

In this section you will replace the date February 19 with February 27.

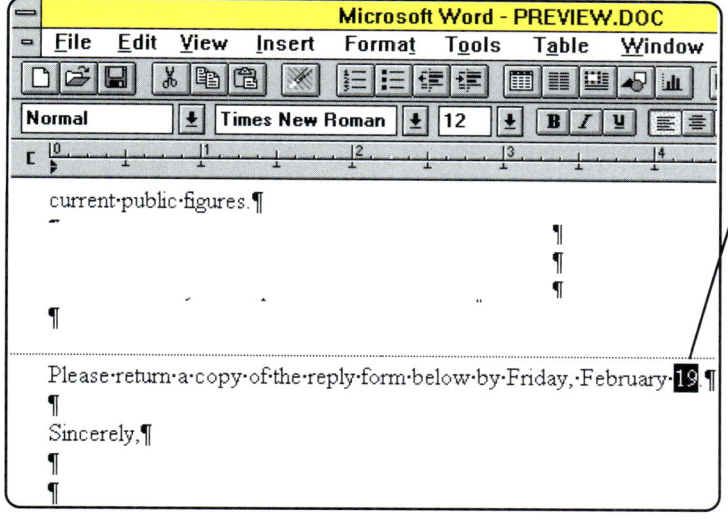

1. Click on the **scroll bar** until you can see the page break line.

2. Place the mouse pointer to the **left of "19." Click** to set the pointer in place.

3. Press and hold the mouse button as you **drag** the pointer **over "19."** It will be highlighted. **Release** the mouse button.

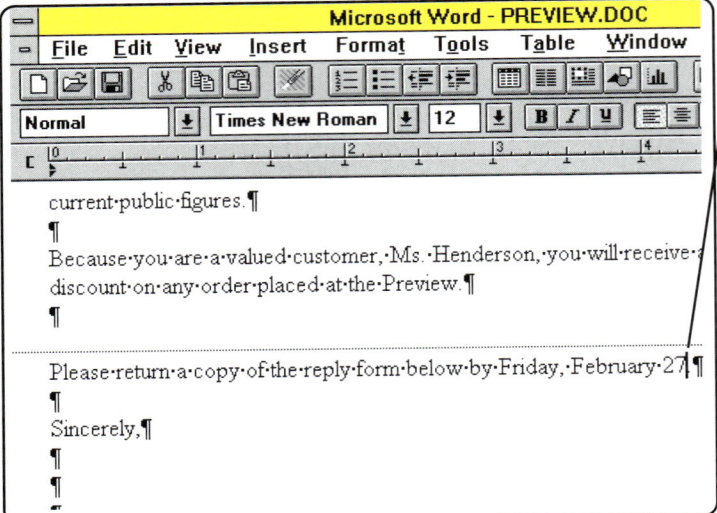

4. Type the number **27**. It will replace the highlighted numbers.

5. Click on the **Save tool** in the toolbar to save your work.

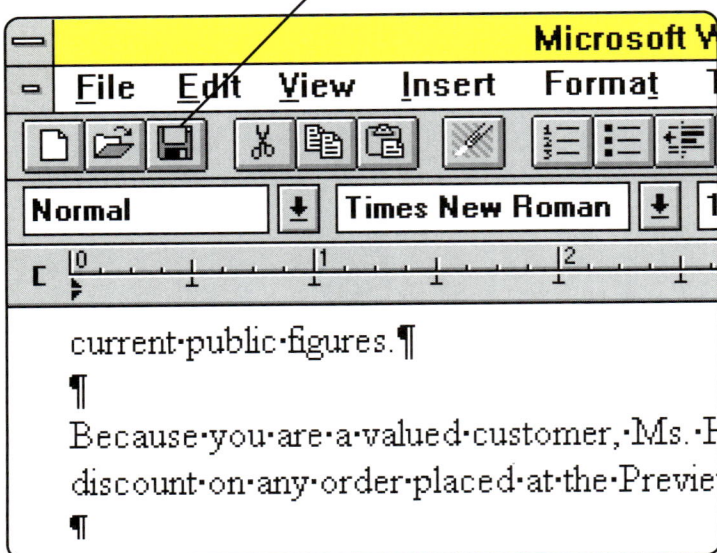

In Chapter 6, "Printing a File," you will print the letter. In Chapter 7, "Customizing Text," you will add some fancy formatting to the letter.

CHAPTER

6

Printing a File

There are several ways to print a file in Word for Windows 2. You can print the entire file by clicking on the Print tool with your mouse. Or you can use the Print command on the File pull-down menu to print a range of pages or to print multiple collated copies of the file. In this chapter you will do the following:

❖ Use the Print tool in the toolbar
❖ Use the Print command on the File pull-down menu

PRINTING WITH THE PRINT TOOL

In this section you will use the Print tool in the toolbar. This allows you to print the entire file at the click of your mouse. If you don't have a file open, open one now. In this example the PREVIEW.DOC is being used.

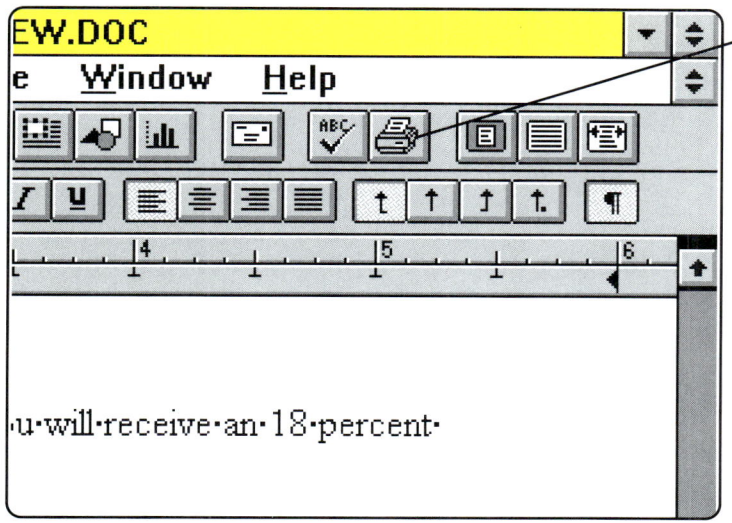

1. **Click** on the **Print tool** on the right side of the toolbar. The Printing message box will appear.

77

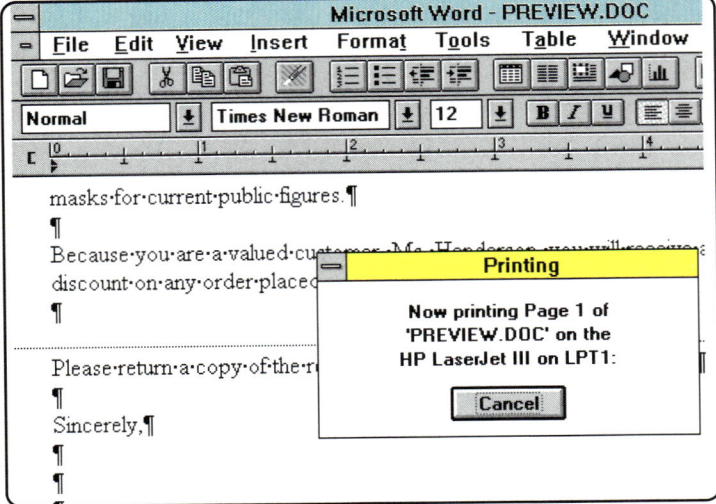

The Printing message box updates you as it prints each page of your document. Notice that you can stop the printing by clicking on Cancel. You must wait until the Printing message box disappears before you can continue to work.

PRINTING FROM THE MENU BAR

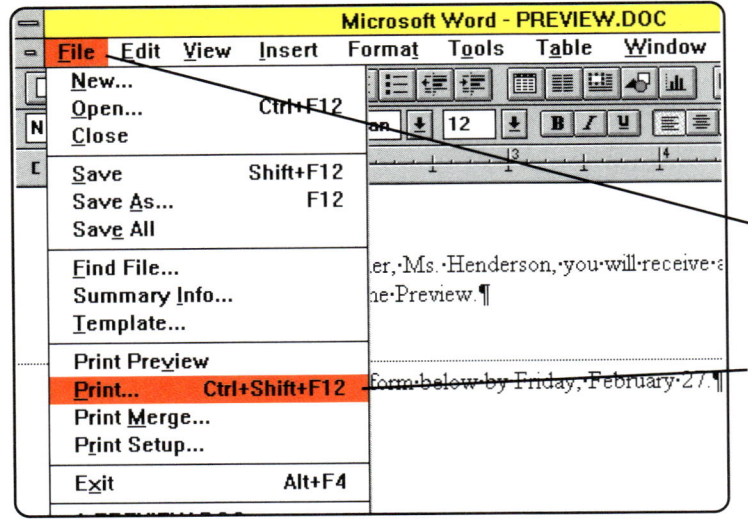

In this section you will use the Print command on the File pull-down menu. Again, if you do not have a file open, open one now.

1. **Click** on **File** in the menu bar. A pull-down menu will appear.

2. **Click** on **Print**. The Print dialog box will appear.

CHAPTER 6: PRINTING A FILE

Printing Selected Pages

In this section you will not actually make any of the following changes in the Print dialog box, but you should be aware of the options available to you.

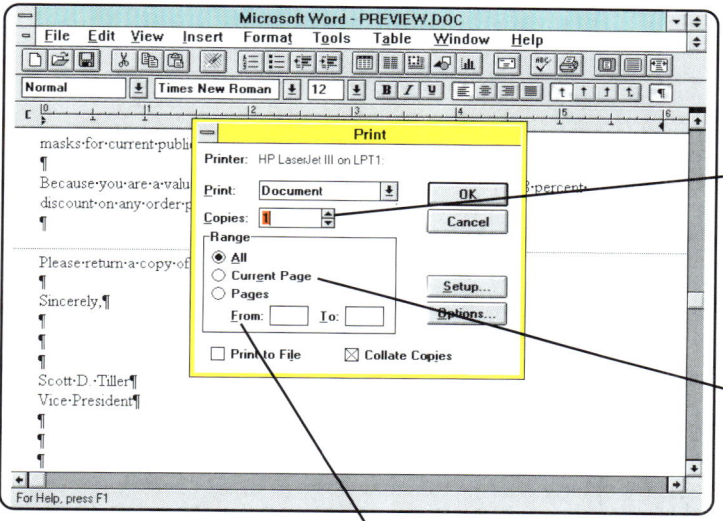

Notice that you can change the number of copies you want to print by clicking on the up arrow in the Copies box.

Notice that you can print only the page where the insertion point is located by clicking on Current Page.

Notice that you can print a range of pages by typing the number of the first page you want to print in the From box, and the number of the last page you want to print in the To box.

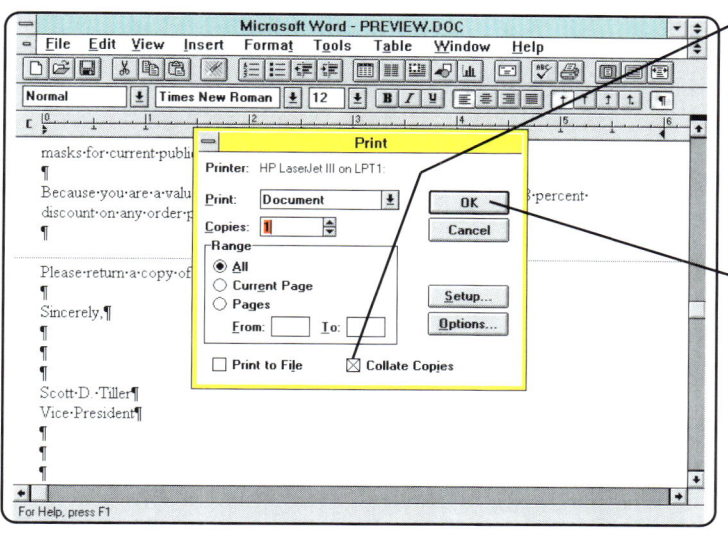

Notice that there is an ✕ in the box beside Collate Copies. This means that multiple copies will be automatically collated as they print.

After you make any of the above changes, click on OK to print.

Printing the Entire Document

In this section you will print all of the pages in the document.

1. **Click** on **All** to insert a dot in the circle if one is not already there.

2. **Click** on **OK**. You will see the Printing message box that you saw when you used the Print tool.

Refer to "Print Preview" in Chapter 10 for directions on how to see a birds-eye overview of your document before it prints.

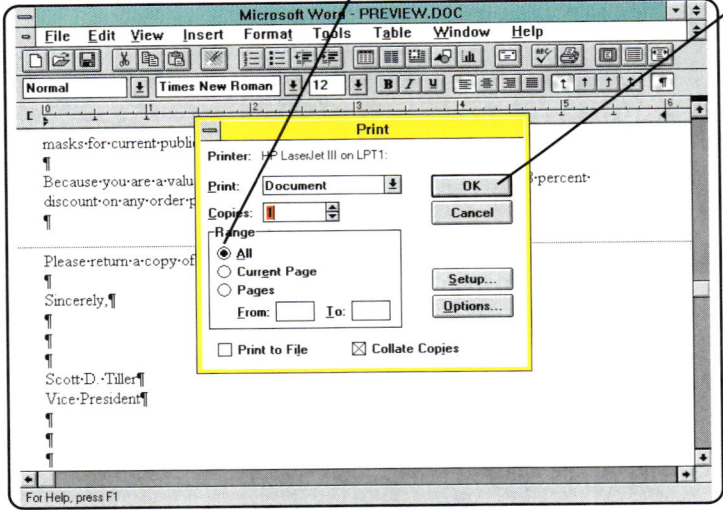

Program Manager

Part II: Formatting a Document

Chapter 7: Customizing Text	Page 83
Chapter 8: Setting and Applying Tabs	Page 95
Chapter 9: Separating a Document into Sections and Adding a Header and Footer	Page 111
Chapter 10: Changing the View	Page 119

CHAPTER 7

Customizing Text

You will love how easy it is to customize the look of your text in Word for Windows 2. With just a click of your mouse button you can change the type size or make type bold or italic. With another click of the mouse button you can center text or create a bulleted list. In addition, you can add special borders around sections of your text, then add shading inside the border to create an exciting visual effect. In this chapter you will do the following:

- ❖ Change type size
- ❖ Make text bold and italic
- ❖ Center text
- ❖ Add a border around text and add shading inside the border
- ❖ Create a bulleted list

CHANGING TYPE SIZE

In this section you will increase the size of the type in the first line of the letter you created in Part I. If you don't already have PREVIEW.DOC open, open it now.

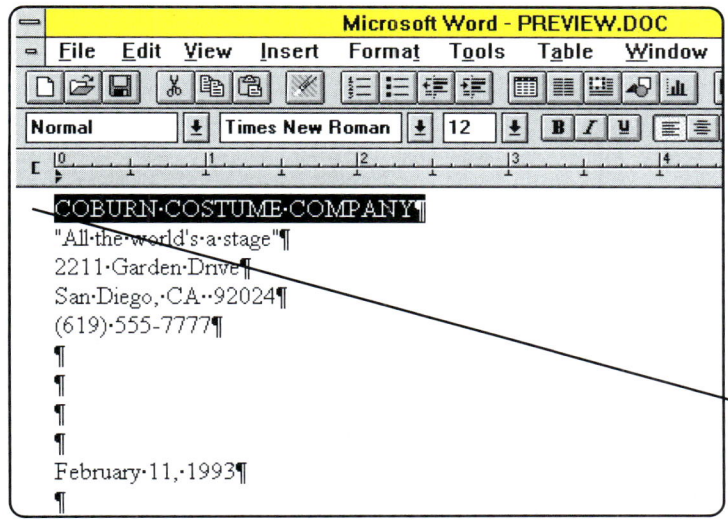

1. **Press and hold Ctrl**, then **press Home** (Ctrl + Home) to go to the top of the file if you are not already there.

2. **Place** the mouse pointer in the left margin **beside "COBURN COSTUME COMPANY."** The pointer will become an arrow.

3. **Click** the mouse button. The line will be highlighted (selected).

83

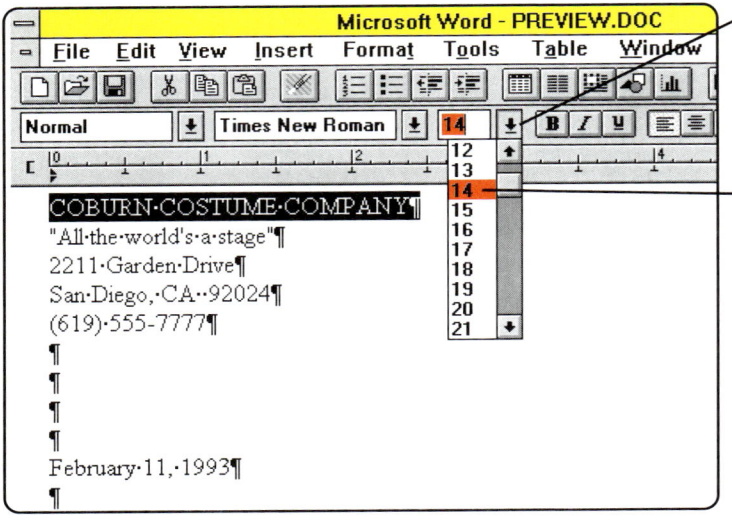

4. Click on ↓ in the Font Size box in the ribbon. A drop-down list box will appear.

5. Click on **14**. The drop-down list box will disappear and the highlighted text will appear in 14-point type.

MAKING TEXT BOLD

In this section you will make the type, "COBURN COSTUME COMPANY," boldface. You must first highlight the text you want to change. If you have been following along with the steps in this chapter, you have already highlighted "COBURN COSTUME COMPANY."

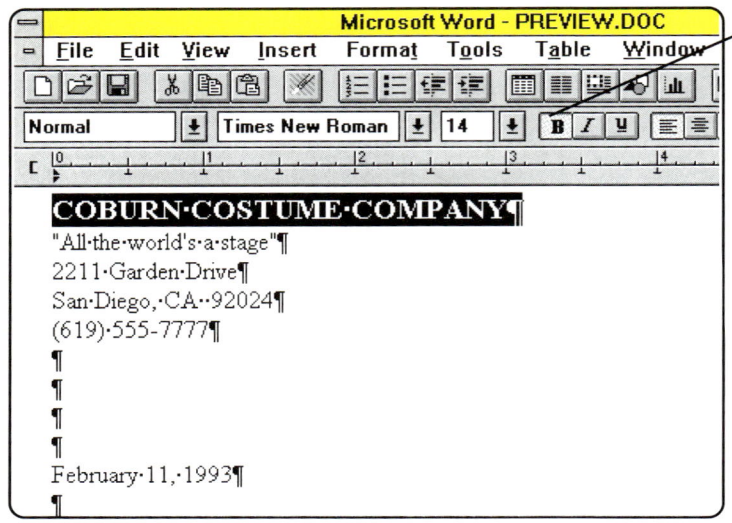

1. Click on the **Bold button** (the capital "B") in the ribbon. The selected text will appear in boldface type.

Notice that the Bold button appears depressed and lighter in color. This tells you that the selected text is now bold. The Bold button works like a toggle switch. With the text still selected, click on the Bold button to turn it off. Click on it a second time to turn it back on.

MAKING TEXT ITALIC

In this section you will add italics to two separate parts of the letter.

1. Click in the left margin **beside "All the world's a stage."** The line will be highlighted.

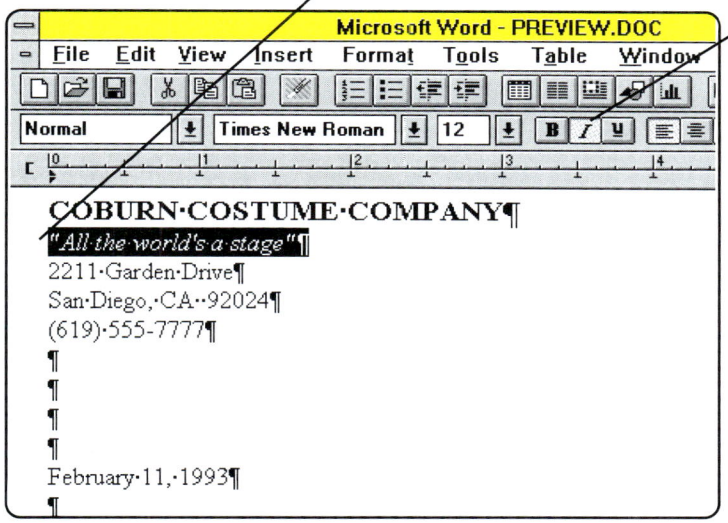

2. Click on the **Italics button** (the slanted capital "*I*") in the ribbon. The selected text will appear in italics. Notice that the Italics button appears depressed and lighter in color. The Italics button also works like a toggle switch.

3. Click on ↓ on the scroll bar to scroll down to the sentence that begins with "We hope you will be here."

4. Place the mouse pointer to the **left of "you."** The pointer will become an I-beam.

5. Press and hold the mouse button and **drag** the pointer **over "you."** It will be highlighted.

6. Click on the **Italics button** in the ribbon. The word "you" will appear in italics.

CENTERING TEXT

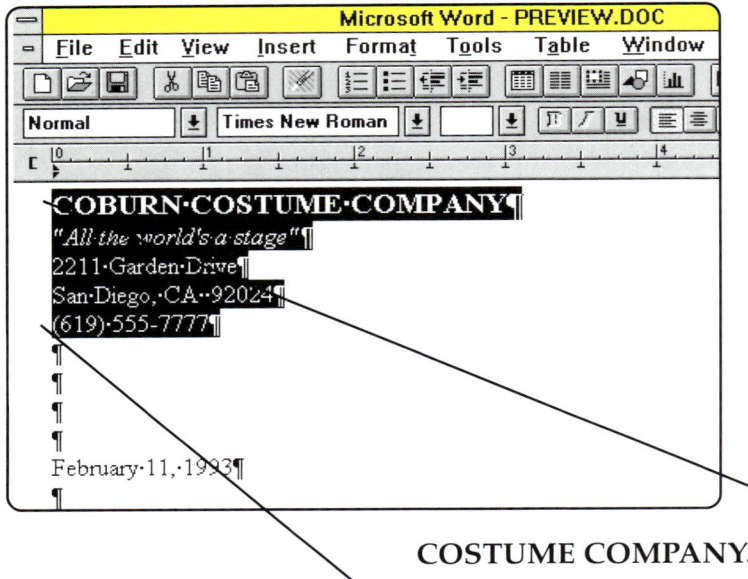

In this section you will center the first four lines of the letter at the top of the page. You can highlight all of the lines and then apply the centering command to all four at the same time.

1. Press and hold Ctrl, then **press Home** (Ctrl + Home) to get back to the beginning of the file.

2. Click in the left margin **beside "COBURN COSTUME COMPANY."** It will be highlighted.

3. Press and hold the **Shift key** and **click** in the left margin **beside "(619) 555-7777."** All the lines between clicks will be highlighted.

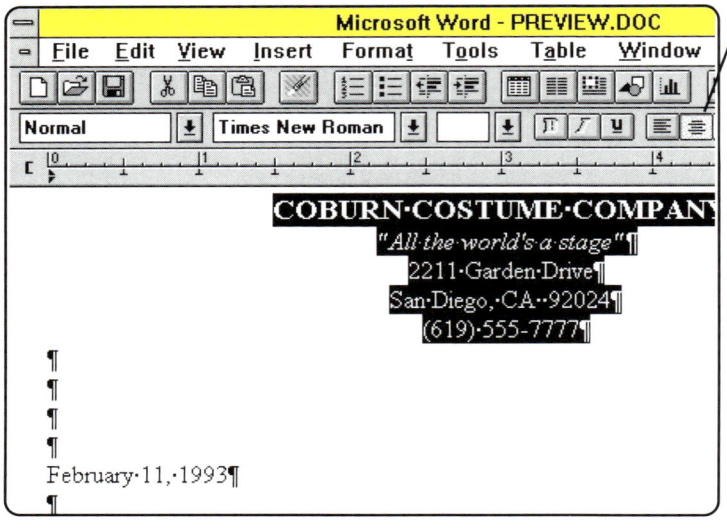

4. Click on the **Center button** in the ribbon. Each line in the highlighted text will be centered across the page. Notice that the Center button appears depressed and lighter in color. The Center button also works like a toggle switch.

You will now apply these same procedures to center two portions of text on page 2 of the letter.

CHAPTER 7: CUSTOMIZING TEXT

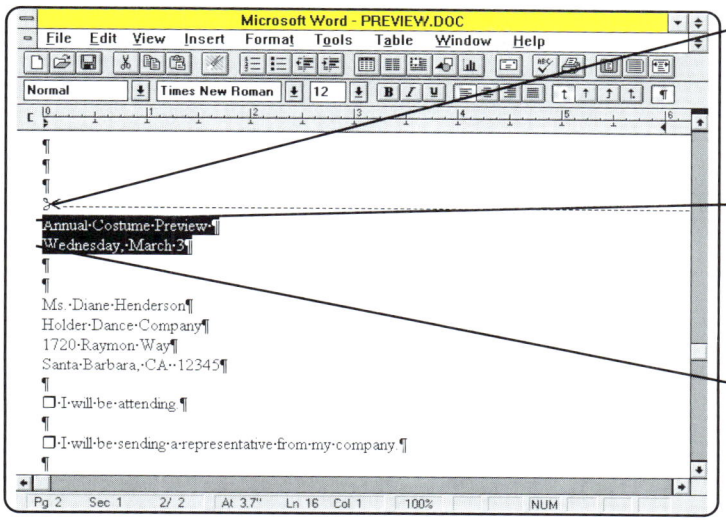

5. Click on the **scroll bar** until you can see the scissors and the two lines below it.

6. Click in the left margin **beside "Annual Costume Preview."** The line will be highlighted.

7. Press and hold Shift and **click** in the left margin **beside "Thursday, March 3."** Both lines will be highlighted.

8. Click on the **Center button** in the ribbon. Both lines will be centered across the page.

9. Press and hold Ctrl, then **press End** (Ctrl + End). You will go to the end of the letter.

10. Click twice in the left margin **beside the last paragraph** in the letter. The entire paragraph (the two lines of text) will be highlighted.

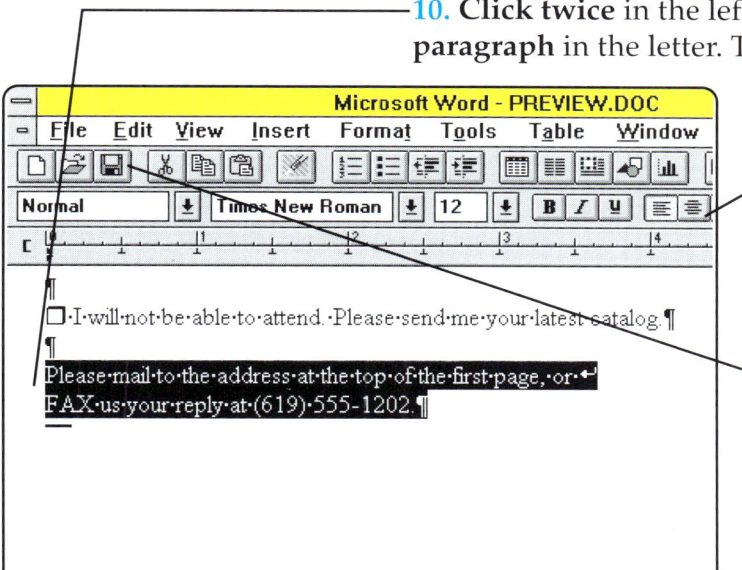

11. Click on the **Center button** in the ribbon. The highlighted lines will be centered across the page.

12. Click on the **Save tool** in the toolbar to save your work.

"READING" THE RIBBON

When you move the insertion point to the beginning of a paragraph, the settings in the ribbon will reflect the formatting or styles in the paragraph. In this section you will see how the ribbon reflects the formatting of "COBURN COSTUME COMPANY."

1. Press and hold Ctrl, then **press Home** (Ctrl + Home) to return to the top of the letter.

These are the settings on the ribbon for the first line of text:

❖ Normal is the standard style of all Word documents, but other styles are available. See Chapter 18 for more information on styles.

❖ Times New Roman and 14 indicate the font and point size of this paragraph. If you select a paragraph that has different fonts or different point sizes, Word will only show the setting of the first word in the paragraph.

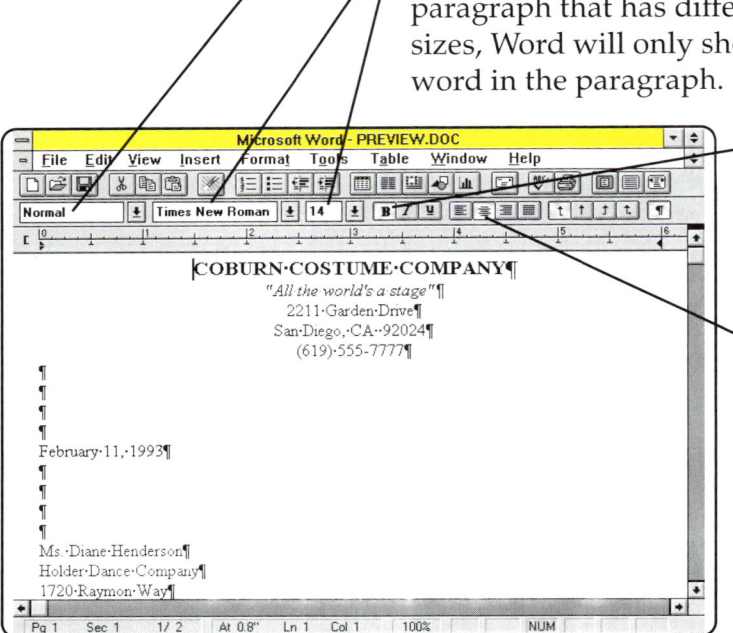

❖ The Bold button is lighter and appears depressed, indicating that the paragraph is bold.

❖ The Center button is lighter and appears depressed, indicating that the paragraph is centered across the page.

CHAPTER 7: CUSTOMIZING TEXT

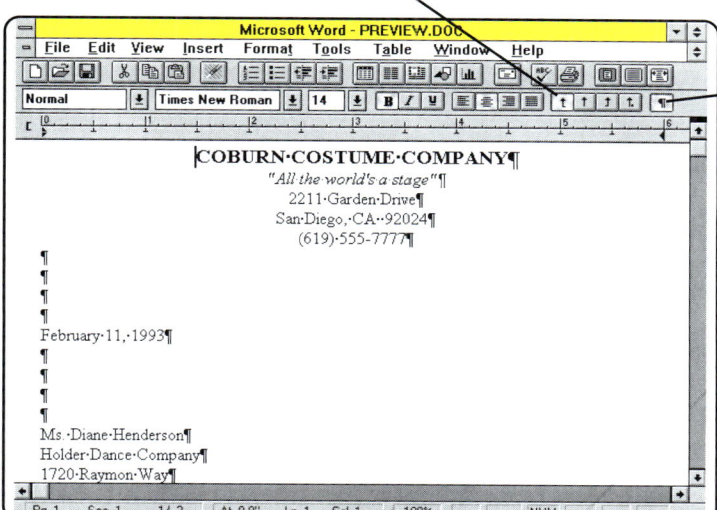

❖ The Tab button is depressed. Since you haven't customized the tab settings, the default tab setting is on. See Chapter 8 for more information on tab settings.

❖ The Show/Hide ¶ button at the end of the ribbon is depressed, which means that paragraph, tab, and space symbols are displayed.

Any time your type doesn't look the way you expect it to, check these buttons. Chances are you clicked on a button for one paragraph and forgot to click it off for the next paragraph.

ADDING A BORDER AND SHADING

In this section you will add a border around the five lines at the top of the letter and shade the boxed text to create a letterhead.

Adding a Border

1. **Click** in the left margin beside "**COBURN COSTUME COMPANY.**" It will be highlighted.

2. **Press and hold** the **Shift key** and **click** in the left margin **beside the telephone number**. All the lines between the clicks will be highlighted.

3. Click on **Format** in the menu bar. A pull-down menu will appear.

4. Click on **Border**. The Border Paragraphs dialog box will appear.

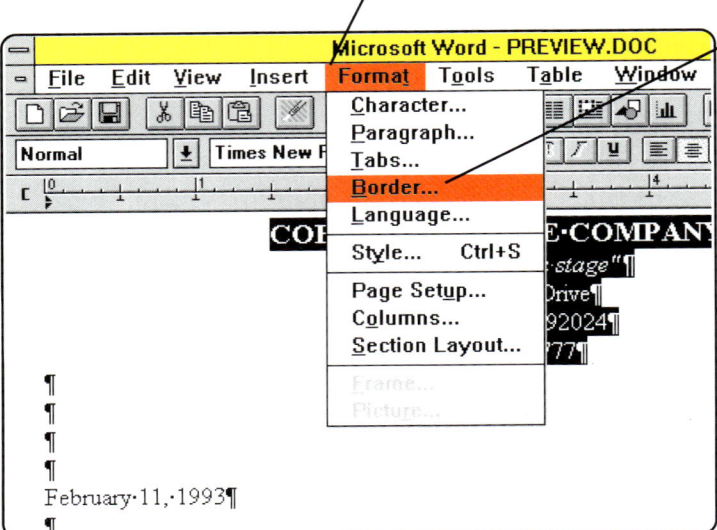

5. Click on **Box** in the Preset area of the dialog box. The box will be surrounded by a selection border.

6. Click on the **Double Line option** in the Line area of the dialog box. It would be surrounded by a selection border.

You could click on OK now and the selected text will be surrounded by a double-line border, but let's add some shading to it first.

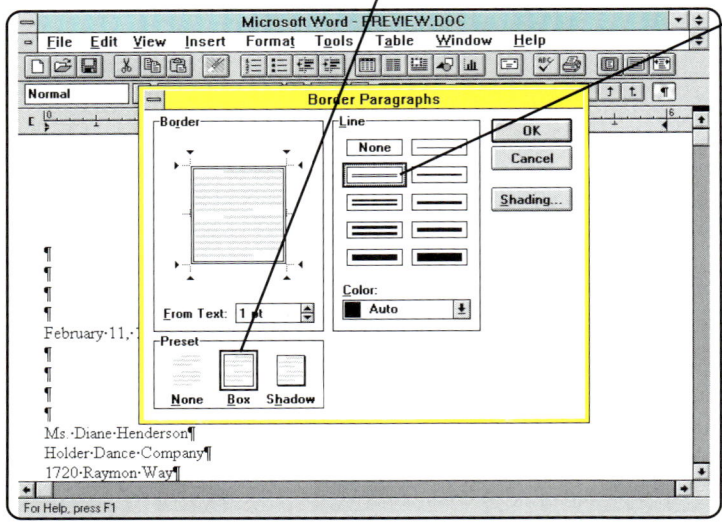

CHAPTER 7: CUSTOMIZING TEXT 91

Shading the Boxed Text

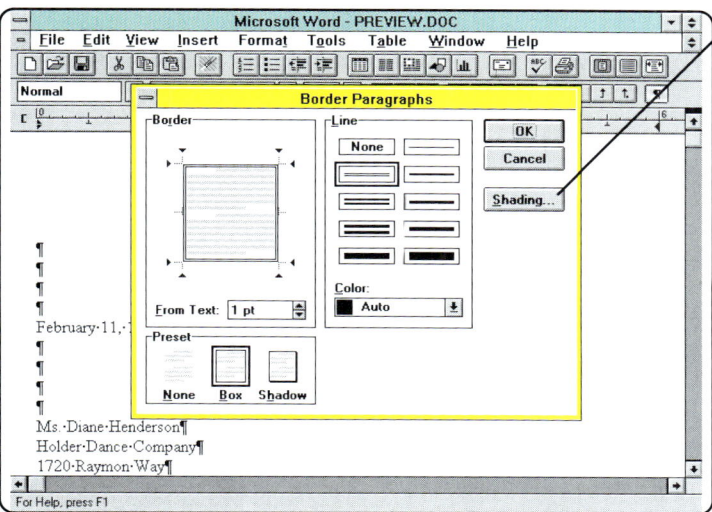

1. **Click** on **Shading**. The Shading dialog box will appear.

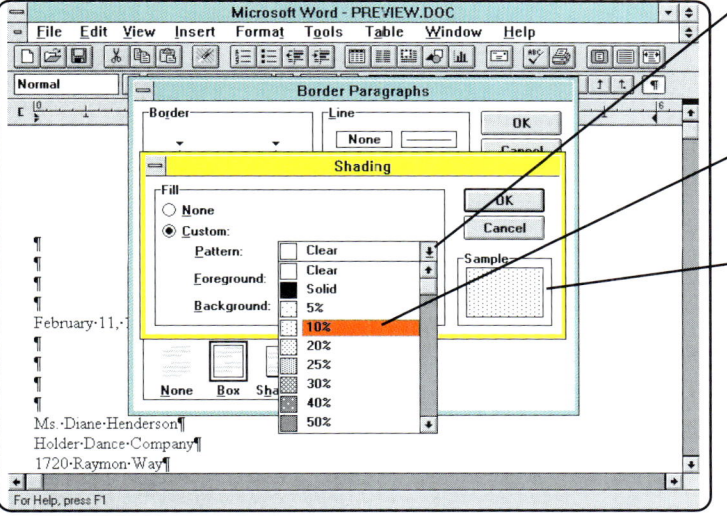

2. **Click** on ↓ to the right of the Pattern box. A drop-down list will appear.

3. **Click** on **10%**. The drop-down list will disappear.

Notice that the Sample box shows what 10% shading will look like. The 10% shading may look like a case of the measles now, but it will look terrific when you print it.

4. **Click** on **OK** in the upper-right corner of the Shading dialog box. The Shading dialog box will disappear and you will again see the Border Paragraphs dialog box.

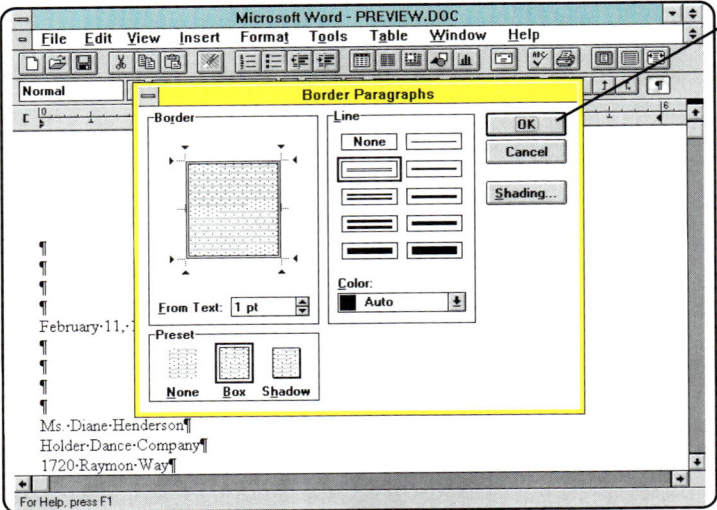

5. Click on **OK** in the Border Paragraphs dialog box. The dialog box will disappear.

6. Click anywhere outside of the border to remove the highlighting.

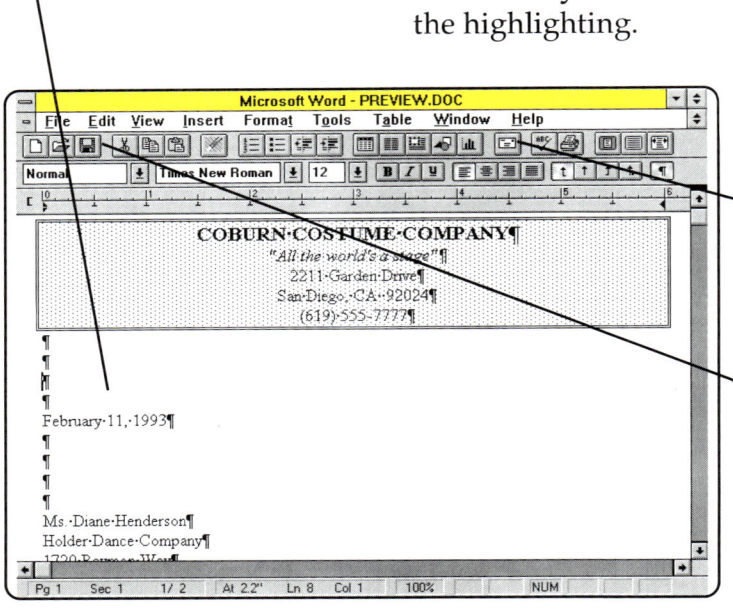

Your letter will look like the example to the left.

7. Click on the **Print tool** in the toolbar if you want to print your letter and see what it looks like.

8. Click on the **Save tool** in the toolbar to save your work.

CHAPTER 7: CUSTOMIZING TEXT 93

CREATING A BULLETED LIST

In this section you will create a bulleted list using the four paragraphs describing the costumes carried by the Coburn Costume Company. It's as easy as clicking your mouse.

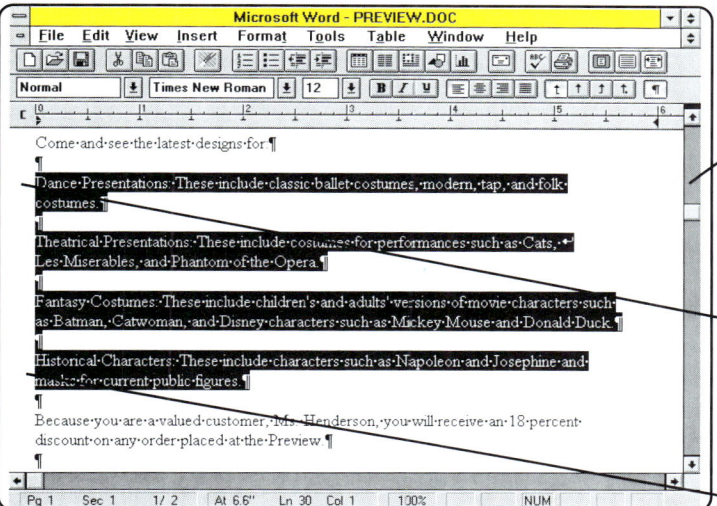

1. **Click** on the **scroll bar** until you can see the four paragraphs that describe the costumes.

2. **Click** in the left margin beside **"Dance Presentations."** The line will be highlighted.

3. **Press and hold** the **Shift** key as you **click** in the left margin **beside "masks for current public figures."** All the lines between the clicks will be highlighted.

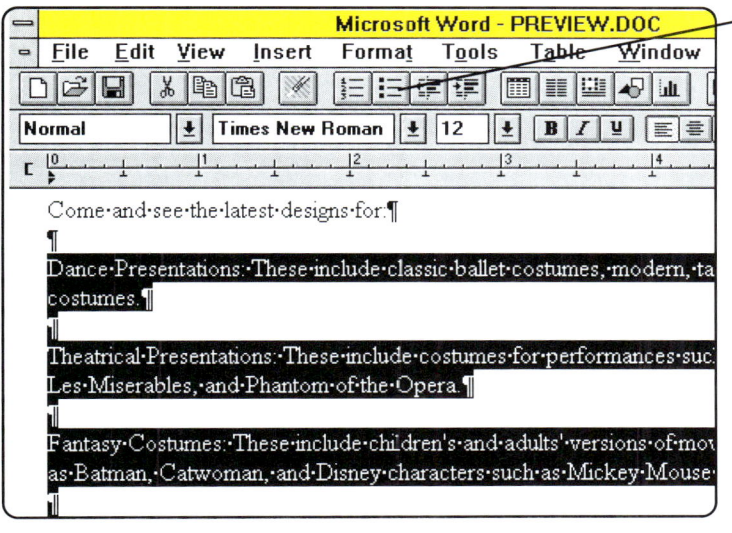

4. **Click** on the **Bulleted List tool** in the toolbar. You will see an hourglass as Word changes the paragraphs into a bulleted list.

5. Click anywhere on the letter to remove the highlighting from the list. Your letter will look like the example to the left.

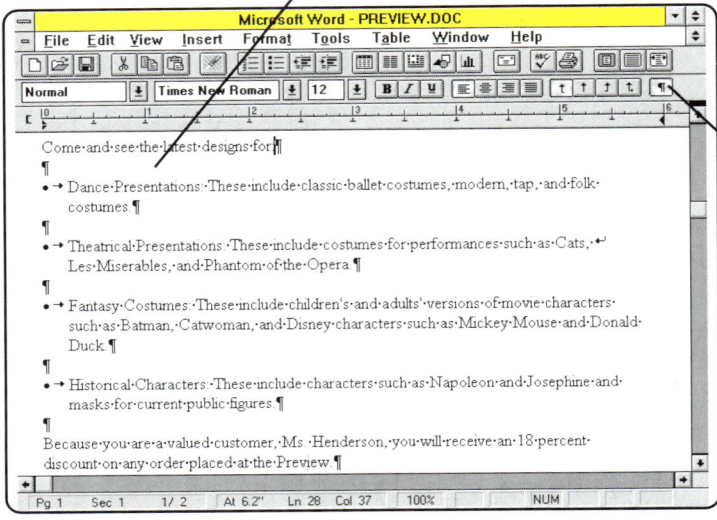

The letter looks a little strange with all of the formatting marks showing.

6. Click on the **Show/Hide ¶ button** in the ribbon to hide the paragraph, space, and tab symbols.

Your screen will look like the example to the left.

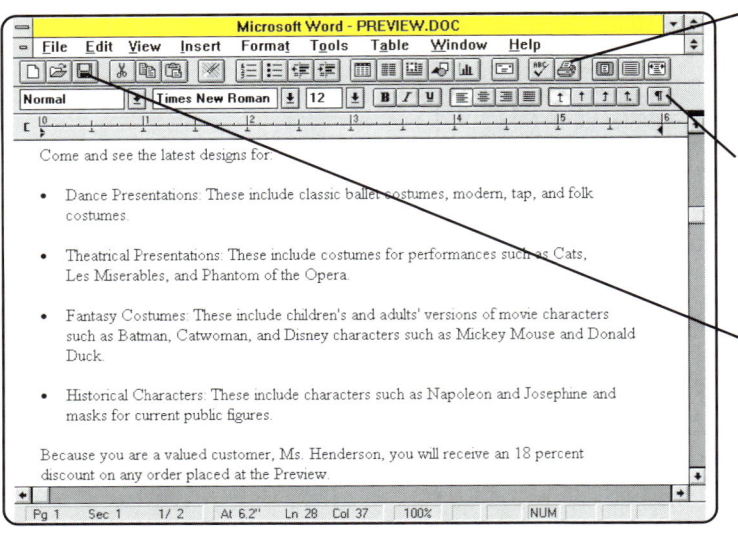

7. Click on the **Print tool** in the toolbar to print the letter.

8. Click on the **Show/Hide ¶ button** in the ribbon so that the symbols show again.

9. Click on the **Save tool** in the toolbar to save your work.

CHAPTER 8

Setting and Applying Tabs

Word for Windows 2 has tabs pre-set at every half inch. To insert a tab, simply press the Tab key. You can also set your own tabs. When you set a tab, the pre-set tabs between the new tab and the left margin disappear. In this chapter you will set and apply the following kinds of tabs:

❖ The standard *left-aligned tab* that lines words up on the first letter: Josh
                                                                              Jessica

❖ A *leader* (line) that ends at a *right-aligned tab*:   Josh _____
                                                         Jessica _____

❖ A right-aligned tab that aligns words on the last letter: Josh
                                                              Jessica

❖ A *center-aligned tab* that centers words: Josh
                                               Jessica

❖ A *decimal tab* that aligns numbers on the decimal point: 13.95
                                                              105.00

SETTING A LEFT-ALIGNED TAB WITH THE RULER

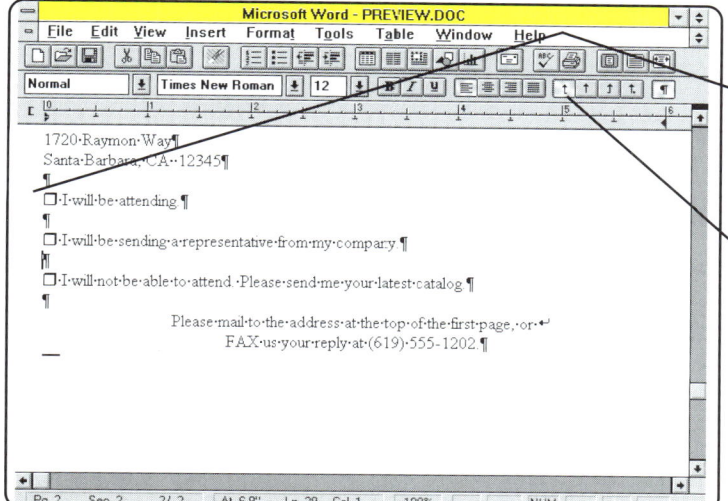

1. **Open** the **PREVIEW.DOC** file you created in earlier chapters if it's not already open.

2. **Place** the mouse pointer to the left of the paragraph mark **above the last check box**. **Click** to set it in place.

3. **Confirm** that the Left-Aligned Tab button on the ribbon appears depressed and is lighter in color than the other buttons. **Click** on the **button** if it is not.

95

4. Place the mouse pointer **in the ruler** (it will become an arrow pointer) so that the arrow points at, *but does not touch*, the .25-inch mark on the ruler. If the arrow touches the .25-inch mark, you will not get a tab mark when you click your mouse button.

5. Click the mouse button. A left-aligned tab mark will appear just below the ruler line. If the tab mark does not appear, you probably placed the arrow too close to the .25-inch mark. Try again.

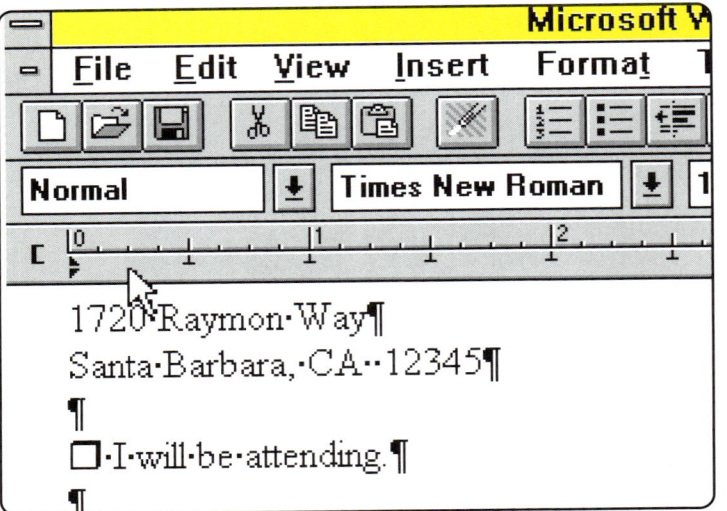

6. Press Tab. A tab mark will appear in the text and the insertion point will tab over .25 inch.

7. Type Name.

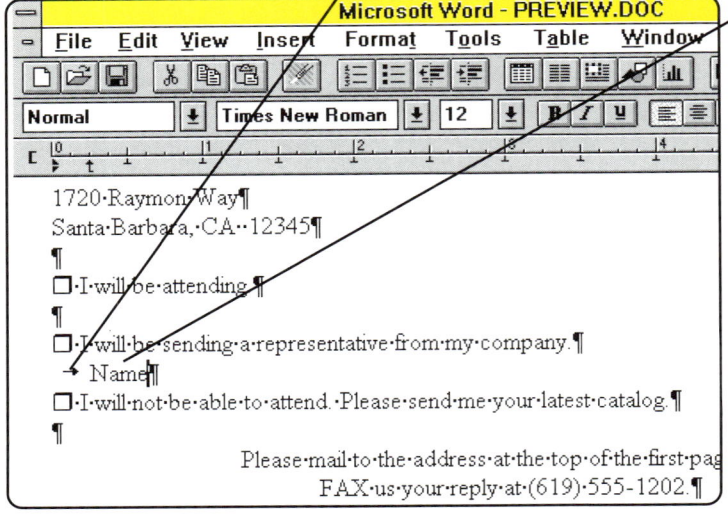

INSERTING A LEADER WITH A RIGHT-ALIGNED TAB

A common example of a *leader* is the dotted line in a table of contents that connects a chapter and its page number, as shown here:

    Chapter 2..34

Another common example of a leader is the fill-in-the-blank solid line seen on forms, for example:

    Name _____

To create these kinds of leaders, use the Right-Aligned Tab button.

In this section you will insert a solid line after "Name."

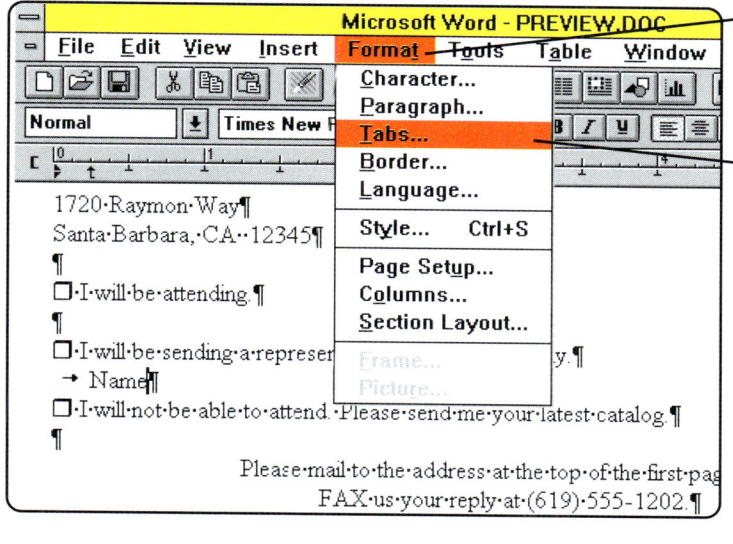

1. **Click** on **Format** in the menu bar. A pull-down menu will appear.

2. **Click** on **Tabs**. The Tabs dialog box will appear.

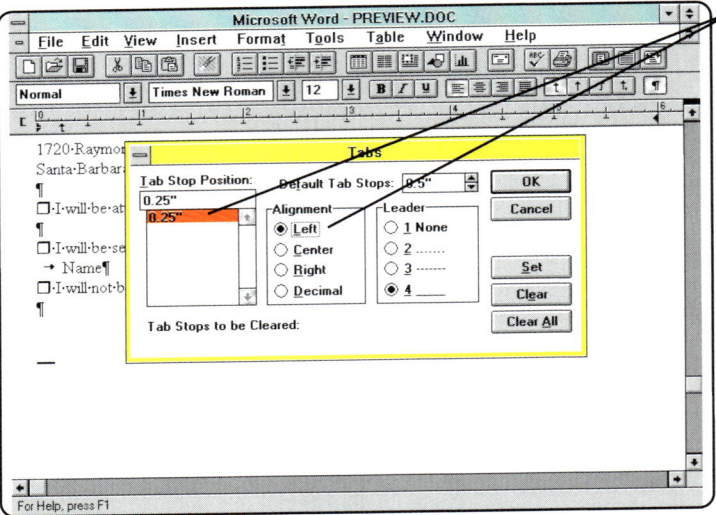

Notice that the left-aligned tab stop at .25 inch that you set in the ruler in the previous section appears in the Tabs dialog box.

3. Since the insertion point is already flashing in the Tab Stop Position box, just **type 4**. You don't have to type the inch symbol ("). The 4 will replace the number in the box but will not replace the tab setting at .25 inch. Both tabs will be set.

4. Click on **Right** in the Alignment box to insert a dot in the circle.

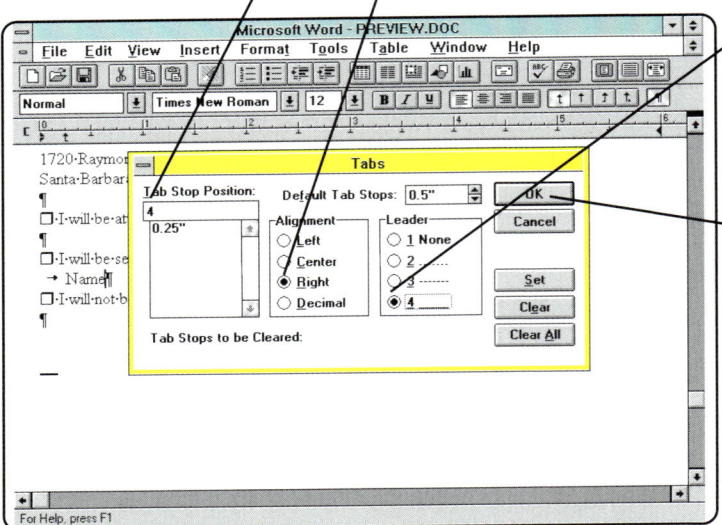

5. Click on **Option 4** (the solid line option) in the Leader box to insert a dot in the circle.

6. Click on **OK**. The dialog box will close and a right-aligned tab mark will appear in the ruler at 4 inches.

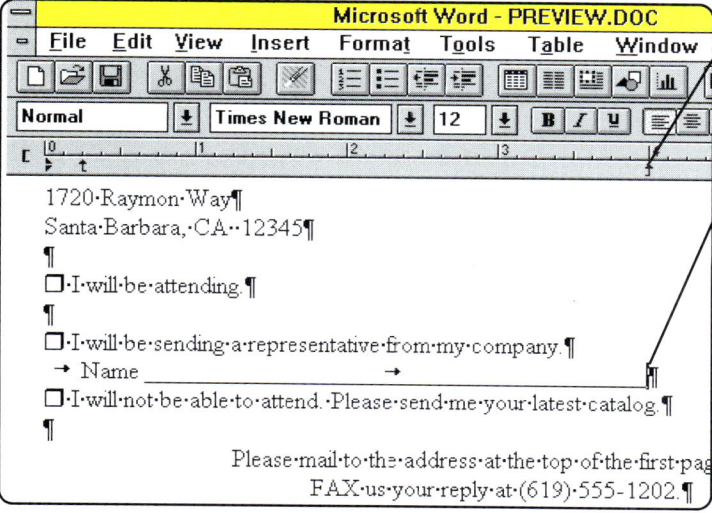

Notice the right-aligned tab mark at 4 inches in the ruler.

7. Press Tab. The insertion point will move to the 4-inch tab stop and a solid line leader will appear between "Name" and the right-aligned tab stop.

8. In preparation for the next section, **press Enter** to move down a line.

SETTING A LEFT-ALIGNED TAB FROM THE MENU BAR

In this section you will add a second blank line to be filled in with the title of the representative coming to the Preview. First, you will set a slightly indented tab under "Name" so you can learn a second way to set a standard tab.

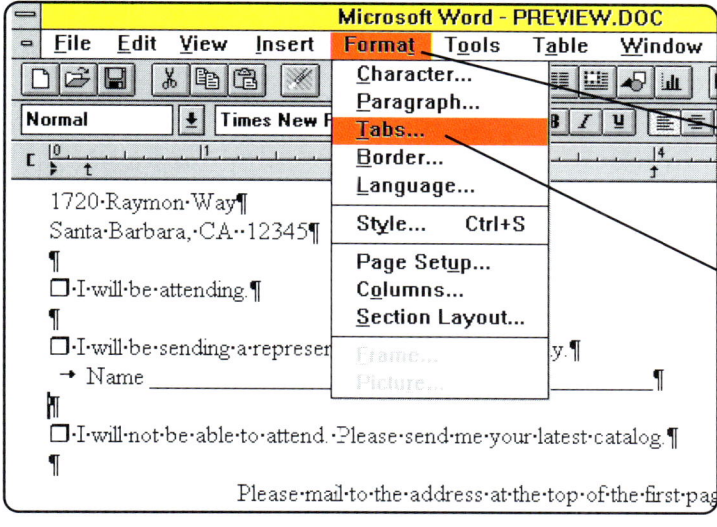

1. Click on **Format** in the menu bar. A pull-down menu will appear.

2. Click on **Tabs**. The Tabs dialog box will appear.

Notice that the Tab Stop Position list box has the two tab settings: .25 and 4 inches.

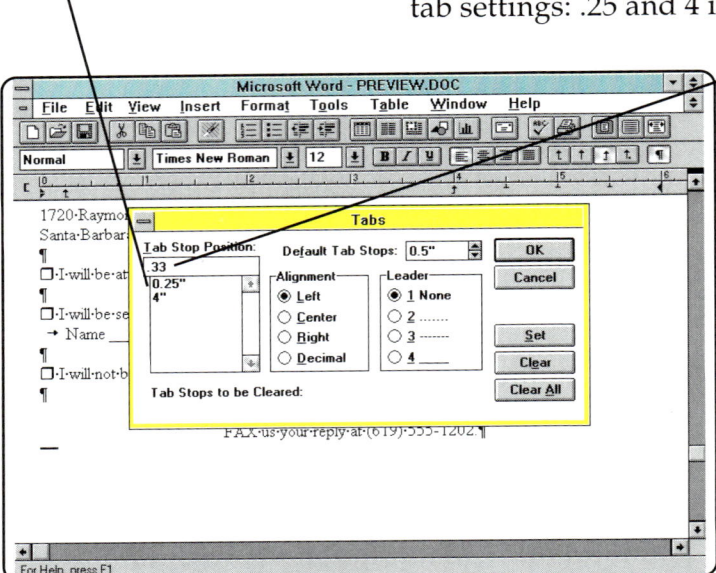

3. **Type .33** in the Tab Stop Position box. It will replace the highlighted text.

4. **Confirm** that Left is selected in the Alignment box (has a dot in the circle). Click on it if it is not selected.

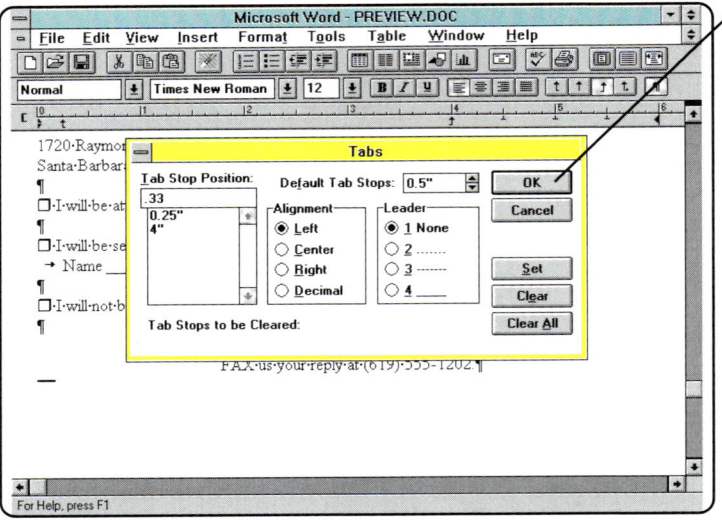

5. **Click** on **OK** to confirm the tab you just set in steps 3 and 4 and close the dialog box.

Notice that two left-aligned tab marks now appear on the ruler, one at .25 inch and one at .33 inch.

6. Press Tab twice to move the insertion point to the .33-inch tab stop.

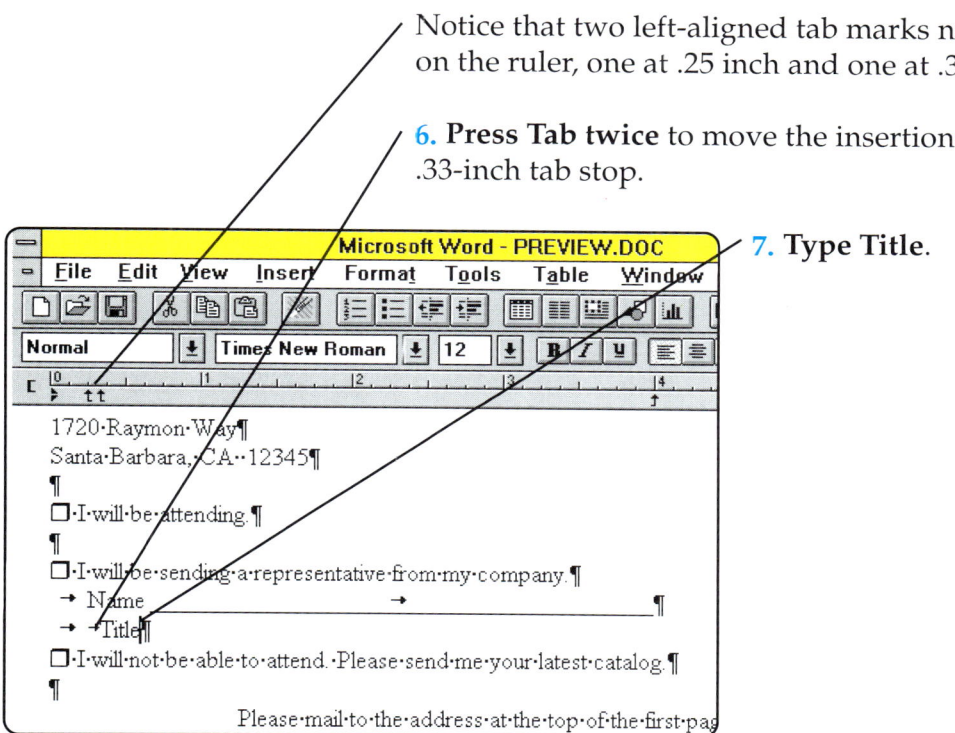

7. Type Title.

In this next step, you will use the right-aligned tab that you set earlier to insert another leader.

8. Press Tab. The leader line will appear and the insertion point will move to the 4-inch tab stop.

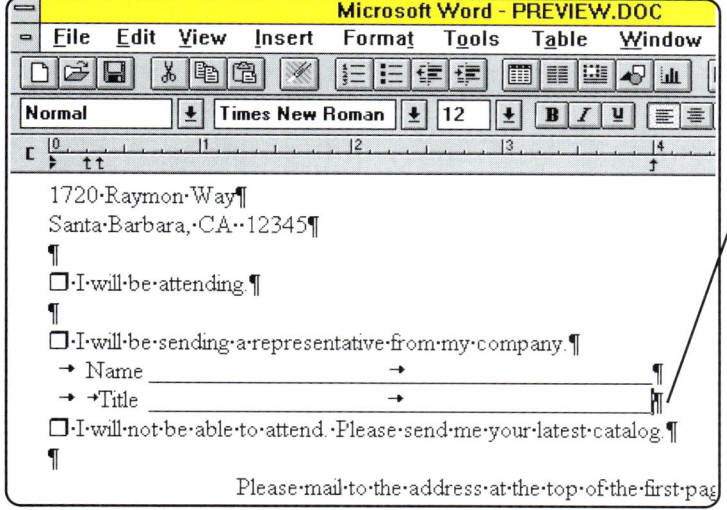

CLEARING A TAB

In this section you will align "Title" under "Name" by clearing the tab you set at .33 inch.

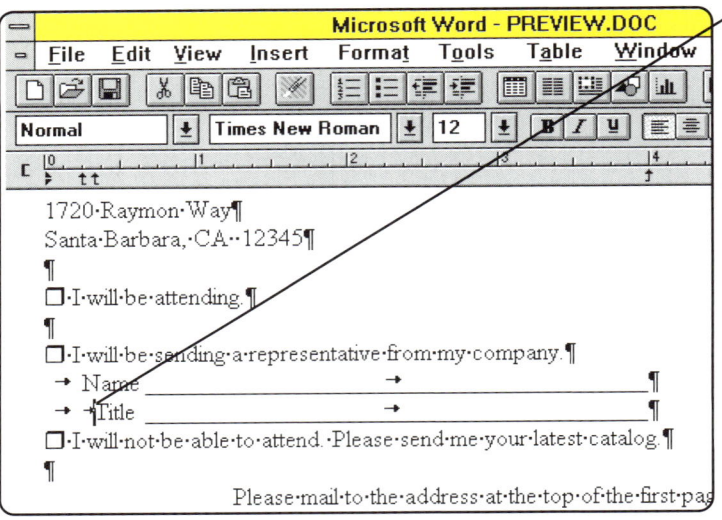

1. **Place** the mouse pointer to the **left of "Title." Click** to set it in place.

2. **Press** the **Backspace key**. "Title" will backspace one tab position and be aligned under "Name."

Now you will clear the tab you set at .33 inch.

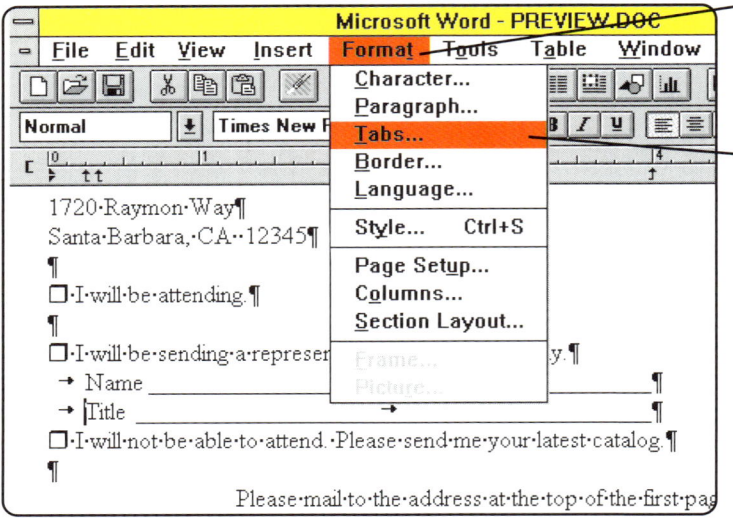

3. **Click** on **Format** in the menu bar. A pull-down menu will appear.

4. **Click** on **Tabs**. The Tabs dialog box will appear.

CHAPTER 8: SETTING AND APPLYING TABS   **103**

5. **Click** on **.33"** (the tab you want to clear) in the Tab Stop Position list box. It will be highlighted.

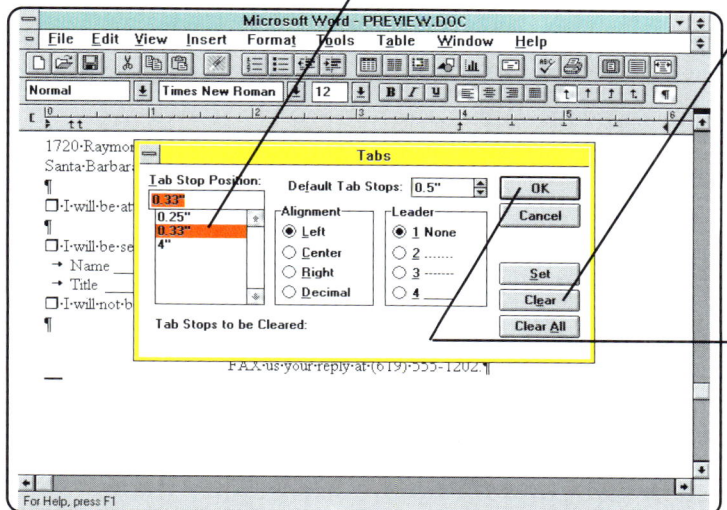

6. **Click** on **Clear**. The .33" tab will disappear from the list box.

Notice that you can clear all tabs at once by clicking on Clear All (located beneath Clear).

7. **Click** on **OK**.

Notice that the .33-inch tab mark on the ruler is gone.

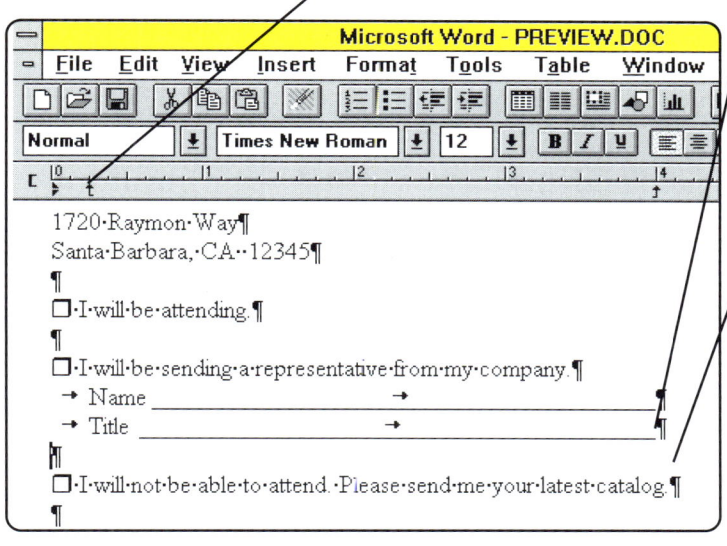

8. **Place** the mouse pointer to the left of the paragraph mark at the **end of the Title line**. **Click** to set it in place.

9. **Press Enter** to insert a blank line after the Title line.

10. **Click** on the **Save tool** in the toolbar to save your work.

OPENING A NEW DOCUMENT

In the remaining sections of the chapter, you'll learn how to set a right-aligned tab and a center-aligned tab with the mouse, and set a decimal tab with the mouse and from the menu bar. Since the tabs will not be used in PREVIEW.DOC, you will open a new document. You don't need to close PREVIEW.DOC in order to open a new document though. Word allows up to nine documents to be open at a time.

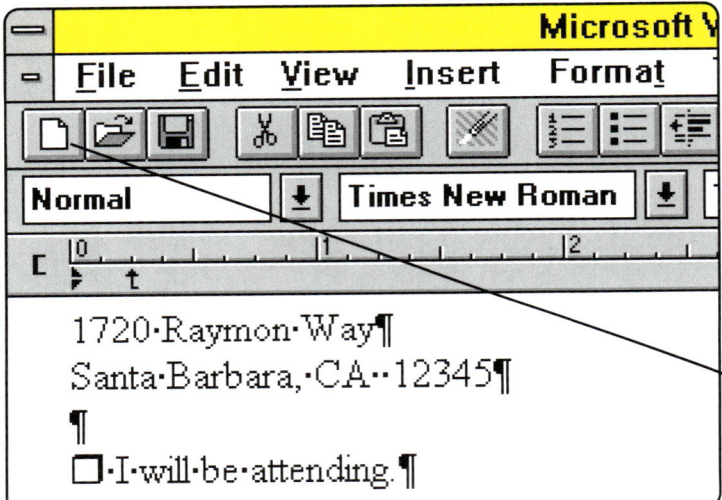

1. Click on the **New Document tool** in the toolbar. A new document will appear on your screen on top of PREVIEW.DOC.

SETTING A RIGHT-ALIGNED TAB WITH THE MOUSE

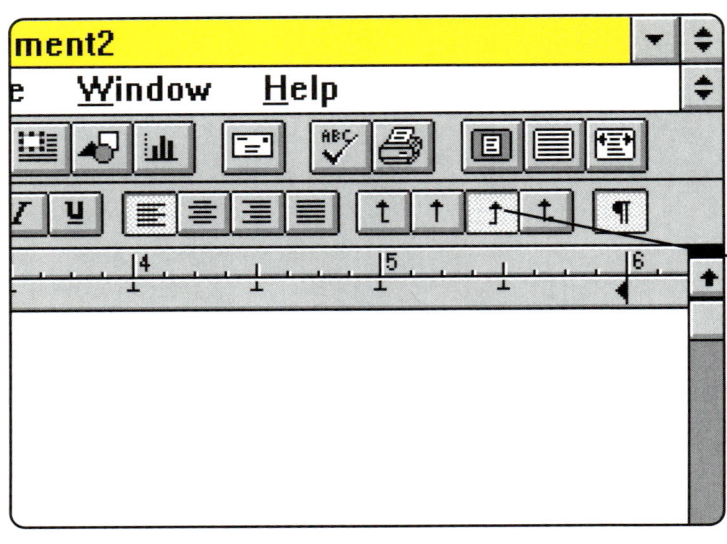

1. Click on the **Right-Aligned Tab button** in the ribbon if it is not already depressed. If you have been following along with the steps in this chapter it will be depressed.

CHAPTER 8: SETTING AND APPLYING TABS 105

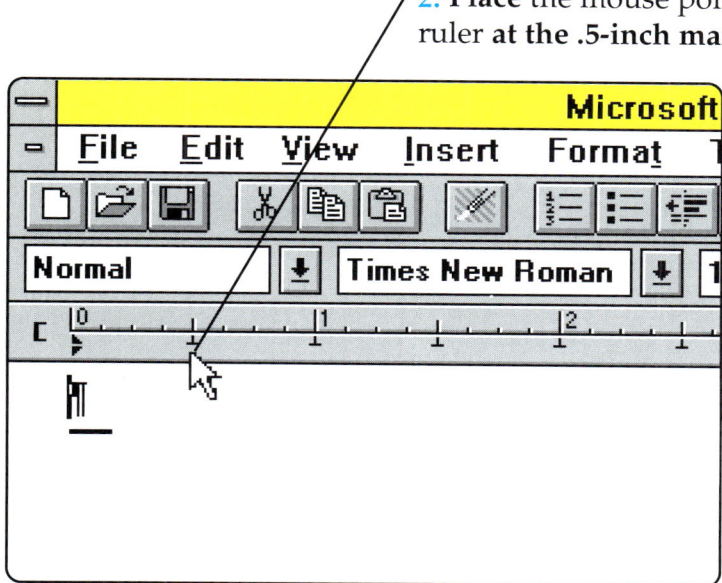

2. **Place** the mouse pointer in the lower-half of the ruler **at the .5-inch mark**. It will become an arrow. Do not let the arrow touch the ruler line itself.

3. **Click** to insert a right-aligned tab at this position. The right-aligned tab mark will appear. (If the tab mark does not appear, you probably placed the arrow too close to the ruler line. Move it slightly and try again.)

You will use this tab setting later in the chapter in the section "Applying Tabs."

SETTING A CENTER-ALIGNED TAB WITH THE MOUSE

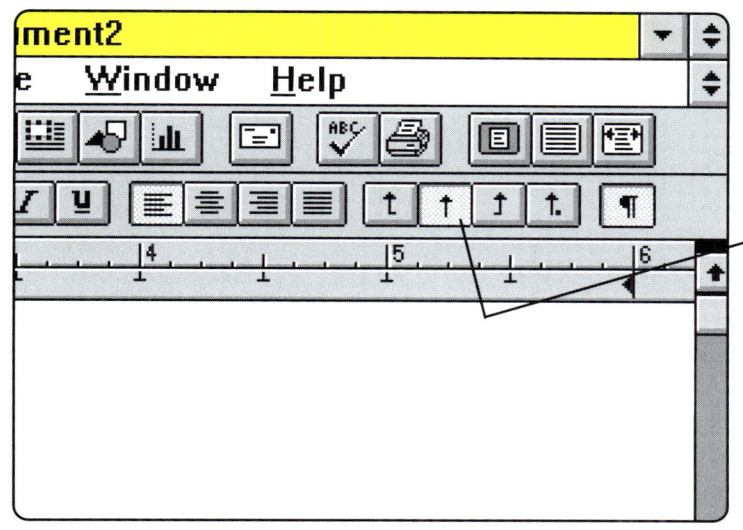

In this section you will use the mouse to set a center-aligned tab at the 2-inch mark.

1. **Click** on the **Center-Aligned Tab button** in the ribbon.

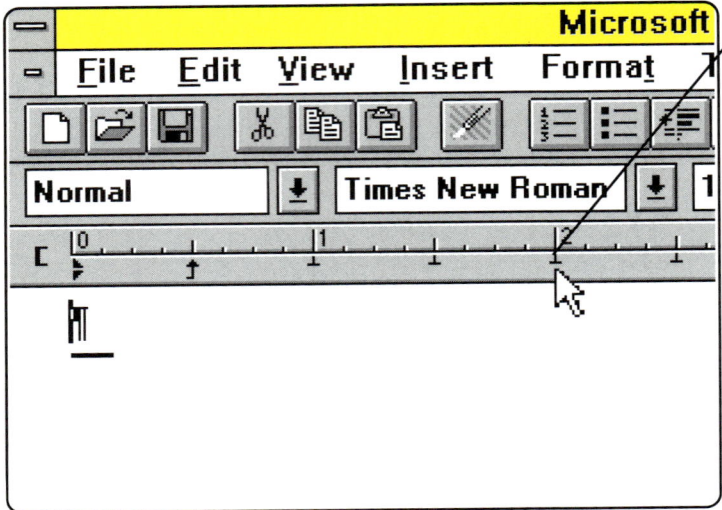

2. **Place** the mouse pointer in the lower-half of the ruler **at the 2-inch mark**. Do not let the arrow touch the ruler line itself.

3. **Click** to set the center-aligned tab in place.

You will use this tab setting later in the chapter in the section "Applying Tabs."

SETTING A DECIMAL TAB WITH THE MOUSE

In this section you will use the mouse to set a decimal tab at 3.5 inches.

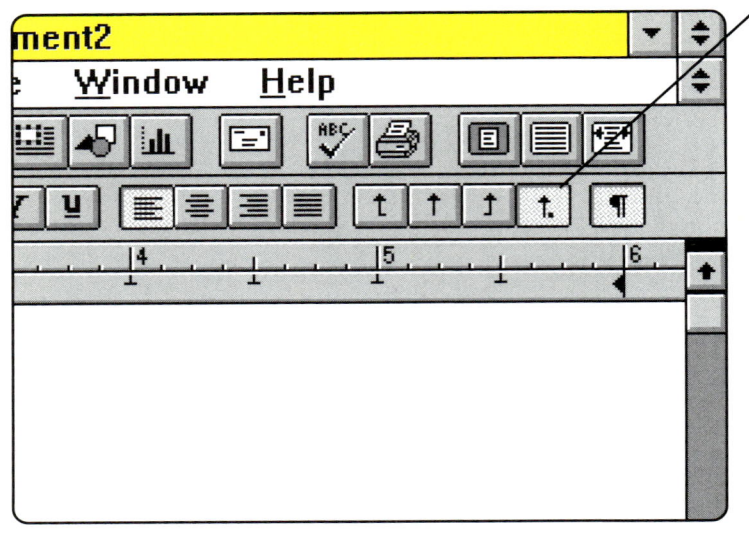

1. **Click** on the **Decimal Tab button** in the ribbon.

CHAPTER 8: SETTING AND APPLYING TABS   107

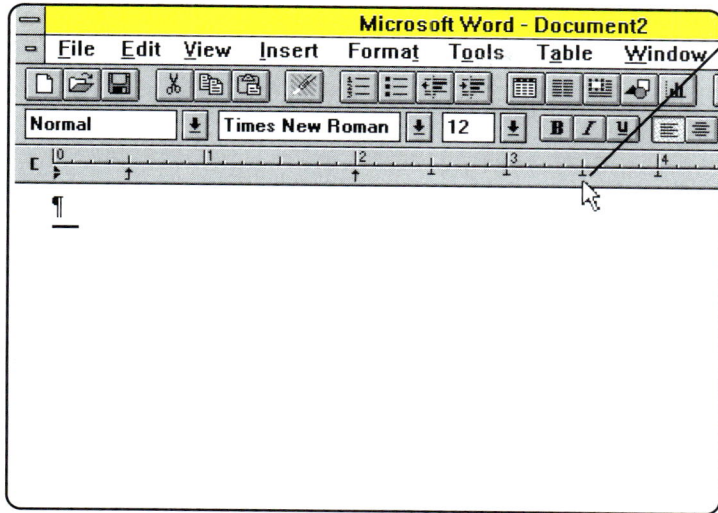

2. Place the mouse pointer in the lower-half of the ruler **at the 3.5-inch mark**. Do not let the arrow touch the ruler line itself.

3. Click to set the decimal tab in place.

You will use this tab setting later in the chapter in the section "Applying Tabs."

SETTING A DECIMAL TAB FROM THE MENU BAR

In this section you will use a menu command to set a decimal tab at 5 inches.

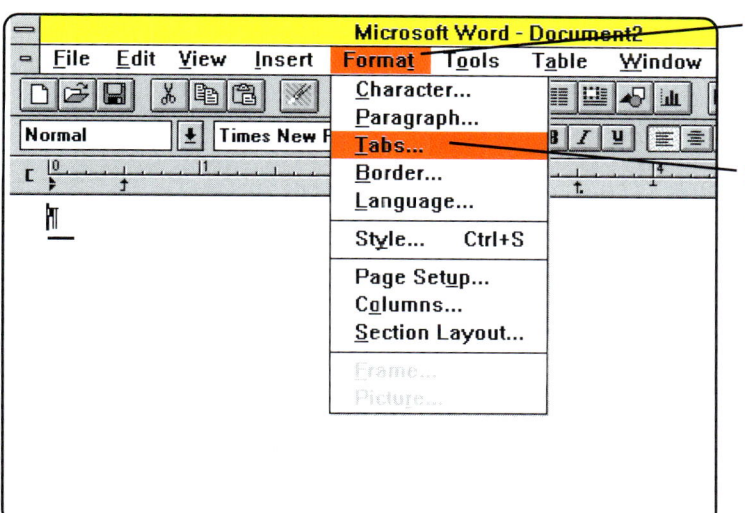

1. Click on **Format** in the menu bar. A pull-down menu will appear.

2. Click on **Tabs**. The Tabs dialog box will appear.

Notice that the tabs you set with the mouse are listed in the Tab Stop Position list box.

3. **Type 5** in the Tab Stop Position box. You don't need to type the inch symbol ("). The number 5 will replace the highlighted text in the box.

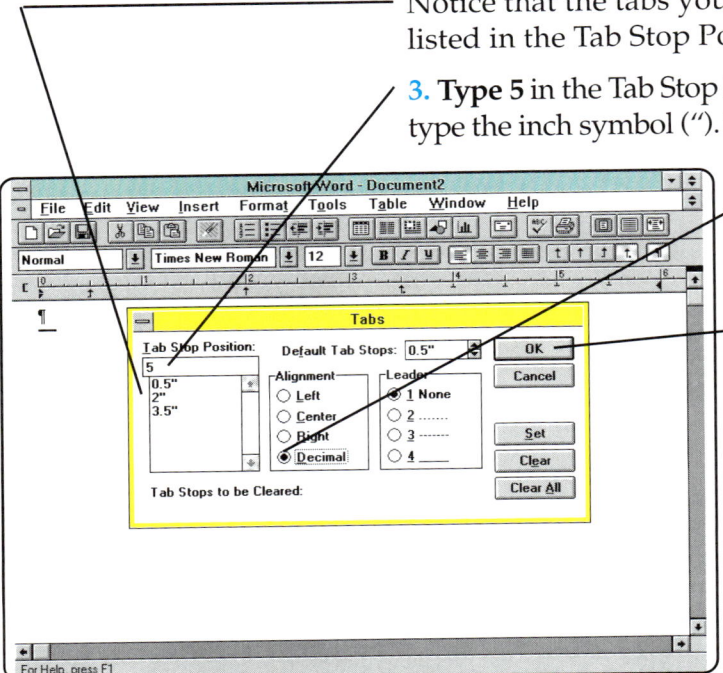

4. **Click** on **Decimal** in the Alignment box to insert a dot in the circle.

5. **Click** on **OK**. The dialog box will close and a decimal tab mark will appear on the ruler line at 5 inches.

You will use this tab setting in the following section.

APPLYING TABS

In this section you will apply the tabs you set in the previous sections. Notice how each text entry aligns on the tab stop in the ruler.

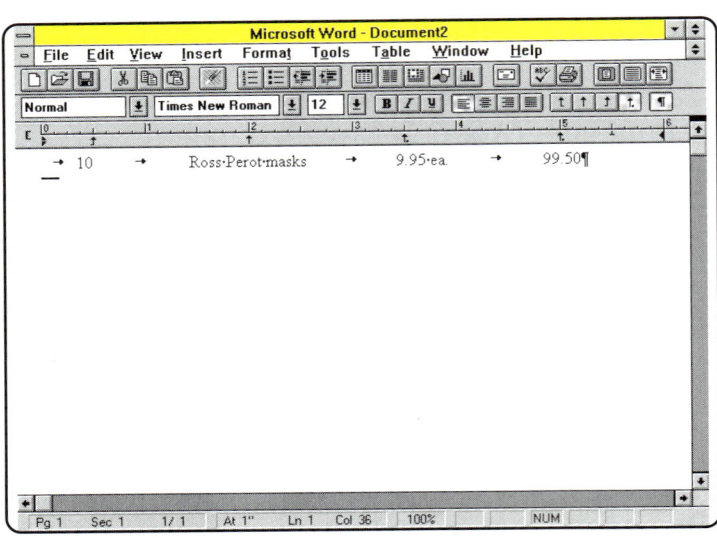

1. **Press Tab** and **type 10**.

2. **Press Tab** and **type Ross Perot masks**. Notice that the text moves to the left as you type.

3. **Press Tab** and **type 9.95 ea.** (don't forget the period).

4. **Press Tab** and **type 99.50**.

CHAPTER 8: SETTING AND APPLYING TABS   **109**

5. **Press Enter** to move to the next line.

6. **Press Tab** and **type 5**. Notice the "5" is right-aligned under "10."

7. **Press Tab** and **type Catwoman costumes**. Notice that it is centered under the entry above it.

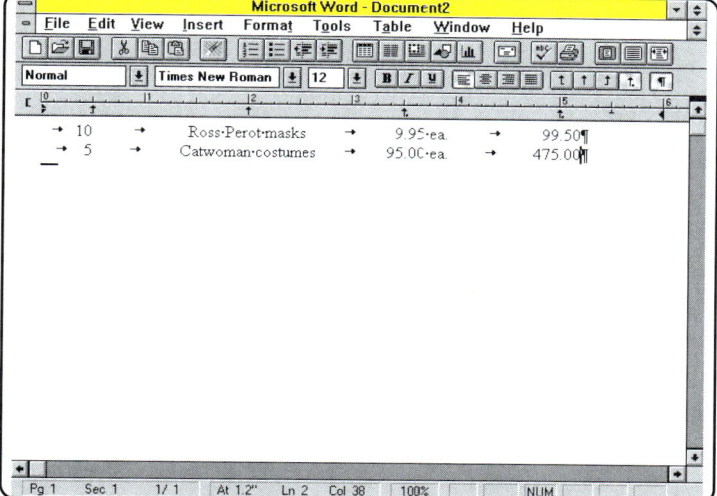

8. **Press Tab** and **type 95.00 ea.** (don't forget the period). Notice that the decimal points are lined up.

9. **Press Tab** and **type 475.00**. Again, notice that the decimal points are lined up. Your screen will look like the example to the left.

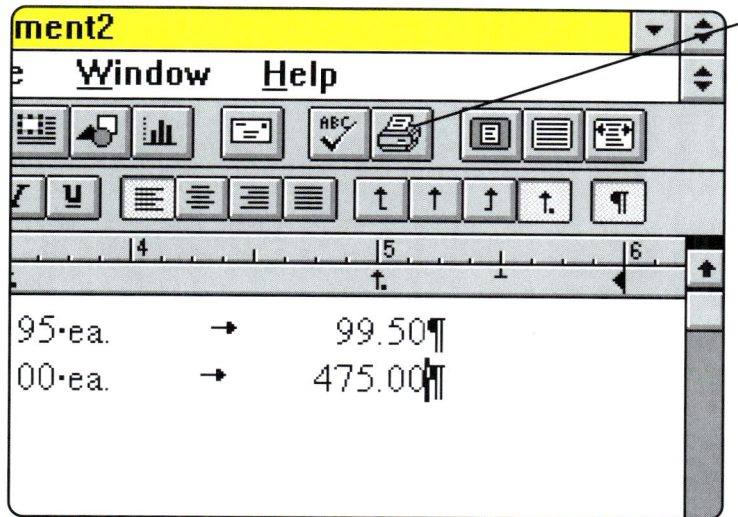

10. **Click** on the **Print tool** in the toolbar if you want to see what the printed document looks like.

CLOSING THE DOCUMENT WITHOUT SAVING

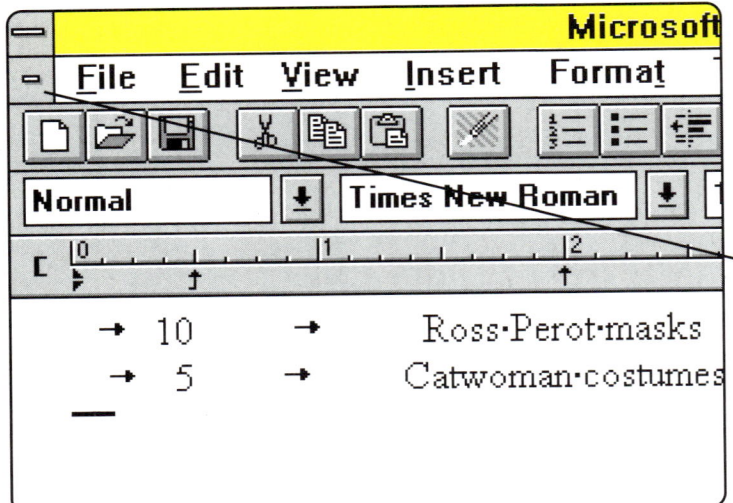

Since this exercise was meant only as practice in setting different types of tabs and will not be used later in the book, you don't need to save the document.

1. **Click twice** on the **Control menu box** (□) to the left of the menu bar to close the document. (Be careful not to click on the Control menu box in the title bar above, which will close Word.)

Since you haven't saved this document, you will see the Microsoft Word dialog box.

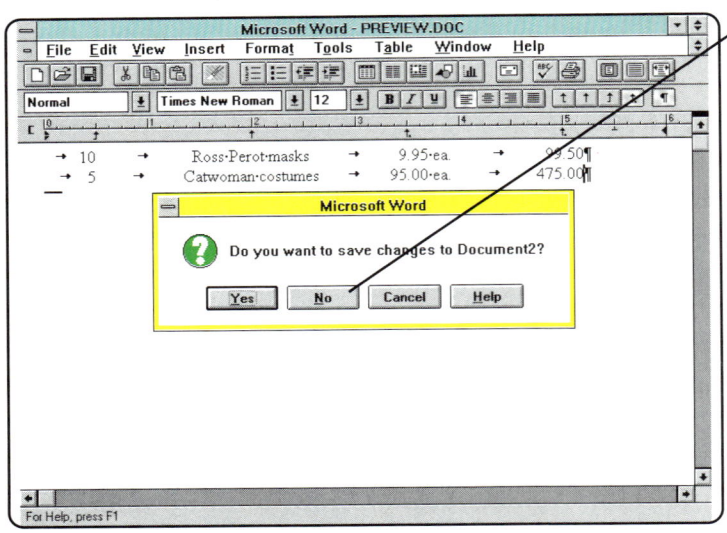

2. **Click** on **No**. The document will close without being saved. You will see PREVIEW.DOC on your screen. It will be exactly as you left it when you opened the new document.

CHAPTER 9

Separating a Document into Sections and Adding a Header and Footer

In Word for Windows 2 you can divide a document into sections and format each section separately, allowing you to make elements like margins, headers, and footers different in each section. A *header* or *footer* is information that is printed at the top or bottom of each page, respectively. For example, in this book the page number and book title is a header on every left page and the chapter title and page number is a header on every right page. In this chapter you will do the following:

❖ Make page 2 of the sample PREVIEW.DOC file into a separate section and change the top margin

❖ Insert a header and footer on page 2 of the sample document

SEPARATING A DOCUMENT INTO TWO SECTIONS

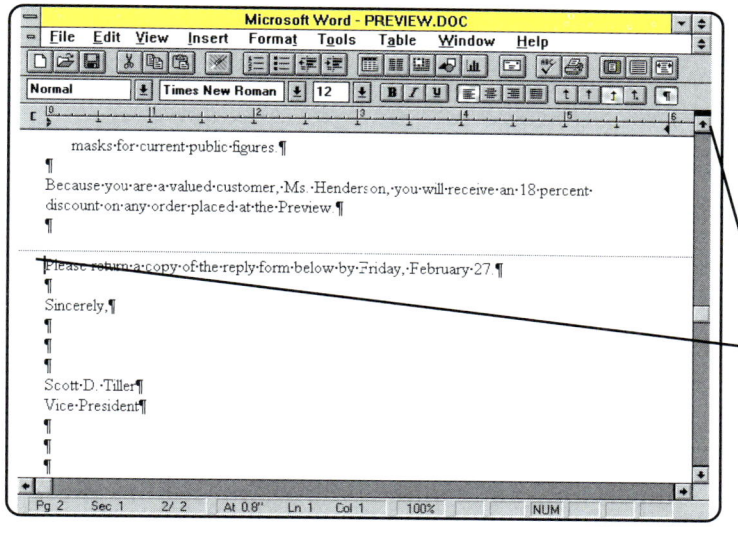

To change the top margin on just the second page of PREVIEW.DOC, you must first separate the document into two sections.

1. **Click** on ↑ to scroll up to the top of page 2.

2. **Place** the mouse pointer to the **left of "Please return"** and **click** to set it in place.

111

3. Click on **Format** in the menu bar. A pull-down menu will appear.

4. Click on **Page Setup**. The Page Setup dialog box will appear.

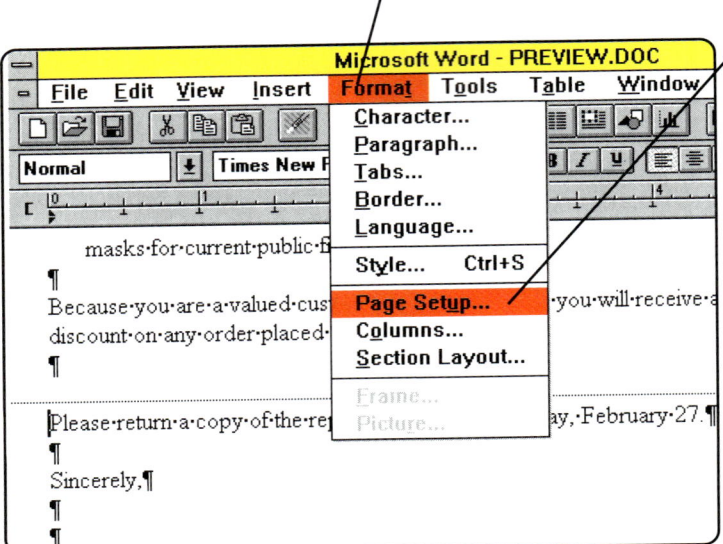

5. Click on **Margins** to insert a dot in the circle if one is not already there.

6. Place the mouse pointer to the **left of 0.75"** in the Top margin box and **click twice**. The 0.75" setting you specified in Chapter 1 will be highlighted.

7. Type 1.5. It will replace the highlighted text.

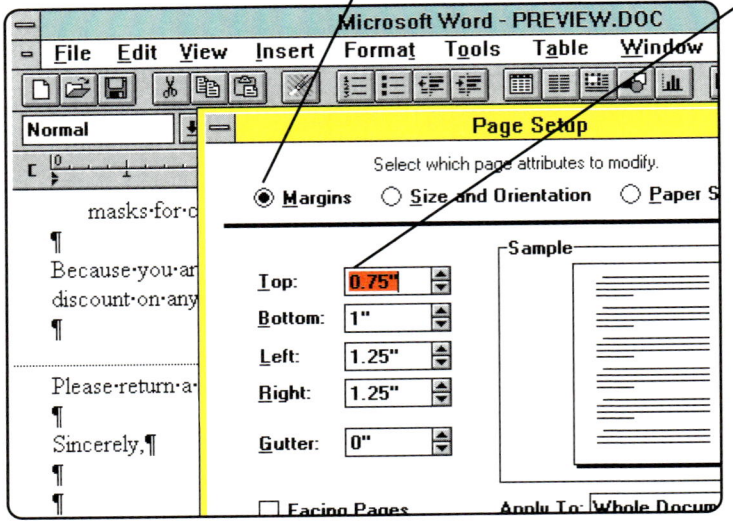

CHAPTER 9: SECTIONS, HEADERS, AND FOOTERS 113

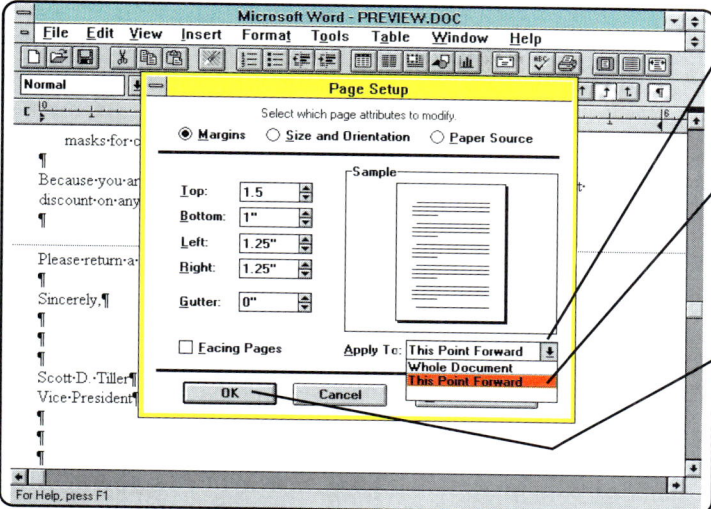

8. **Click** on ↓ to the right of the Apply To box. A drop-down list will appear.

9. **Click** on **This Point Forward** to apply the margin change only to page 2 of the document.

10. **Click** on **OK** to confirm the changes you just made and close the dialog box.

Notice that the page break you inserted is still there. You will delete it in the next procedure.

Notice the double line indicating the start of a new section in the document.

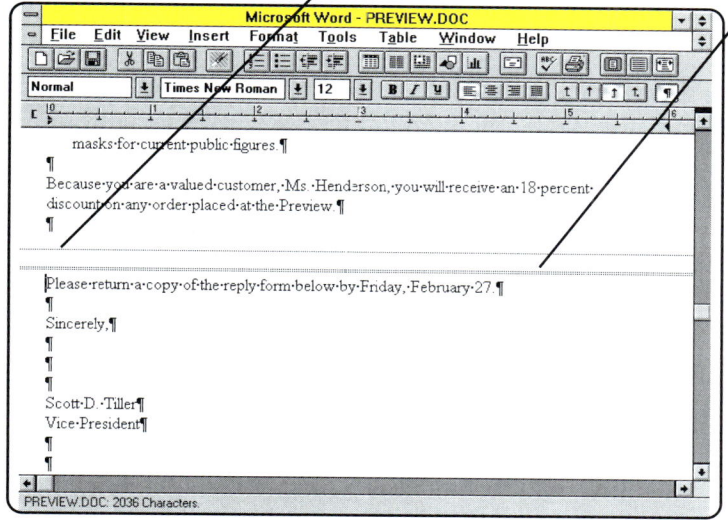

Deleting the Page Break

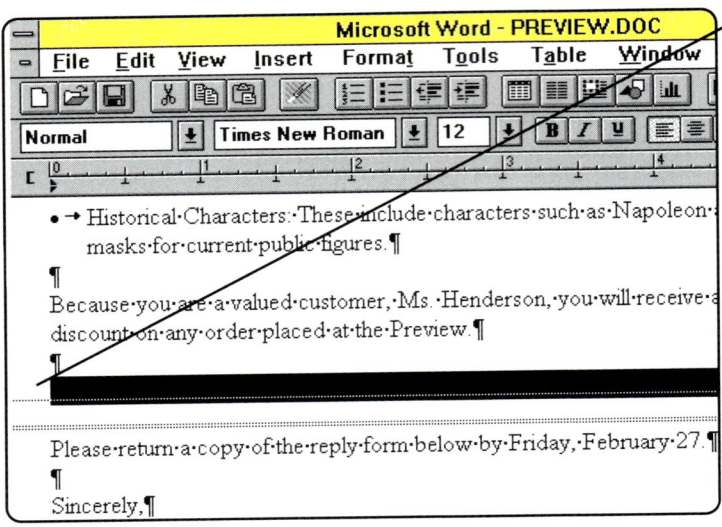

1. **Place** the mouse pointer in the left margin **on top of the page break line**. The pointer will change to an arrow.

2. **Click** on the **page break line**. The line will be highlighted.

3. **Press** the **Del key**. The page break line will disappear. The double line indicating the new section is still there.

CREATING A HEADER

When you create a header in Word, it will appear at the top of *every* page of the document. You can change this. In this section you will create a header using the words "Ms. Diane Henderson" and the date. You will also set up Word to print the header only on page 2. Although there are several ways to do this, the following steps will be appropriate for most situations.

Notice that the insertion point is on page 1 of the document.

CHAPTER 9: SECTIONS, HEADERS, AND FOOTERS

1. **Click** on **View** in the menu bar. A pull-down menu will appear.

2. **Click** on **Header/Footer**. The Header/Footer dialog box will appear.

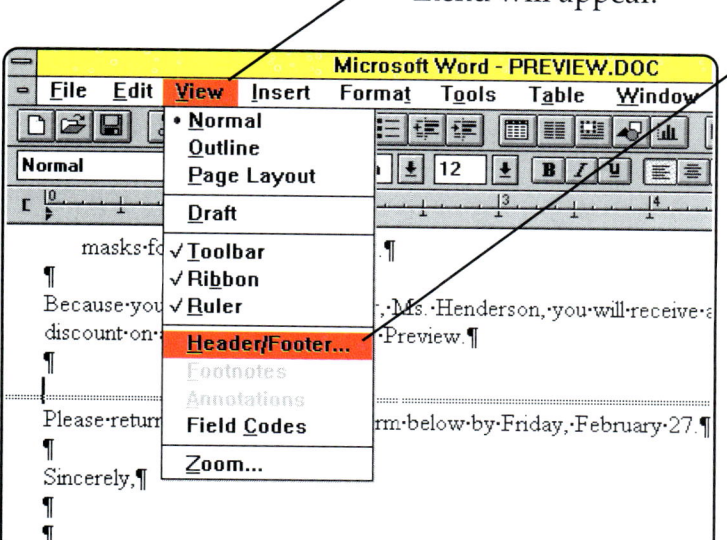

Notice that Header is already highlighted.

3. **Click** on **Different First Page** to insert an ✗ in the check box. When you do this, "First Header" and "First Footer" will appear in the Header/Footer list box. By clicking on Different First Page you are telling Word that you do not want the header to go on page 1 of the letter.

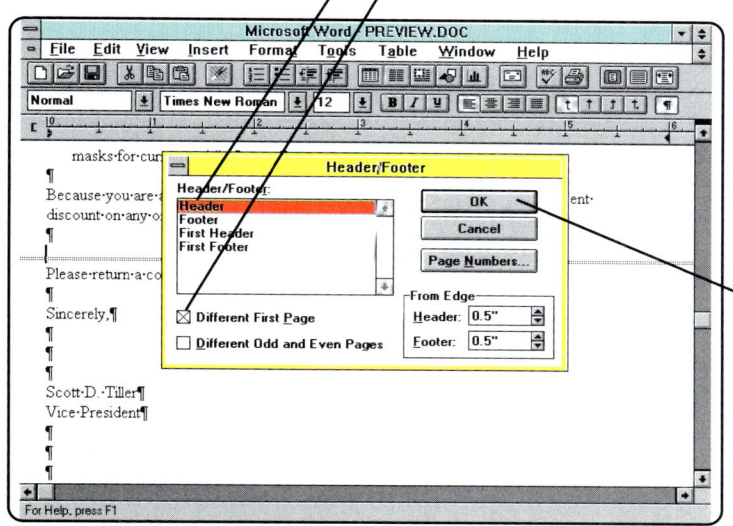

4. **Click** on **OK**. The Header/Footer dialog box will disappear and the header pane will appear.

WORD FOR WINDOWS 2: THE VISUAL LEARNING GUIDE

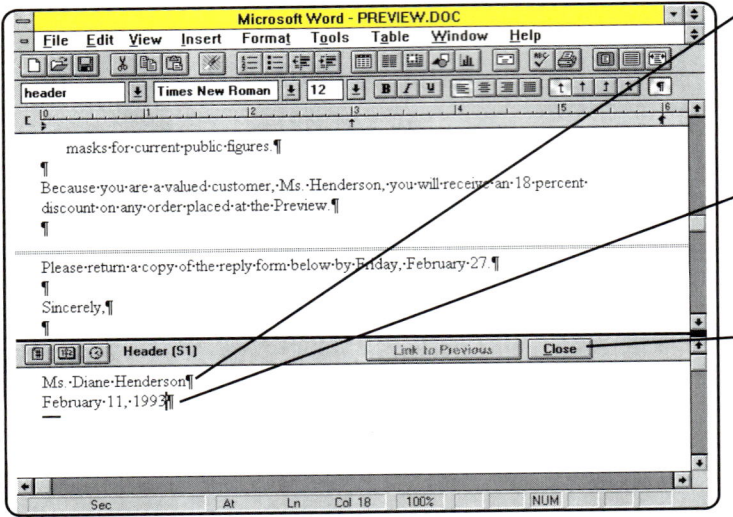

5. Type **Ms. Diane Henderson** and **press Enter** to move the insertion point to the next line.

6. Type the current date (rather than the date you see in the example).

7. Click on **Close**. The header pane will disappear.

Although the header will print, you will not see it on your screen. In the next chapter, "Changing the View," you will change the view so that you can see the header.

CREATING A FOOTER

In this example you will create a footer just for page 2, using the document's page number, and center it at the bottom of the page.

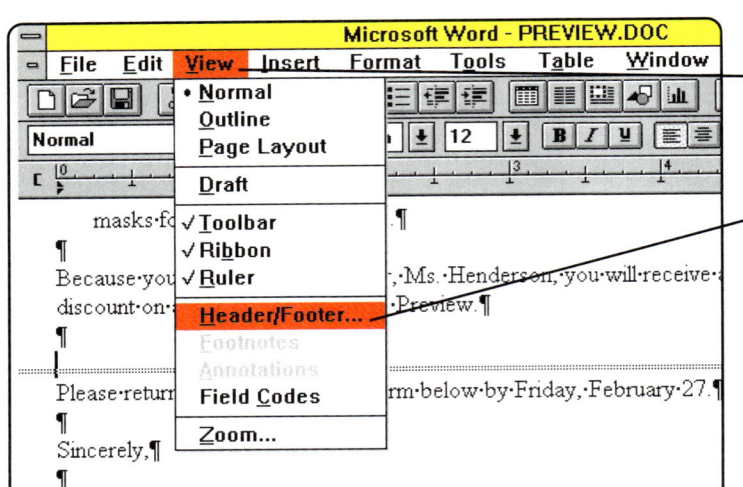

1. Click on **View** in the menu bar. A pull-down menu will appear.

2. Click on **Header/Footer**. The Header/Footer dialog box will appear.

CHAPTER 9: SECTIONS, HEADERS, AND FOOTERS

3. **Click** on **Footer**. It will be highlighted.

Notice the X in the Different First Page check box. You inserted the X earlier when you created the header.

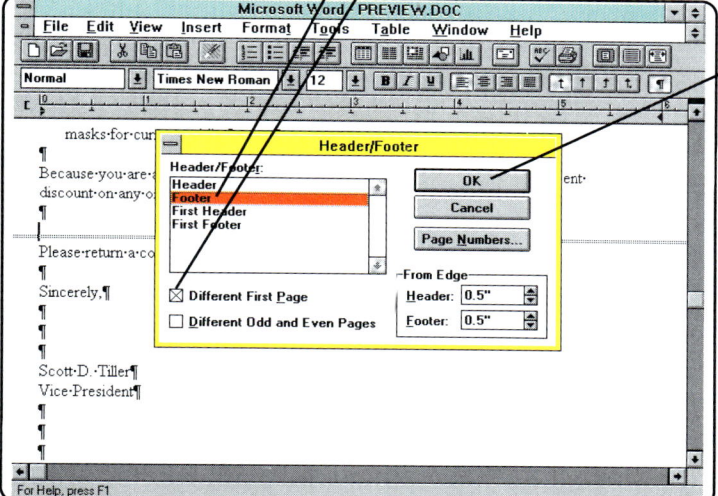

4. **Click** on **OK**. The footer pane will appear.

The header and footer panes have two pre-set (default) tabs. The first tab centers text, the second aligns the text at the right margin.

5. **Press Tab**. The insertion point will move to the center of the page.

6. **Click** on the **Page Number tool** to insert the page number in the footer. You will see the number "1" appear because the insertion point is on page 1. However, the footer will not print on page 1, and page 2 will be numbered correctly. (It's a little strange but it works.)

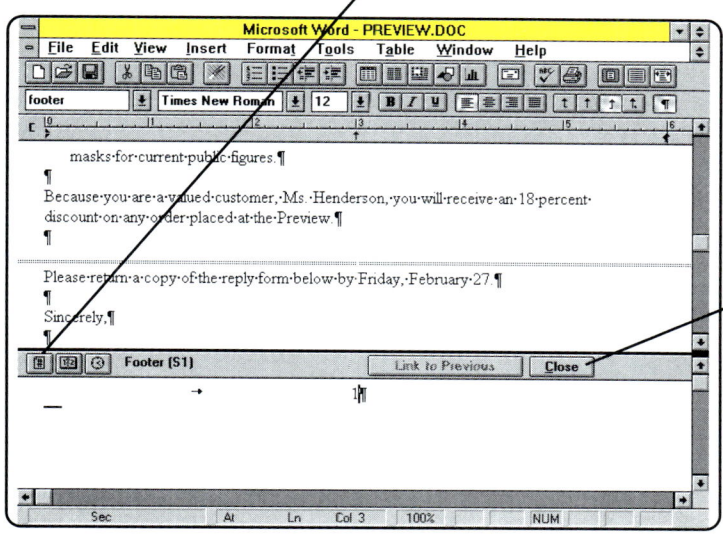

7. **Click** on **Close**.

You will learn how to view the header and footer in the next chapter.

CHAPTER 10

Changing the View

In Chapters 1 through 9 you've been working in *Normal view*, the Word for Windows 2 standard (default) onscreen display of a document. Normal view is the best view for everyday work. As you saw in Chapter 9, however, Normal view doesn't display headers or footers onscreen. To see these and other special screen elements, as well as to get different perspectives of a document, Word provides a variety of views. You can, for example, zoom in on a document and magnify a portion of the screen, or zoom out to get a broader view of the document. In this chapter you will learn how to work in the following views:

❖ Page Layout
❖ Print Preview
❖ Draft
❖ Zoom

PAGE LAYOUT VIEW

Page Layout view shows you how a document, including headers and footers, will look when it is printed. You can edit the document while in this view.

1. **Press and hold Ctrl** as you **press Home** (Ctrl + Home) to move the mouse pointer to the beginning of the document if you are not already there. In this case, you are working with the PREVIEW.DOC file created earlier.

2. **Click** on **View** in the menu bar. A pull-down menu will appear.

3. **Click** on **Page Layout**. You will see an hourglass as the view changes to Page Layout.

119

This is the view you will see in Page Layout.

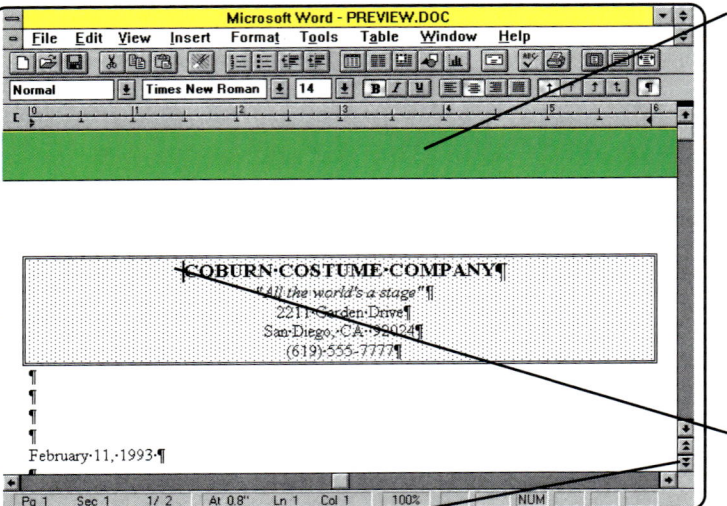

Notice that your desktop color appears at the top of the document. (The exact colors of the desktop, title bars, and highlight bars you see on your screen depend on the colors you set in Windows. Refer to *Windows 3.1: The Visual Learning Guide* to learn how to change the colors on your screen.)

Notice that the insertion point is in the same place it was in the Normal view. If you had placed the insertion point on page 2, you would see page 2 in Page Layout.

Scrolling Through Pages in Page Layout View

1. **Click** on the **Page Down double arrow** at the bottom of the scroll bar to move the view down an entire page. (Clicking on the Page Down double arrow on the scroll bar will not move you within a page, but to the next page.)

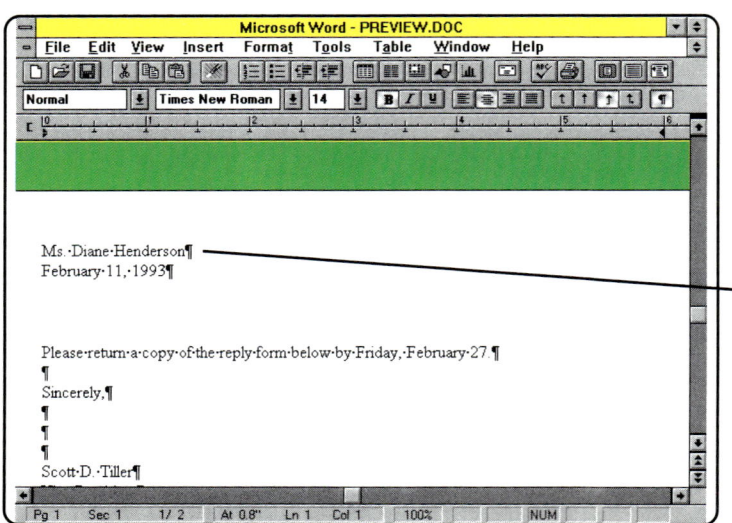

Notice the header you created earlier appears where you placed it.

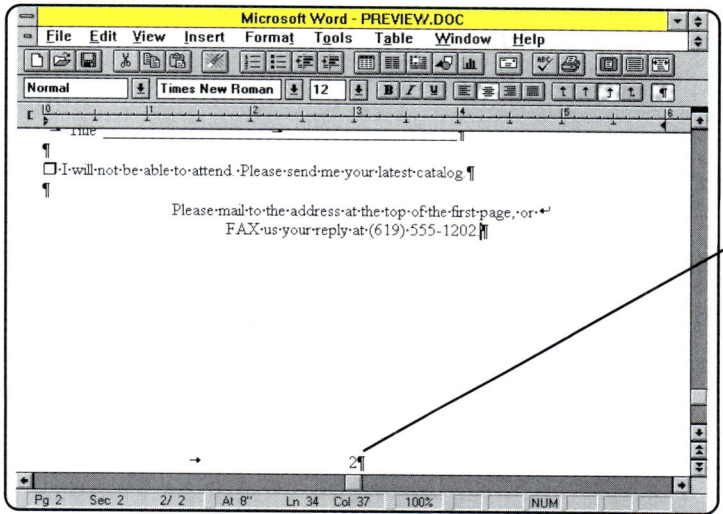

2. **Press and hold Ctrl** as you **press** the **End key** (Ctrl + End) to move the insertion point to the end of the document.

Notice the page number footer in the center of the page.

Remember, you can edit the document while in this view.

PRINT PREVIEW

Print Preview gives you a bird's-eye view of what your printed document will look like. You can see up to two pages at a time. Although you cannot edit text in Print Preview, you can change margins, adjust the position of headers and footers, and change page breaks.

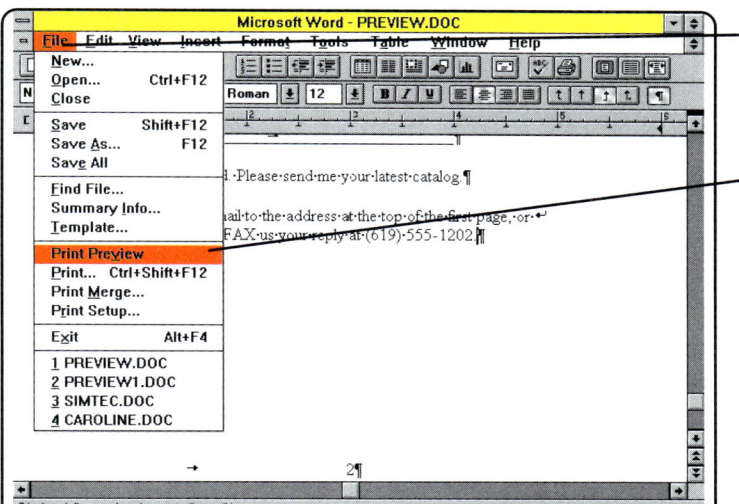

1. **Click** on **File** in the menu bar. A pull-down menu will appear.

2. **Click** on **Print Preview**. The Print Preview screen will appear.

Scrolling Through Pages in Print Preview

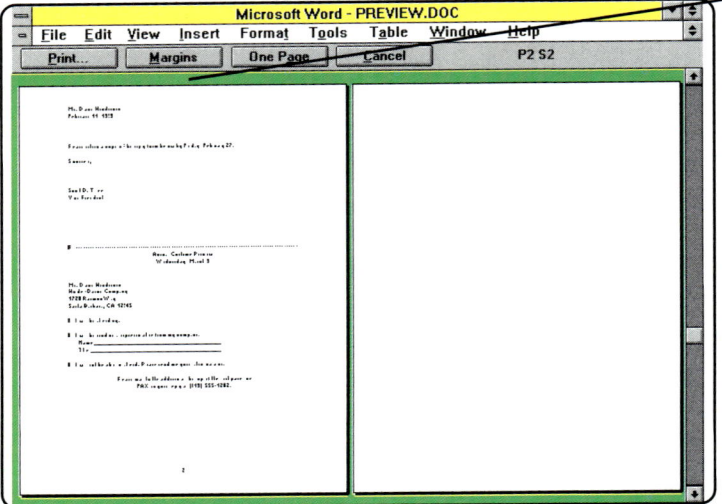

Notice that page 2 is the only page you see. This is because the insertion point was located on page 2 when you opened the Print Preview screen.

1. **Press** the **PgUp key** on your keyboard to go to page 1. Since Page Preview can show two consecutive pages at once, you will see pages 1 and 2 on your screen, as in the example below.

If your document is more than two pages long, simply press PgDn and PgUp to scroll through the document.

Displaying Margins in Print Preview

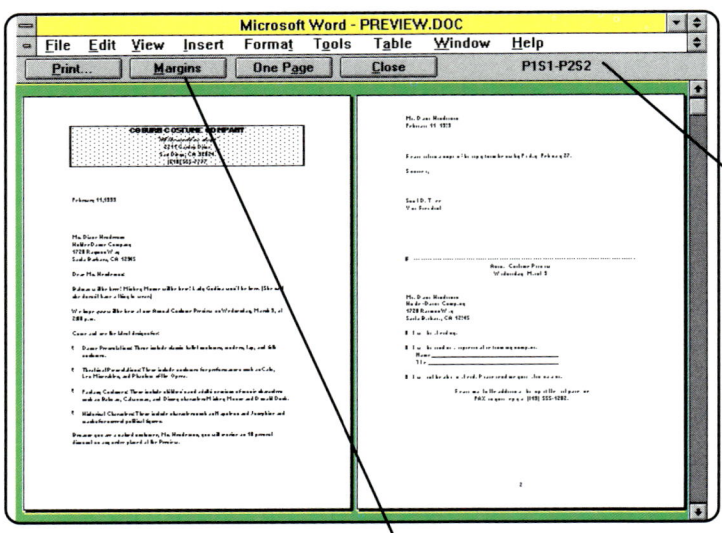

Notice the range of pages currently being displayed. Besides telling you that you are viewing pages 1 and 2, it also indicates that page 1 is *in* section 1 (P1S1) and page 2 is *in* section 2 (P2S2)—just as you had divided the document in Chapter 9.

1. **Click** on the **Margins** button.

Dotted lines showing the placement of the margins appear on page 1.

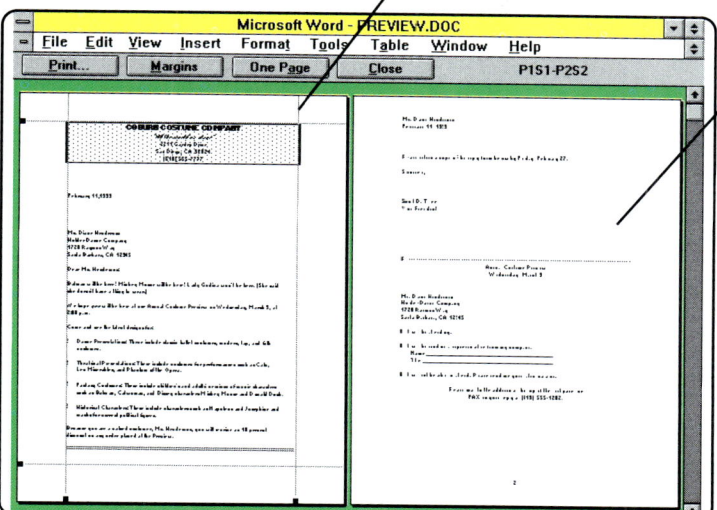

2. Click anywhere on **page 2** to display the margin lines on page 2.

You can change the placement of the margins, as well as the placement of headers and footers, while you are in this view. Refer to the *Microsoft Word for Windows 2 User's Guide* for more details.

Printing in Print Preview

1. Click on the **Print button**. The Print dialog box will appear.

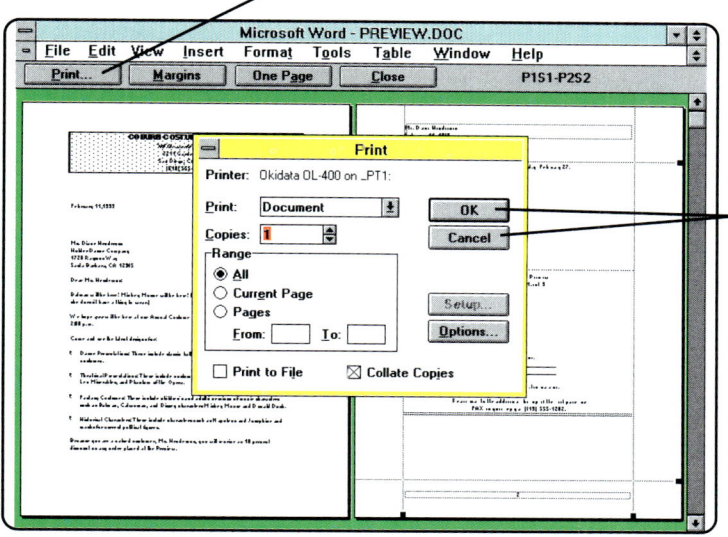

Refer to Chapter 6, "Printing a File," for details on the Print dialog box if you need help.

After you click on either OK or Cancel, the Print dialog box will disappear and the Print Preview window will be on your screen.

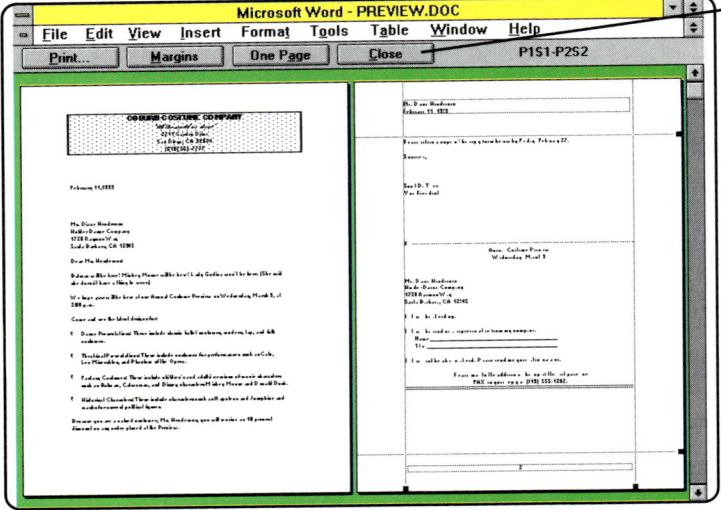

2. Click on the **Close button** to close the Print Preview window. (If you did not print the letter, this will be a Cancel button.) You will be returned to the Page Layout view of the letter because that was the view you were in when you selected Print Preview.

DRAFT VIEW

Draft view shows text in a single font and point size regardless of any font and point size changes you may have made. This allows your computer to display text quickly since it doesn't have to perform the complex computations necessary to display text on screen as it will print on paper (called WYSIWYG—pronounced wiz-ee-wig—or "What You See Is What You Get").

This is especially helpful if you need to edit only text and are not concerned about formats.

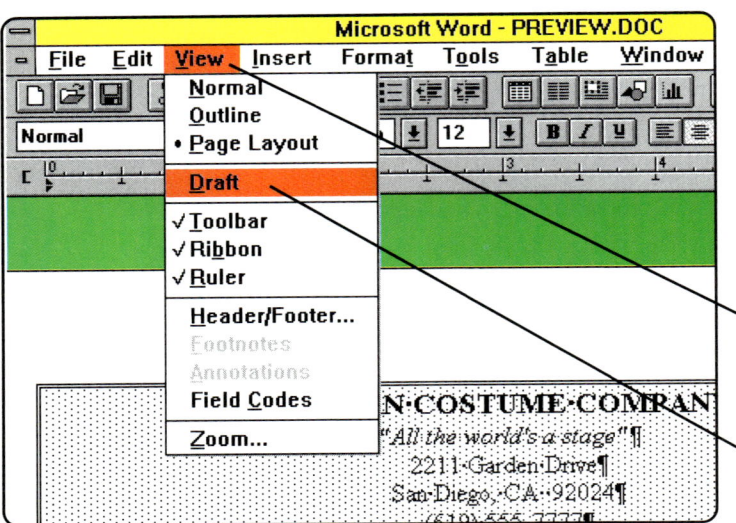

1. Click on **View** in the menu bar. A pull-down menu will appear.

2. Click on **Draft**. The Draft view of the document will appear.

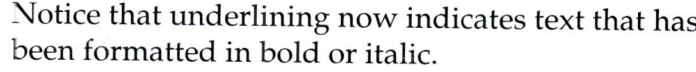

Notice that underlining now indicates text that has been formatted in bold or italic.

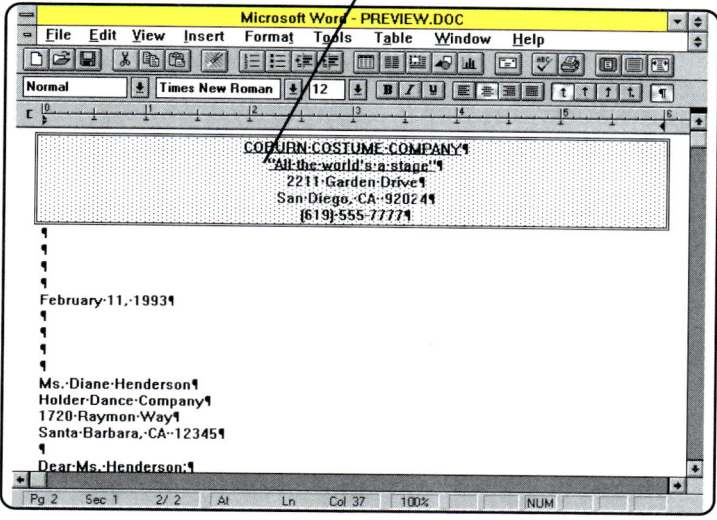

Returning to Normal View from the Menu Bar

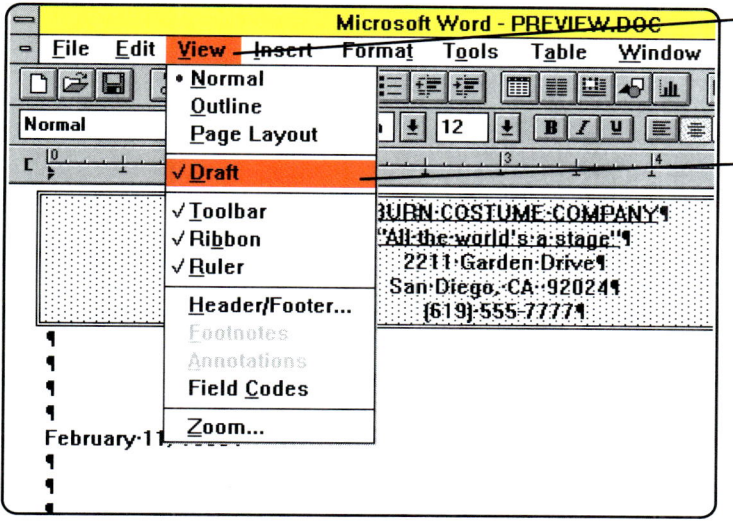

1. **Click** on **View** in the menu bar. A pull-down menu will appear.

2. **Click** on **Draft** to remove the check mark. Your screen will return to Normal view.

ZOOM VIEW

Zoom view works like the zoom lens on a camera. You can zoom in on the document to magnify a portion of the screen or zoom out to get a broader view. You can edit text in Zoom view.

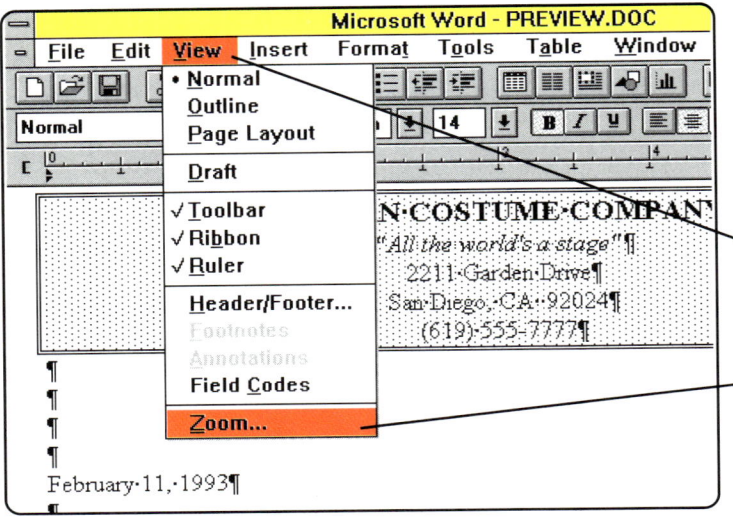

1. **Click** on **View** in the menu bar. A pull-down menu will appear.

2. **Click** on **Zoom**. The Zoom dialog box will appear.

Magnifying the View (Zooming In)

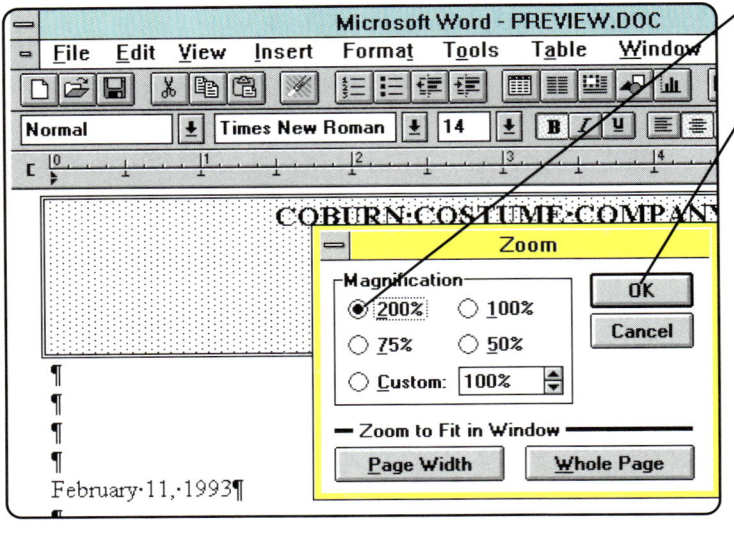

1. **Click** on **200%** to insert a dot in the circle.

2. **Click** on **OK**. The area around the insertion point will be magnified 200 percent.

Reducing the View (Zooming Out)

1. **Click** on **View** in the menu bar. A pull-down menu will appear.

2. **Click** on **Zoom**. The Zoom dialog box will appear.

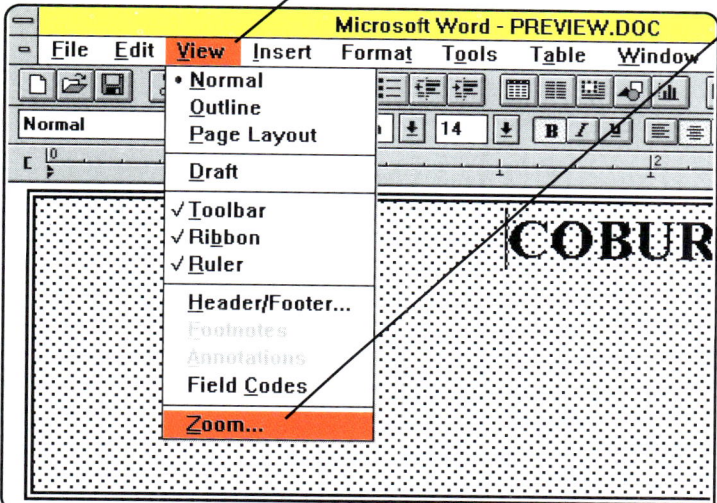

3. **Click** on **50%**.

4. **Click** on **OK**. The document will appear on your screen at 50 percent of its normal size.

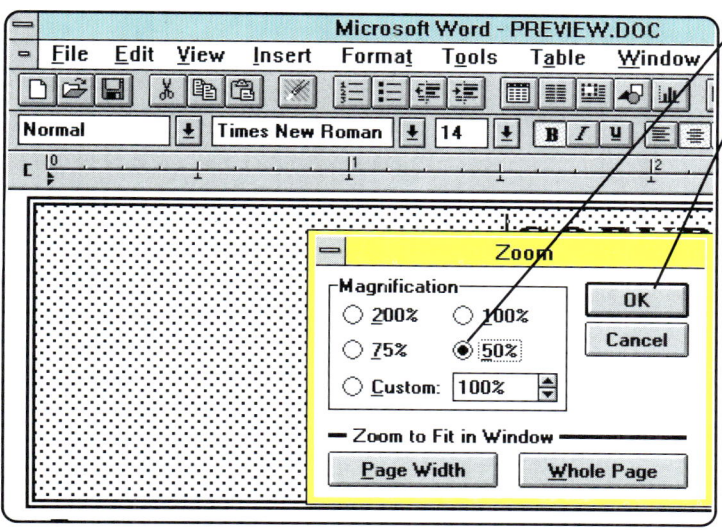

Returning to Normal View Using the Zoom 100 Percent Tool

You can use the Zoom 100 Percent tool to return to Normal view from Zoom view or from Page Layout view. (Unfortunately, the button doesn't work from Print Preview or Draft view.)

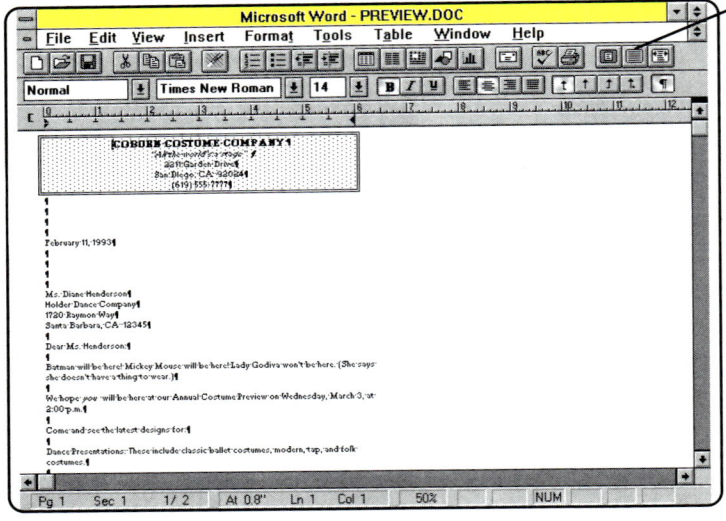

1. **Click** on the **Zoom 100 Percent tool** in the toolbar. You will be returned to the standard-sized screen in Normal view.

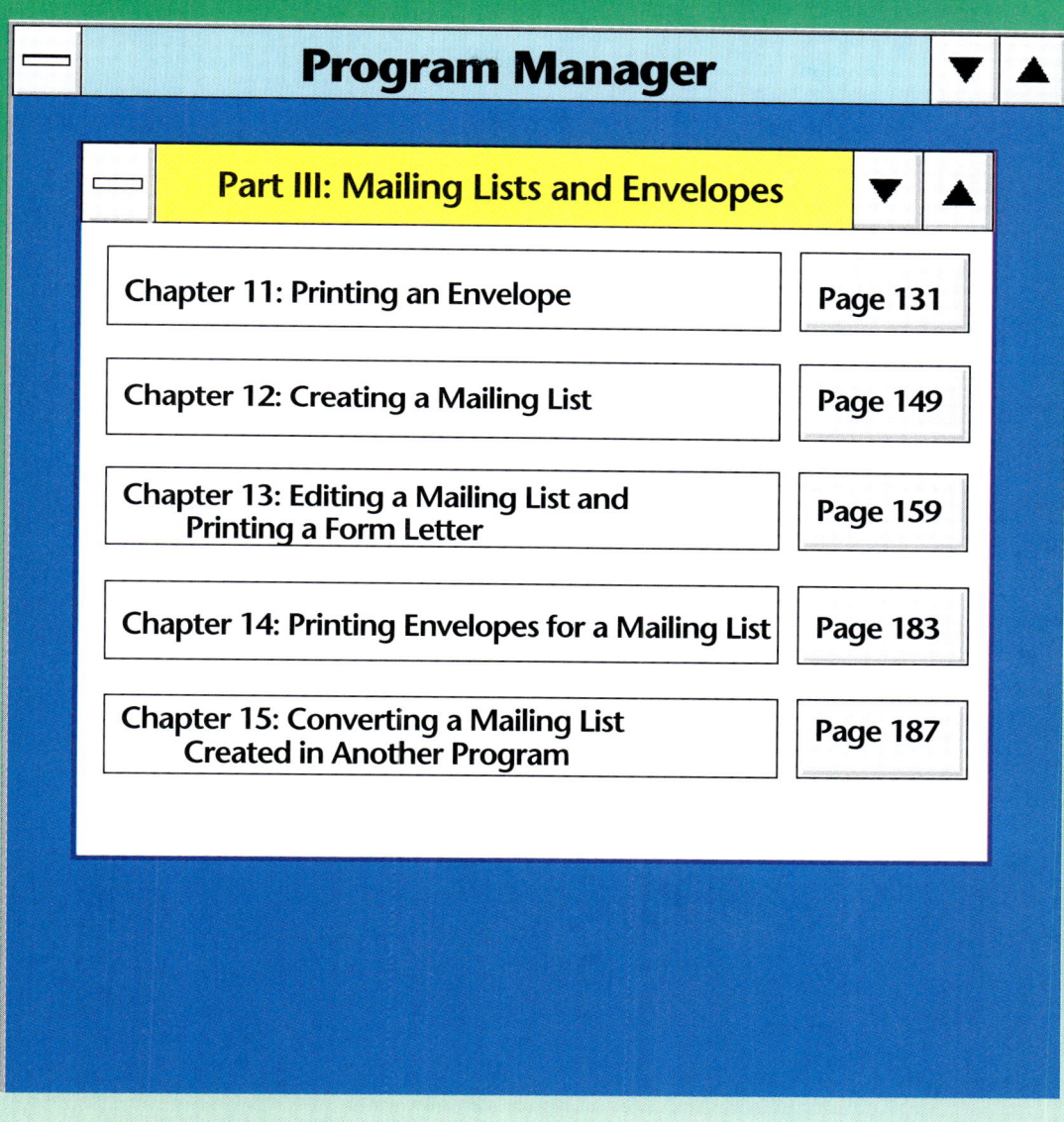

Program Manager

Part III: Mailing Lists and Envelopes

Chapter 11: Printing an Envelope	Page 131
Chapter 12: Creating a Mailing List	Page 149
Chapter 13: Editing a Mailing List and Printing a Form Letter	Page 159
Chapter 14: Printing Envelopes for a Mailing List	Page 183
Chapter 15: Converting a Mailing List Created in Another Program	Page 187

CHAPTER 11

Printing an Envelope

Unlike most word processing programs, Word for Windows 2 makes it as easy to print an envelope as clicking your mouse. But to customize an envelope, you must first attach it to a document and then customize it, which is still an easy process. In this chapter you will do the following:

❖ Use the Envelope tool to quick-print a standard business envelope on a LaserJet Series printer and a dot-matrix printer
❖ Print the return address
❖ Customize the return address
❖ Print an envelope that has been permanently attached to a document

USING THE ENVELOPE TOOL

In this section you will print a standard business envelope with a preprinted return address. After you complete the step below, refer to the directions for either LaserJet Series II and III printers (and printers that emulate them) or dot-matrix printers.

1. **Open the PREVIEW.DOC** file if it is not already on your screen.

131

Printing with a LaserJet Series II or III Printer

1. Place an **envelope tray** into your printer. If you do not have an envelope tray, **place a single envelope in the manual feed slot** on your printer's paper tray. Since each brand of printer operates slightly differently, consult your printer manual for the exact placement of the envelope as you feed it into the printer.

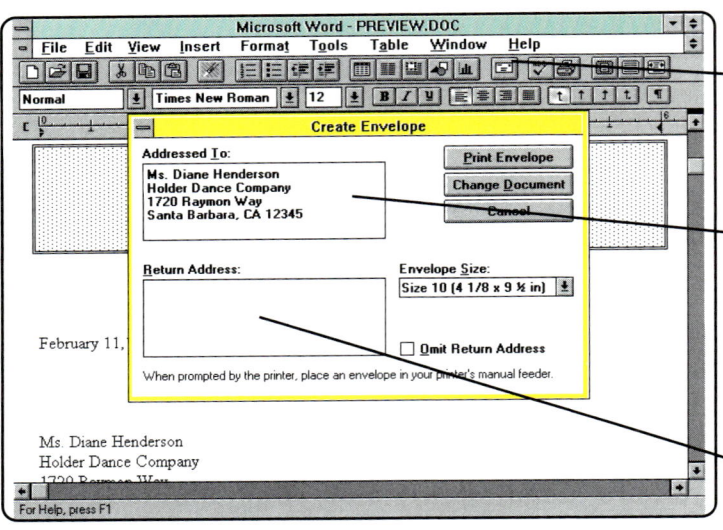

2. Click on the **Envelope tool** in the toolbar. The Create Envelope dialog box will appear.

Notice that the address on your letter appears in the Addressed To box. Word automatically searches for the address in the letter and enters it here.

Notice that the Return Address box is empty. Later in this chapter you will put a return address in this box.

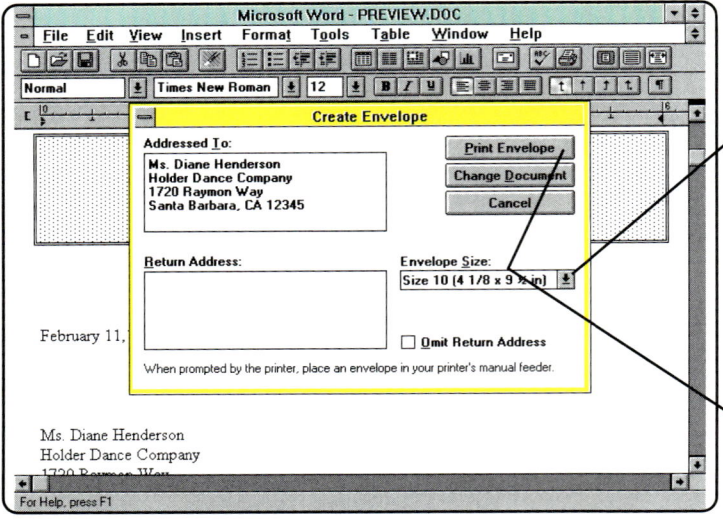

Notice that Word automatically selects the standard size business envelope. If you want to select another envelope size, click on ↓ on the right of the Envelope Size box.

3. Click on **Print Envelope**. The Printing message box will appear.

CHAPTER 11: PRINTING AN ENVELOPE 133

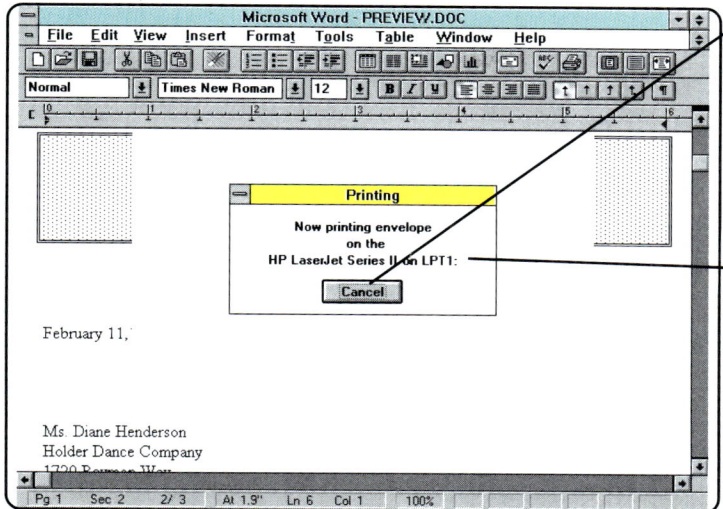

If you change your mind, click on Cancel.

When the Printing message box disappears, your printer will begin printing the envelope. Slick!

Notice that the name of your laser printer appears in this box.

Printing with a Dot-Matrix Printer

Since each brand of printer operates slightly differently, consult your printer manual for the exact placement of the envelope as you feed it into the printer.

1. Remove the **tractor feed paper** from your printer and **insert an envelope**. Word tells most dot-matrix printers to feed the envelope through half an inch before beginning to print. If you want the return address to be printed further down on the envelope, adjust the envelope's position manually before printing. Your printer may allow you to feed an envelope without removing the tractor feed paper. Check your printer manual for help.

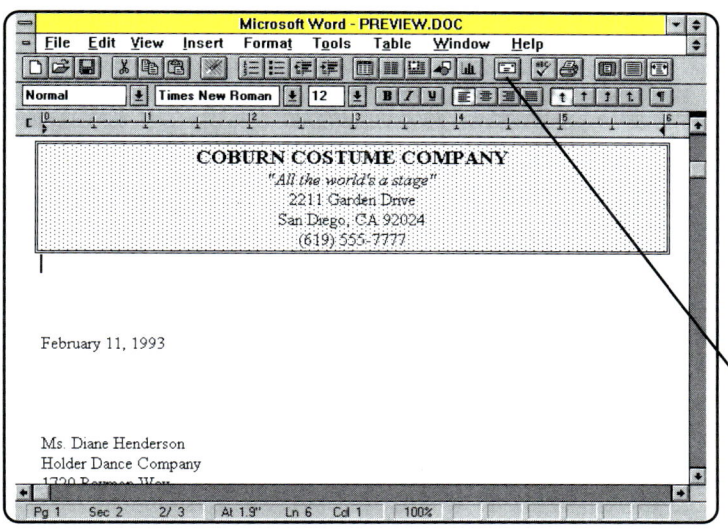

2. Click on the **Envelope tool** in the toolbar. The Create Envelope dialog box will appear.

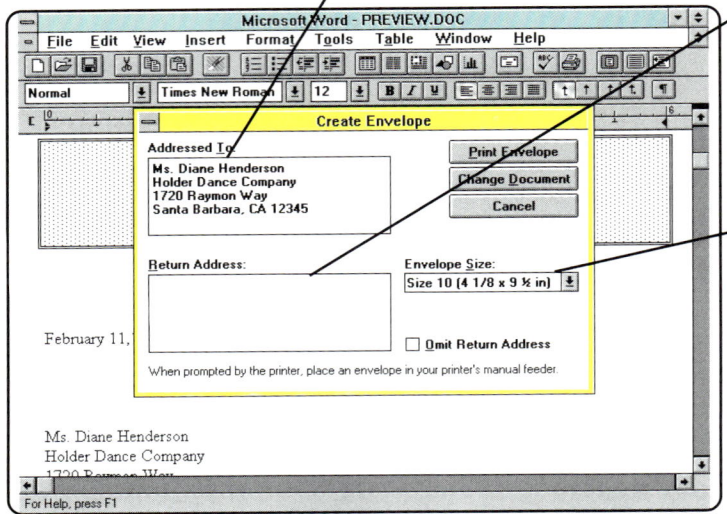

Notice that the address on your letter appears in the Addressed To box. Word automatically searches for the address in the letter and enters it here.

Notice that the Return Address box is empty. In the next section you will put the return address in this box.

Notice that Word automatically selects the standard size business envelope. If you want to select another envelope size, click on ↓ on the right of the Envelope Size box.

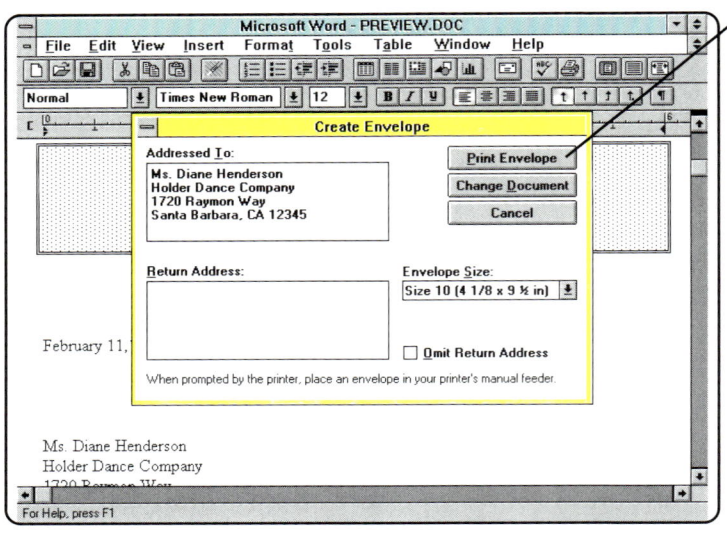

3. **Click** on **Print Envelope**. The Printing message box will appear.

CHAPTER 11: PRINTING AN ENVELOPE

If you change our mind, click on Cancel.

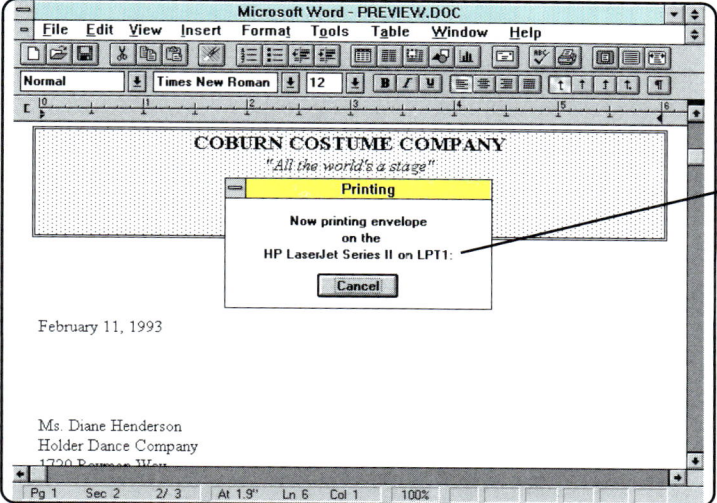

When the Print message box disappears, your printer will begin printing the envelope. Slick!

Notice that the name of your dot-matrix printer appears in this box.

You may have to fiddle with the position and alignment of your envelope in the printer to get it to print properly.

PRINTING THE RETURN ADDRESS

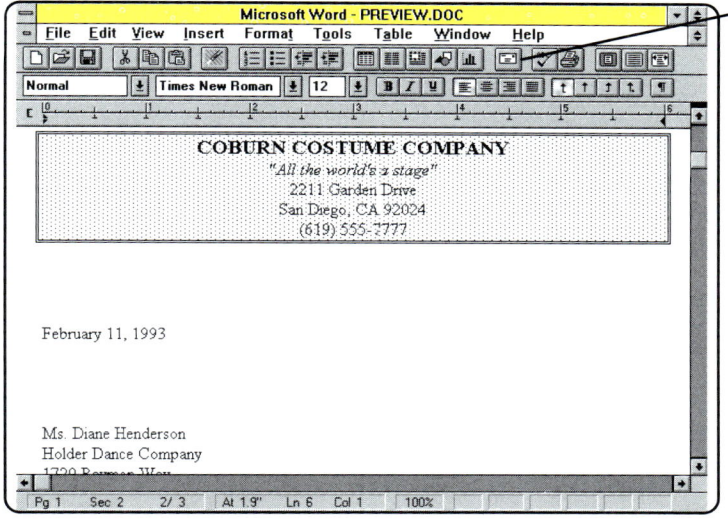

1. Click on the **Envelope tool** in the toolbar. The Create Envelope dialog box will appear.

2. Click on the **Return Address box** to set the insertion point in the box.

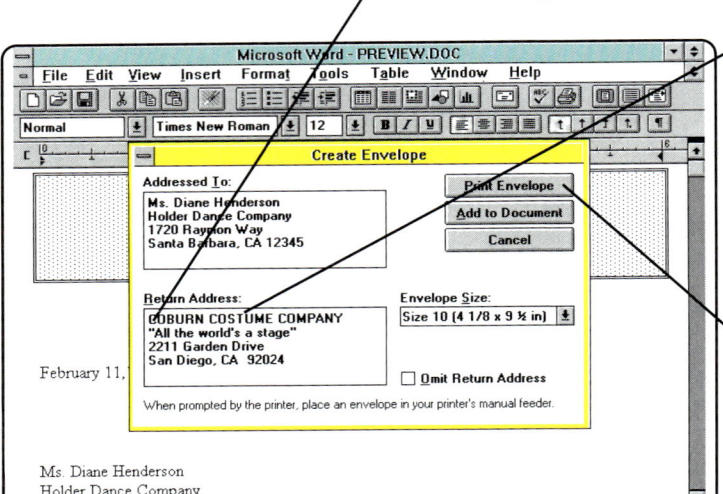

3. Type the following return address:
COBURN COSTUME COMPANY
"All the world's a stage"
2211 Garden Drive
San Diego, CA 92024

4. Click on **Print Envelope**. A Microsoft Word dialog box will appear.

5. Click on **Yes** if you want to make this your standard (default) return address when printing envelopes. **Click** on **No** if you do not want to save this address as your standard return address. The Printing message box will appear.

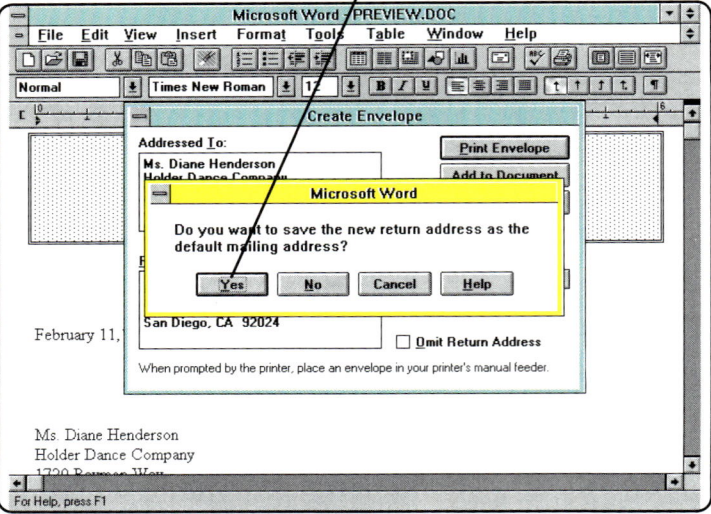

Omitting and Restoring the Standard (Default) Return Address

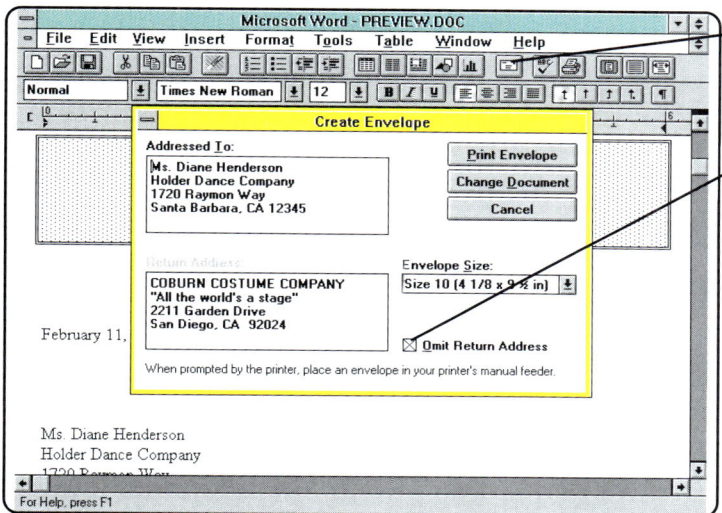

1. **Click** on the **Envelope tool**. The Create Envelope dialog box will appear.

2. **Click** on **Omit Return Address** to place an ✕ in the box if you want to omit the return address.

3. **Click** on **Omit Return Address** again to remove the ✕ and restore the address. Go on to the next section to customize the return address.

CUSTOMIZING THE RETURN ADDRESS

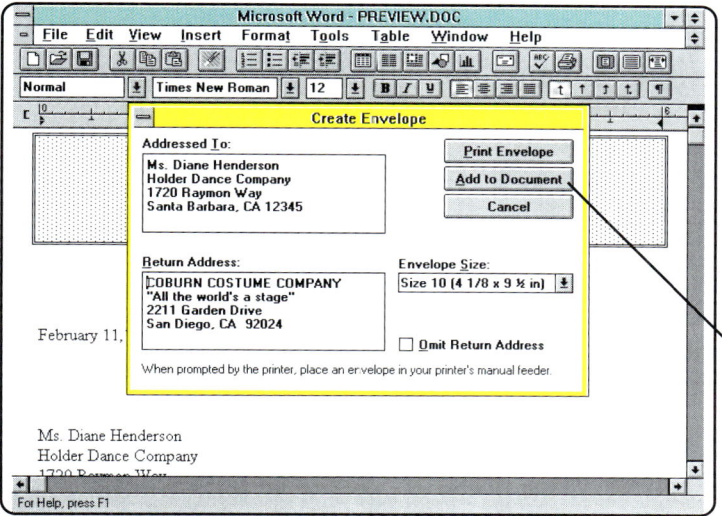

To make changes to Word's return address format, you must first attach the envelope to the document.

Attaching the Envelope to the Letter

1. **Click** on **Add to Document**. The envelope will appear attached to the top of the PREVIEW.DOC page.

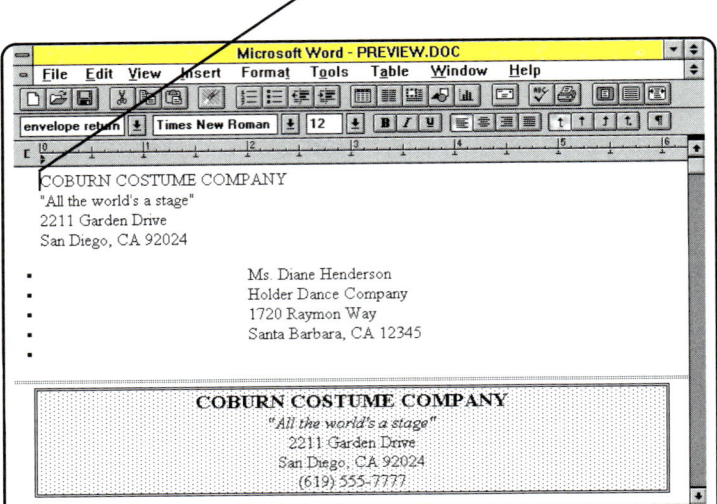

Notice that the insertion point is flashing in the return address.

Opening the Style Dialog Box

1. Click on **Format** in the menu bar. A pull-down menu will appear.

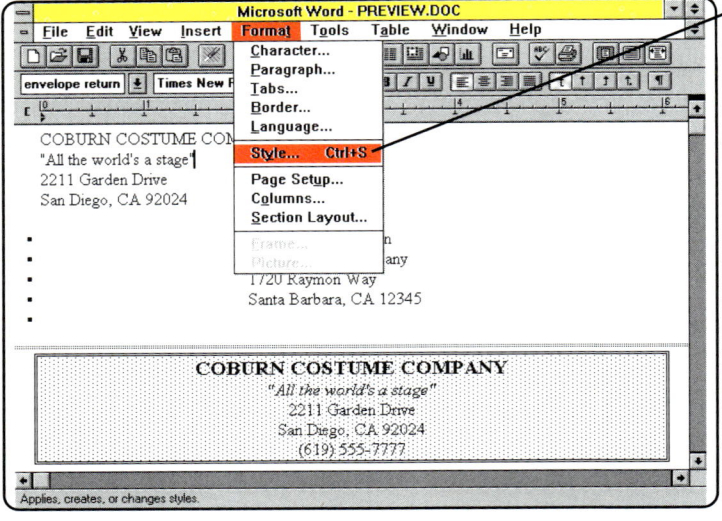

2. Click on **Style**. The Style dialog box will appear.

CHAPTER 11: PRINTING AN ENVELOPE 139

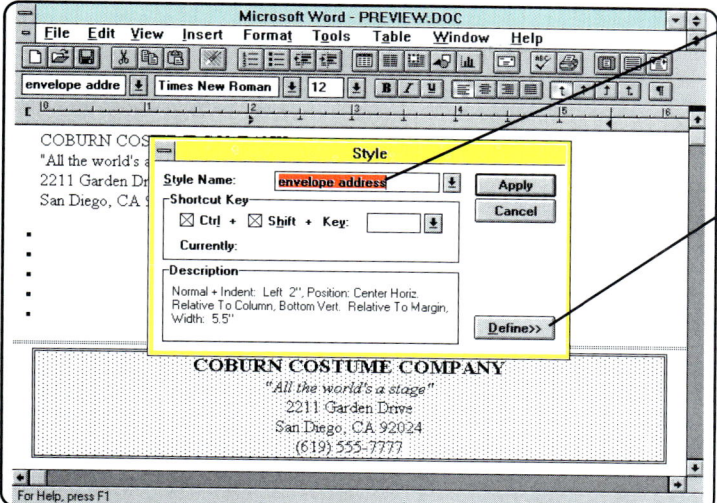

Notice that the phrase "envelope return" is highlighted in the Style Name box.

3. Click on **Define**. A Change Formatting area will appear at the bottom of the Style dialog box.

Changing the Font and Point Size

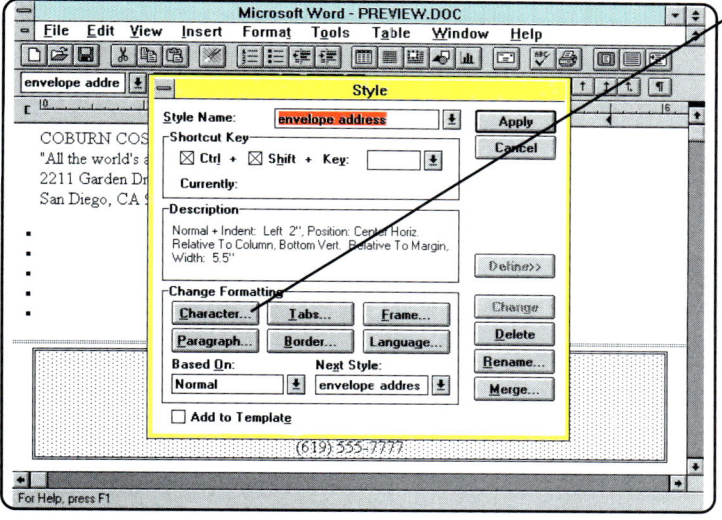

1. Click on **Character**. The Character dialog box will appear.

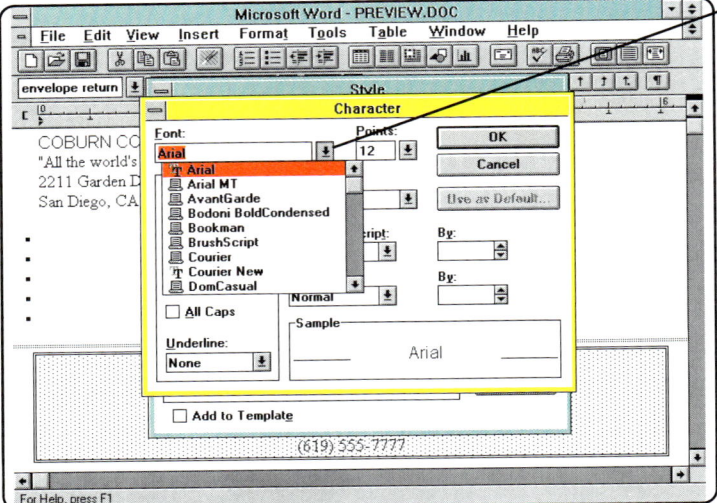

2. Click on ↓ to the right of the Font box. A drop-down list box will appear.

3. Click on ↑ on the scroll bar to scroll up the list of available fonts. Your list of fonts may be different from the one shown here.

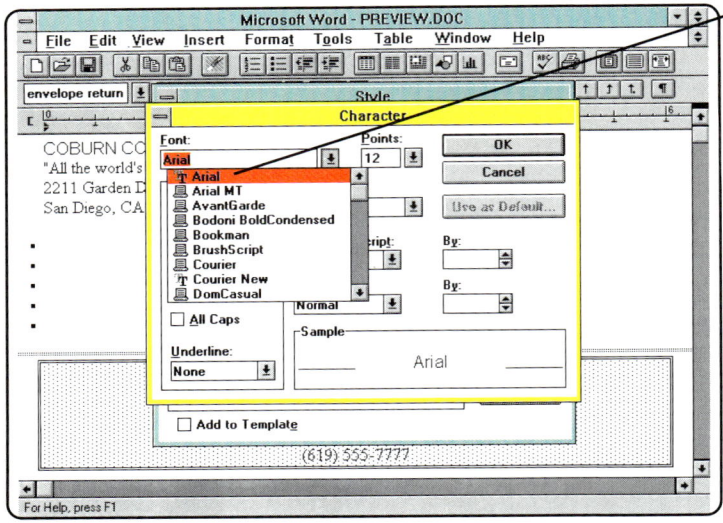

4. Click on **Arial**. The drop-down list box will disappear and "Arial" will appear in the Font box.

CHAPTER 11: PRINTING AN ENVELOPE 141

5. Click on ↓ to the right of the Points box. A drop-down list of point sizes will appear.

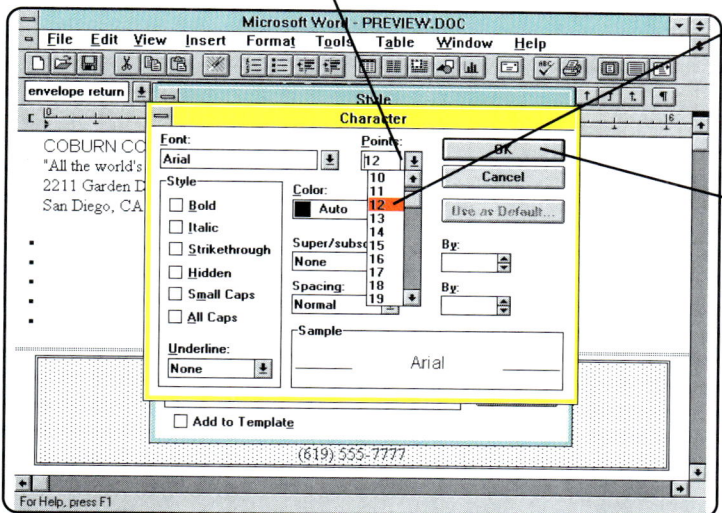

6. Click on **12**. The drop-down list will disappear and the number "12" will appear in the Points box.

7. Click on **OK**. The Style dialog box will appear.

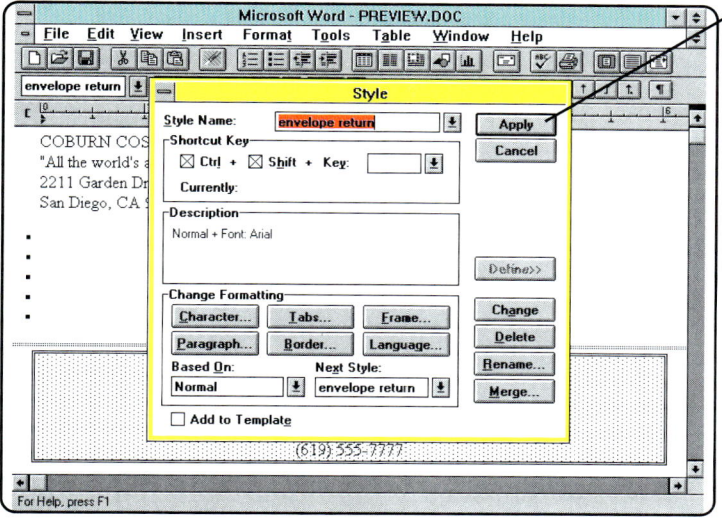

8. Click on **Apply**. A Microsoft Word dialog box will appear in the foreground of the Style dialog box.

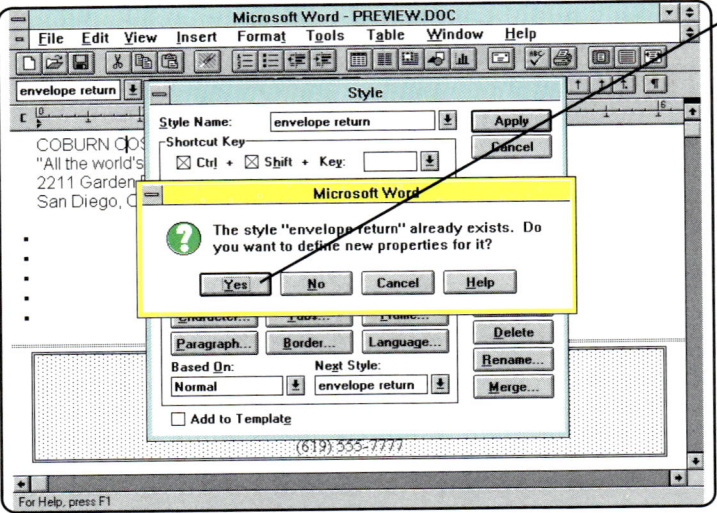

9. Click on **Yes**. The envelope will appear. The text in the return address is now set as 12-point Arial font.

Making the First Line of the Address Bold

1. Place the cursor to the **left of "COBURN"** and **click** to set the cursor.

2. Press and hold the mouse button and **drag** the cursor to highlight the company name.

3. Click on the **Bold button**. The highlighted text will change to bold.

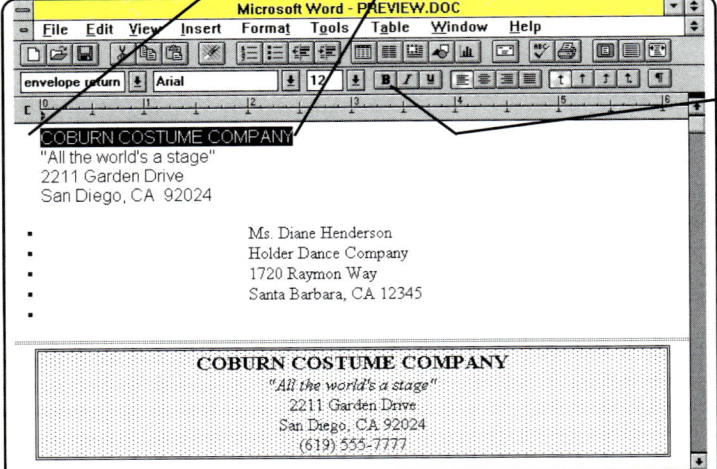

CHAPTER 11: PRINTING AN ENVELOPE   143

4. Click anywhere off the text to remove the highlighting. The company name is now Arial, 12 points, bold.

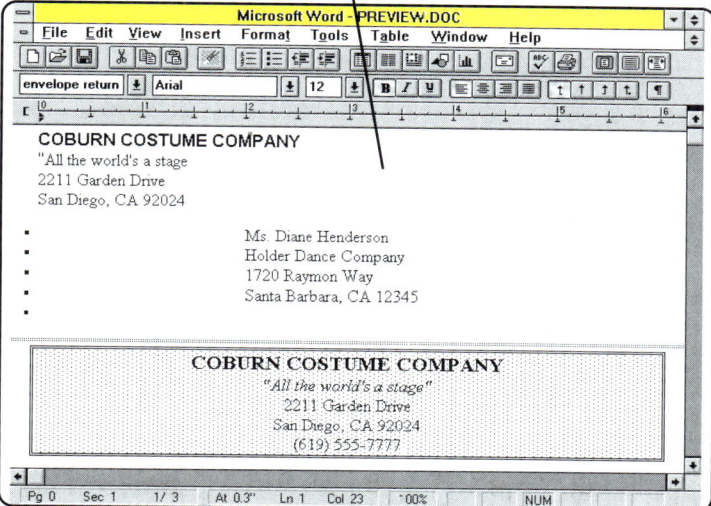

To make changes to the return address, repeat steps 1 through 8 in the "Changing the Font and Point Size" section of this chapter.

Do not save this letter when you close the file if you plan to follow through the rest of the chapters. If you do save it, the envelope with the customized return address will be permanently attached to the letter. This means that each time you open this letter, the envelope will appear at the top of the screen.

PRINTING THE LETTER AND THE ATTACHED ENVELOPE

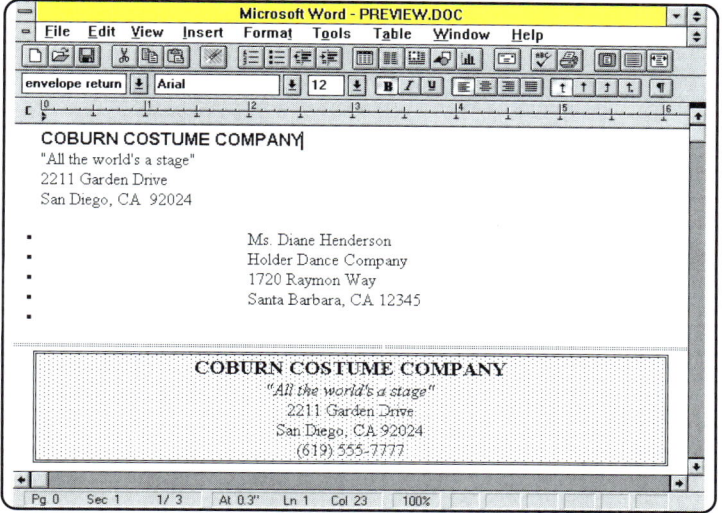

When you attach an envelop to a Word document, the envelope becomes page "0" of the document. When you print with the Envelope tool or the Print tool the envelope will automatically be printed first, followed by the letter. If you want to print only the letter or only the envelope, go to the following sections.

1. **Click** on **File** in the menu bar. A pull-down menu will appear.

2. **Click** on **Print**. The Print dialog box will appear.

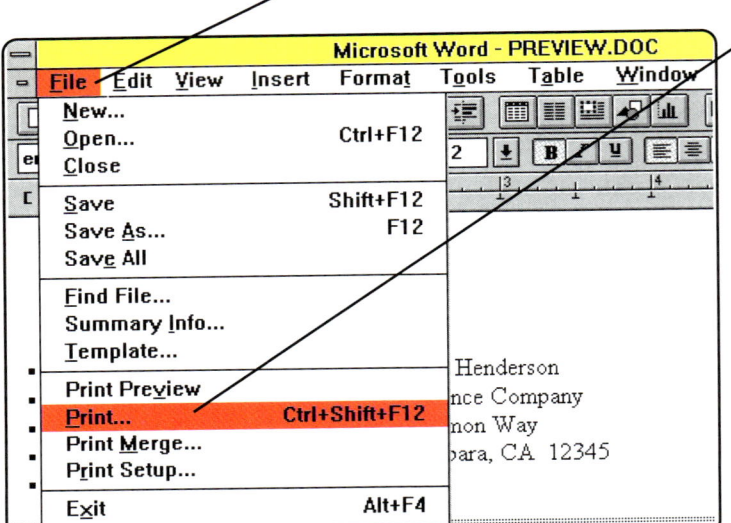

Notice that in the Range area, the circle next to All has a dot in it. This means that if you click on OK, Word will print both the envelope and the letter.

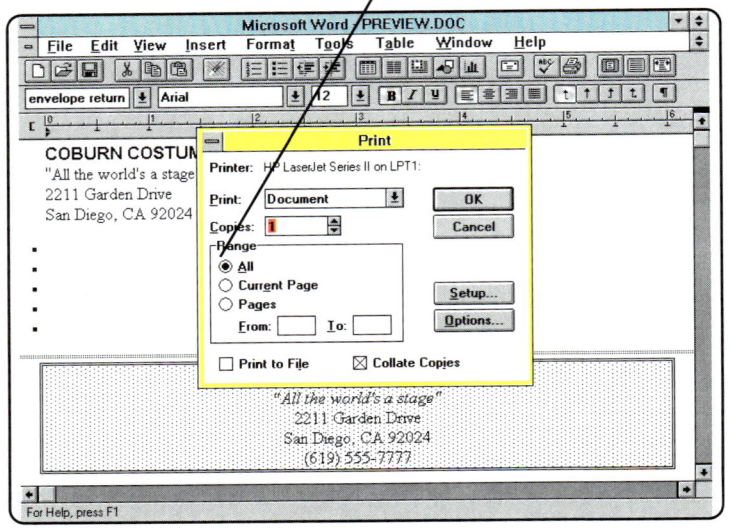

CHAPTER 11: PRINTING AN ENVELOPE

PRINTING THE ATTACHED ENVELOPE WITHOUT THE LETTER

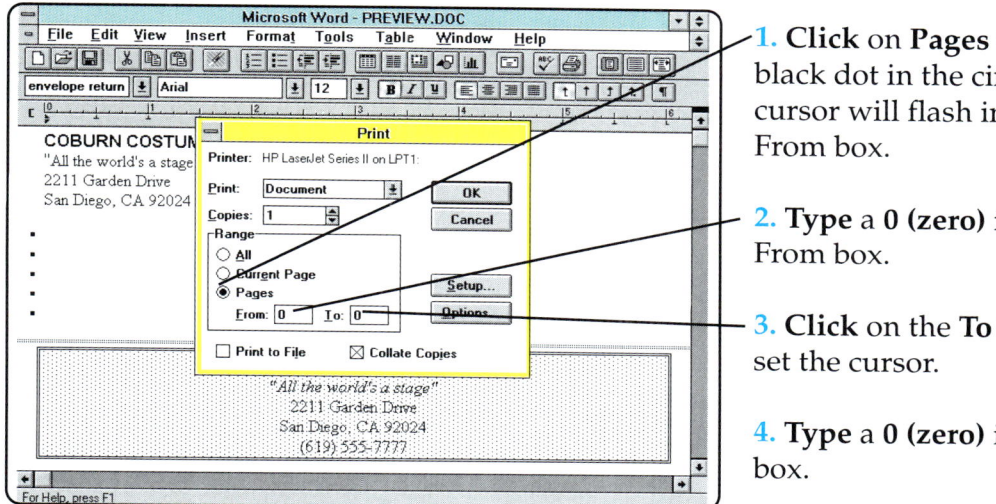

1. **Click** on **Pages** to put a black dot in the circle. The cursor will flash in the From box.

2. **Type** a **0 (zero)** in the From box.

3. **Click** on the **To box** to set the cursor.

4. **Type** a **0 (zero)** in the To box.

5. **Click** on **OK**. The Printing message box will appear. Only the attached envelope will be printed.

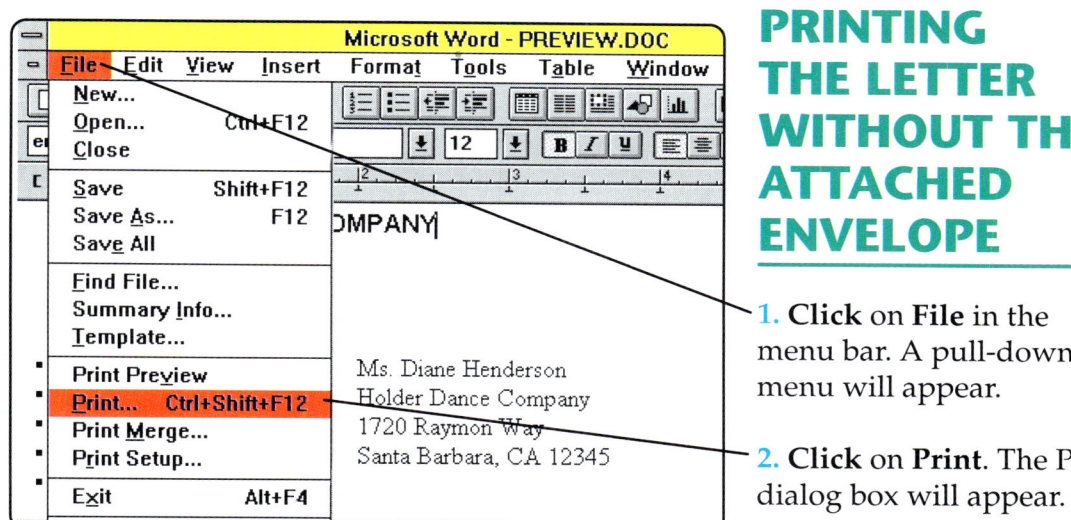

PRINTING THE LETTER WITHOUT THE ATTACHED ENVELOPE

1. **Click** on **File** in the menu bar. A pull-down menu will appear.

2. **Click** on **Print**. The Print dialog box will appear.

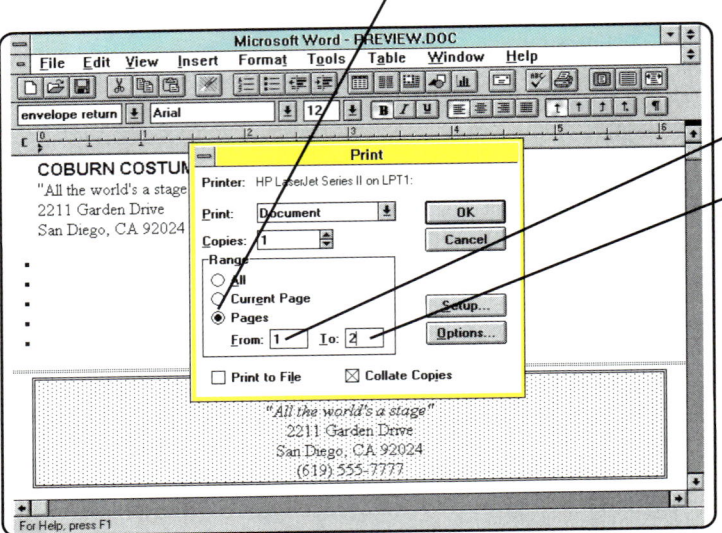

3. **Click** on **Pages** to place a black dot in the circle if the dot is not already there. The cursor will flash in the From box.

4. **Type 1** in the From box.

5. **Click** on the **To box** to set the cursor.

6. **Type 2** in the To box.

7. **Click** on **OK**. The Printing message box will appear.

Only the letter will print.

CLOSING WITHOUT SAVING THE ATTACHED ENVELOPE

1. **Click** on the **Control menu box** (□) to the left of the title bar. A pull-down menu will appear.

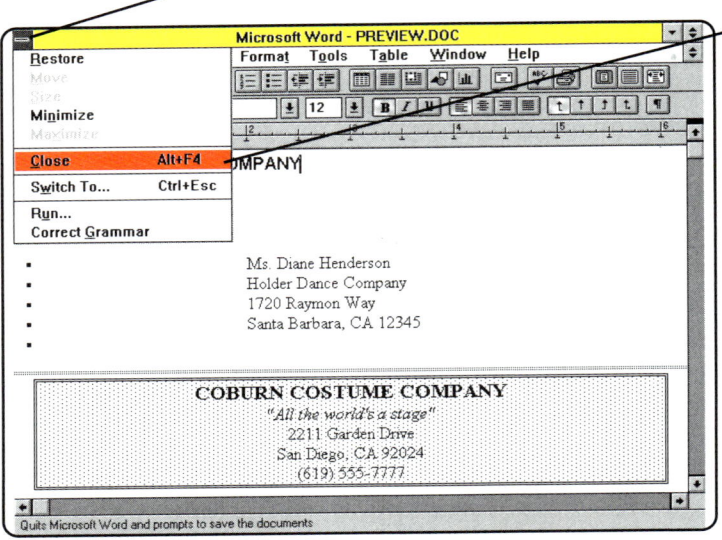

2. **Click** on **Close**. A Microsoft Word dialog box will appear.

CHAPTER 11: PRINTING AN ENVELOPE   **147**

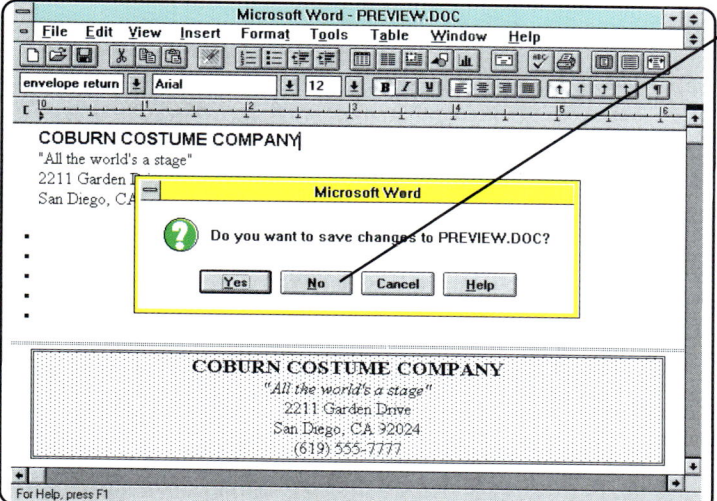

3. Click on **No**. The letter will close and the envelope will not be attached when you reopen the letter in later chapters.

CHAPTER 12

Creating a Mailing List

With the Word for Windows 2 Print Merge feature, you can send the same letter (a form letter, for example) to different people and have the individual's name, address, salutation, and other information personalized on each letter without having to retype each letter. After you've written the letter, begin the print merge process by first creating a mailing list, as shown in this chapter. Then you edit the mailing list (Chapter 13), attach, code, and print the letters (Chapter 13). Finally you print personalized envelopes (Chapter 14).

Even if you have a mailing list already created in another non-Windows (DOS-based) word processing program, such as WordPerfect or WordStar, work through Chapters 12 and 13 first to learn how Word's Print Merge feature works. Then go to Chapter 15, "Converting a Mailing List Created in Another Program," to convert your mailing list to Word. In this chapter you will do the following:

❖ Create a data entry table
❖ Create a mailing list

SETTING UP A DATA ENTRY TABLE

To create a mailing list in Word, you must first enter the information for your mailing list into a *data entry table*.

Opening a New Document File

1. **Click** on **File** in the menu bar. A pull-down menu will appear.

2. **Click** on **New**. The New dialog box will appear with the word "Normal" highlighted.

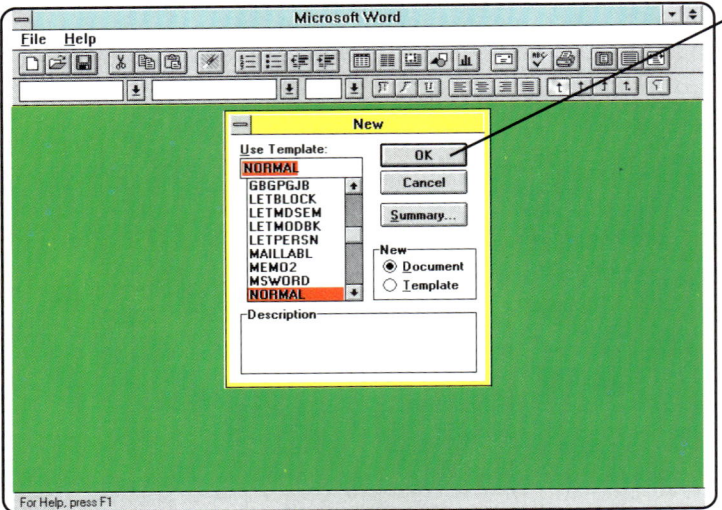

3. **Click** on **OK**. A blank document screen will appear.

Opening the Print Merge Setup Dialog Box

1. **Click** on **File** in the menu bar. A pull-down menu will appear.

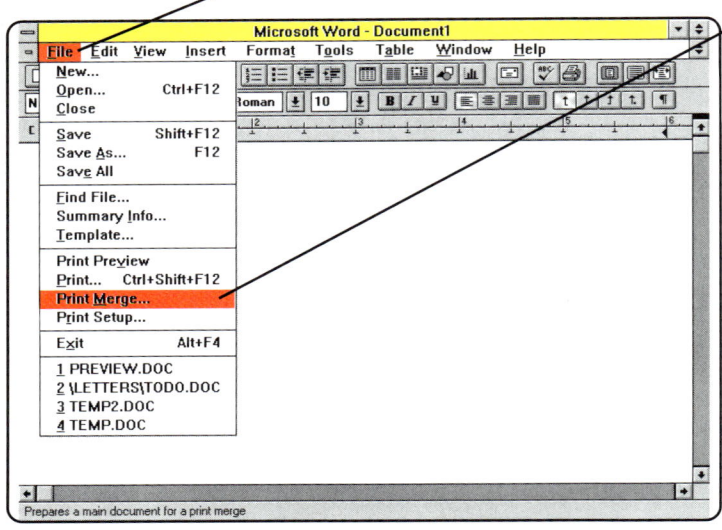

2. **Click** on **Print Merge**. The Print Merge Setup dialog box will appear.

CHAPTER 12: CREATING A MAILING LIST   151

Entering the Field Names for the Data Entry Table

1. **Click** on **Attach Data File**. The Attach Data File dialog box will appear.

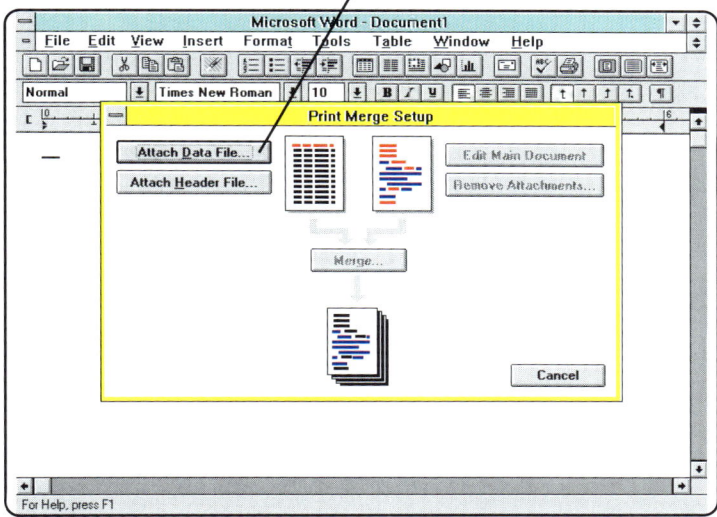

2. **Click** on **Create Data File**. The Create Data File dialog box will appear. The cursor will be flashing in the Field Name box.

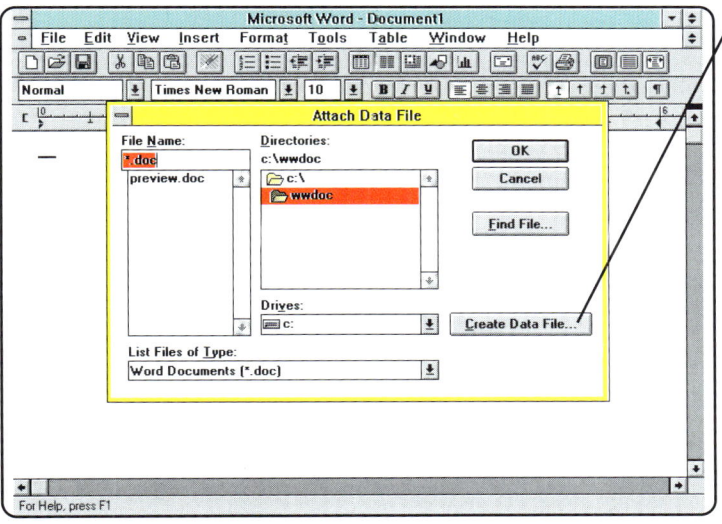

3. **Type** the word **Last** in the Field Name box.

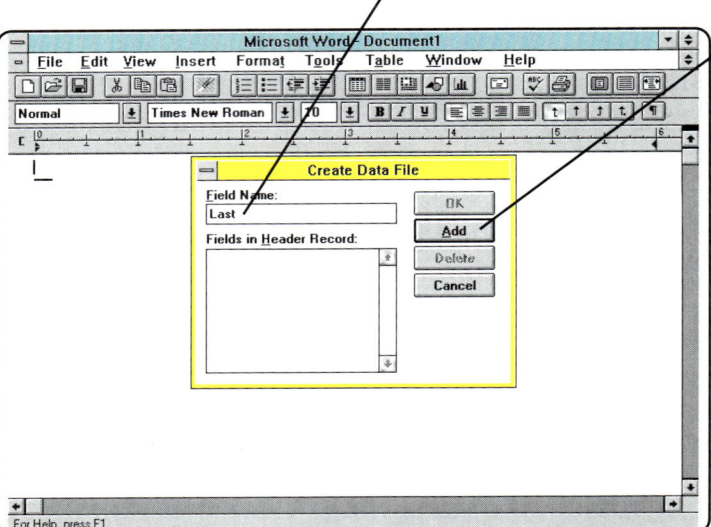

4. **Click** on **Add**. The word "Last" will appear in the Fields in Header Record box. The cursor will be flashing in the Field Name box.

5. **Type** the word **First** in the Field Name box.

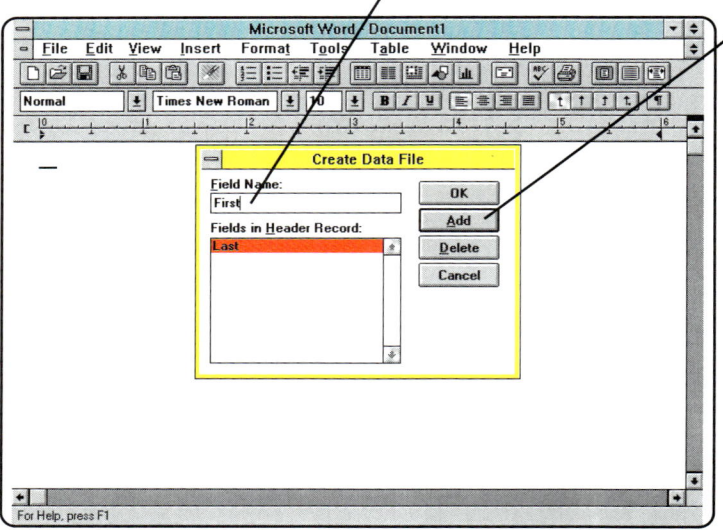

6. **Click** on **Add**. The word "First" will appear in the Fields in Header Record box. The cursor will be flashing in the Field Name box.

CHAPTER 12: CREATING A MAILING LIST 153

7. **Repeat steps 3 and 4** to enter the following words (field names) in the Fields in Header Record box:

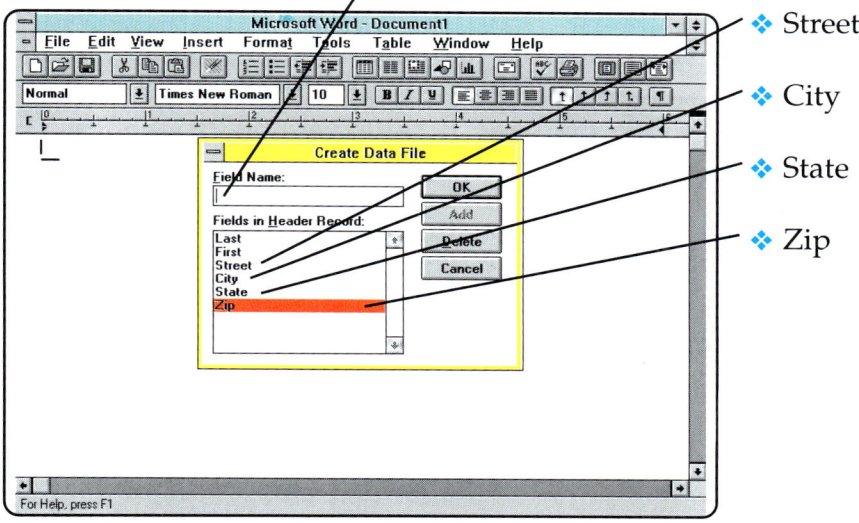

❖ Street

❖ City

❖ State

❖ Zip

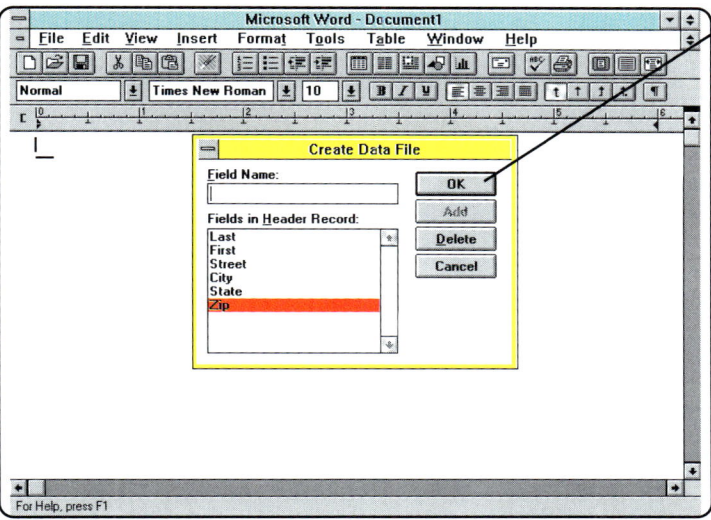

8. **Click** on **OK**. The Save As dialog box will appear.

9. **Type mylist** in the File Name box.

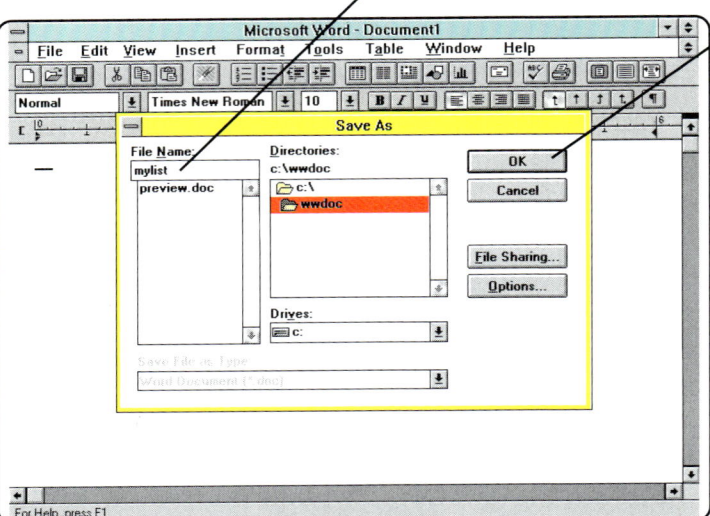

10. **Click** on **OK**. An hourglass will appear briefly. The MYLIST.DOC will appear with a table across the top of the screen.

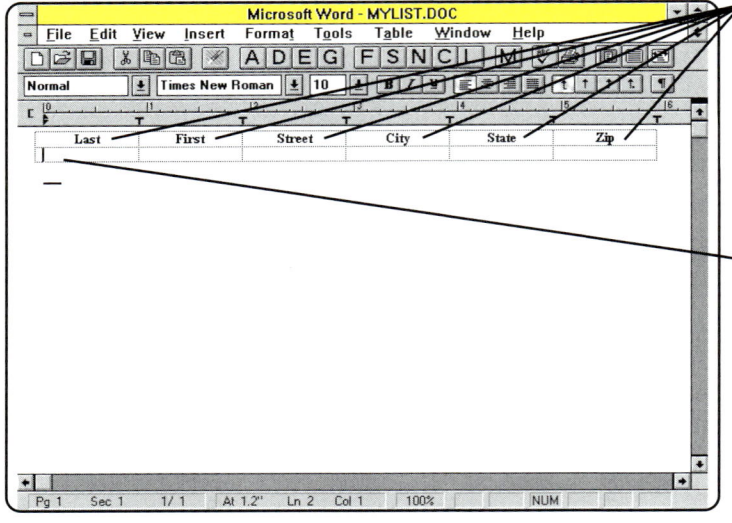

Notice that the first row of the table contains the names of the fields you just typed. This row is called the *header record* for this data file (your mailing list).

Notice that the cursor is flashing in the first empty box in the second row of the table. Each of these boxes is called a *cell*.

CHAPTER 12: CREATING A MAILING LIST 155

ENTERING NAMES AND ADDRESSES INTO THE DATA ENTRY TABLE

1. Type Chambers in the cell labeled "Last."

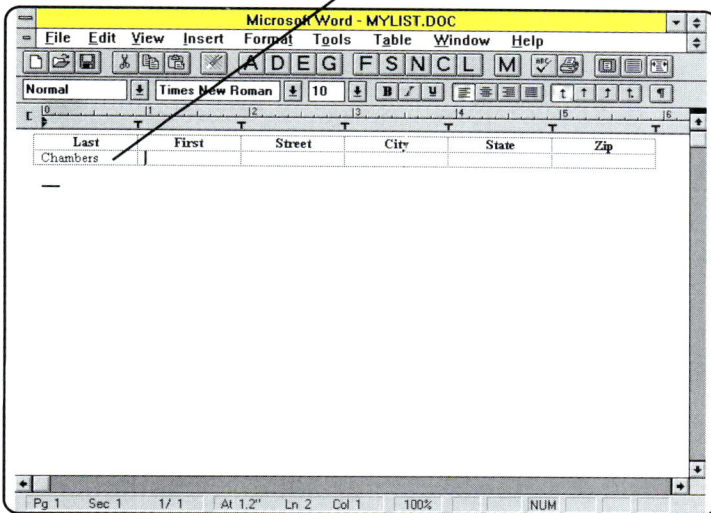

2. Press Tab. The cursor will move to the next cell.

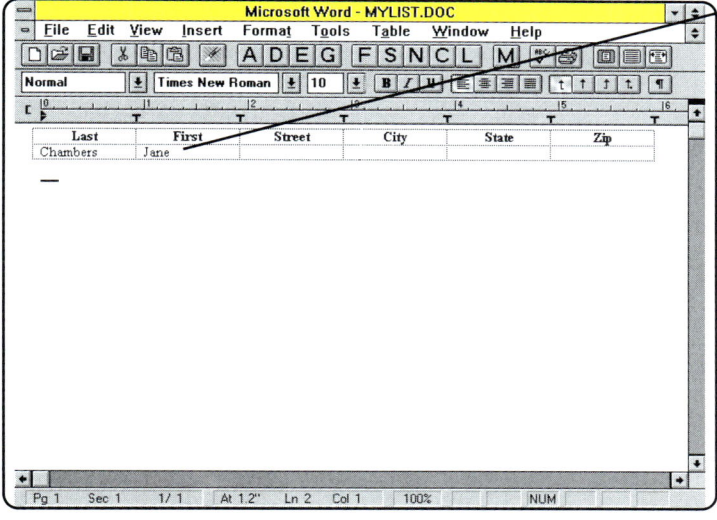

3. Type Jane in the cell labeled "First."

4. Press Tab. The cursor will move to the next cell.

5. **Continue** to enter the following information in the remaining cells:

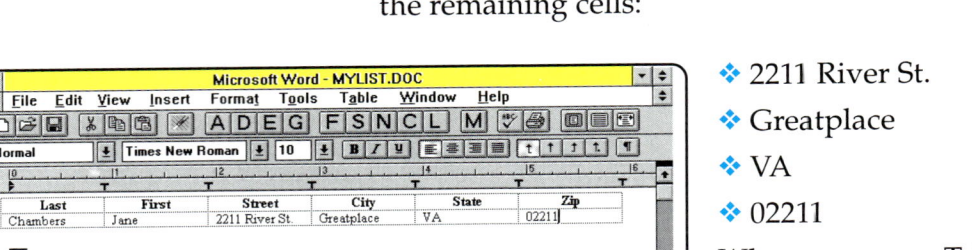

- 2211 River St.
- Greatplace
- VA
- 02211

When you press Tab after the last entry in the row (the "Zip" cell), Word automatically creates a new empty row in the table.

6. **Type Avery** in the cell labeled "Last."

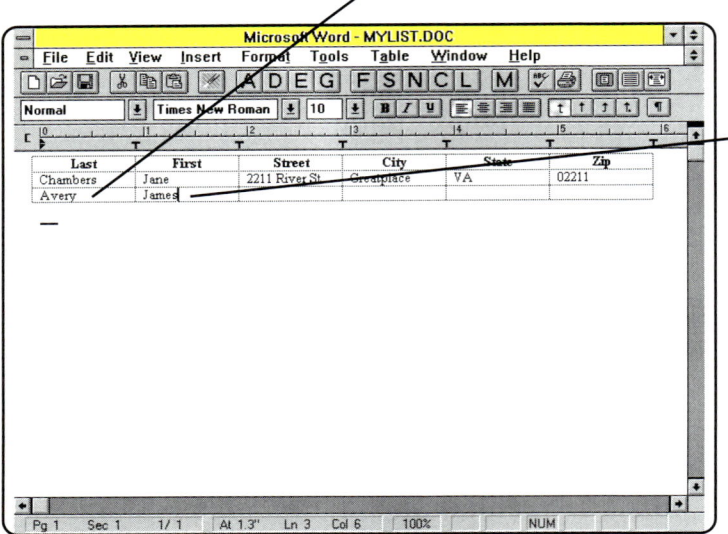

7. **Press Tab**. The cursor will move to the next cell.

8. **Type James** in the cell labeled "First."

9. **Press Tab**. The cursor will move to the next cell.

CHAPTER 12: CREATING A MAILING LIST   **157**

10. Type 32234 Tar Heel Drive in the cell labeled "Street."

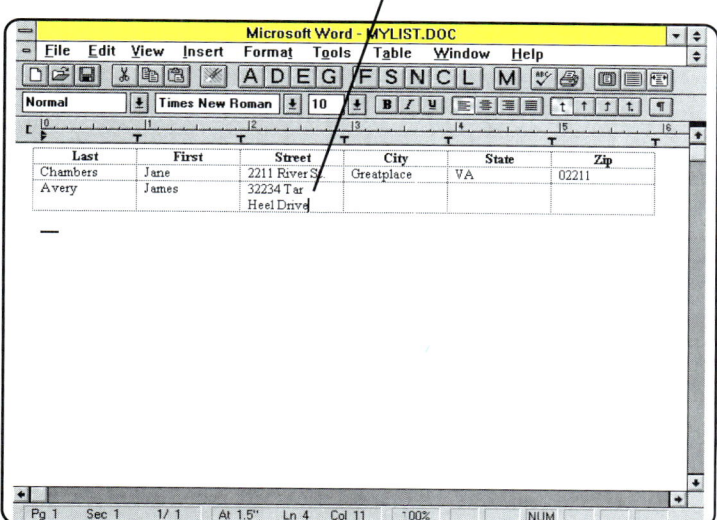

Notice that Word automatically enlarges the cell so that the text you enter fits.

11. Press Tab. The cursor will move to the next cell.

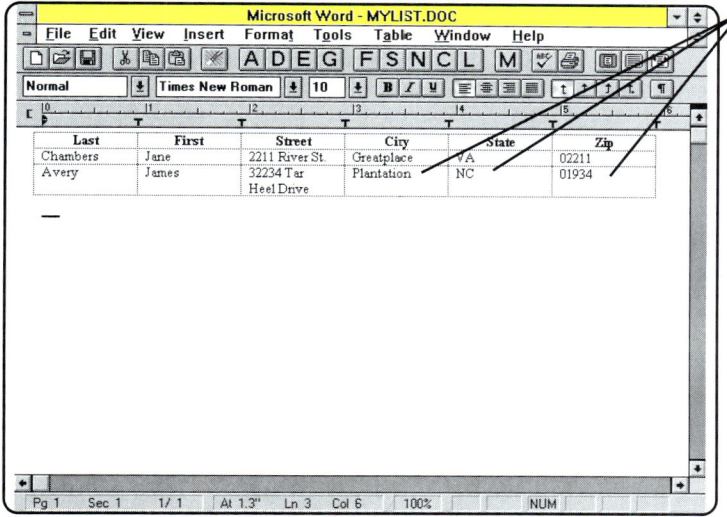

12. Continue to enter the rest of the address information in the remaining cells, as shown in this example. You will enter only these two names now. When you are making up your own mailing list, you can enter as many names as you like. If you do not have information to enter into a particular cell, just press the Tab key to leave that cell empty. Do not use the Spacebar to put spaces in an empty cell, or Word will enter the spaces into your document when you print.

SAVING THE MAILING LIST

1. Click on the **Save tool** in the toolbar. The Summary Info dialog box will appear.

2. Type information about the file, as shown in this example, or skip this step.

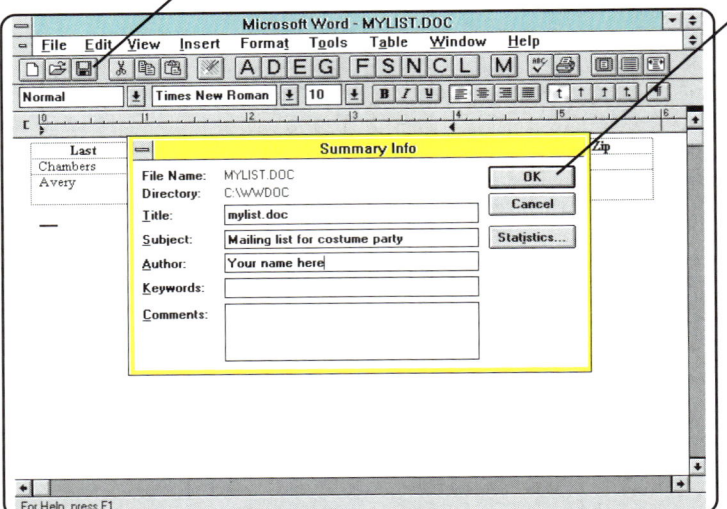

3. Click on **OK**. Your mailing list data file is now saved.

If you plan to go on to Chapter 14 to merge this list with a form letter and print the letter, do not exit or close this file at this time. If you plan to continue later, you can exit now. See Chapter 3 if you need help closing or exiting a Word document.

CHAPTER 13

Editing a Mailing List and Printing a Form Letter

Suppose you created and saved a mailing list, as you did in Chapter 12, and then discover that you didn't include fields for the company name and the person's title, for example. In order to edit a mailing list to add these fields, you must first attach the list to a document. Then in order to print the additional fields on the letter, you must code the letter to match the mailing list. In this chapter you will do the following:

❖ Attach a mailing list file to a letter
❖ Add additional fields to the mailing list
❖ Code a letter so that it will merge with the mailing list properly
❖ Print multiple personalized copies of the letter using the mailing list

ADDING FIELDS TO A MAILING LIST

To add additional fields to a mailing list, the mailing list must be attached to a letter.

Attaching a Mailing List to a Letter

1. **Open** the **mailing list** file (MYLIST.DOC) and then open the **letter** file (PREVIEW.DOC) that you created earlier if they are not already open.

2. **Click** on **File** in the menu bar of the letter file. A pull-down menu will appear.

3. **Click** on **Print Merge**. The Print Merge Setup dialog box will appear.

159

4. Click on **Attach Data File**. The Attach Data File dialog box will appear.

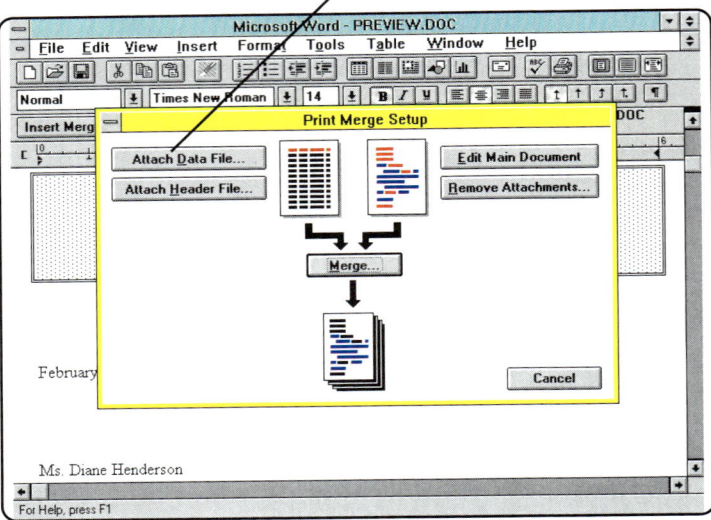

5. Click on **mylist.doc**.

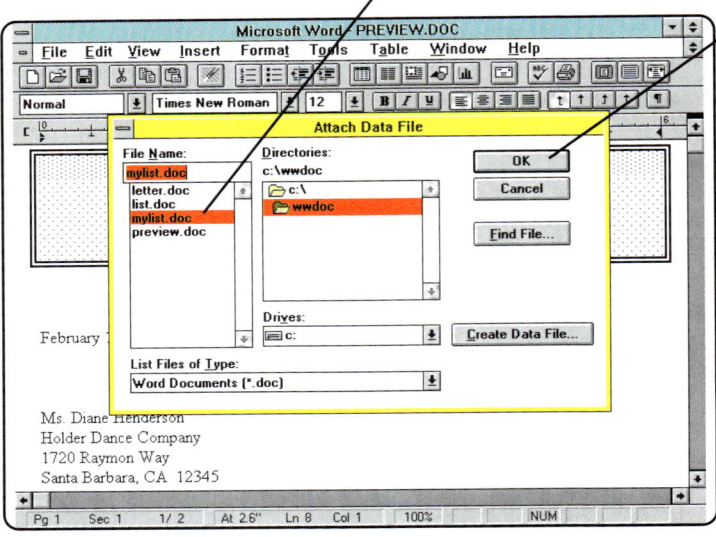

6. Click on **OK**. The PREVIEW.DOC letter will appear in the foreground. The MYLIST.DOC mailing list data file is now attached (linked) to the PREVIEW.DOC letter.

Adding Fields to the Attached Mailing List

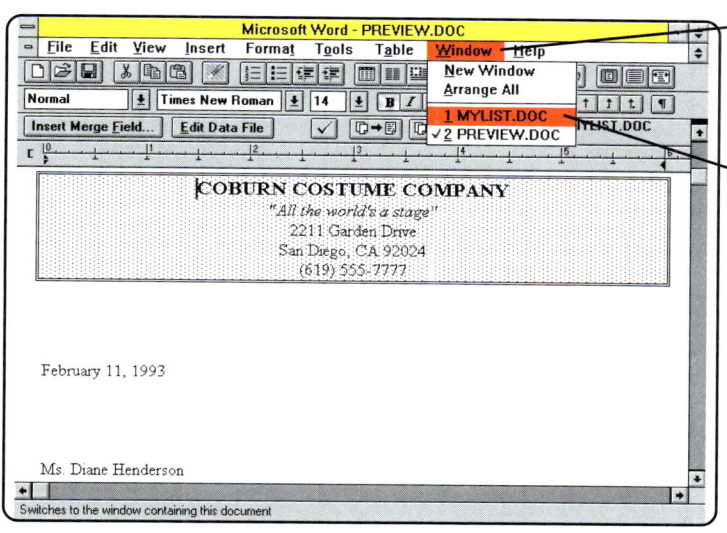

1. **Click** on **Window** in the menu bar. A pull-down menu will appear.

2. **Click** on **MYLIST.DOC**. The MYLIST.DOC window will appear.

3. **Click** on **Tools** in the menu bar. A pull-down menu will appear.

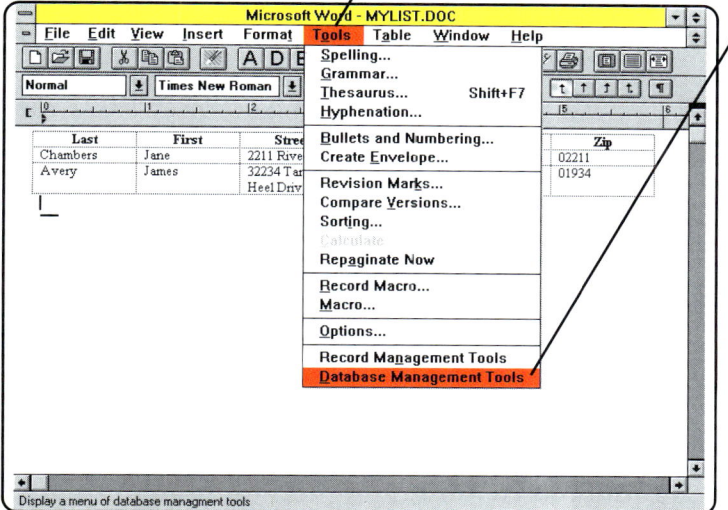

4. **Click** on **Database Management Tools**. The Database Management Tools dialog box will appear.

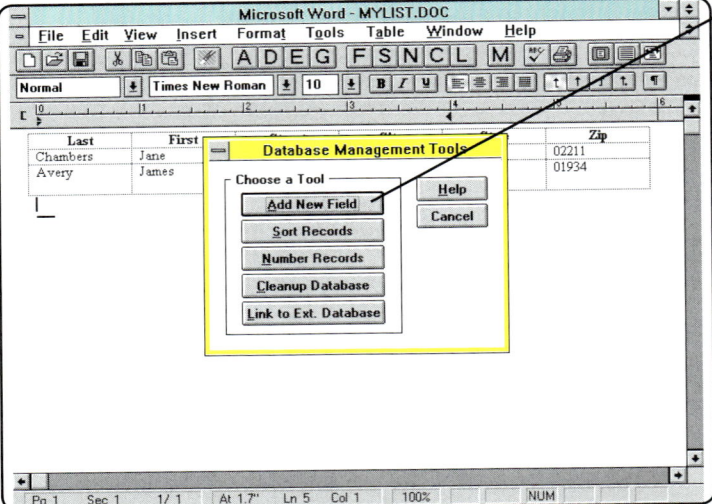

5. Click on **Add New Field**. A Microsoft Word dialog box will appear.

6. Type Prefix in the Merge Field box.

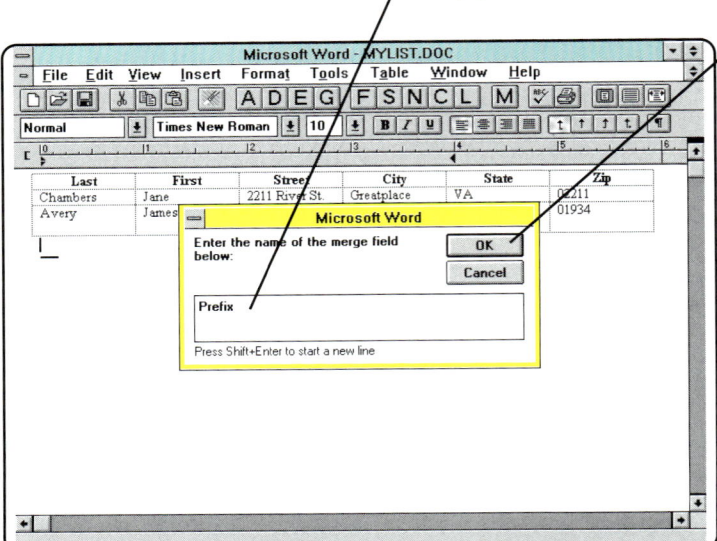

7. Click on **OK**. The MYLIST.DOC window will appear. The new Prefix merge field header will not be shown on your screen, but you can bring it into view.

CHAPTER 13: EDITING A MAILING LIST AND PRINTING A FORM LETTER

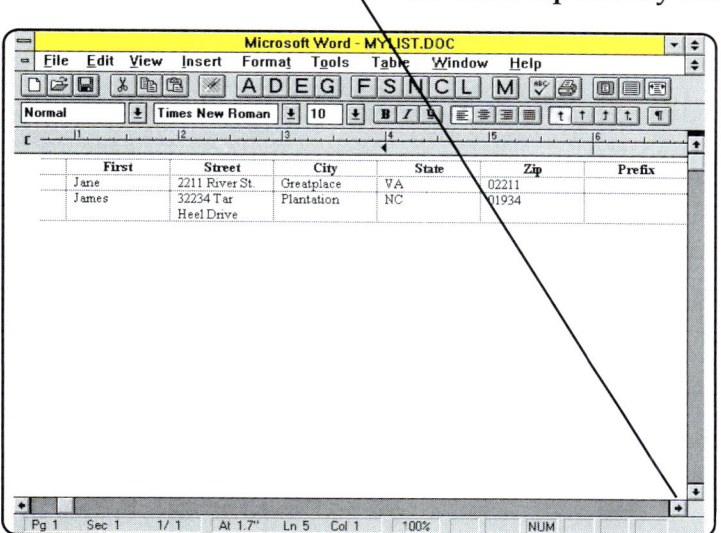

8. **Click repeatedly** on the ➡ on the **horizontal scroll bar** to bring the Prefix field into view.

The position of a field in the mailing list table's header record does not affect its position in the letter itself. The position of the field in the letter is set when you place a merge field in the letter, which you will do in the section entitled "Setting Up a Form Letter" later in this chapter.

9. **Click** on **Tools** in the menu bar. A pull-down menu will appear.

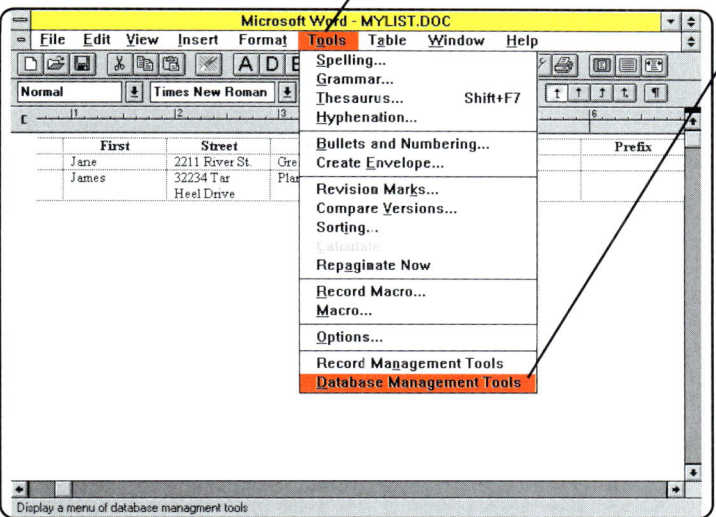

10. **Click** on **Database Management Tools**. The Database Management Tools dialog box will appear.

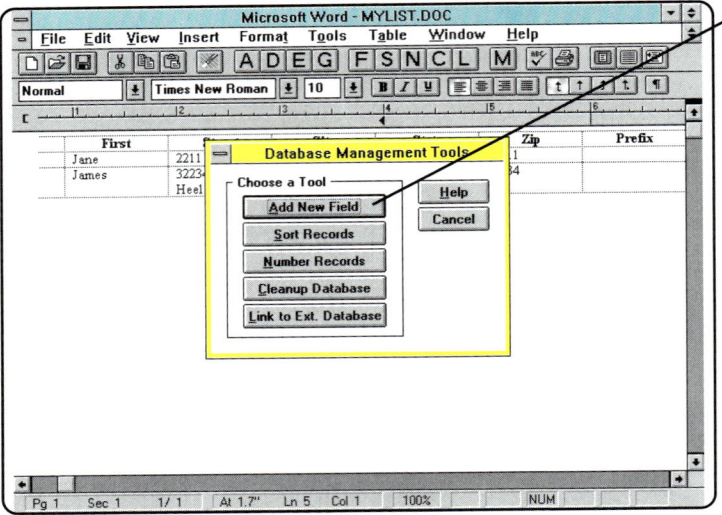

11. Click on **Add New Field**. A Microsoft Word dialog box will appear.

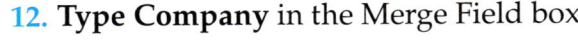

12. Type Company in the Merge Field box.

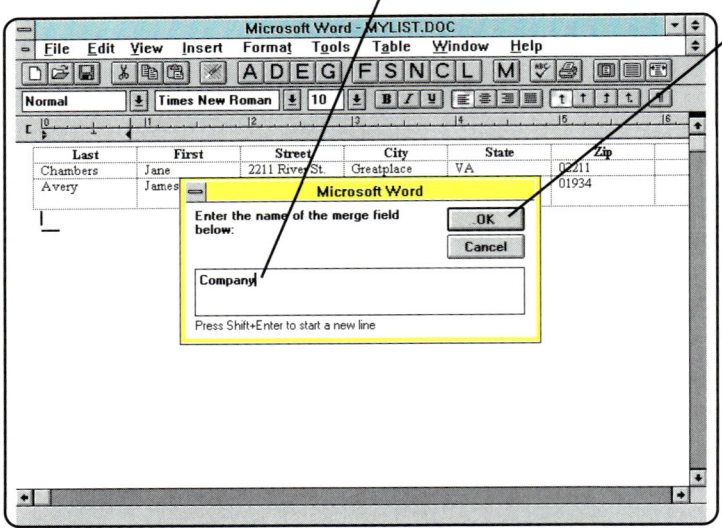

13. Click on **OK**. The MYLIST.DOC window will appear in the foreground. The new Company merge field header will not be shown on your screen. **Repeat step 8** to bring it into view.

CHAPTER 13: EDITING A MAILING LIST AND PRINTING A FORM LETTER

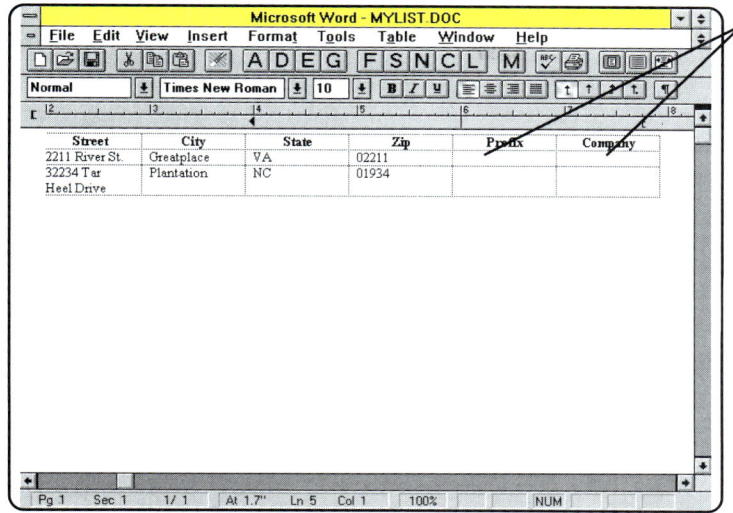

Congratulations. You have successfully added two merge fields to your mailing list.

Entering More Data in a Mailing List Data File

1. **Click** on **Tools** in the menu bar. A pull-down menu will appear.

2. **Click** on **Record Management Tools**. The Record Management Tools dialog box will appear.

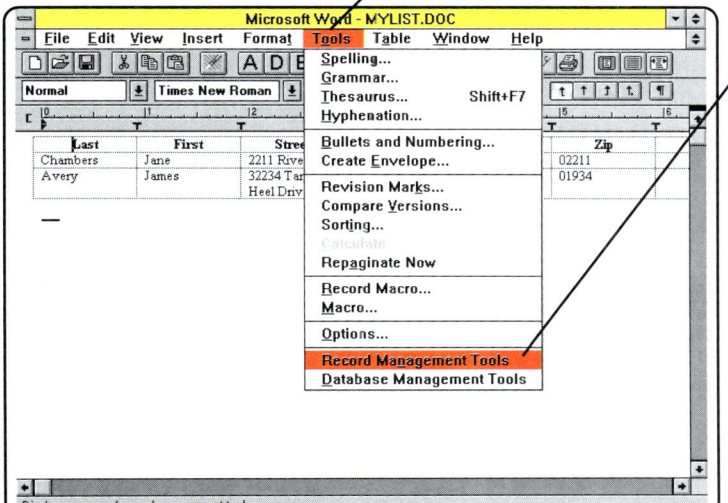

3. Click on **Goto Record**. A Microsoft Word dialog box will appear. The cursor will be flashing in the Goto Record # box.

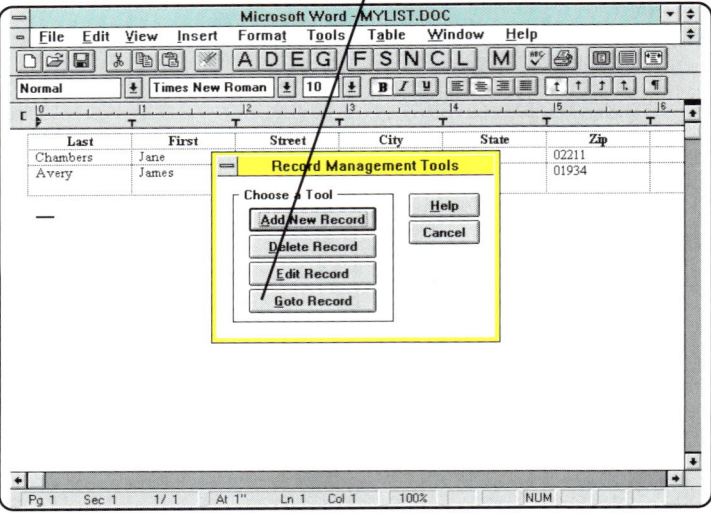

4. Type 1 in the Goto Record # box.

5. Click on **OK**. The dialog box will disappear and the cursor will begin flashing in the first field (Chambers) of the first row of the mailing list table.

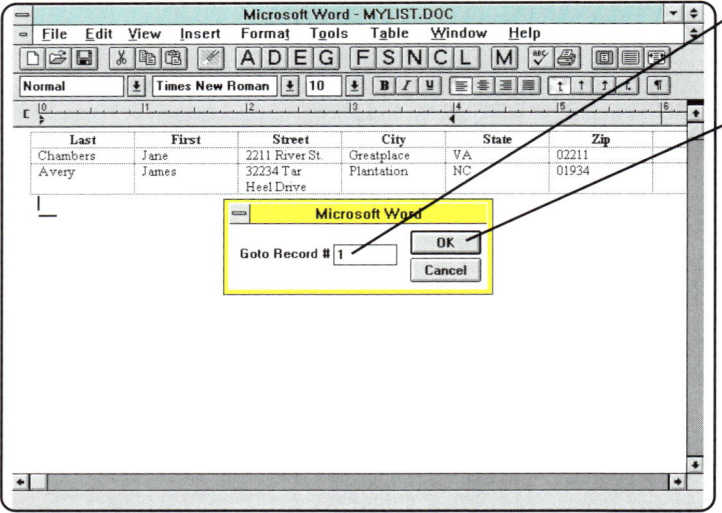

CHAPTER 13: EDITING A MAILING LIST AND PRINTING A FORM LETTER

6. **Press** and **hold** the → key on your keyboard. The cursor will move rapidly to the right.

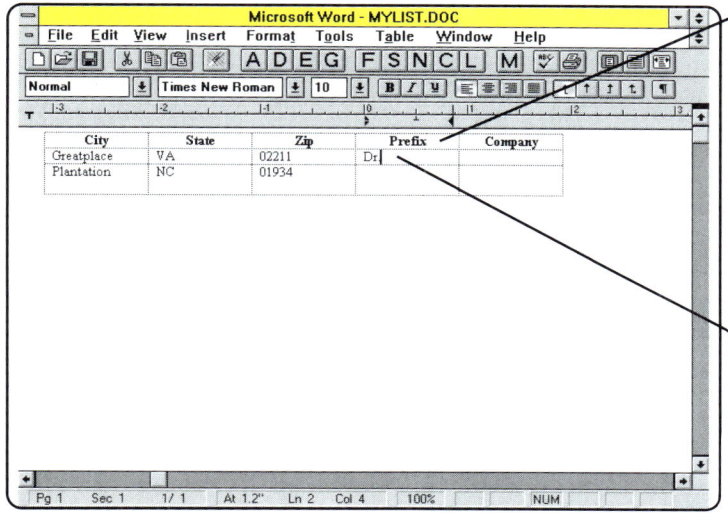

7. **Release** the key when the Prefix cell comes into view, then press the → again until the cursor is positioned in the first Prefix cell. (If you go past the cell, simply press the ← to go back.)

8. **Type Dr.** (include the period).

9. **Press Tab**. The cursor will be flashing in the first "Company cell."

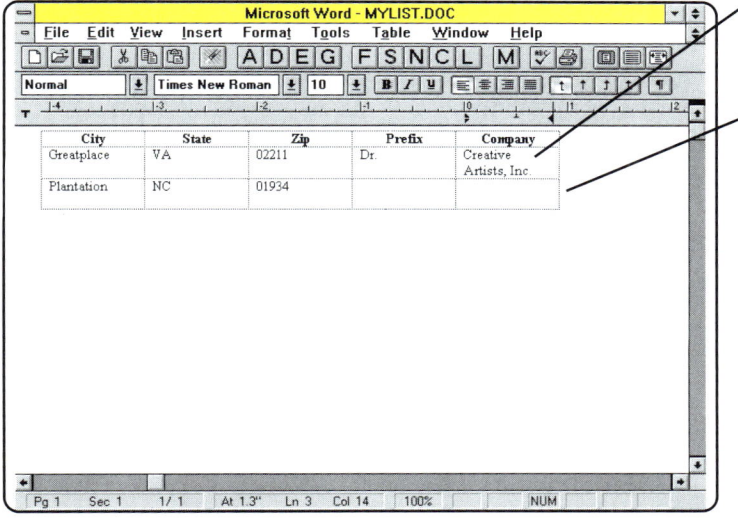

10. **Type Creative Artists, Inc.** (include the period).

Notice that Word automatically adjusts the cell size to accommodate the company name.

11. **Press Tab**. The cursor will move to the first cell (Avery) of the next row.

12. **Press** and **hold** →. The cursor will move rapidly to the right.

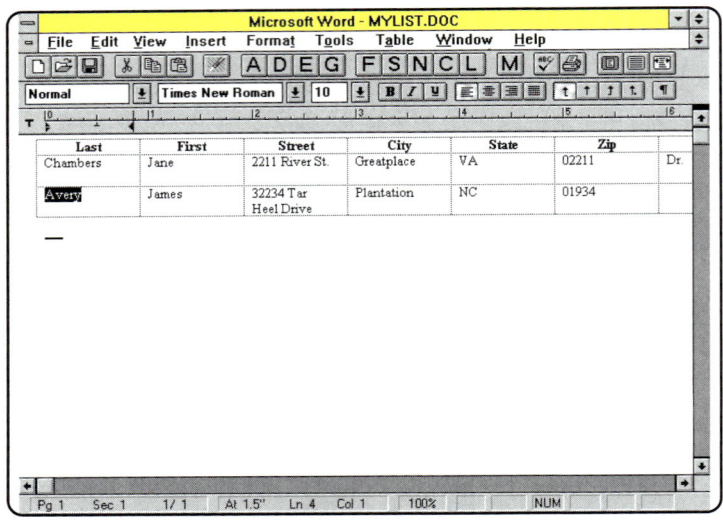

13. **Release** the key when the Prefix cell comes into view, then press the → again until the cursor is positioned in the Prefix cell. (If you go past the cell, simply press the ← to go back.)

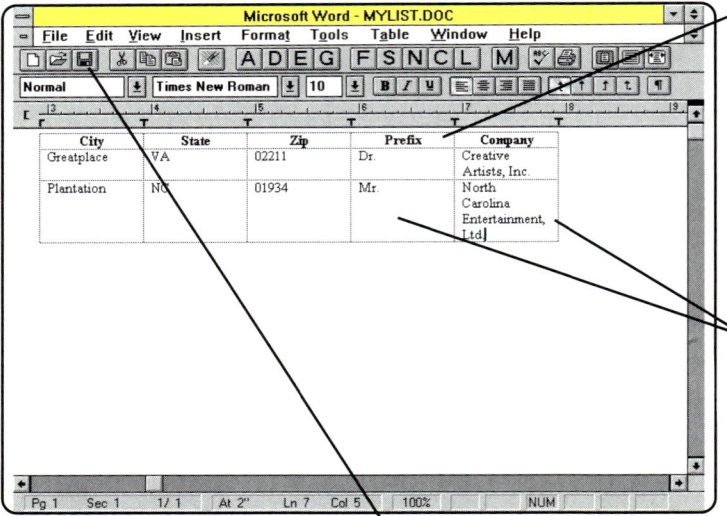

14. **Repeat steps 8 and 9** and **type Mr.** in the Prefix cell and **North Carolina Entertainment, Ltd.** in the Company cell.

15. **Click** on the **Save tool**. Your mailing list is now updated. In the next section you will set up your letter (PREVIEW.DOC) as a form letter, ready for printing with this mailing list.

SETTING UP A FORM LETTER

To set up a form letter in Word, you first attach (link) the mailing list to the letter. If you have been following along in this chapter, MYLIST.DOC is already attached to PREVIEW.DOC. In that case, go to the next section, "Inserting Merge Fields into a Form Letter."

Attaching a Mailing List to a Letter

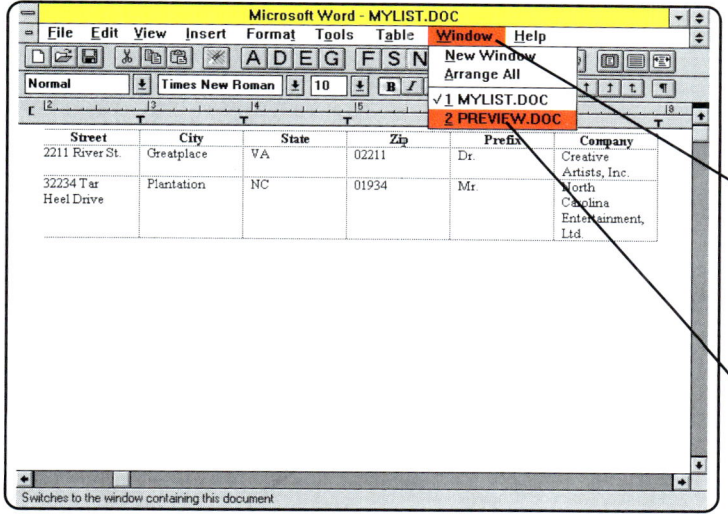

1. With the mailing list already open, **click** on **Window** in the menu bar. A pull-down menu will appear.

2. **Click** on **PREVIEW.DOC**. The first page of PREVIEW.DOC will appear.

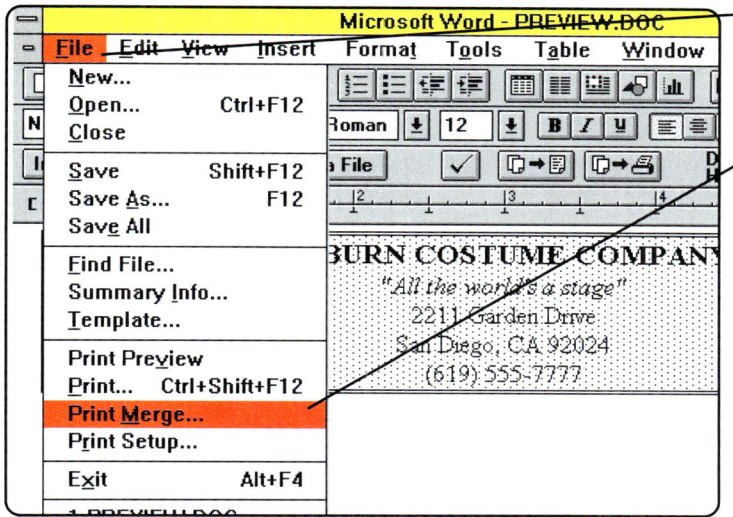

3. **Click** on **File** in the menu bar. A pull-down menu will appear.

4. **Click** on **Print Merge**. The Print Merge Setup box will appear.

5. Click on **Attach Data File**. The Attach Data File dialog box will appear.

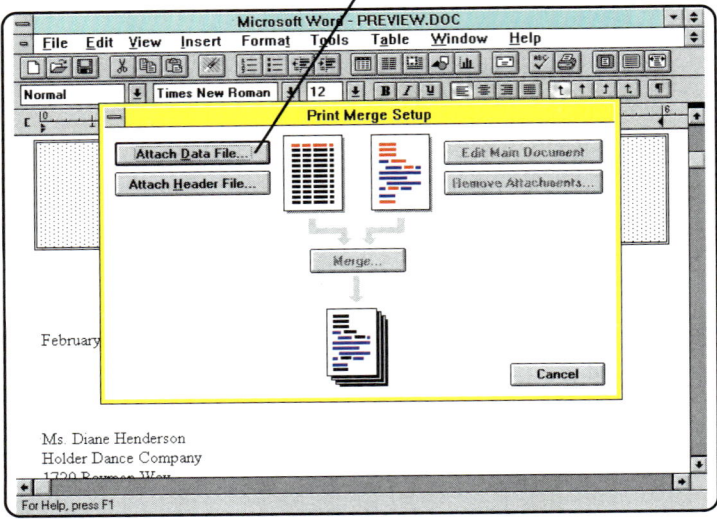

6. Click on **mylist.doc** in the File Name box. The filename, mylist.doc, will appear highlighted in the File Name box.

7. Click on **OK**. The first page of PREVIEW.DOC will appear.

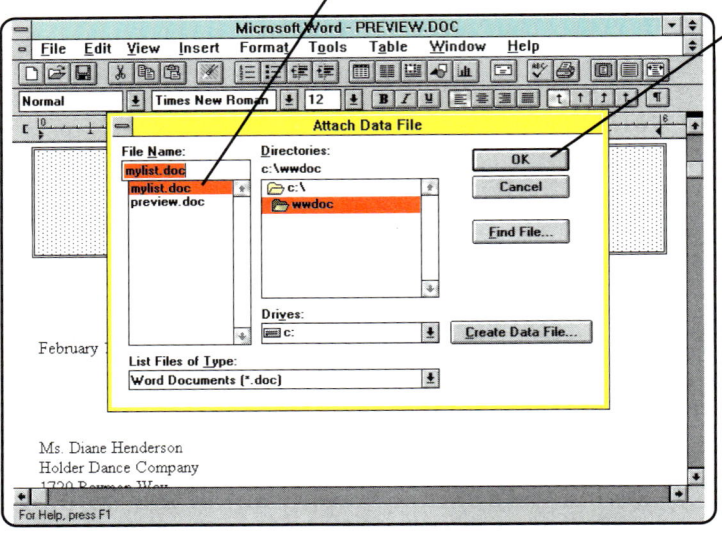

CHAPTER 13: EDITING A MAILING LIST AND PRINTING A FORM LETTER

Inserting Merge Fields into a Form Letter

1. **Move** the mouse pointer to the **left of "Ms."**

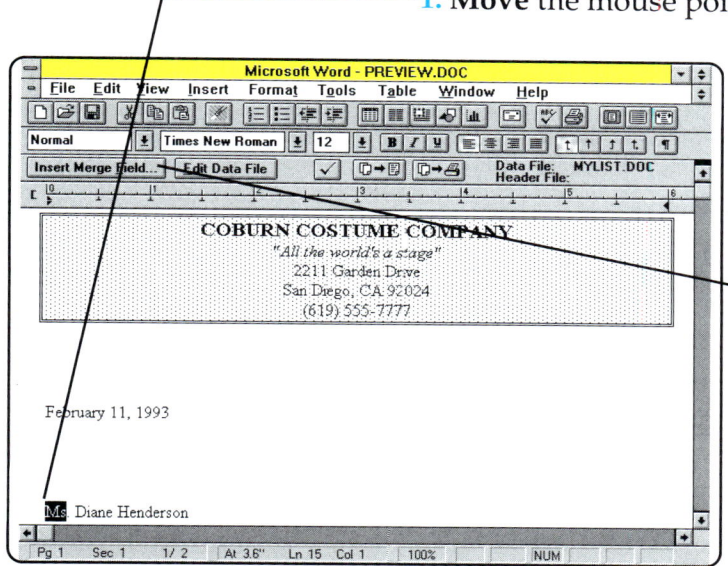

2. **Press and hold** the mouse button as you **drag** to the right to highlight **"Ms." Release** the mouse button.

3. **Click** on **Insert Merge Field**. The Insert Merge Field dialog box will appear.

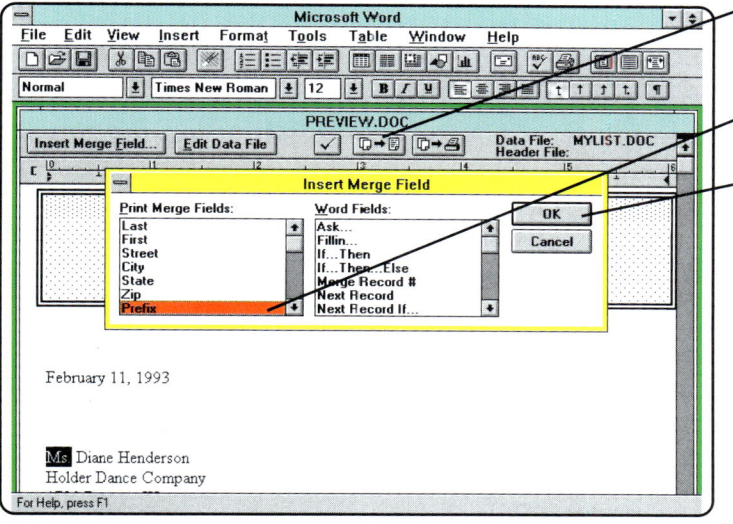

Notice that a new toolbar appears.

4. **Click** on **Prefix**.

5. **Click** on **OK**. The first page of PREVIEW.DOC will appear. The "Ms." prefix will be replaced with the merge field <<Prefix>>. This means that when you print the form letter, the prefix (Dr., Mrs., Mr., etc.) will be inserted in the letter for each person on the list.

6. **Move** the mouse pointer to the **left of "Diane."**

7. **Press** and **hold** the mouse button as you **drag** to the right to highlight **"Diane." Release** the mouse button.

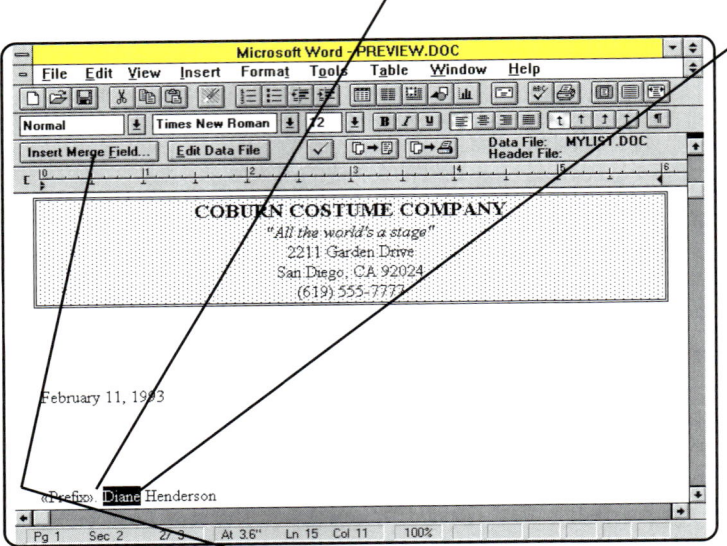

8. **Click** on **Insert Merge Field**. The Insert Merge Field dialog box will appear.

9. **Click** on **First**.

10. **Click** on **OK**. The first page of PREVIEW.DOC will appear. "Diane" will be replaced with the merge field <<First>>. This means that when you print the form letter, the first name of each person in your mailing list will be inserted in the letter printed for that person.

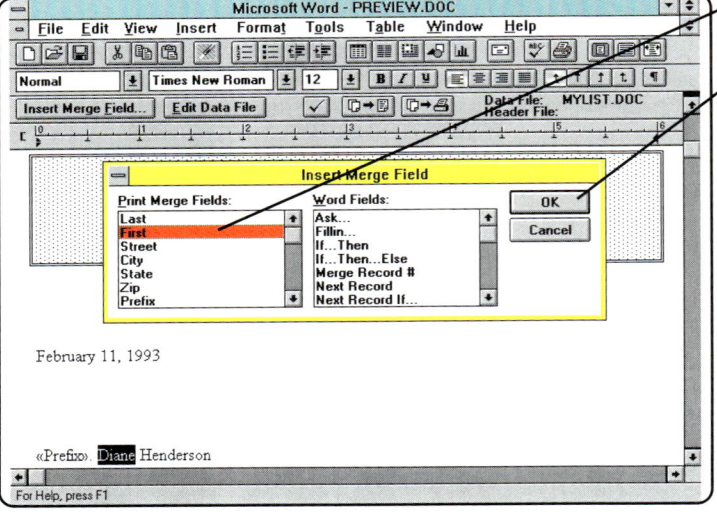

CHAPTER 13: EDITING A MAILING LIST AND PRINTING A FORM LETTER   173

11. **Move** the mouse pointer to the **left of** "Henderson."

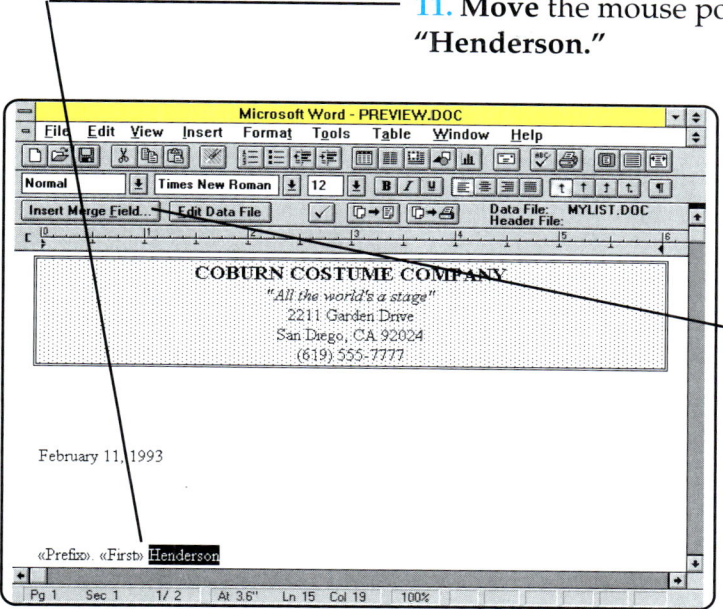

12. **Press and hold** the mouse button as you **drag** to the right to highlight **"Henderson." Release** the mouse button.

13. **Click** on **Insert Merge Field**. The Insert Merge Field dialog box will appear.

14. **Click** on **Last**.

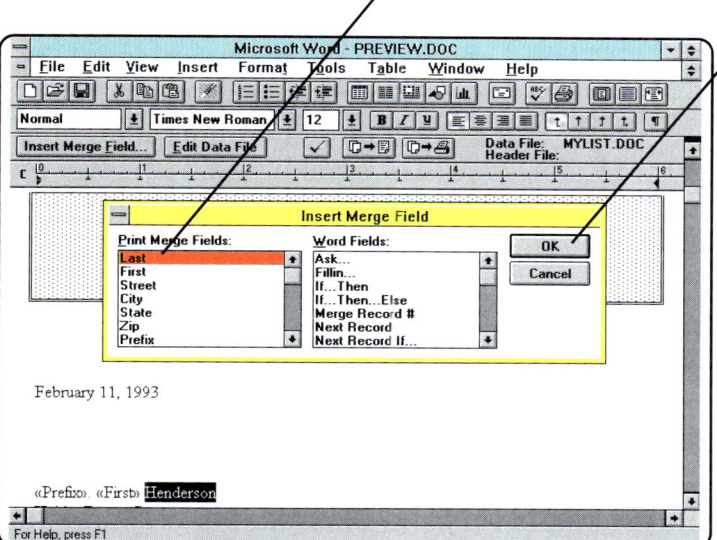

15. **Click** on **OK**. The first page of PREVIEW.DOC will appear. "Henderson" will be replaced with the merge field <<Last>>. This means that when you print the form letter, the last name of each person in your mailing list will be inserted in the letter printed for that person.

16. **Move** the mouse pointer to the **left of "Holder."**

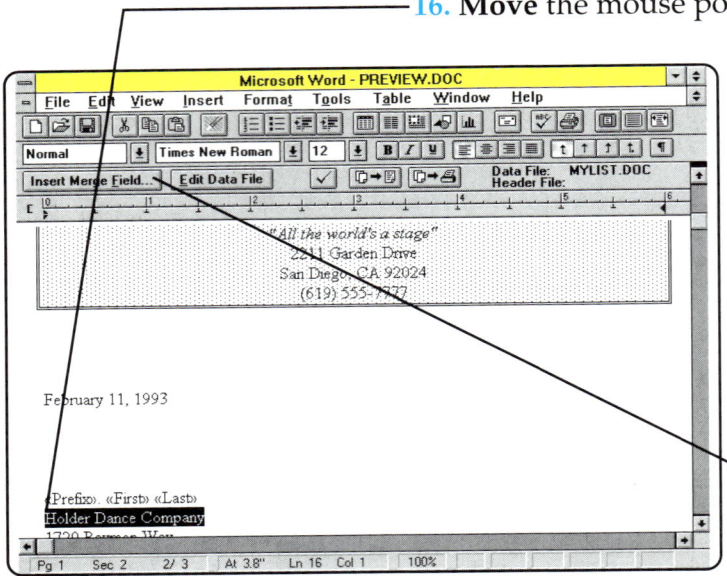

17. **Press and hold** the mouse button as you **drag** to the right to highlight **"Holder Dance Company." Release** the mouse button. (Or, place the mouse pointer in the left margin beside "Holder." It will change to an arrow. Click to highlight the entire line.)

18. **Click** on **Insert Merge Field**. The Insert Merge Field dialog box will appear.

19. **Click** on the ↓ to scroll to the bottom of the Print Merge Field box.

20. **Click** on **Company**.

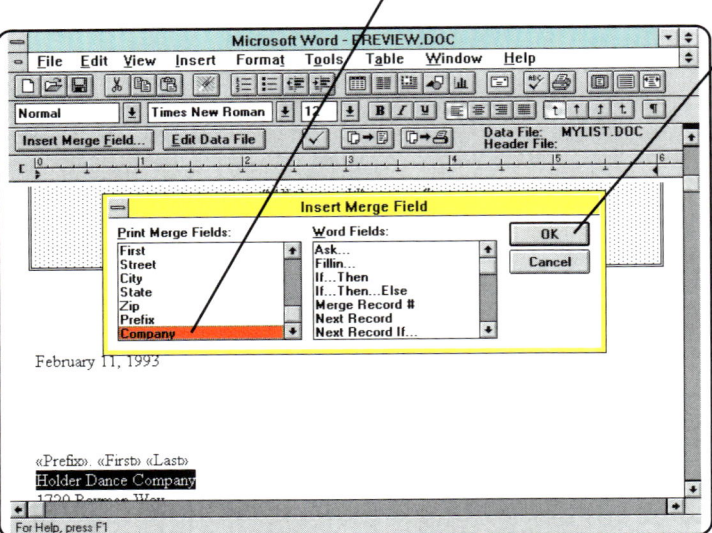

21. **Click** on **OK**. The first page of PREVIEW.DOC will appear. "Holder Dance Company" will be replaced with the merge field <<Company>>. This means that when you print the form letter, the company name for each person in your mailing list will be inserted in the letter printed for that person.

CHAPTER 13: EDITING A MAILING LIST AND PRINTING A FORM LETTER

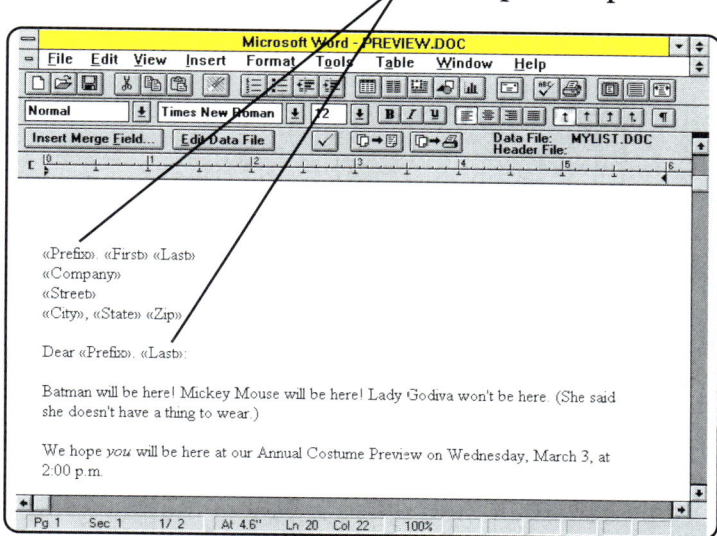

22. Repeat steps 16 through 21 to insert the other merge field codes into the remaining address and salutation sections of the form letter. Make certain you do not highlight the comma after "Santa Barbara" or the colon after "Henderson." If you goof and put a merge field in the wrong place, highlight it and repeat steps 16 through 21 to replace it with the correct merge field. Be careful not to add or delete spaces.

Inserting Personalized Information into the Body of the Letter

Just as you've personalized the letter by adding a name, address, and salutation to the first page of the letter, you can also insert personal touches in the body of the letter using the same kinds of fields used on page 1 of the letter.

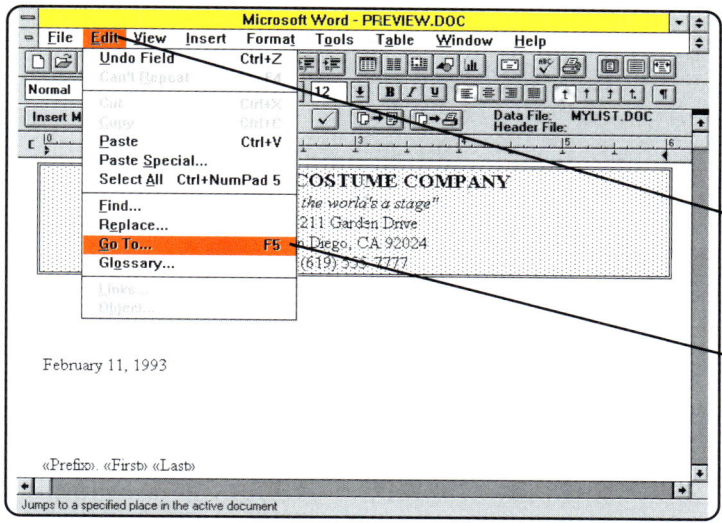

1. Click on **Edit** in the menu bar. A pull-down menu will appear.

2. Click on **Go To**. The Go To dialog box will appear. The cursor will be flashing in the Go To box.

3. **Type 2** in the Go To box.

4. **Click** on **OK**. Page 2 of PREVIEW.DOC will appear.

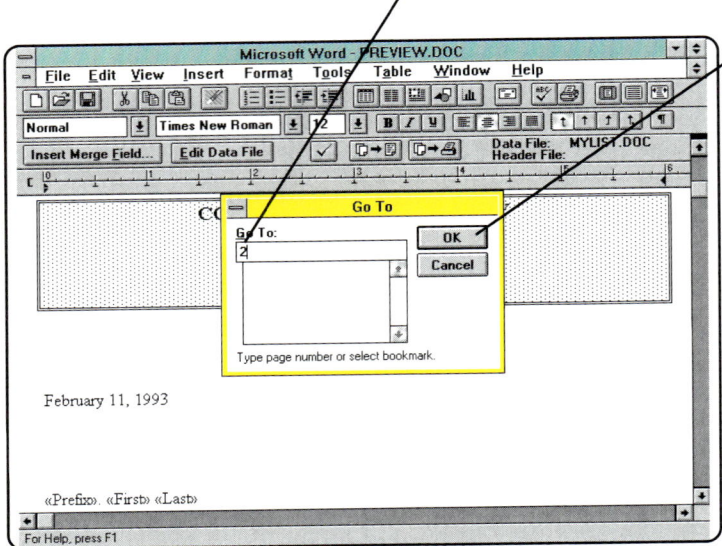

5. **Repeat steps 16 through 21** in the previous section, "Inserting Merge Fields into a Form Letter," to insert the other merge field codes in the body of the form letter.

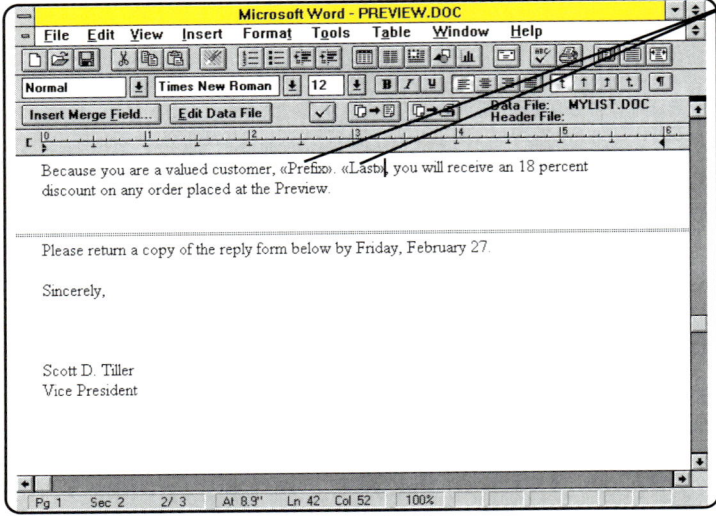

CHAPTER 13: EDITING A MAILING LIST AND PRINTING A FORM LETTER

177

Inserting Personalized Information into the Header

You can also individualize the headers of a letter.

1. Click on **View** in the menu bar. A pull-down menu will appear.

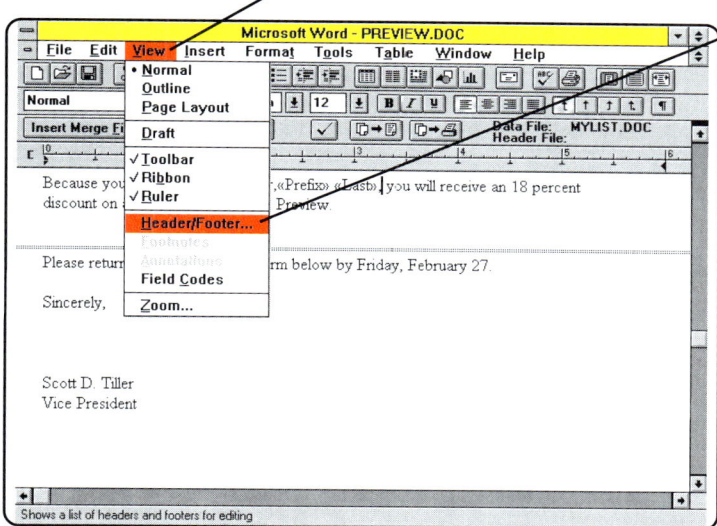

2. Click on **Header/Footer**. The Header/Footer dialog box will appear.

Notice that "Header" is highlighted.

3. Click on **OK**. The Header pane will appear at the bottom of PREVIEW.DOC.

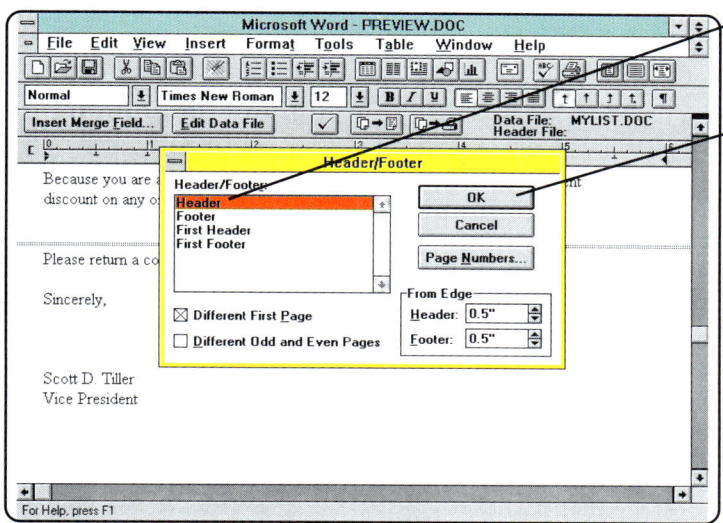

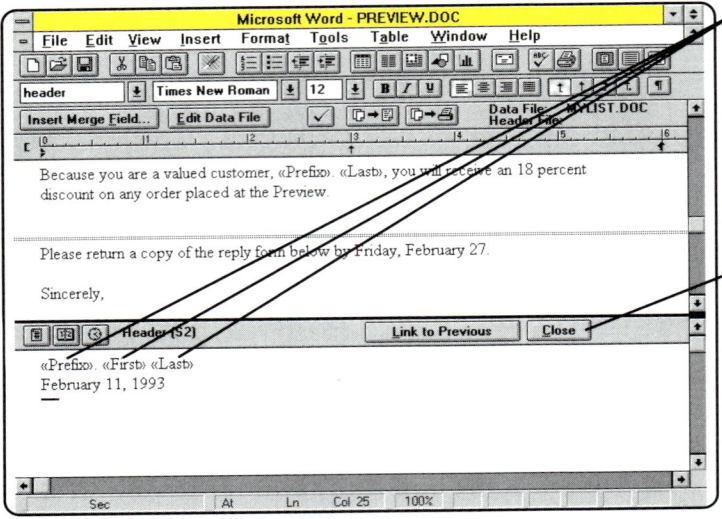

4. **Repeat steps 16 through 21** in the section entitled "Inserting Merge Fields into a Form Letter" to insert the merge field codes into the header.

5. **Click** on **Close**.

6. **Repeat steps 16 through 21** in the section entitled "Inserting Merge Fields into a Form Letter" once again to insert the merge field codes into the reply form on page 2. (Unfortunately, the copy/paste function cannot be used in the print merge process. You must insert each merge field code individually.)

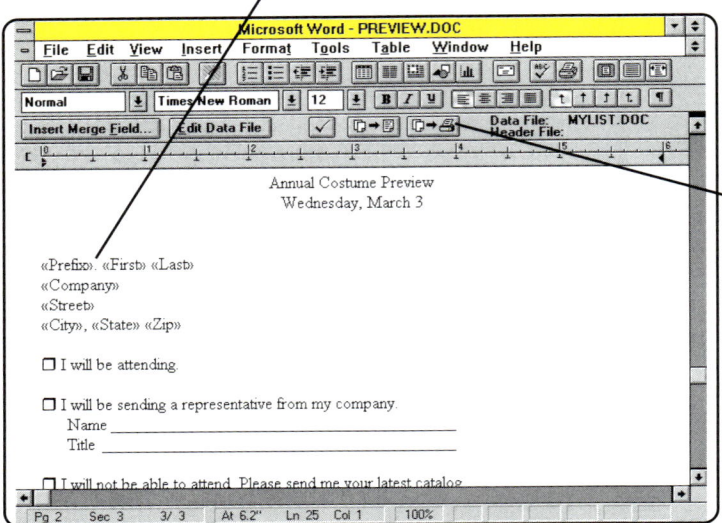

PRINTING THE FORM LETTER

1. **Click** on the **Print Merge tool**. The Print dialog box will appear.

CHAPTER 13: EDITING A MAILING LIST AND PRINTING A FORM LETTER 179

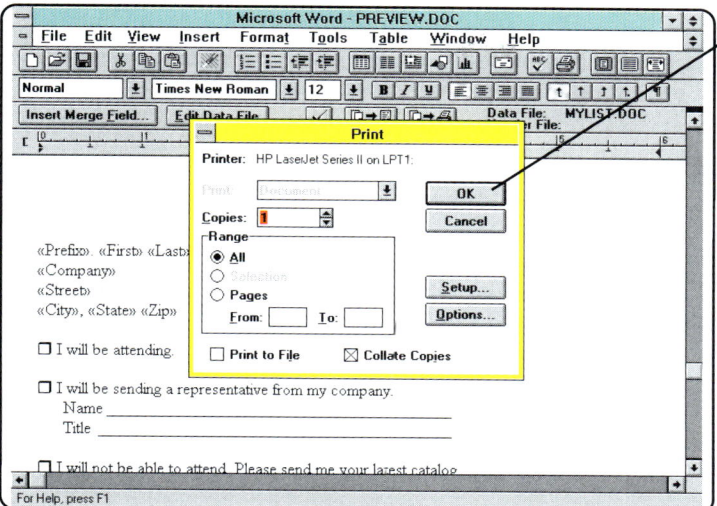

2. Click on **OK**.

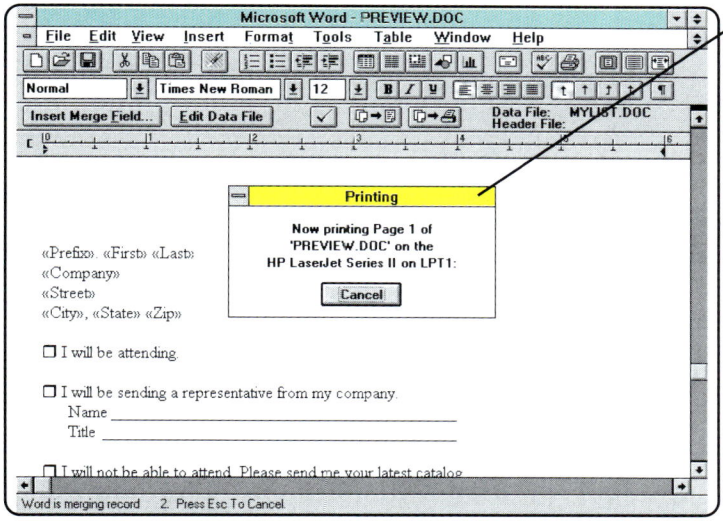

The Printing message box will stay on the screen until both pages of the document have been sent to the printer. Your printer will now print two, two-page form letters using the personalized information that you entered into the MYLIST.DOC mailing list file.

Isn't this great?

SAVING YOUR FORM LETTER

1. **Click** on **File** in the menu bar.

2. **Click** on **Save As**. The Save As dialog box will appear.

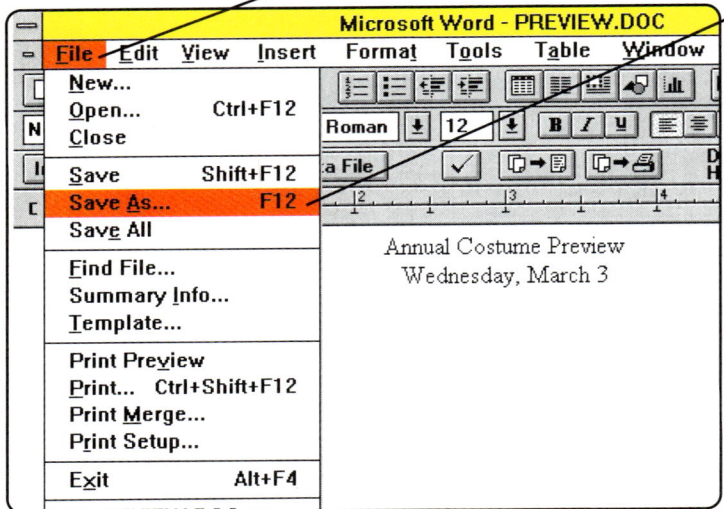

3. **Type myform.doc** in the File Name box.

4. **Click** on **OK**. The Summary Info dialog box will appear.

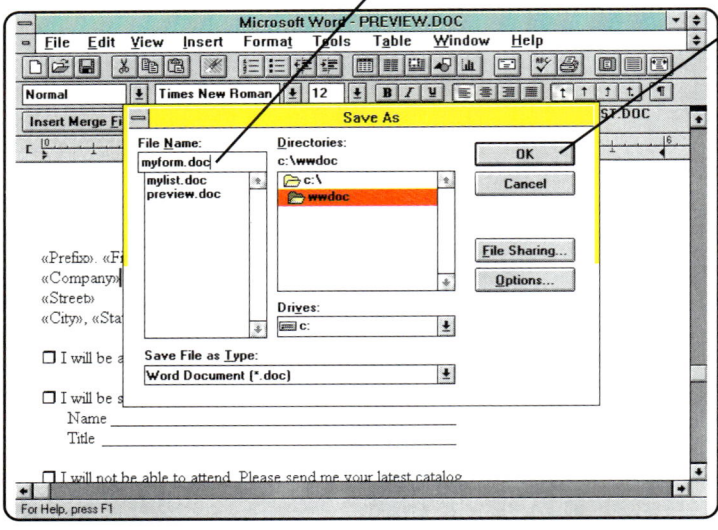

CHAPTER 13: EDITING A MAILING LIST AND PRINTING A FORM LETTER 181

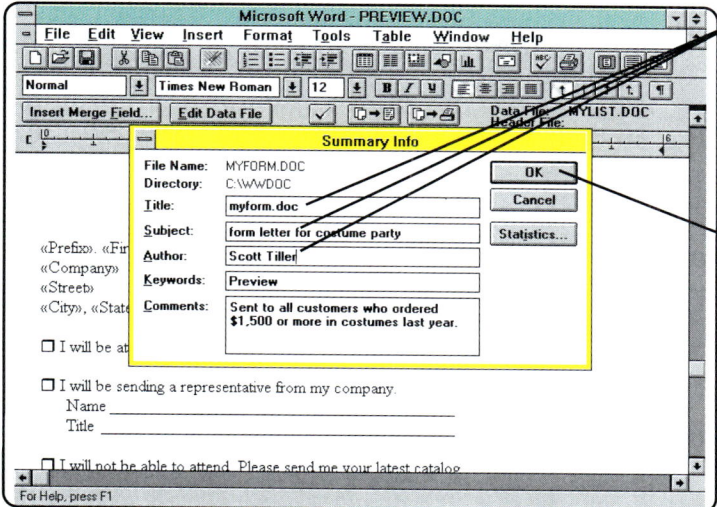

5. Type in the **information** in the boxes as shown here. If you do not want summary information for this file, skip this step.

6. Click on **OK**. Your form letter is now saved as a separate file.

CHAPTER 14

Printing Envelopes for a Mailing List

Once you have created a mailing list (Chapter 12) and coded a form letter for merge printing (Chapter 13), printing envelopes for a mailing list is easy. We recommend that you do this chapter only if you have an envelope feeder for a laser printer or tractor feed envelopes for a dot-matrix printer. In this chapter you will do the following:

❖ Address an envelope for merge printing
❖ Add the envelope to the form letter
❖ Merge print the envelopes
❖ Save the coded envelope with the form letter, or remove the coded envelope from the form letter

ADDRESSING THE ENVELOPE

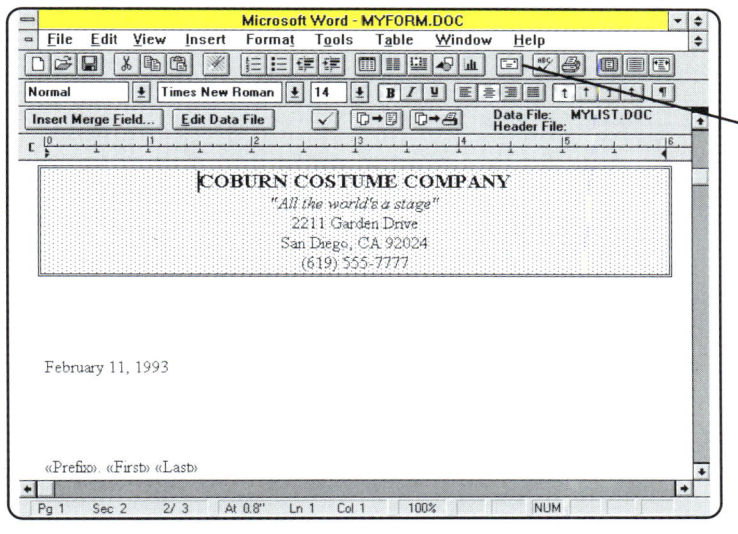

1. **Open MYFORM.DOC** if it is not already open.

2. **Click** on the **Envelope tool**. The Create Envelope dialog box will appear.

183

184 **WORD FOR WINDOWS 2: THE VISUAL LEARNING GUIDE**

Notice that the merge field codes have been automatically placed in the Addressed To box.

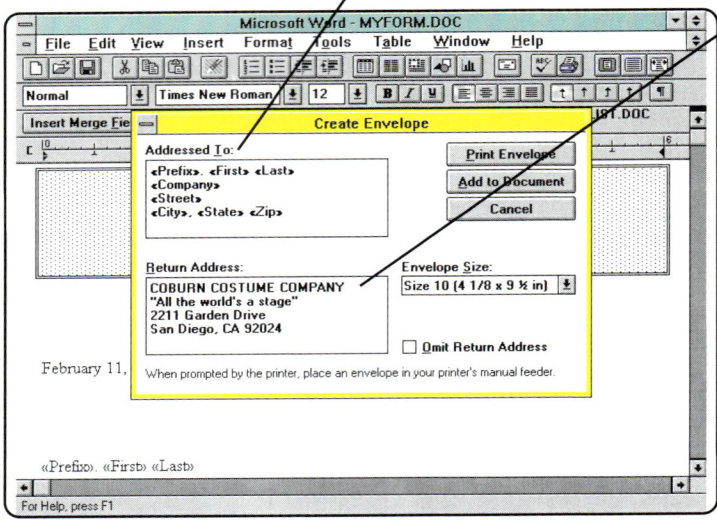

3. **Type** in the **return address** in the Return Address box. If you made this your permanent return address in Chapter 11, skip this step since it will already appear here.

ATTACHING THE ENVELOPE TO THE FORM LETTER

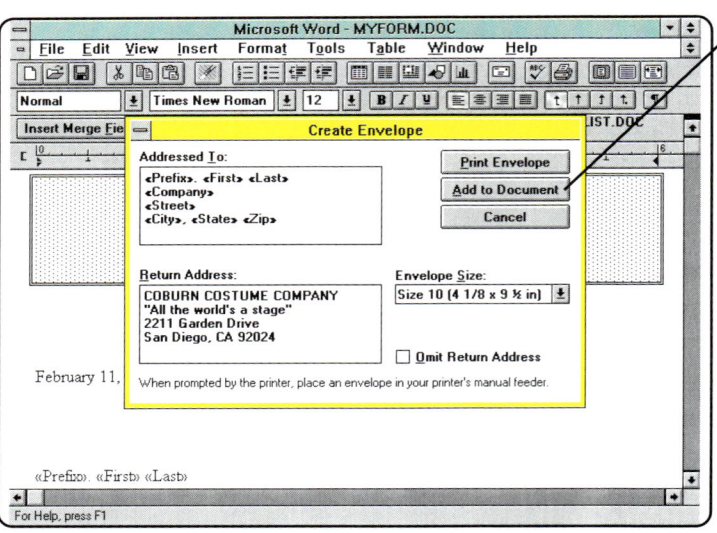

1. **Click** on **Add to Document**. The envelope will appear at the top of MYFORM.DOC.

CHAPTER 14: PRINTING ENVELOPES FOR A MAILING LIST

MERGE PRINTING THE ENVELOPES

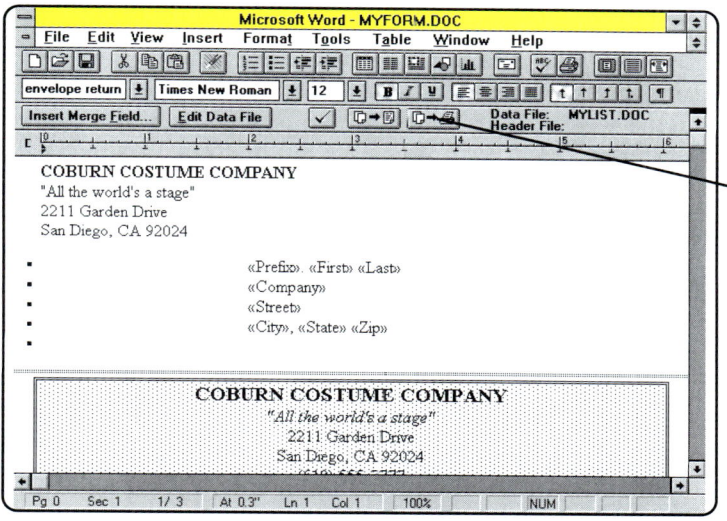

Insert an envelope tray in your laser printer (or put tractor feed envelopes in your dot-matrix printer).

1. **Click** on the **Print Merge tool**. The Print dialog box will appear.

2. **Click** on **Pages** to place a black dot in the circle. The cursor will begin flashing in the From box.

3. **Type 0** (zero). The envelope is considered to be page 0 in the letter file.

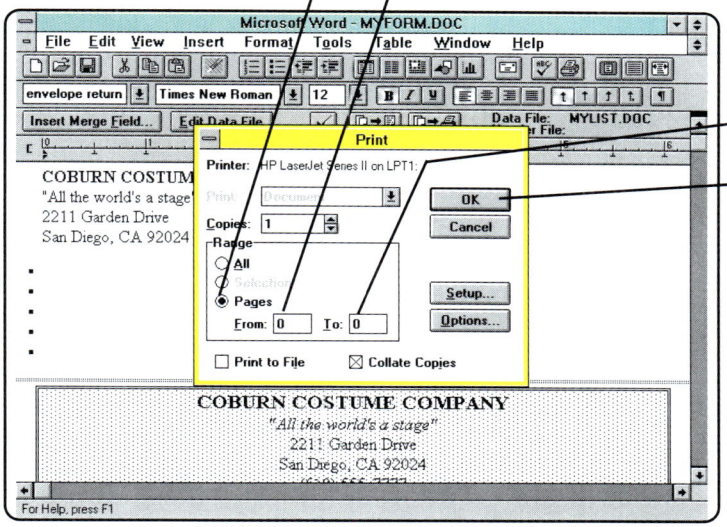

4. **Press Tab**. The cursor will move to the To box.

5. **Type 0** (zero).

6. **Click** on **OK**. Your printer will print an envelope for each person on the mailing list.

TO SAVE OR NOT TO SAVE...

If you save the envelope with the letter, it will be permanently attached and you will see it every time you open the letter. There is no way to remove it. You can exit the mailing list without saving the envelope, but this means you will have to recreate the envelope if you need it again. The choice is yours.

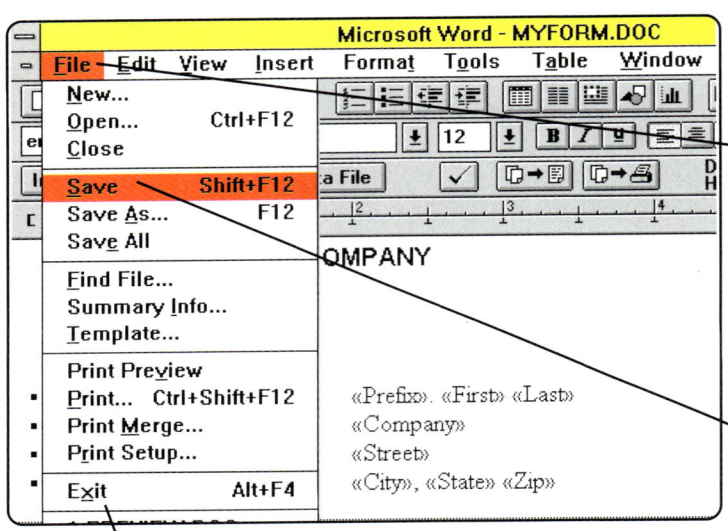

1. **Click** on **File** in the menu bar. A pull-down menu will appear.

Saving the Attached Envelope

1. **Click** on **Save** if you want the envelope to remain attached to the document.

Exiting Without Saving the Attached Envelope

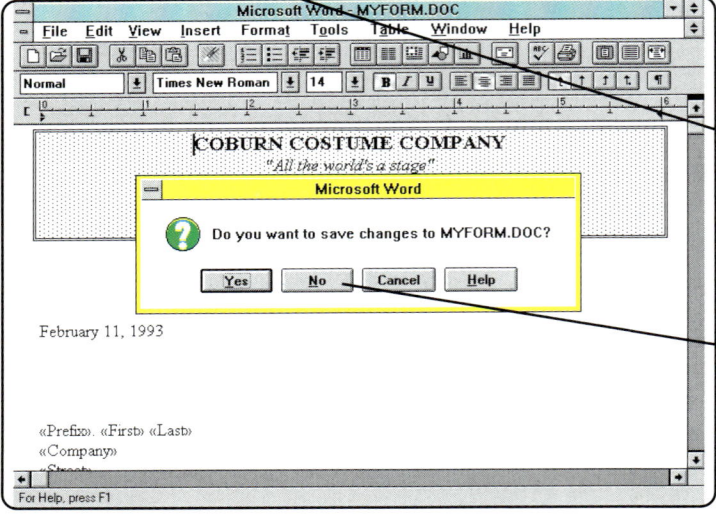

1. **Click** on **Exit** if you do not want to save the attached envelope. A Microsoft Word dialog box will appear.

2. **Click** on **No**. The envelope will no longer be attached to the document and you will be returned to Program Manager.

Converting a Mailing List Created in Another Program

CHAPTER 15

If you have a mailing list created in another word processing program that you want to use with a form letter created in Word for Windows 2, you can simply convert the mailing list into a Word file. You don't have to create the list all over again. In this chapter you will do the following:

❖ Convert a mailing list from a DOS-based program
❖ Add a header row to the converted mailing list
❖ Save the mailing list as a Word file

CONVERTING A DOS-BASED MAILING LIST

For the sake of visual clarity, this section will begin with a blank Word screen. In actuality, however, you can start with a blank Word screen, an empty document, or even a letter or other file on your screen. Since Word allows you to have multiple files open at the same time, the process of opening a file can be done at any time.

1. **Click** on **File** in the menu bar. A pull-down menu will appear.

2. **Click** on **Open**. The Open dialog box will appear.

In this example we moved a mailing list file (called DOS.DAT) from a DOS-based program to the WWDOC directory.

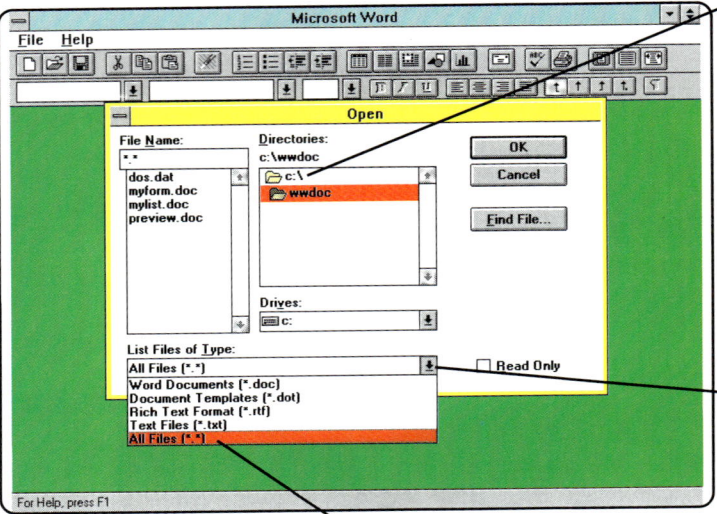

If the file you want to convert is in another directory, click twice on c:\ to open a list of all directories on the C drive. Then scroll through the list until you can click twice on the appropriate directory. You will then see a list of all files in that directory in the File Name box.

3. Click on ↓ to the right of the List Files of Type box. A drop-down list of file types will appear.

4. Click on **All Files (*.*)**. All Files in the directory, regardless of the extension, will appear in the list box.

5. Click twice on the **filename** of the file you want to convert (in this example, DOS.DAT). The Convert File dialog box will appear.

Note: Word versions 2.0 and 2.0a will not convert an Excel 4.0 file, but 2.0b will.

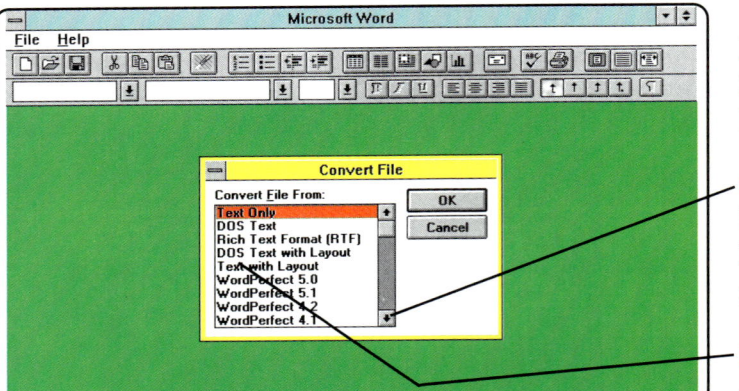

6. Click on ↓ on the scroll bar until you can see the DOS program in which the file was created.

7. Click twice on the **DOS program** and the DOS file will be converted. The newly converted file will appear on your screen.

Saving the Converted File

1. **Click** on **File** in the menu bar. A pull-down menu will appear.

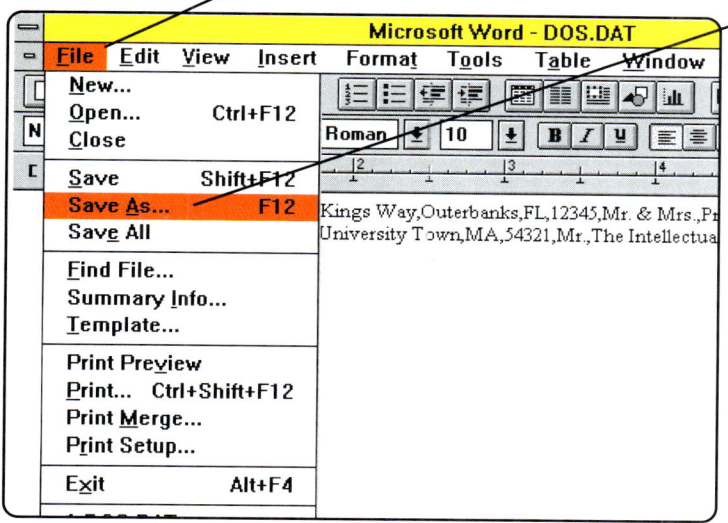

2. **Click** on **Save As**. The Save As dialog box will appear.

Notice that the name of the file created in a DOS-based program appears in the File Name box.

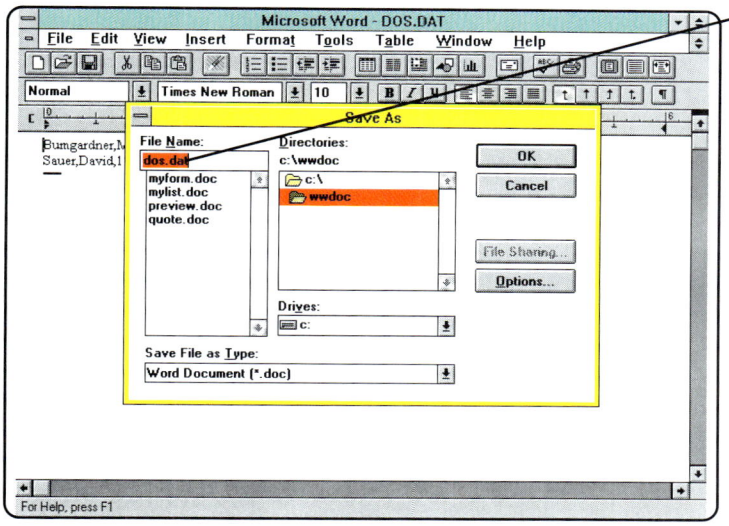

3. **Click** to the **left of the extension** (in this example, **.dat**) to set the cursor. The cursor will begin flashing and the highlighting will disappear.

4. **Press and hold** the mouse button as you **drag** the mouse to highlight the extension.

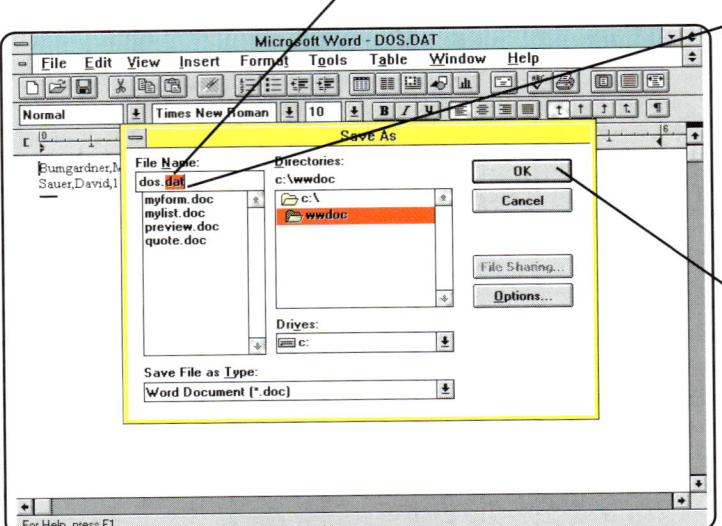

5. **Type doc**. The .dat extension is replaced with the .doc extension. This means that a new file is created, without making changes to the original DOS-based file.

6. **Click** on **OK**. The Summary Info dialog box will appear.

7. **Click** on **OK**. Word will save the document as DOS.DOC and your original DOS-based document will be intact.

ATTACHING THE CONVERTED MAILING LIST TO A FORM LETTER

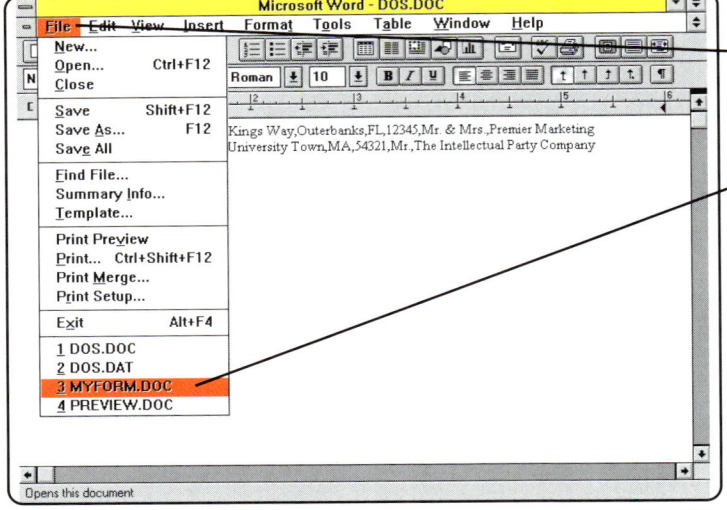

1. **Click** on **File** in the menu bar. A pull-down menu will appear.

2. **Click** on **MYFORM.DOC**. This is the letter you created in Chapter 13. If it is not displayed on this list, open it by clicking on Open. If you need help opening a file, see the "Opening a Saved File" section in Chapter 3.

CHAPTER 15: CONVERTING A MAILING LIST   **191**

3. **Click** on **File** in the menu bar. A pull-down menu will appear.

4. **Click** on **Print Merge**. The Print Merge Setup dialog box will appear.

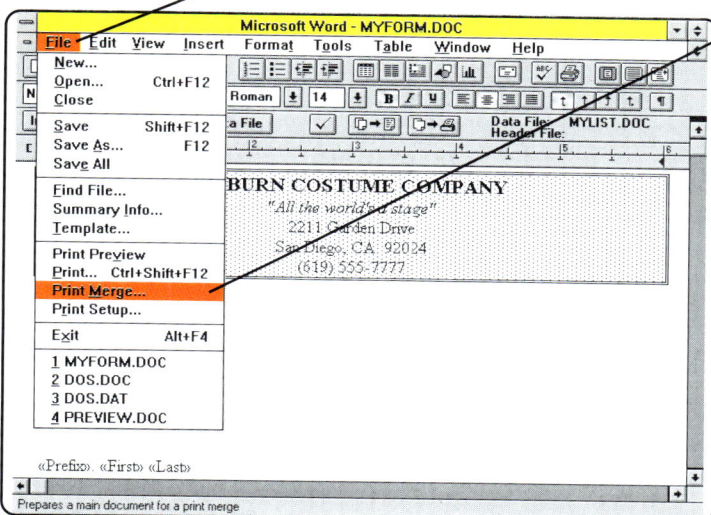

5. **Click** on **Attach Data File**. The Attach Data File dialog box will appear.

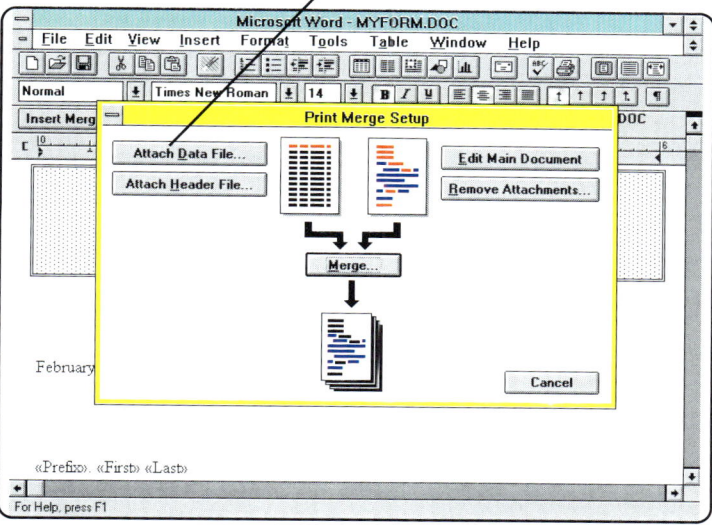

6. **Click** on the name of the **newly converted file**. (In this example it is DOS.DOC.) If you saved the converted file to another directory, you will have to open it from that directory.

7. **Click** on **OK**. A Microsoft Word dialog box may appear with an error message. Don't panic! Everything is okay. The error message may appear because Word is programmed to look for a specific format in the first line of a mailing list. (See Chapter 12 for details.) Since other word processing programs may not require the same format, Word will detect this "error" in the converted mailing list and give you this message.

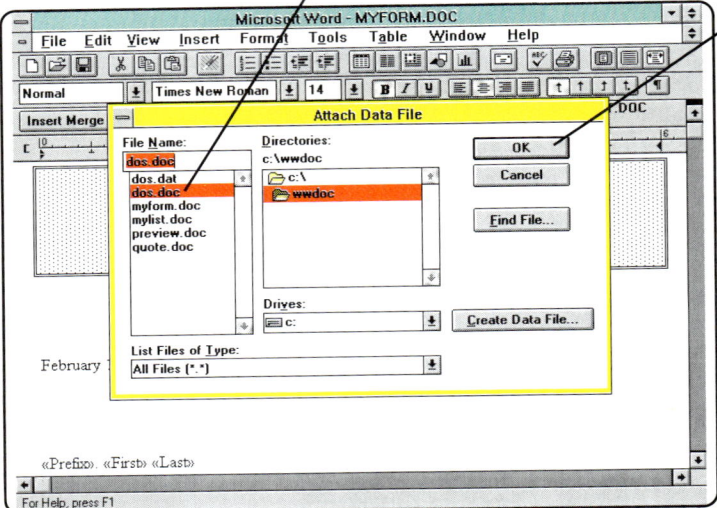

(If you don't get an error message, go on to the next section.)

8. **Click** on **Fix Error Now** to tell Word that you want to fix the error. DOS.DOC will appear on your screen. Now go to the next section to add a header record.

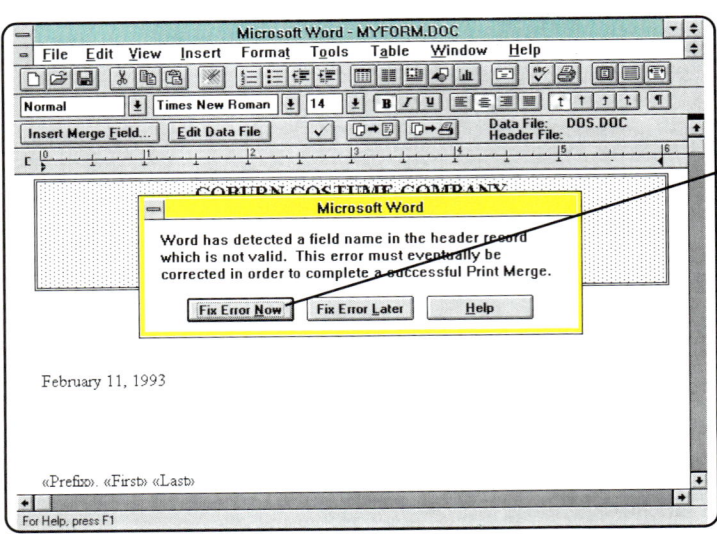

ADDING A HEADER RECORD TO A CONVERTED MAILING LIST

1. Click to the **left of the first row** of your converted file.

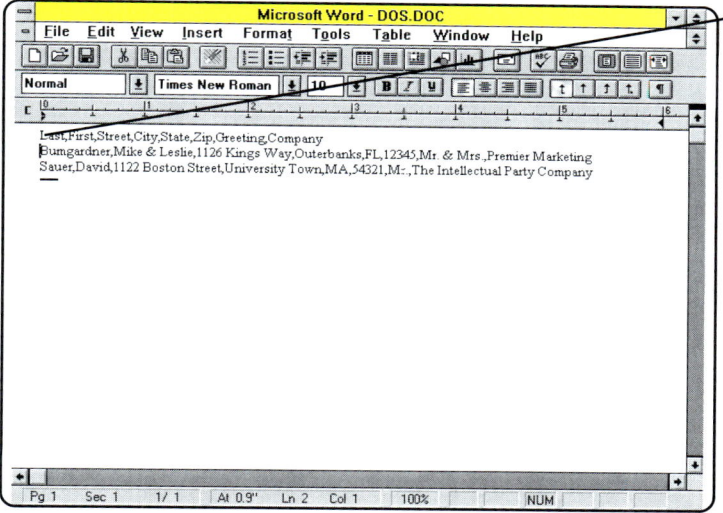

2. Type a **header record** like the one shown here. Type a comma after each field, but do not put a space after the comma. Immediately type the next field name. Do not type an ampersand (&), period(.), or space within a given field name. When you type the last field name, *do not* follow it with a comma.

3. Press Enter. The converted mailing list now has a header record and can be used to print a form letter.

Checking the Header Record

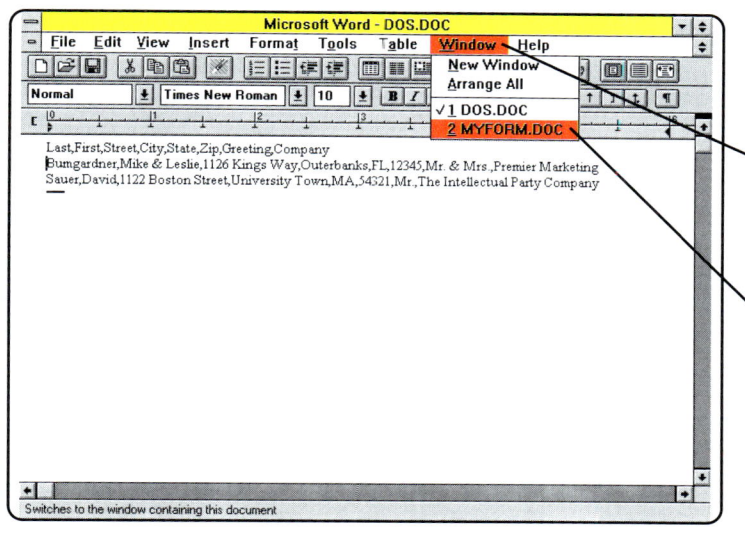

1. Click on **Window** in the menu bar. A pull-down menu will appear.

2. Click on **MYFORM.DOC**. MYFORM.DOC will appear on your screen.

3. Click on **Insert Merge Field**. The Insert Merge Field dialog box will appear. If you get an error message box, your header record may contain a spacing error or an unacceptable character.

Notice that the fields you typed in the converted mailing list's header record are listed in the Print Merge Fields box.

Notice that the DOS.DOC mailing list (or the converted mailing list you used) is still attached to the MYFORM.DOC form letter.

3. Click on ↓ to scroll to the bottom of the list.

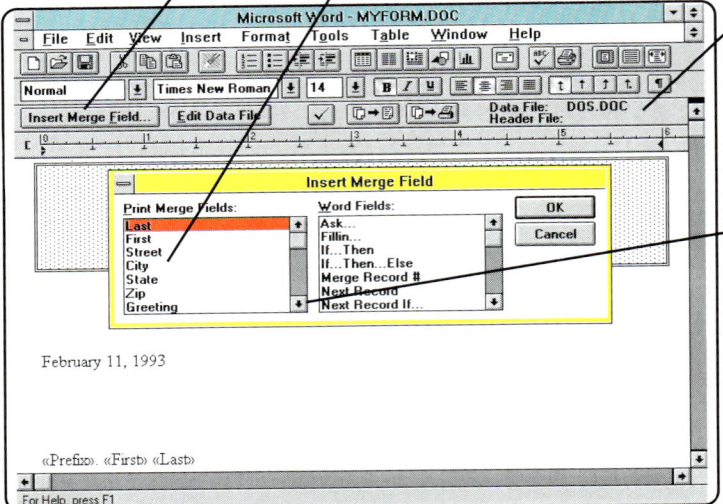

CHAPTER 15: CONVERTING A MAILING LIST

Notice that the remainder of the field names you typed in the header record are in the list.

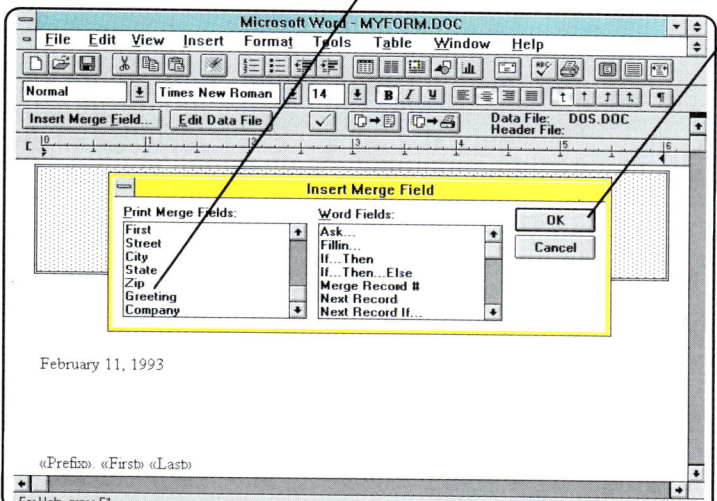

4. Click on **OK**. MYFORM.DOC will appear.

Congratulations. You have successfully converted a DOS-based mailing list to a Word for Windows 2 document. It is now ready for printing in any form letter using any or all the merge fields you put in the header record.

If you want to use this mailing list to print a form letter, see Chapter 13.

EXITING WORD

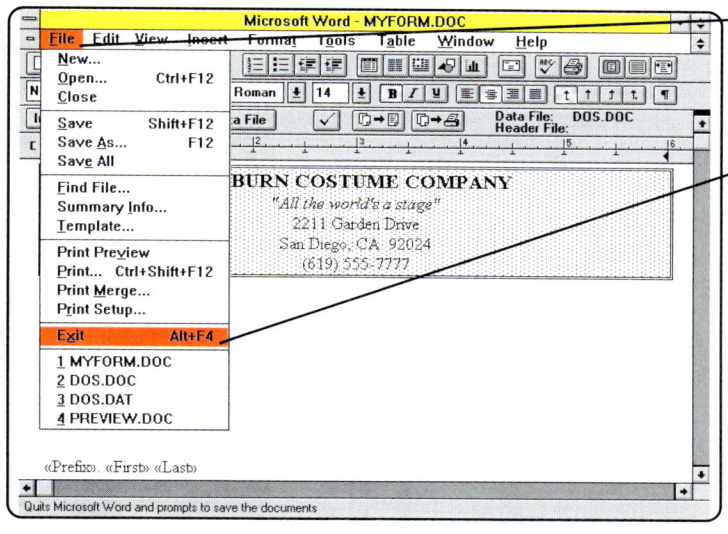

1. Click on **File** in the menu bar. A pull-down menu will appear.

2. Click on **Exit**. If you have previously saved your work, Word will close and return to the Program Manager. If you have not previously saved, you will be asked to if you want to save the file(s) before exiting. **Click** on **Save** if you want to save the new file.

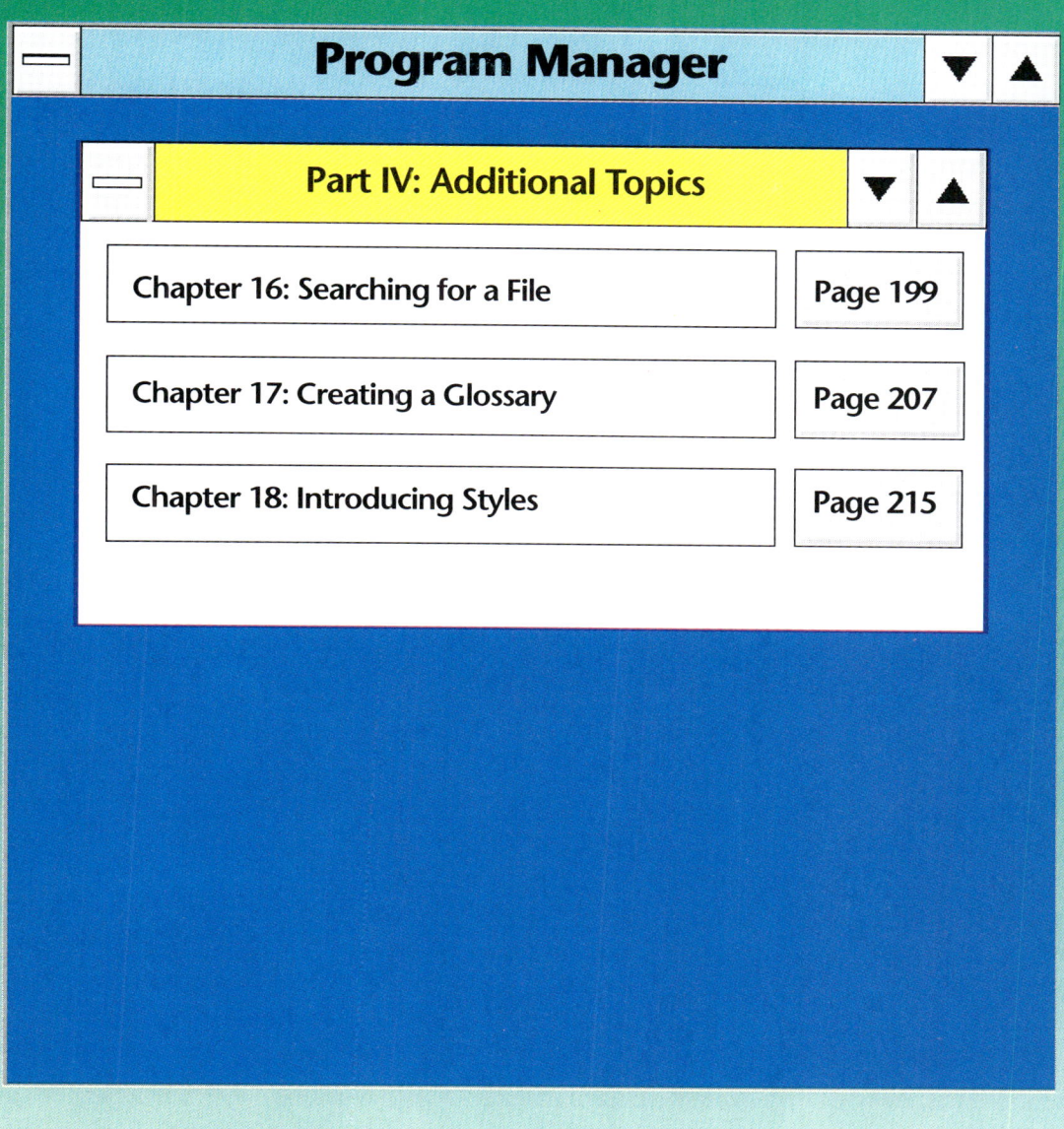

CHAPTER 16

Searching for a File

When you have many files in your directories, you may forget the name of a specific file. Luckily the Word for Windows 2 Find File option allows you to locate files easily. You can use the Find File option to search your current directory, other directories, and/or find a file using a keyword. In this chapter you will do the following:

❖ Find a file in your current directory
❖ Find a file in a different directory
❖ Find a file using a keyword

OPENING THE FIND FILE DIALOG BOX

You can open the Find File dialog box from any Word document. In this example, you should begin your search with a new document on your screen. See "Opening a New Document" in Chapter 8 if you need help.

1. **Click** on **File** in the menu bar. A pull-down menu will appear.

2. **Click** on **Find File**. The Find File dialog box will appear.

FINDING A FILE IN YOUR CURRENT DIRECTORY

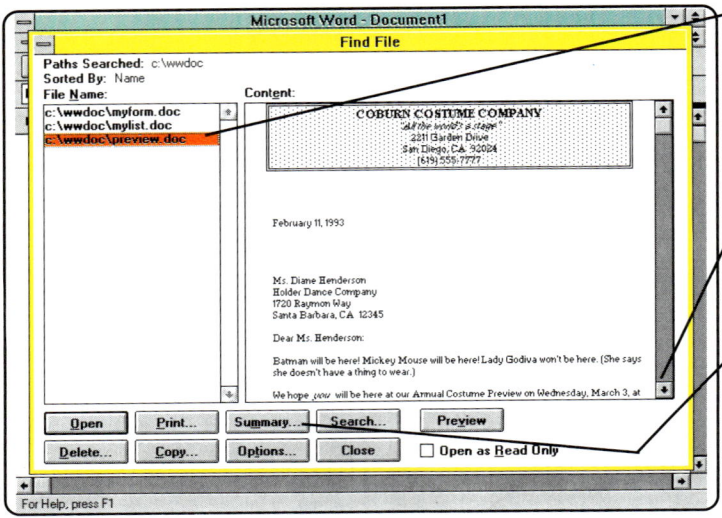

1. **Click** on **preview.doc**. The top of the first page of PREVIEW.DOC will appear in the Content box.

You can scroll through the text by clicking repeatedly on the ⬇.

2. **Click** on **Summary**. The Summary Info dialog box will appear.

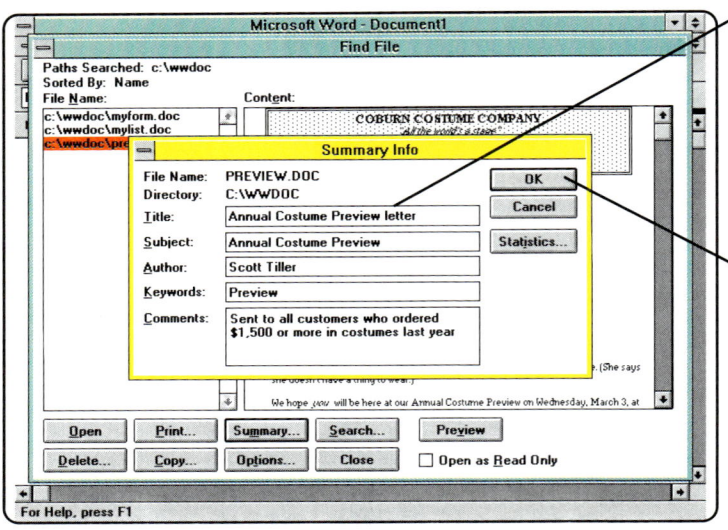

Notice that you can view the notes you made about the file the first time you saved it. You can also edit the information in this box if you want to.

3. **Click** on **OK**. The Find File dialog box will appear.

CHAPTER 16: SEARCHING FOR A FILE

4. Click on **mylist.doc**. The first page of MYLIST.DOC will appear in the Content box.

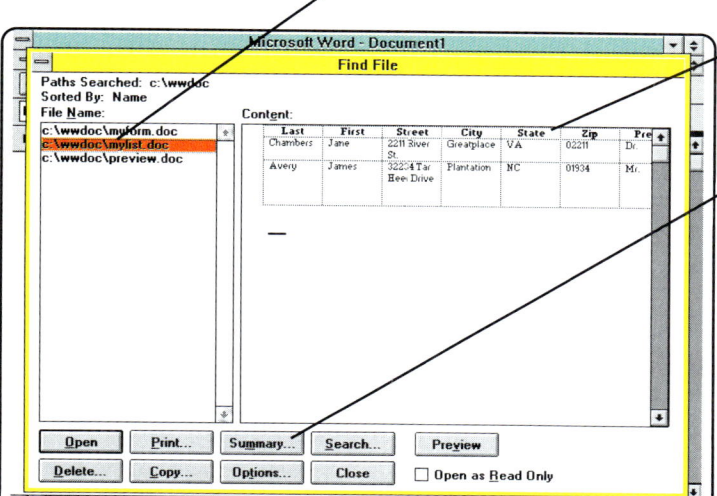

Notice that you can read the text to see if it is the file you want to open.

You can also click on Summary to view the information in the Summary Info dialog box you entered when you first saved this mailing list.

If you can't find the file you want in the current directory, you can search another directory for the file you are seeking.

SEARCHING FOR A FILE IN A DIFFERENT DIRECTORY

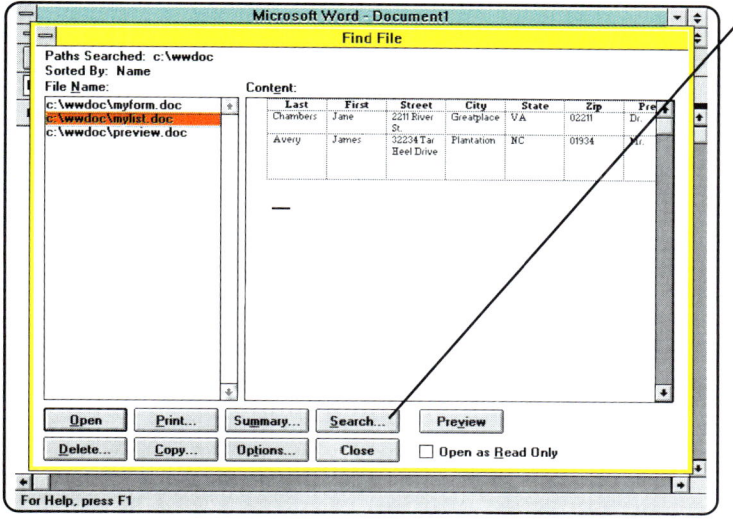

1. Click on **Search**. The Search dialog box will appear.

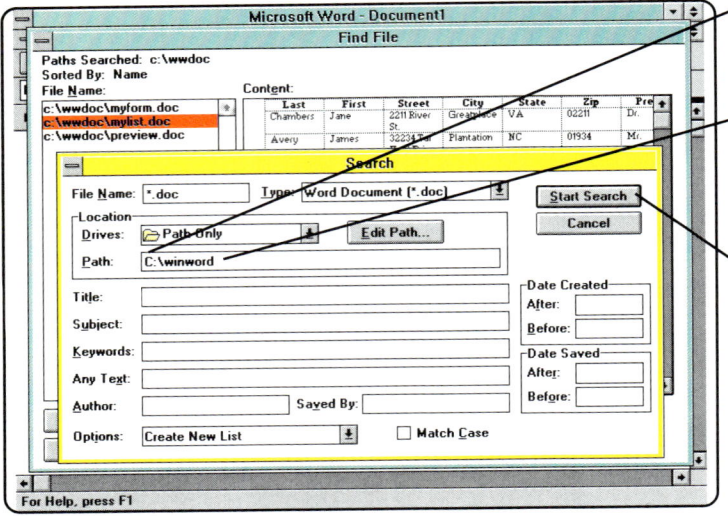

2. Click in the **Path box** to set the cursor.

3. Type C:\winword to search the WINWORD directory on the C drive.

4. Click on **Start Search**. The Find File dialog box will appear.

Notice that the names of the files in this directory are displayed in the File Name box.

Notice that the content of the highlighted filename is displayed in the Content box.

If you cannot find the file you are seeking, try the keyword method discussed in the next section.

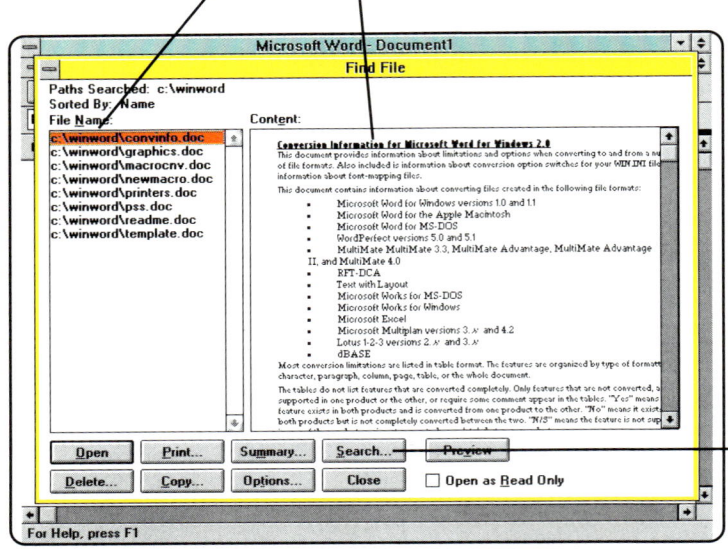

SEARCHING WITH A KEYWORD

You can search for a file by title, subject, keyword, author, or specific text in the file. In this section you will use a keyword to search for a file in a specific drive.

1. Click on **Search**. The Search dialog box will appear.

2. Click on the ⬇ on the Drives box. A drop-down list of available drives will appear.

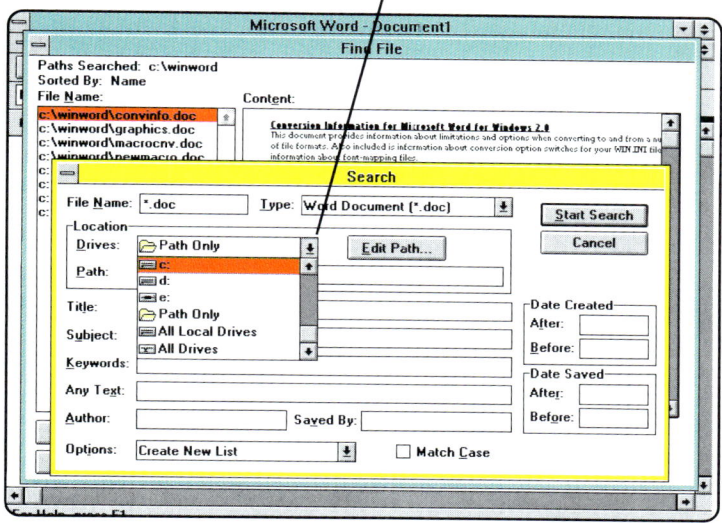

3. Click on **c:**. The drive letter "c:" will now appear in the Drives box.

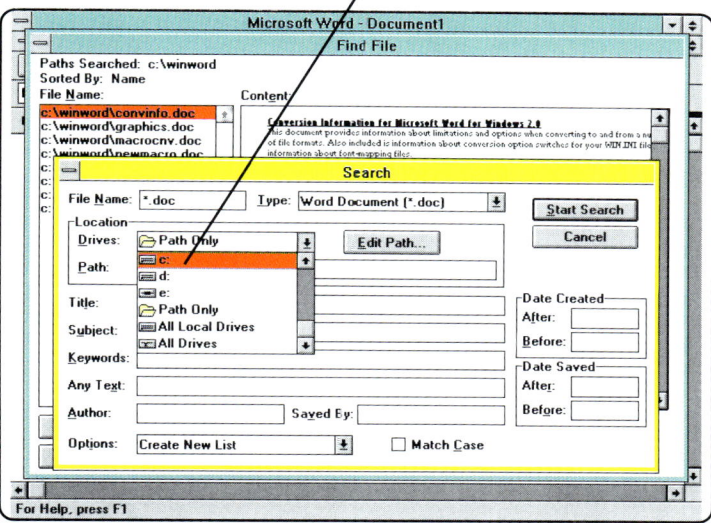

4. Click on the **Keywords box** to set the cursor.

5. Type preview. This is the keyword you put in the Summary Info Keyword box of PREVIEW.DOC when you saved it in Chapter 2.

6. Click on **Start Search**. The Building Search Path message box will appear.

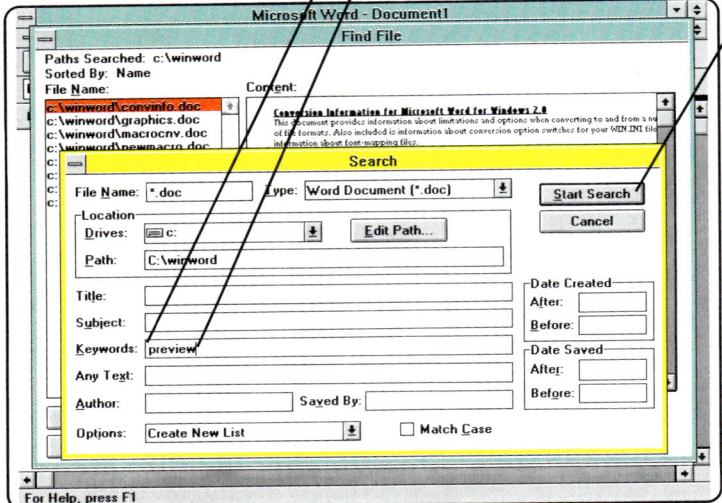

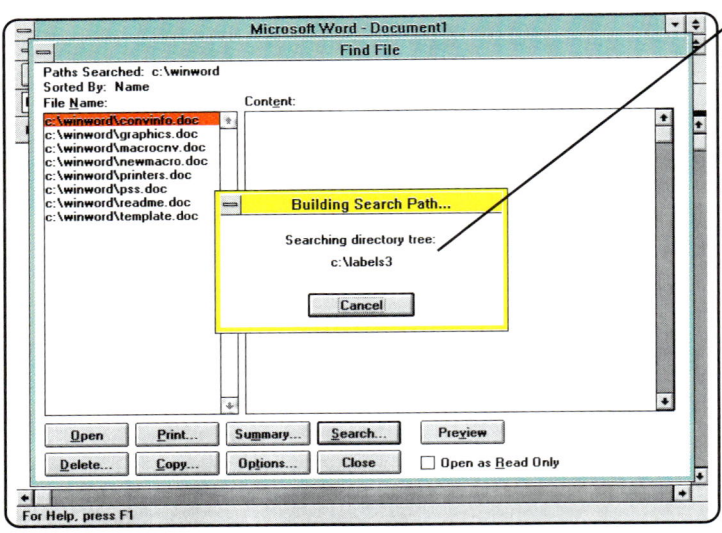

Notice that Word searches the Directory Tree for files with the .DOC extension and the keyword "preview." When the search is complete, the Building File List message box will appear.

CHAPTER 16: SEARCHING FOR A FILE 205

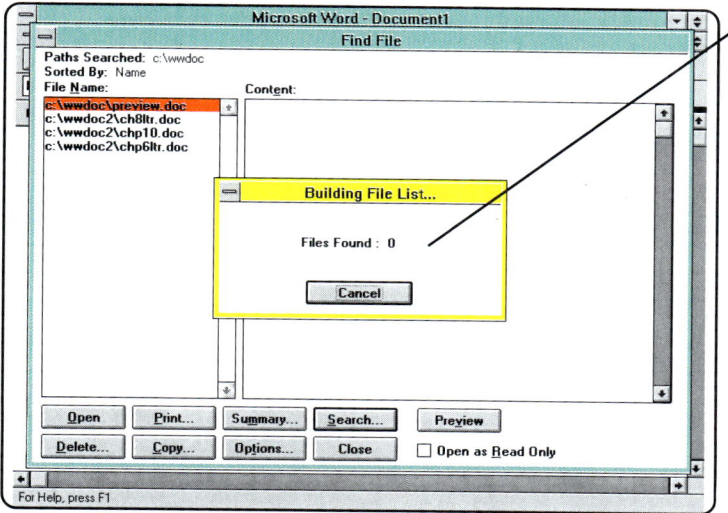

Notice that the message box displays the number of files that Word is searching. When the search is complete, the Find File dialog box will appear.

Notice that "preview.doc" appears in the File Name box. If you have other documents with the keyword "preview," the list will include those filenames as well. In that case you can click on each of them individually to view the contents of each until you find the file you are seeking.

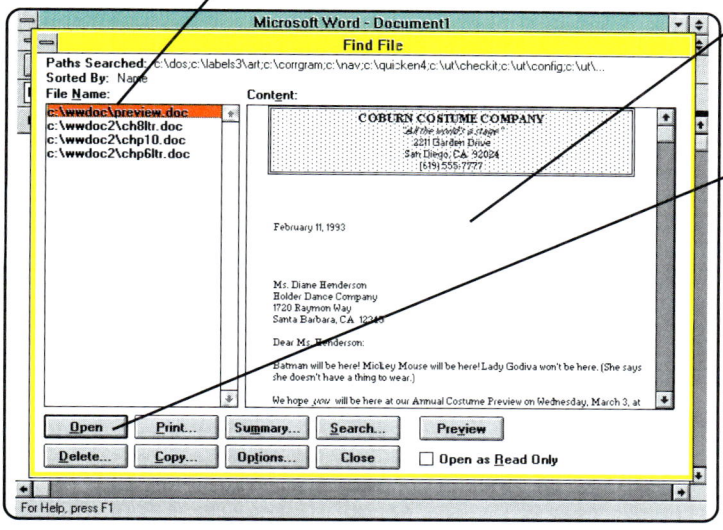

Notice that the first page of PREVIEW.DOC appears in the Content box.

7. Click on **Open**. The first page of PREVIEW.DOC will appear.

Don't you love this feature? Now you don't have to go to File Manager or DOS to find a file anymore!

WORD FOR WINDOWS 2: THE VISUAL LEARNING GUIDE

EXITING WORD

1. **Click** on the **Control menu box** (□) on the left of the PREVIEW.DOC title bar. A pull-down menu will appear.

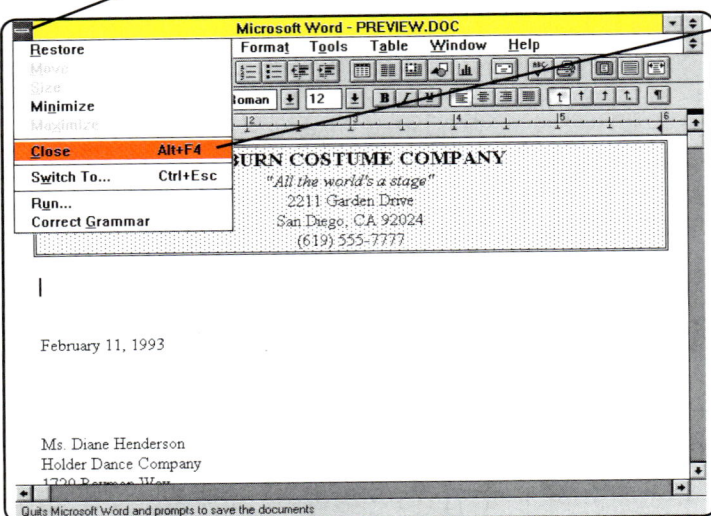

2. **Click** on **Close**. Unless you have other unsaved files open, you will exit Word.

CHAPTER 17

Creating a Glossary

If you find yourself using certain words, phrases, paragraphs, or even graphics over and over again, you will love the Word for Windows 2 Glossary option. This option allows you to save those often-used items to a "glossary" and insert them into a document with just a few clicks of your mouse.

In this chapter you will do the following:

❖ Create a Glossary item
❖ Insert a Glossary item into a new document
❖ Save a Glossary item and exit Word

CREATING A GLOSSARY ITEM

1. **Open PREVIEW.DOC** if it is not already open. If you need help opening a file, see the section entitled "Opening a Saved File" in Chapter 3.

2. **Click** to the **left of "COBURN"** to place the insertion point if it is not already there.

207

WORD FOR WINDOWS 2: THE VISUAL LEARNING GUIDE

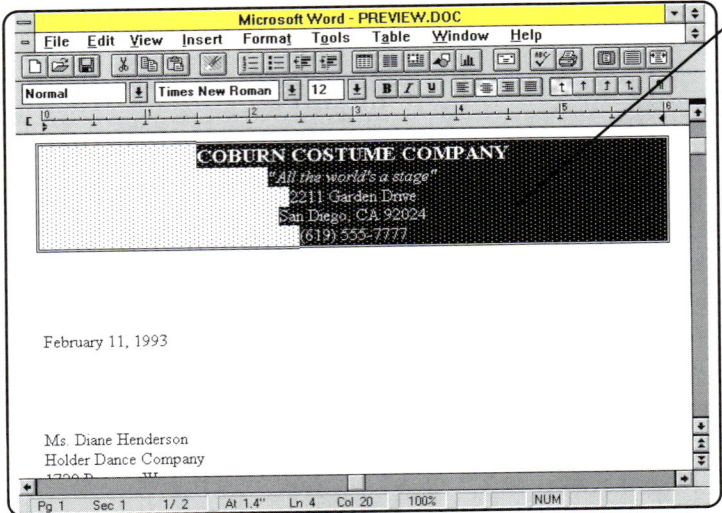

3. **Press and hold** the left mouse button as you **drag** the mouse pointer **down** and to the **right** until the company address and phone number are highlighted. (You can also click to the left of the first line, then hold the Shift key as you click to the left of the last line in the letterhead.)

4. **Click** on **Edit** in the menu bar. A pull-down menu will appear.

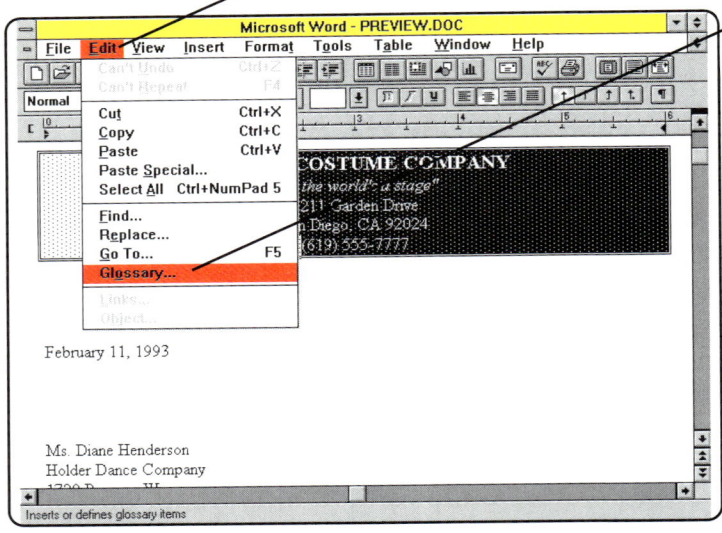

5. **Click** on **Glossary**. The Glossary dialog box will appear. The cursor will be flashing in the Glossary Name box.

CHAPTER 17: CREATING A GLOSSARY 209

6. **Type Letterhead** in the Glossary Name box.

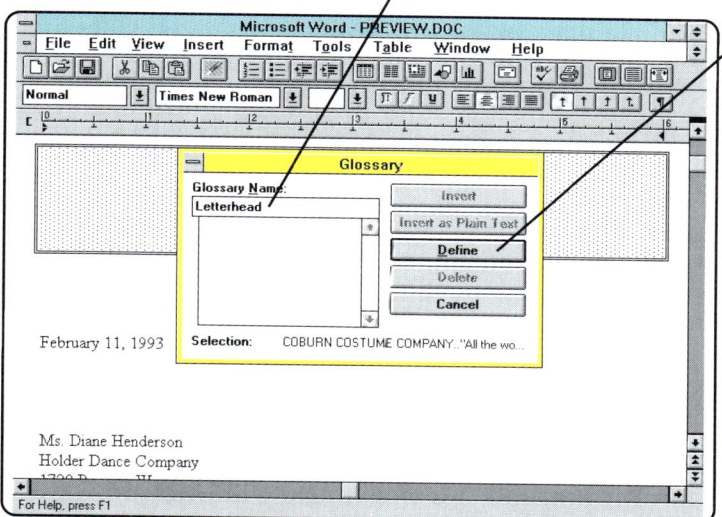

7. **Click** on **Define**. The dialog box will disappear. The Coburn letterhead and the shaded border are now saved to the Glossary.

INSERTING A GLOSSARY ITEM IN A NEW FILE

1. **Click** on **File** in the menu bar. A pull-down menu will appear.

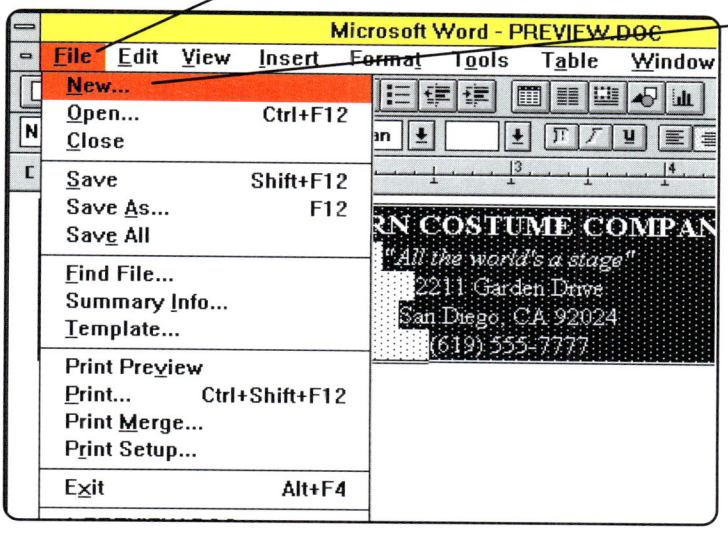

2. **Click** on **New**. The New dialog box will appear.

WORD FOR WINDOWS 2: THE VISUAL LEARNING GUIDE

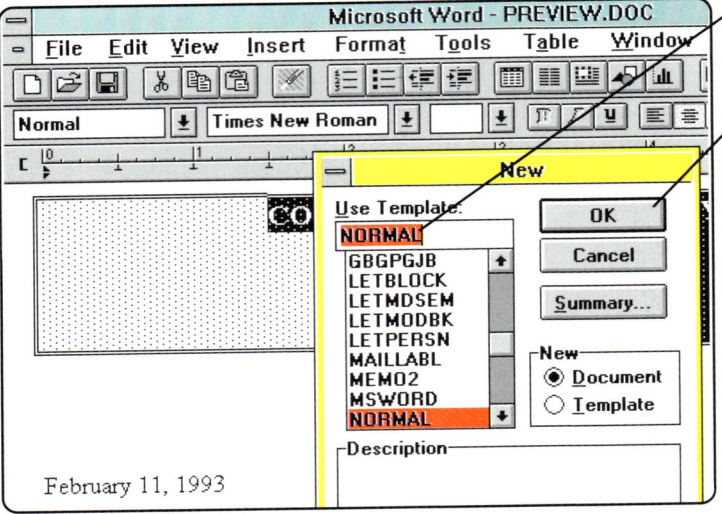

Notice that "Normal" is already highlighted.

3. **Click** on **OK**. A blank Word for Windows document screen will appear.

Notice that this document is labeled "Document2." If you had already opened several documents, this one might have been labeled "Document3" or "Document4," and so on.

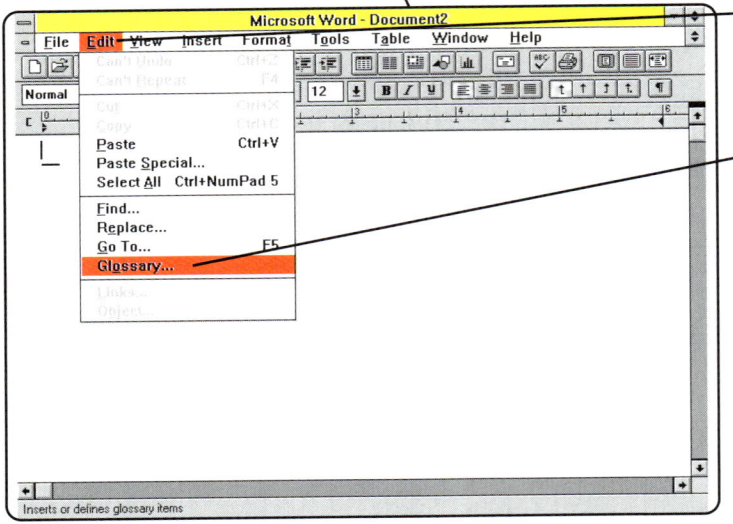

4. **Click** on **Edit** in the menu bar. A pull-down menu will appear.

5. **Click** on **Glossary**. The Glossary dialog box will appear.

CHAPTER 17: CREATING A GLOSSARY

6. Click on **Letterhead**. "Letterhead" will move to the Glossary Name box, as shown here.

Notice that the Glossary dialog box also has a Delete option, which lets you delete a Glossary item, and an Insert as Plain Text option, which, for example, allows you to insert only the letterhead text and not the shading or border.

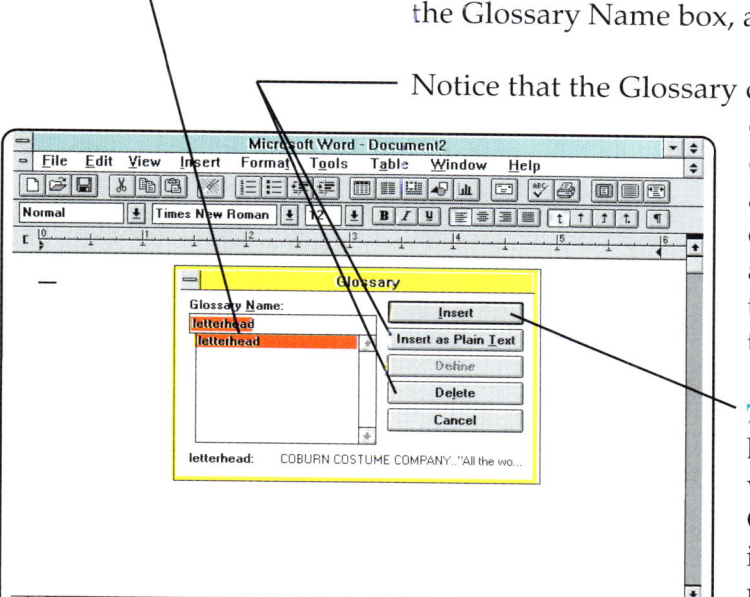

7. Click on **Insert**. Document2 will reappear with the Coburn Costume Company letterhead inserted at the top of the page.

SAVING A GLOSSARY ITEM AND EXITING WORD

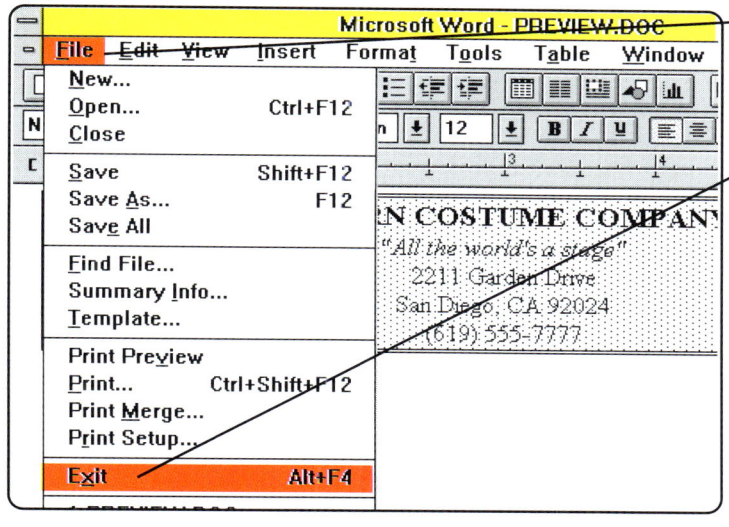

1. Click on **File** in the menu bar. A pull-down menu will appear.

2. Click on **Exit**. A Microsoft Word dialog box will appear.

3. Since you opened this document and inserted the letterhead Glossary item only for practice, **click** on **No** so that you do not save the document. Another Microsoft Word dialog box will appear.

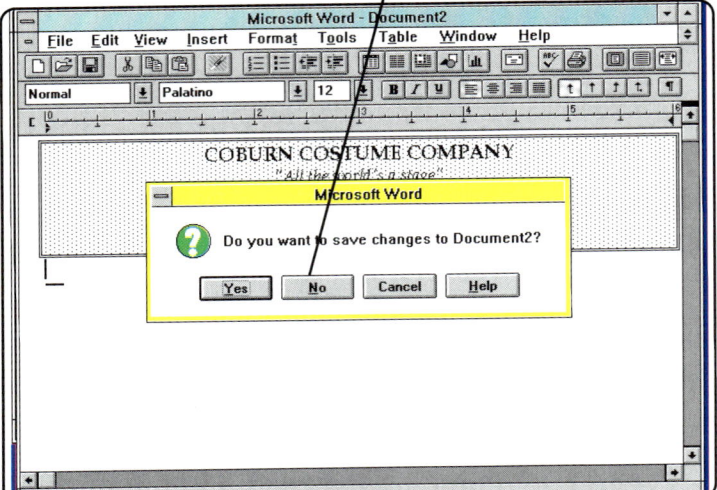

4. Click on **No** so that you do not save any changes to PREVIEW.DOC.

Another dialog box appears, asking you if you'd like to save the Glossary item.

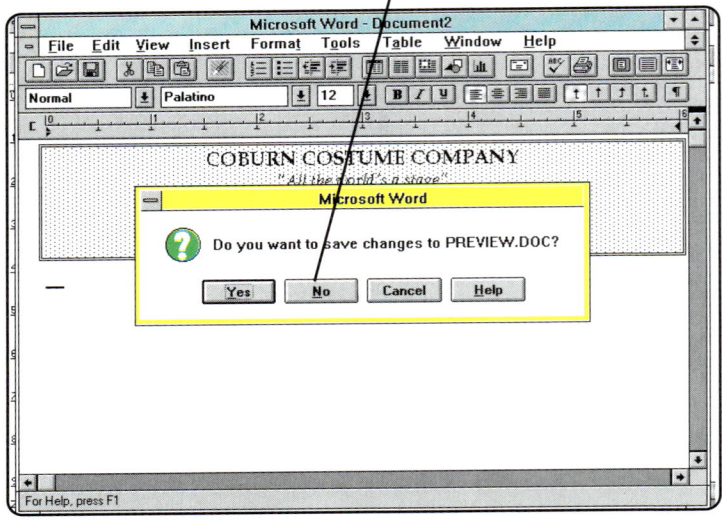

CHAPTER 17: CREATING A GLOSSARY

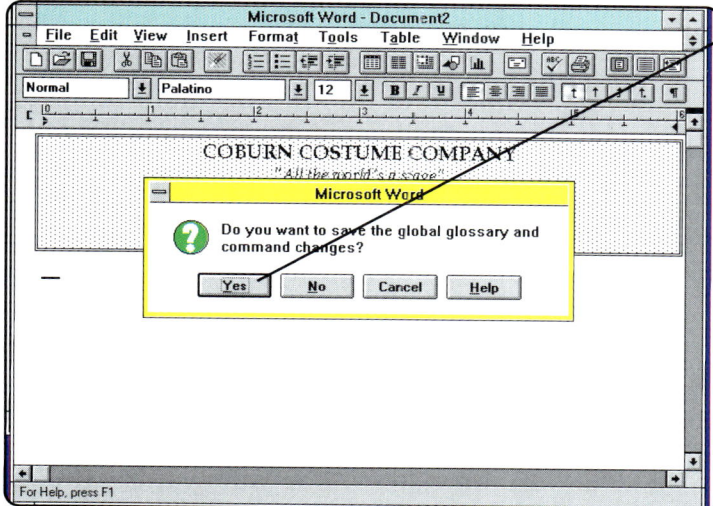

5. Click on **Yes** so that the Coburn Costume Company letterhead and its shaded border become a permanent part of the Glossary. Microsoft Word will close and you will be returned to Program Manager.

CHAPTER 18

Introducing Styles

Formatting text to look the way you want it to look with appropriate fonts, point sizes, spacing, margins, and so forth can be time-consuming. Word for Windows 2 allows you to save a special format or combination of formats as a style and then apply that style to a new paragraph. The formatting of the new paragraph will be changed before your eyes to match the selected style. In this chapter you will do the following:

❖ Create two styles
❖ Apply the new styles to different text
❖ Copy the styles to another document

CREATING TWO NEW STYLES

Opening a New Document

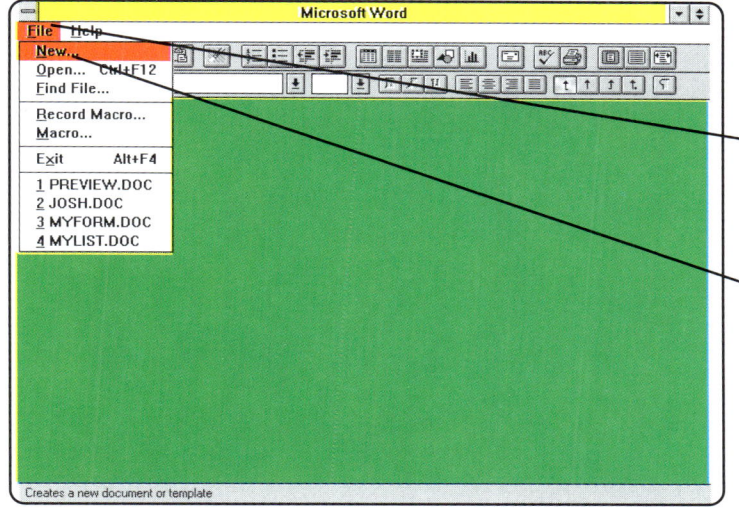

1. **Click** on **File** in the menu bar. A pull-down menu will appear.

2. **Click** on **New**. The New dialog box will appear.

215

Notice that "Normal" is highlighted.

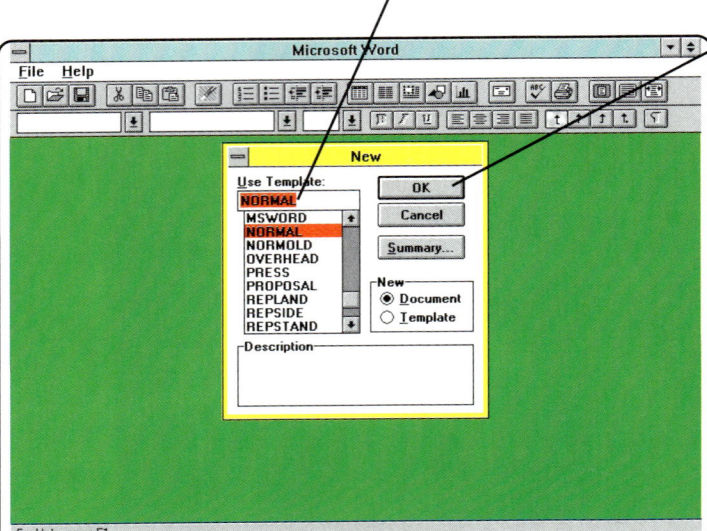

3. **Click** on **OK**. A new document screen will appear, entitled "Document1." If you have opened other documents in your work session, this document will be labeled "Document2," or "Document3," and so on, based on how many documents you opened prior to this one.

Setting Up a New Style for a Heading in the Document

1. **Type** the following text:

Persistence...

"Nothing in the world can take the place of persistence. Talent will not; nothing is more common than unsuccessful men with talent. Genius will not; unrewarded genius is almost a proverb. Education will not; the world is full of educated derelicts. Persistence and determination alone are omnipotent."
Calvin Coolidge

Life...

"Life is either a daring adventure or nothing."
Helen Keller

CHAPTER 18: INTRODUCING STYLES 217

2. **Place** the mouse pointer in the left margin **beside** "**Persistence...**" It will change to an arrow.

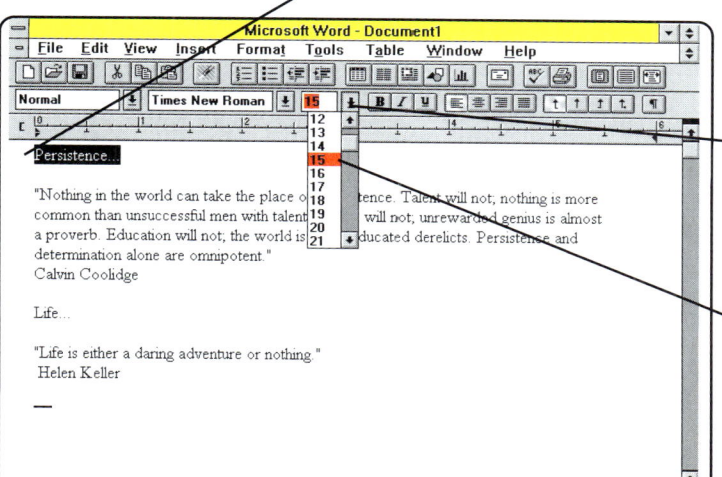

3. **Click** to highlight the word.

4. **Click** on ↓ to the right of the Font Size box. A drop-down list of available font sizes will appear.

5. **Click** on **15**. The number "15" will appear in the Font Size box and "Persistence..." will appear in 15-point type.

6. With the text still highlighted, **click** on the **Bold button** in the ribbon to bold the text. (The Bold button is the bold, capital "B.")

Adding the New Style to the Style List

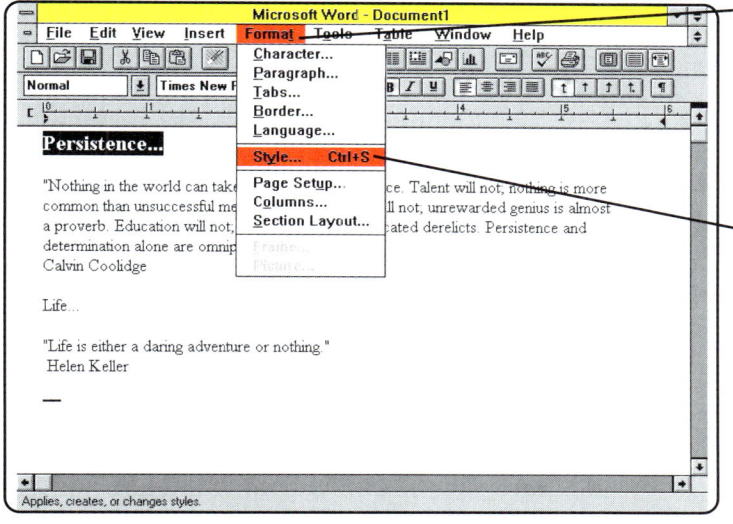

1. With "Persistence..." still highlighted, **click** on **Format** in the menu bar. A pull-down menu will appear.

2. **Click** on **Style**. The Style dialog box will appear.

Notice that "Normal" is highlighted in the Style Name box. This is the style that Word uses to set up new documents.

Notice the description of the Normal style matches the font selection you made in Chapter 1.

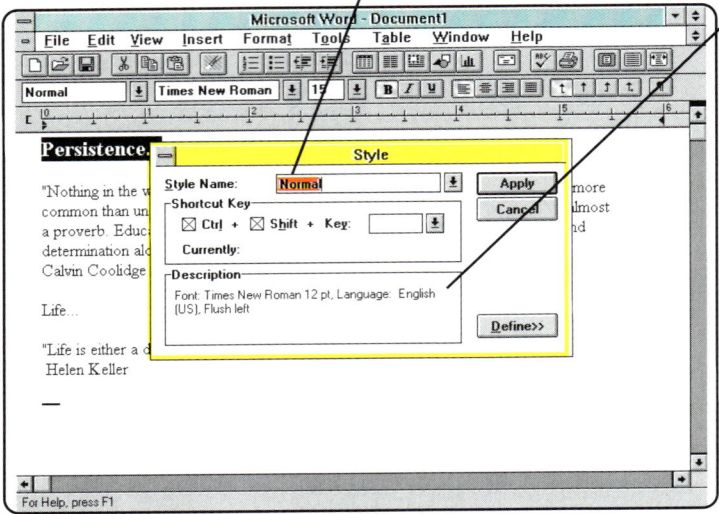

3. **Type quoteheader**. It will replace the highlighted text.

Notice the description changes to match the font style of "Persistence..."

4. **Click** on **Apply**. The Style dialog box will disappear.

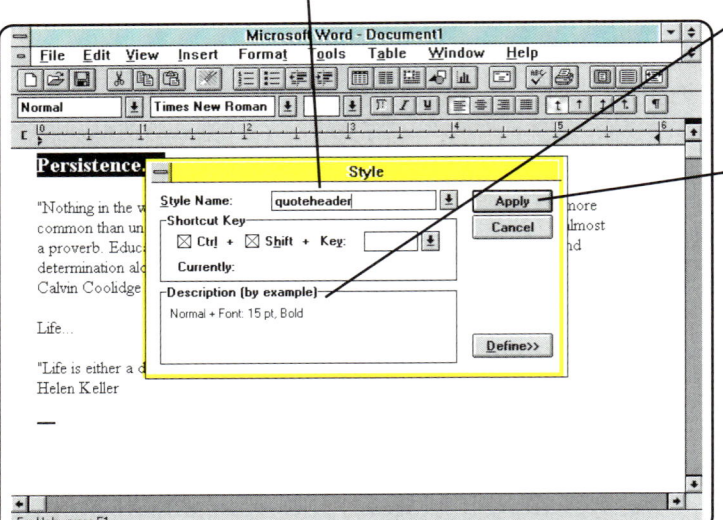

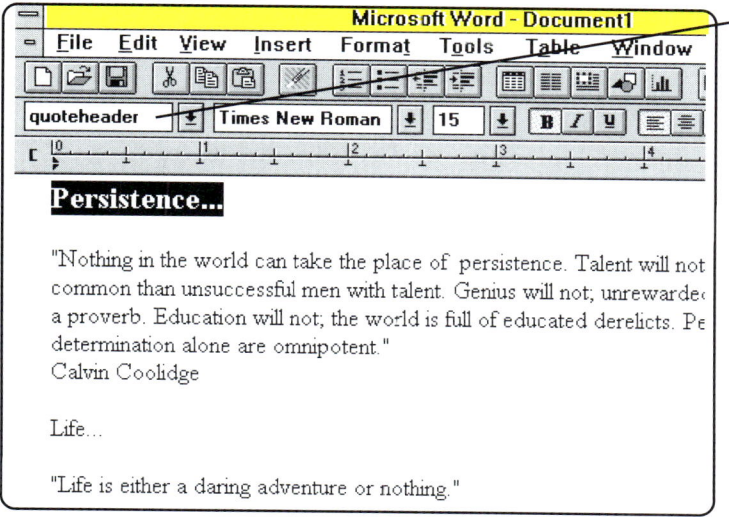

Notice that the quoteheader style you just created is shown in the Style box on the ribbon because the highlighted word is in the quoteheader style.

Setting Up a New Style for the Body Text

In this section you will create a new style for the body of the text.

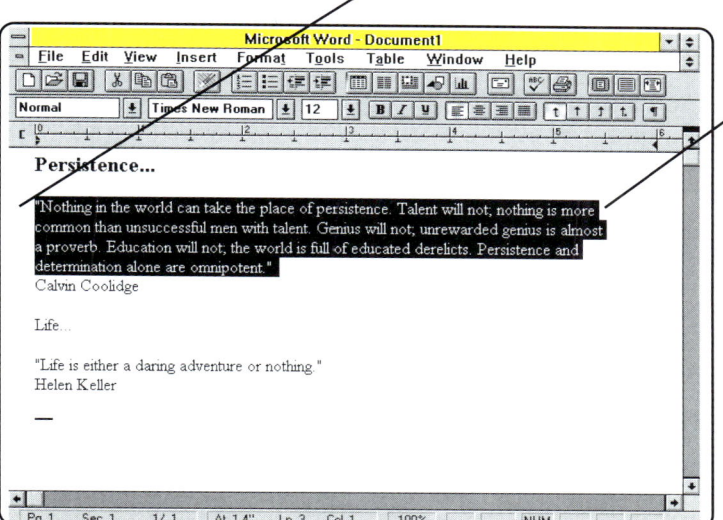

1. **Place** the mouse pointer in the left margin **beside the first line** of the quote. It will change to an arrow.

2. **Click twice** to highlight the entire paragraph.

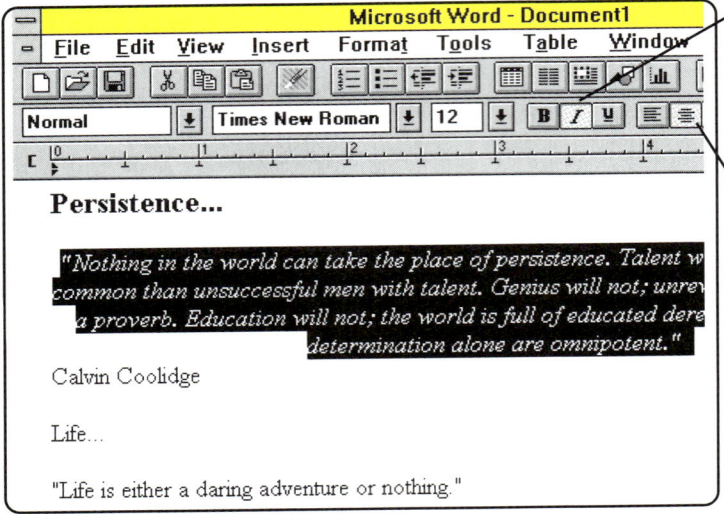

3. Click on the **Italics button** in the ribbon to change the highlighted text to italics.

4. Click on the **Center button** in the ribbon to center the highlighted text.

5. Click on **Format** in the menu bar. A pull-down menu will appear.

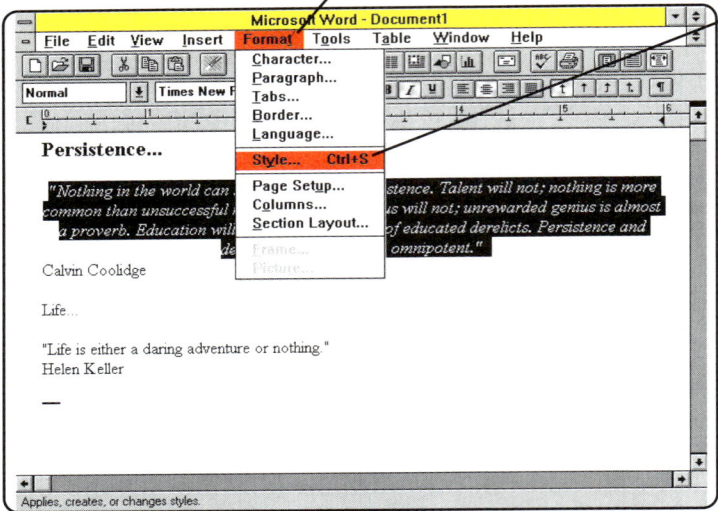

16. Click on **Style**. The Style dialog box will appear.

CHAPTER 18: INTRODUCING STYLES

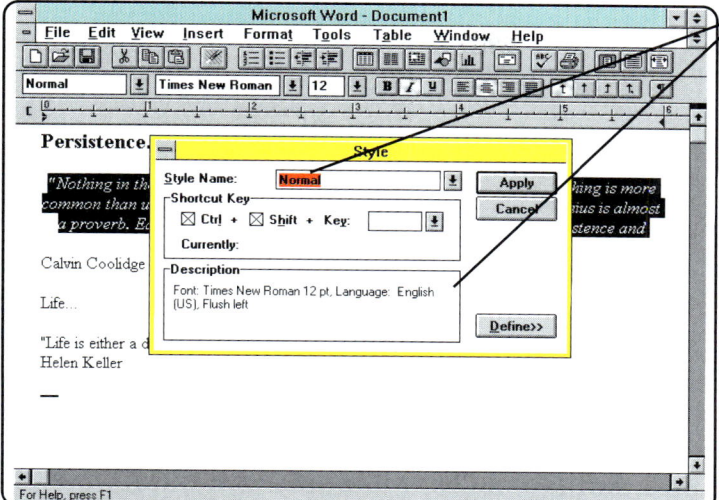

Notice that the style name is Normal and the description matches the font selection you made in Chapter 1.

7. Type quote. It will replace the highlighted text in the Style Name box.

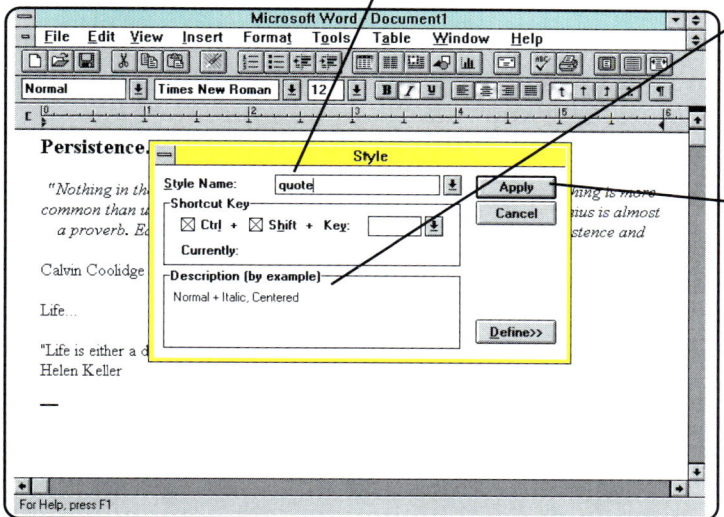

Notice that the description changes to reflect the style of the highlighted text in the document.

8. Click on **Apply**. The dialog box will disappear.

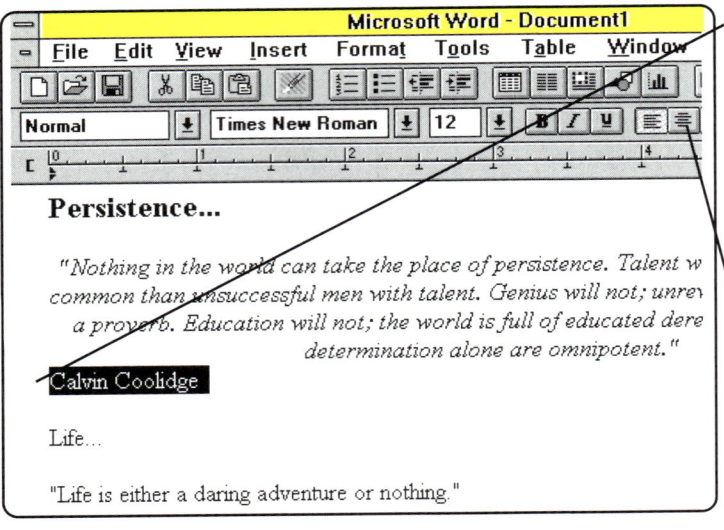

9. Place the mouse pointer in the left margin **beside "Calvin Coolidge."** It will change to an arrow.

10. Click to highlight the name.

11. Click on the **Center button** in the ribbon to center the name.

Viewing the Style List

Now you should open the Styles list box to make sure the two styles that you just created are on the list.

1. Click anywhere on the letter to remove the highlighting from "Calvin Coolidge."

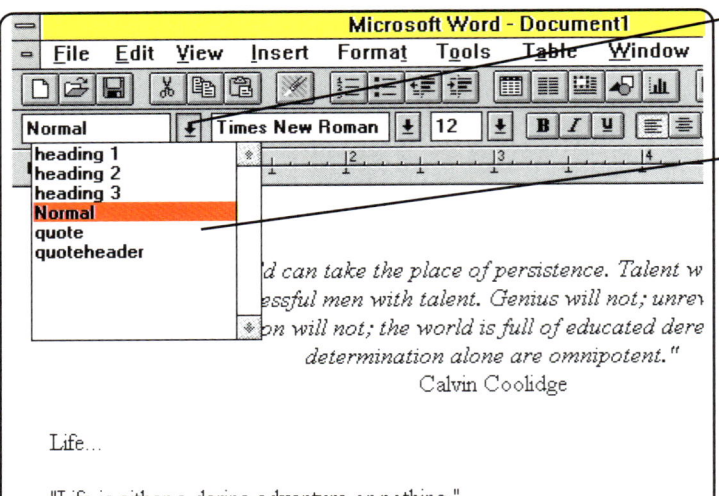

2. Click on ↓ to the right of the Style box. A drop-down list of styles will appear.

Notice that the styles you just created, quote and quoteheader, are on the list of styles available for this document.

3. Click anywhere on the letter to close the drop-down list.

APPLYING THE NEW STYLES TO DIFFERENT TEXT

1. **Place** the mouse pointer in the left margin **beside** "**Life...**" It will change to an arrow.

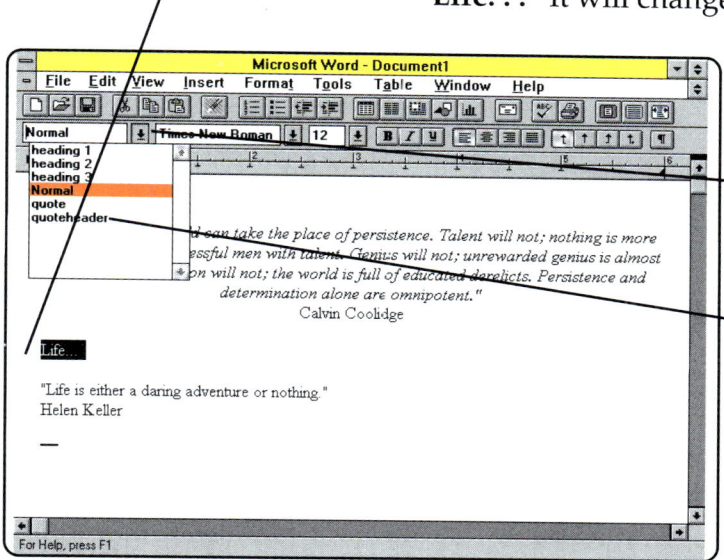

2. **Click** to highlight the line.

3. **Click** on ↓ to the right of the Style box. A drop-down list of styles will appear.

4. **Click** on **quoteheader** to change the style of "Life..."

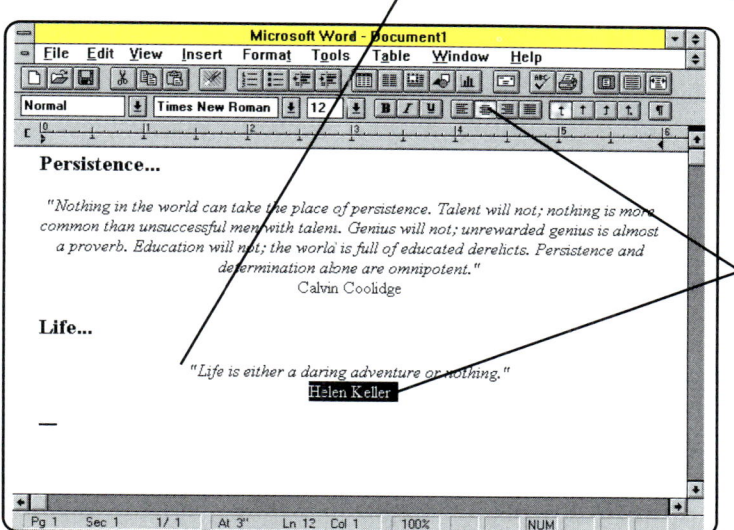

5. **Repeat steps 1 through 4** to apply the quote style to the text. The text will appear in italics and centered as shown here.

6. **Repeat steps 1 and 2** to highlight "Helen Keller."

7. **Click** on the **Center button** to center the name.

PERMANENTLY SAVING THE NEW STYLES

If you create a new style and would like to use it in other documents, you must first save it as part of the current document and then copy the style to the new document.

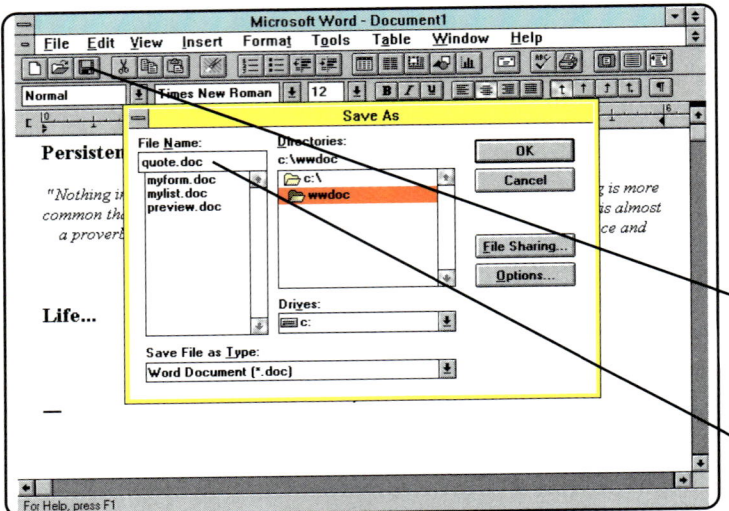

1. Click on the **Save tool**. The Save As dialog box will appear.

2. Type quote.doc in the File Name box.

3. Click on **OK**. The Summary Info dialog box will appear.

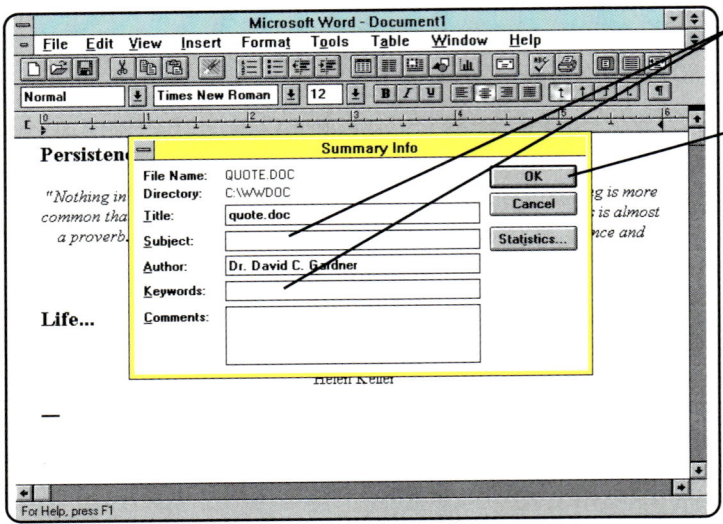

4. Type the appropriate information if desired.

5. Click on **OK**. Word will save the document along with the new styles you created.

COPYING THE NEW STYLES TO ANOTHER DOCUMENT

The best way to transfer styles to another document is to use the Windows Copy and Paste option.

1. Click in the left margin **beside "Persistence."** The line will be highlighted.

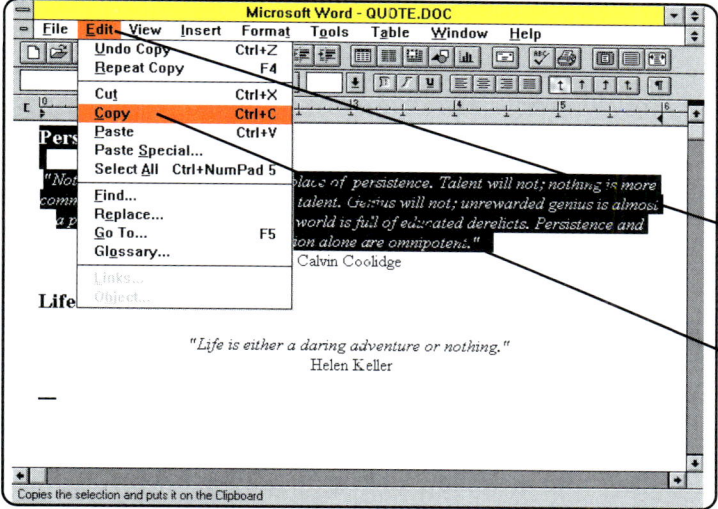

2. Press and hold the **Shift key** and **click** in the left margin **beside the last line** of the quotation. The heading and the quotation will be highlighted.

3. Click on **Edit** in the menu bar. A pull-down menu will appear.

4. Click on **Copy**. You will not see any change on your screen, but the highlighted text is now copied to the Clipboard.

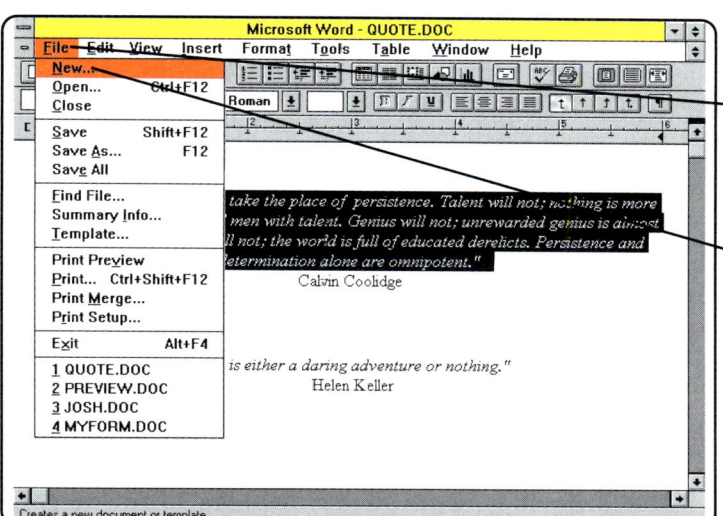

5. Click on **File** in the menu bar. A pull-down menu will appear.

6. Click on **New**. The New dialog box will appear.

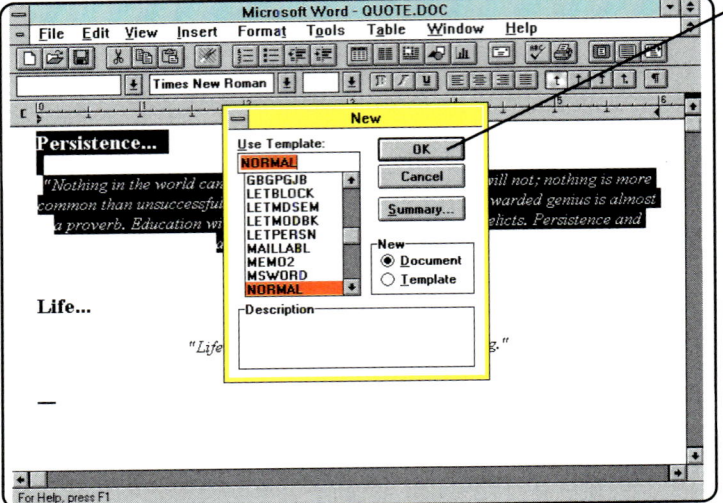

7. **Click** on **OK**. A new document screen, entitled "Document2" will appear.

It's okay if your document has another number.

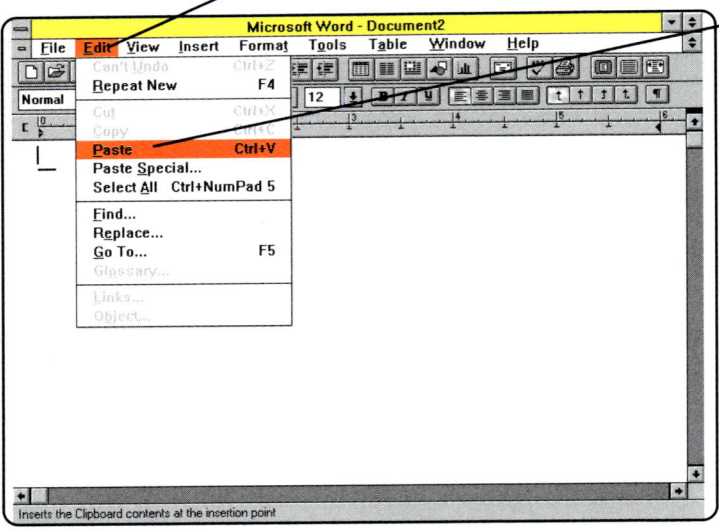

8. **Click** on **Edit** in the menu bar. A pull-down menu will appear.

9. **Click** on **Paste**. The heading and the quotation will appear in the document.

Viewing the Style List

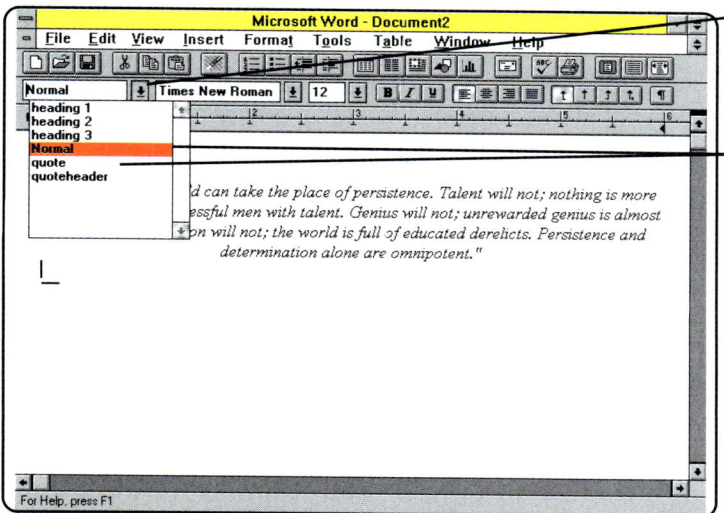

1. **Click** on ↓ to the right of the Style box. A drop-down list of styles will appear.

Notice that the new styles, quote and quoteheader, are now on the list of available styles in this second document.

Since you copied the text to this document just to transfer the styles, you should highlight and delete the text now. The text will be deleted, but the styles remain in the new document. Now you can apply the new styles to any text in this document by repeating steps 1 through 5 in the "Applying the New Styles to Different Text" section earlier in this chapter.

EXITING WORD

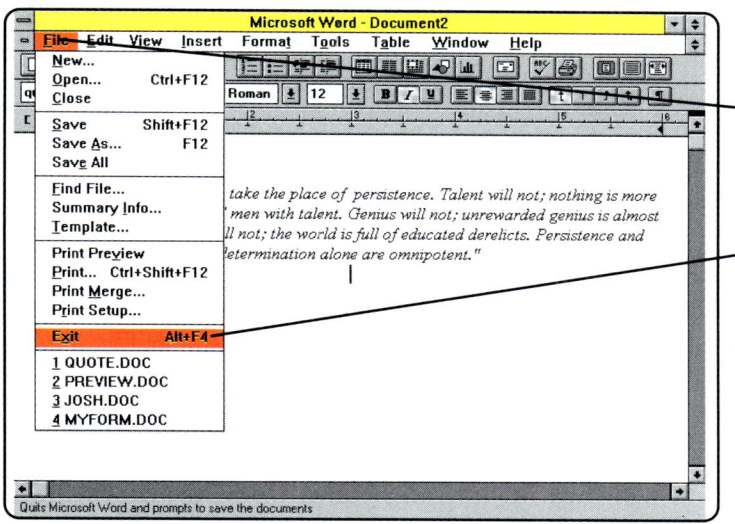

1. **Click** on **File** in the menu bar. A pull-down menu will appear.

2. **Click** on **Exit**. A Microsoft Word dialog box will appear.

Since you created this document simply to practice transferring a style to a new document, you don't need to save this document.

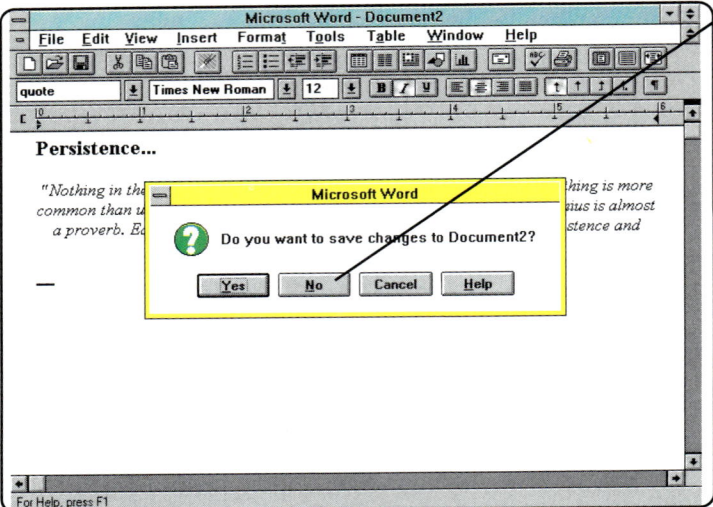

3. **Click** on **No**. You will be returned to the Program Manager.

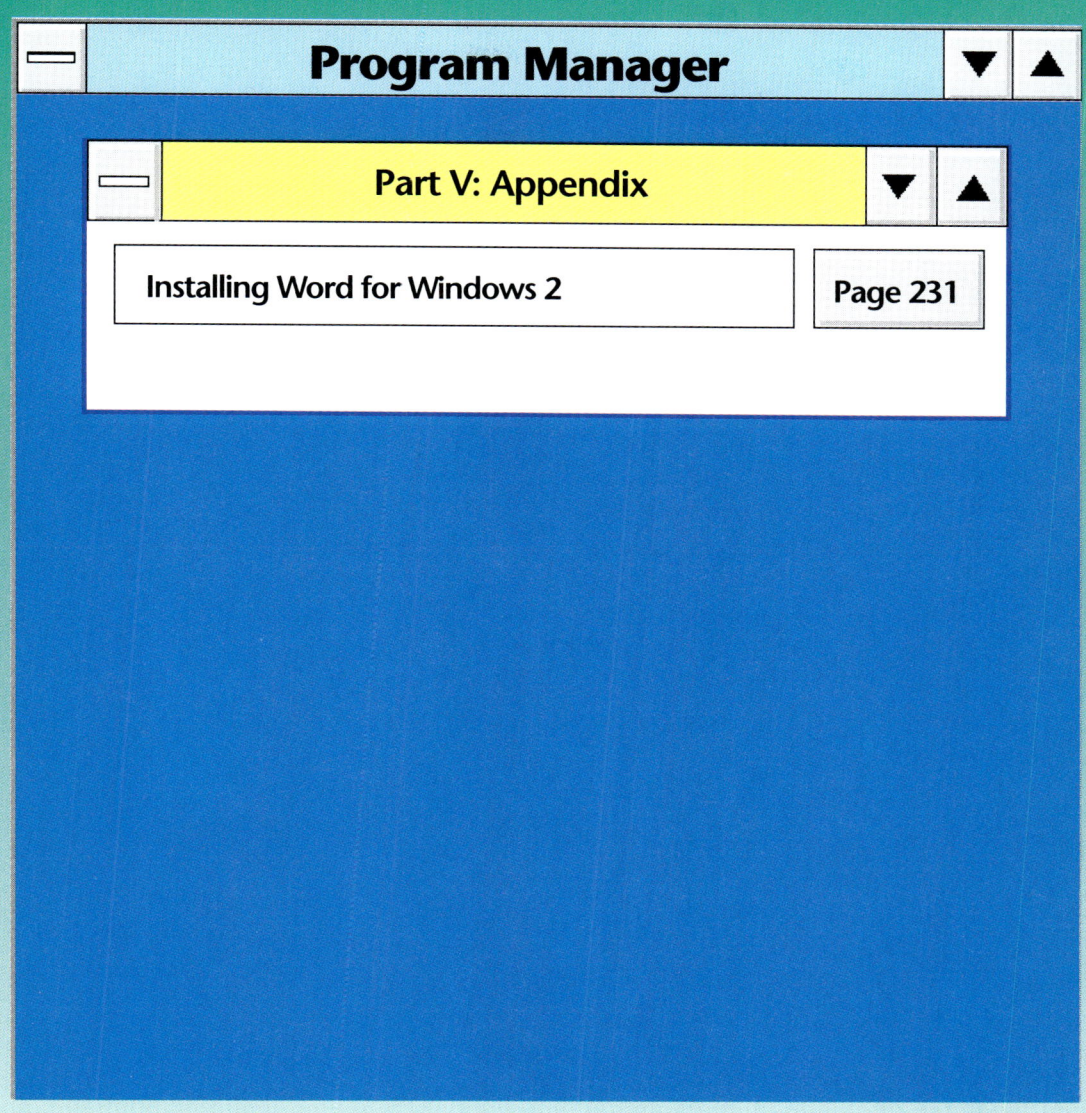

APPENDIX

Installing Word for Windows 2

In this appendix you will:

❖ Make backup copies of your Word for Windows 2 disks
❖ Install Word
❖ Move Word to your customized group window

Note: If you are using a screen saver, we recommend turning it off before installing. In some cases, screen savers can interfere with the installation.

BACKING UP YOUR WORD DISKS

Before you start, make certain that you have a supply of formatted disks handy!

1. Type diskcopy a: a: (or b: b:) and **press Enter**. There is a space after "diskcopy" and after the first "a:". The message, "Insert SOURCE diskette in drive A: (or B:)" will appear.

```
C:\>diskcopy a: a:

Insert SOURCE diskette
in drive A:

Press any key to continue . . .

Copying 88 tracks
18 sectors per track,
2 side(s)

Insert TARGET diskette
in drive A:
```

2. Insert the **Word disk** to be copied in **drive A** (or B). Remember, if you are copying *from* a 1.4MB (megabyte) floppy, you must copy to a 1.4MB floppy. If you try *to* use the Diskcopy command to copy to a different capacity floppy, DOS will not let you do so. (If you are familiar with File Manager or have a copy program such as CopyQM, feel free to use a different method.)

WORD FOR WINDOWS 2: THE VISUAL LEARNING GUIDE

3. **Press Enter and follow the directions** on your screen. Remember, the *SOURCE* diskette is the Word disk. The *TARGET* diskette is the blank formatted disk. It takes a number of passes to copy a disk completely. Continue to insert the same SOURCE disk and the same TARGET disk until you are asked if you want to copy another diskette.

```
Insert SOURCE diskette in drive A:
Press any key to continue. . .
Insert TARGET diskette in drive A:
Press any key to continue. . .
Insert SOURCE diskette in drive A:
Press any key to continue. . .
Insert TARGET diskette in drive A:
Press any key to continue. . .
Volume Serial Number is 22DG-1J1B
Copy another diskette (Y/N)?
```

4. **Type y** to begin the process again with the second Word disk and a second blank TARGET disk. Repeat the process until all the Word disks are copied.

5. When you have copied all of the disks, **put your original disks in a safe place!**

INSTALLING WORD FOR WINDOWS 2

1. **Open** Windows by **typing win** at the DOS prompt (C:\>). The Program Manager opening screen will appear. Your screen may look different from this one.

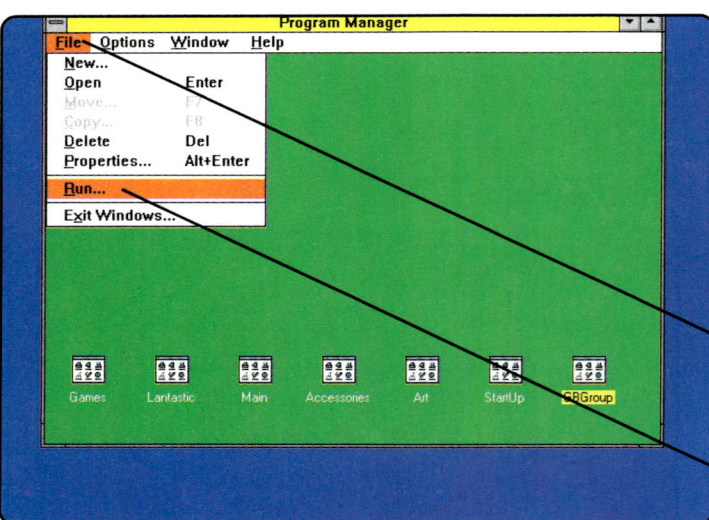

2. **Insert your backup copy of Word Disk 1-Setup** in drive A. (Be certain to use your *backup* copies throughout the installation.)

3. **Click** on **File** in the menu bar. A pull-down menu will appear.

4. **Click** on **Run**. The Run dialog box will appear.

APPENDIX: INSTALLING WORD FOR WINDOWS 2   233

Notice that the cursor is flashing in the Command Line box. When you start typing, the cursor will disappear.

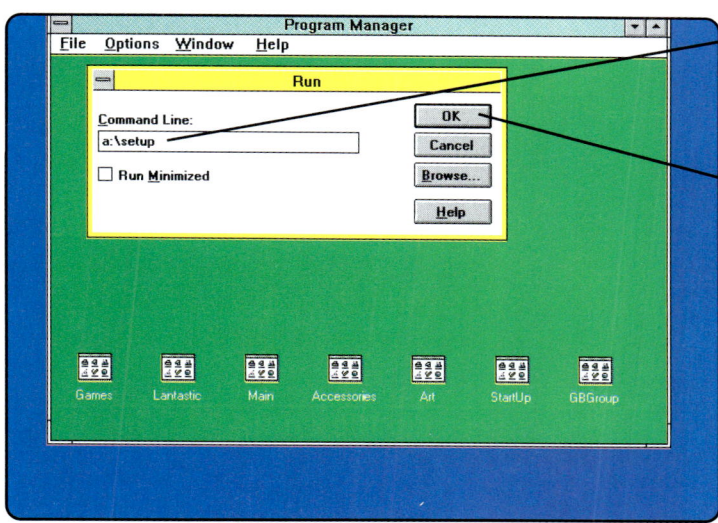

5. **Type a:\setup** (or b:\setup) in the Command Line box.

6. **Click** on **OK**. The hourglass will appear briefly along with a Microsoft Setup message box that says "Initializing Setup..." Next, the User Information for Microsoft Word dialog box will appear.

Notice that the cursor is flashing in the Name box. When you start typing, the cursor will disappear.

7. **Type** your **full name** in the Name box and then **press Tab** to move the cursor to the Organization box.

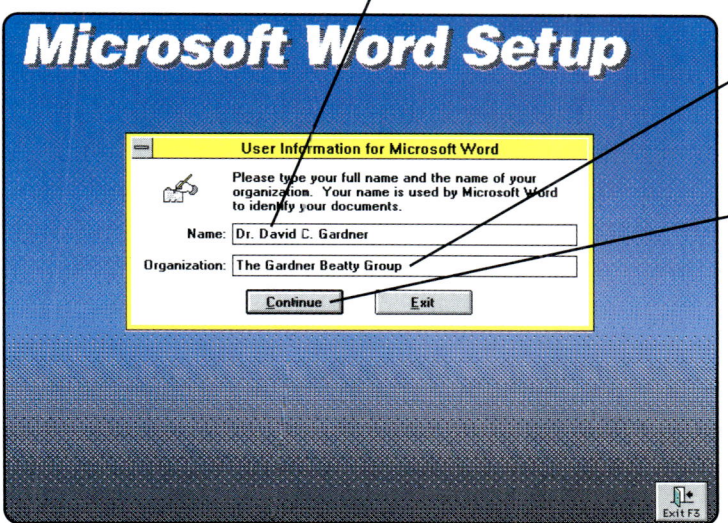

8. **Type** the **name of your organization** in the Organization box.

9. **Click** on **Continue**. A second User Information for Microsoft Word dialog box will appear asking you to verify that the information you typed is correct.

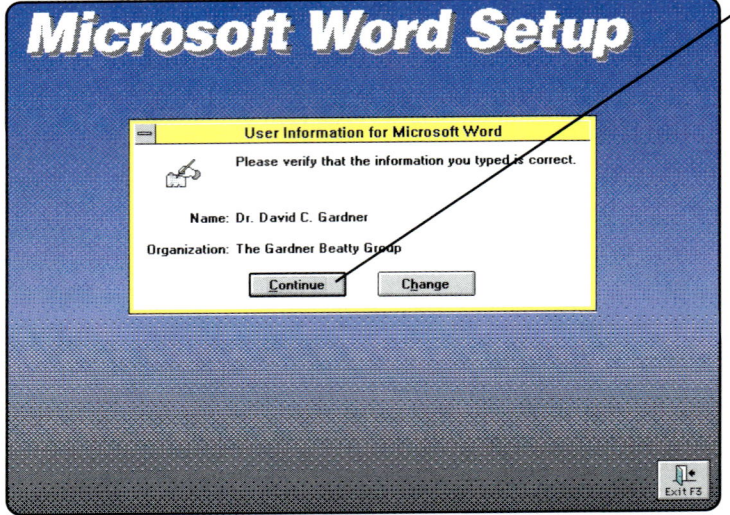

10. **Click** on **Continue** if the information is correct. The Microsoft Word 2.0 Setup dialog box will appear.

If the information is not correct, **click** on **Change**. The previous dialog box will appear. After making your corrections, **click** on **Continue** to return to this dialog box. If you do not type text in the Organization box, the installation will not continue.

11. **Click** on **Continue**. A smaller Microsoft Word 2.0 Setup dialog box will appear in the foreground.

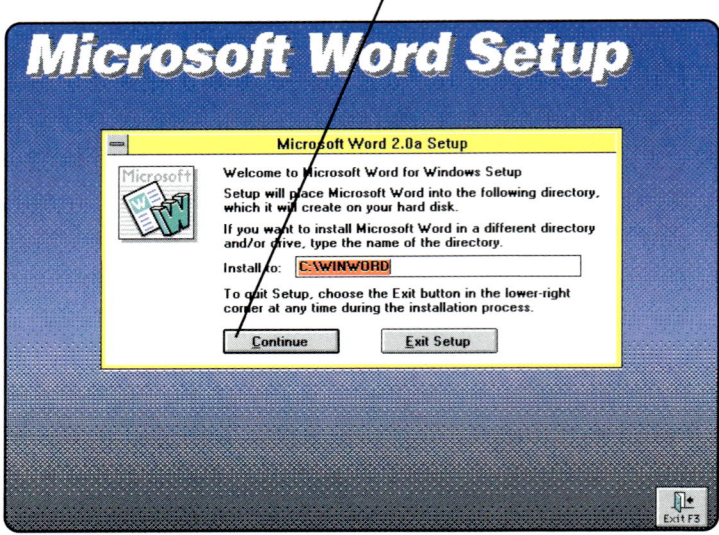

APPENDIX: INSTALLING WORD FOR WINDOWS 2   235

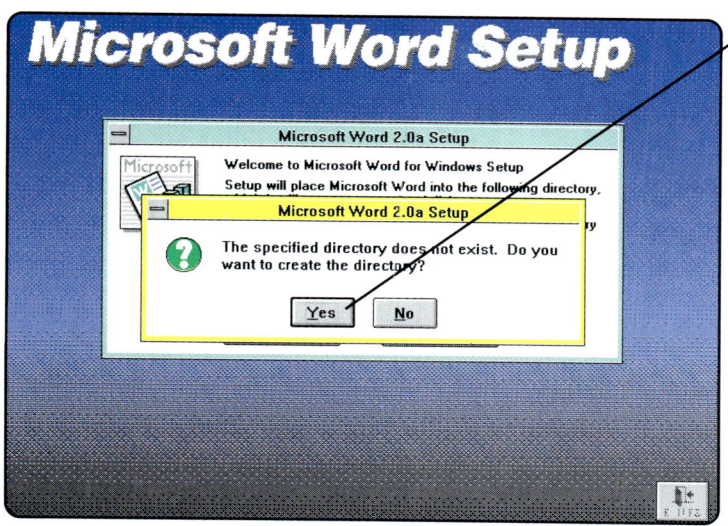

12. Click on **Yes**. A message box saying "Please wait while Setup checks for available disk space" will appear briefly. Then the Microsoft Word for Windows 2.0 dialog box will appear.

13. Click on **Complete Installation** to follow the procedures in this book.

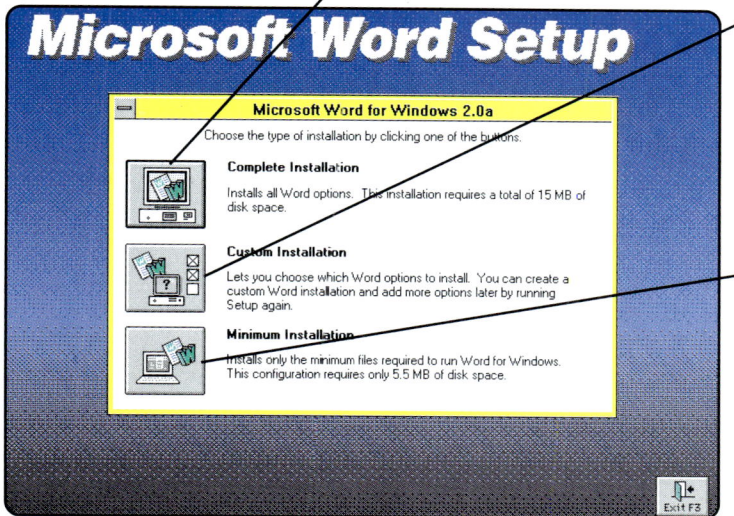

❖ If you are an experienced Word user you may **click** on the **Custom Installation option**. The Custom Installation procedure is not covered in this book.

❖ If you are worried about how much disk space you have, **click** on the **Minimum Installation option**. The Minimum Installation procedure is not covered in this book.

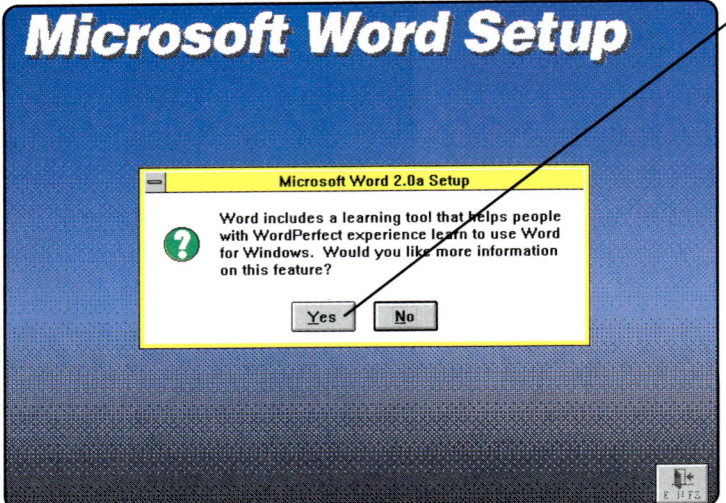

14. **Click** on **Yes** if you have had experience with WordPerfect. The Enable WordPerfect Help System dialog box will appear. Otherwise, **click** on **No**.

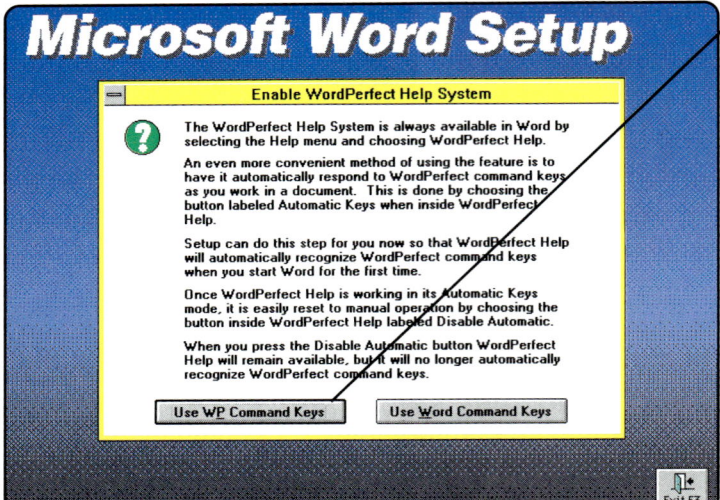

15. **Click** on **Use WP Command Keys** if you want to use the WordPerfect options described on the screen. If you are an experienced Word user (or have never used WordPerfect), **click** on **Use Word Command Keys**. The Microsoft Word 2.0 Setup box will appear.

APPENDIX: INSTALLING WORD FOR WINDOWS 2   237

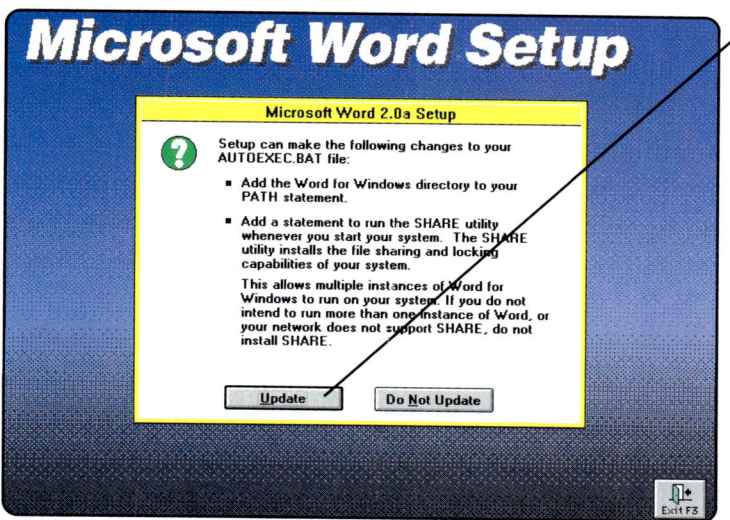

16. Click on **Update**. Word will begin copying files from Disk 1.

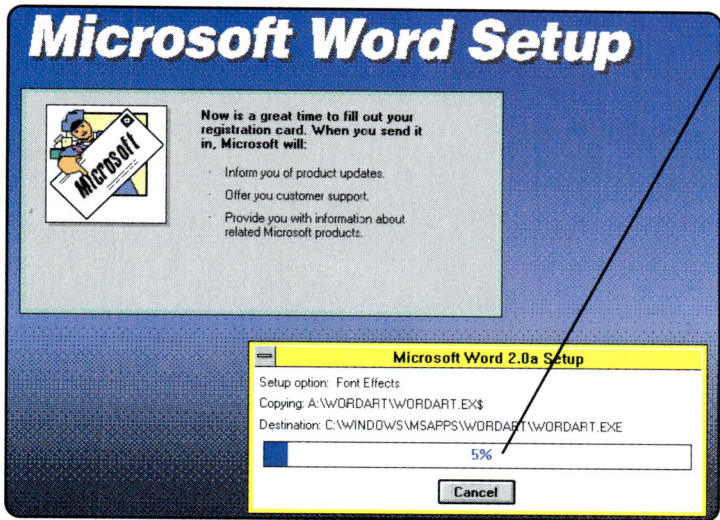

Notice that Word shows you the percentage of files copied as it copies them from the disk in drive A. This may take a while, so be patient. The first time we installed Word we thought something was wrong because nothing seemed to be happening for quite some time. Then all of a sudden Word began to whiz through the copying!

When the files on Disk 1 have been copied, an additional Microsoft Word 2.0 Setup dialog box will appear in the center foreground of your screen. If you have not turned off your screen saver, the appearance of this dialog box may blank your screen. If this happens, press any key to return to the installation screen.

17. Remove Disk 1 from drive A and **insert Disk 2** in drive A.

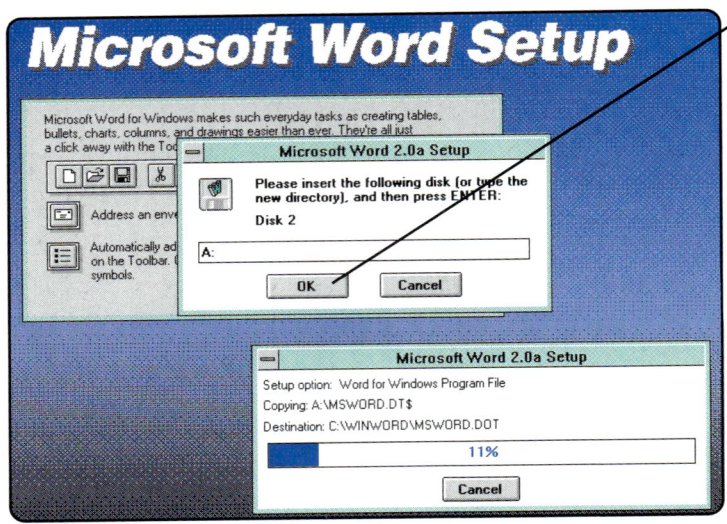

18. Click on **OK** or **press Enter**. The second Setup dialog box will disappear. Word will begin copying the files on Disk 2.

If copying seems to take forever, just hang in there. You are doing fine!

19. Remove Disk 2 from drive A and **insert Disk 3** in drive A.

20. Click on **OK**. Word will begin copying the files on Disk 3. **Repeat** this process for Disks 4, 5, and 6.

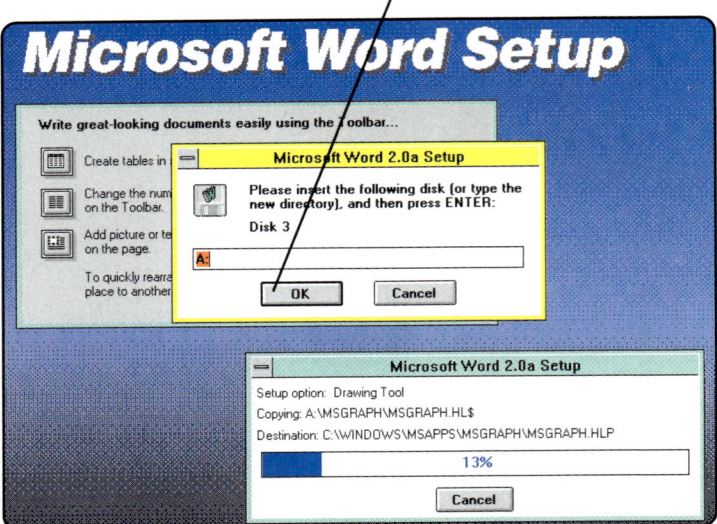

When Word has completed copying all the files in Disk 6, the following message will appear briefly on the screen: "Please wait while Setup updates WIN.INI and other settings."

Then the Microsoft Word Setup is complete! dialog box will appear.

APPENDIX: INSTALLING WORD FOR WINDOWS 2   239

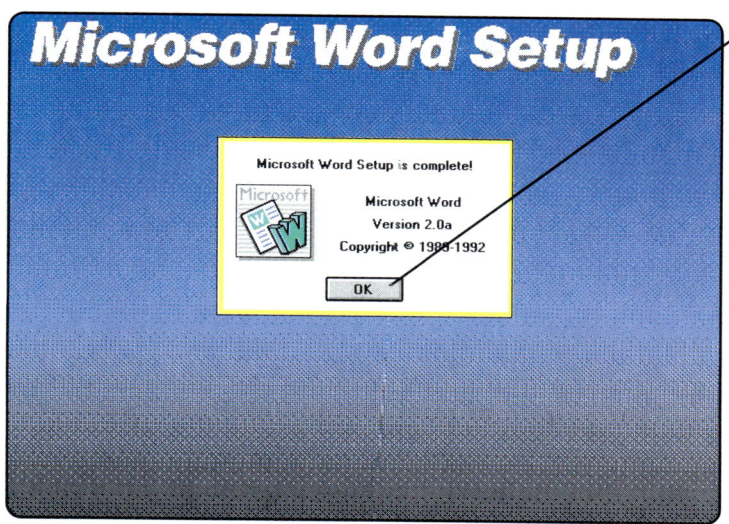

21. Click on **OK**. The Word for Windows 2.0 group window will appear. It may appear in a different size or location than the one shown here.

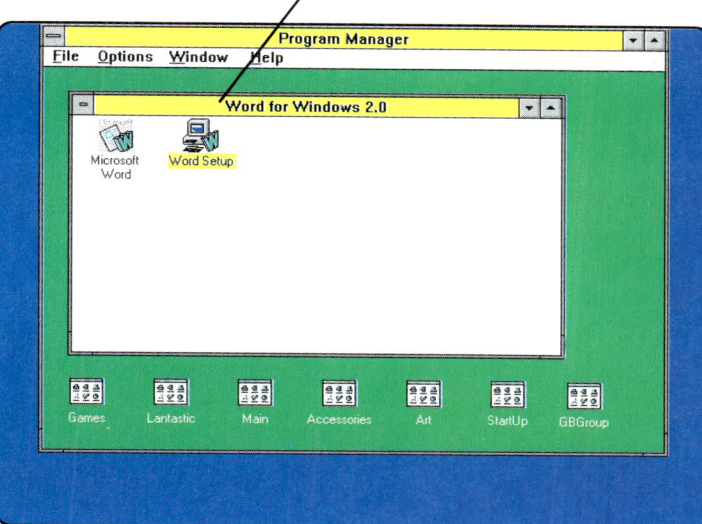

Congratulations! You have successfully installed Word.

You can leave the Word program icons in this group window or move them to another group window. Many people store the programs they use most in a customized group window. If you want to do that, go on to the next page to move the Word program icons to your own customized group window. If not, you can go to the "Introduction" at the beginning of this book, select your first learning goal, and have fun.

MOVING WORD TO YOUR CUSTOMIZED GROUP WINDOW

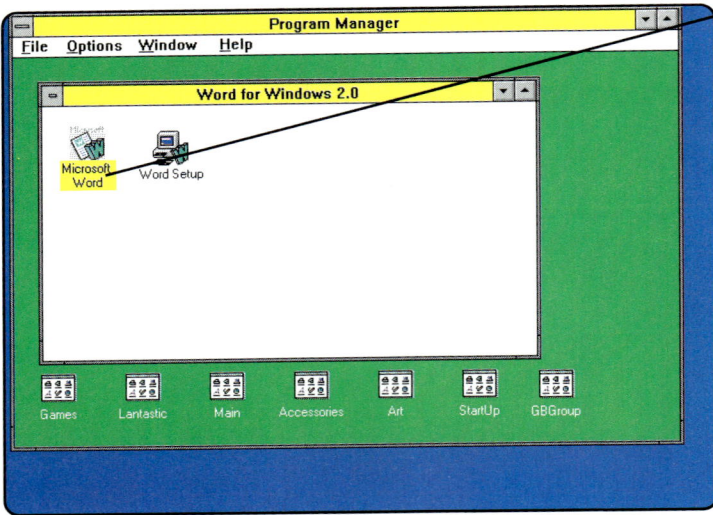

1. **Move** the mouse arrow to the **Word program icon**.

2. **Press and hold** the mouse button as you **drag** the **Word program icon** to your customized group icon at the bottom of your Program Manager screen. The icon will change briefly to a circle and then change back to the Word program icon. Your screen and group icons may be different from those you see here.

3. **Release** the mouse button when the Word icon is on top of your customized group icon. The Word icon will disappear into your customized group icon. In this example, the Word icon is now located in the GBGroup icon.

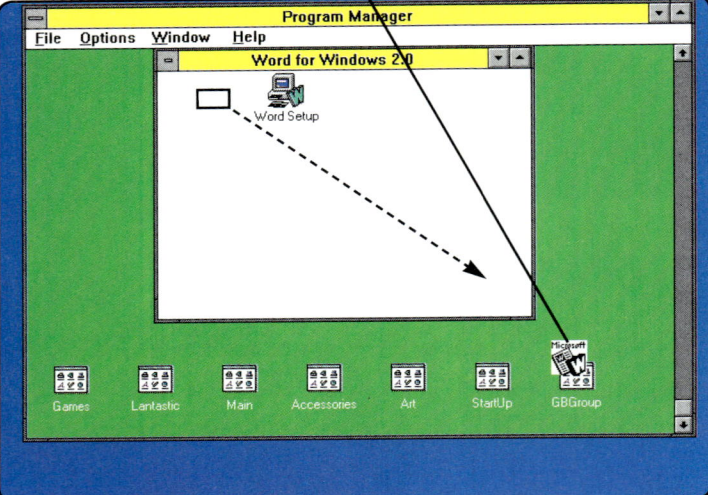

4. **Repeat** the process for the Word Setup icon. We suggest that you place the Word Setup icon in the Windows Main group as a matter of convenience. (**Note:** you can also perform this procedure with other desktop programs.)

APPENDIX: INSTALLING WORD FOR WINDOWS 2   241

Deleting the Word Group Icon

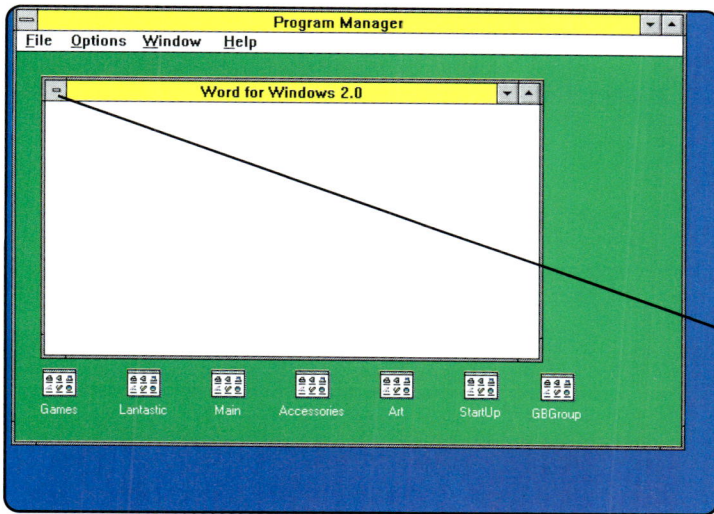

You have moved the Word program icons to your customized group window and Main group window. Now, you can delete the Word for Windows 2.0 group since it no longer serves a useful purpose.

1. **Click twice** on the **Control menu box** (□) on the left of the Word group window title bar. The Word group icon will appear at the bottom of your Program Manager screen.

2. **Click once** on the **Word group icon**. (Make certain that you do not click twice.) The Word group icon title will be highlighted and a pop-up menu will appear. Ignore the pop-up menu and go on to step 3.

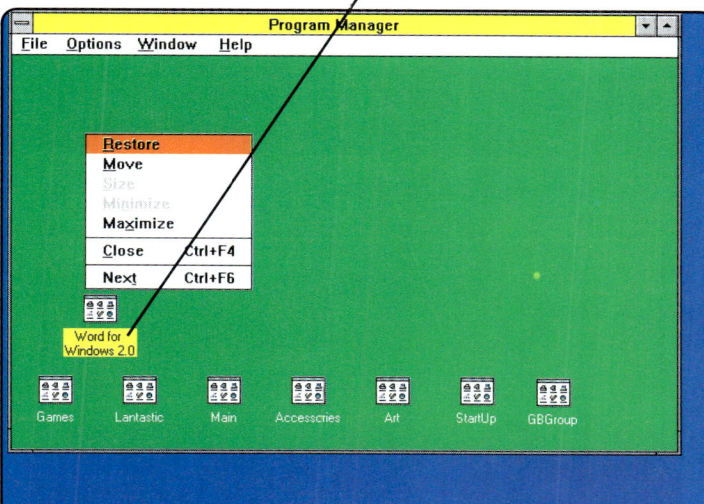

3. **Click** on **File** in the menu bar. A pull-down menu will appear and the pop-up menu will disappear.

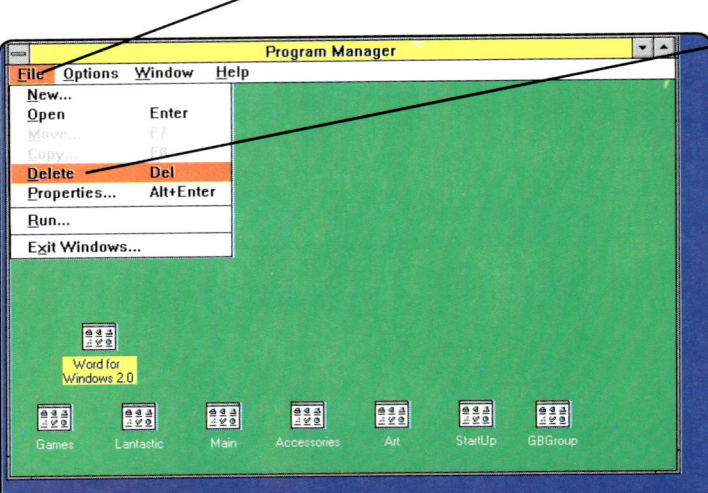

4. **Click** on **Delete**. The pull-down menu will disappear. The Delete dialog box will appear. Don't panic when you see the next message. You are only erasing an *empty* group window.

5. **Click** on **Yes**. The Delete dialog box will disappear, the Word for Windows 2.0 group window will be deleted and you will be returned to Program Manager.

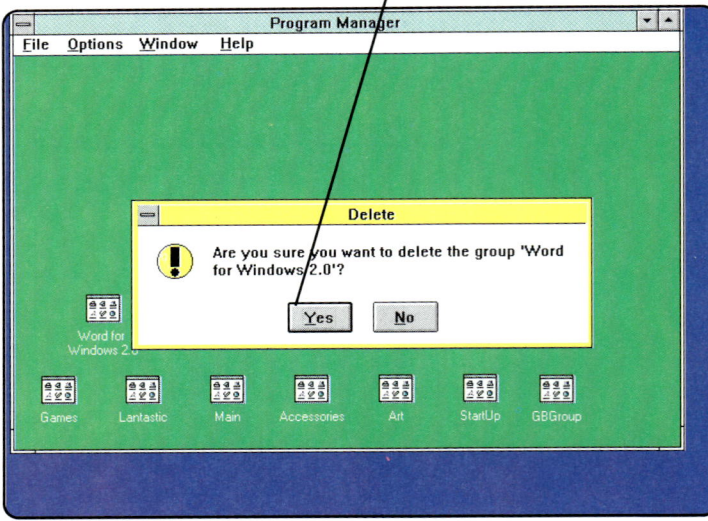

Index

A

Adding letters and words to text, 55-57
Addresses. *See also* Envelopes; Form letters; Return address
   entering address, 14
   mailing lists, entering names and addresses for, 155-157
Automatic page break, 16
Automatic saving, 37-38

B

Backing up work disks, 231-232
Bird's eye view. *See* Print Preview
Boldfacing
   in Draft view, 125
   return address, first line of, 142-143
   text, 84
Booting up Word, 3, 41
Borders, 89-90
   shading boxed text, 91-92
Bulleted lists, 93-94

C

Cells, 154
Center-aligned tabs set with mouse, 105-106
Centering text, 86-87
Clearing tabs, 102-103
Clicking, 4
Clipboard. *See* Copying and pasting text
Closing
   attached envelope, closing without saving, 146-147
   File Manager, 30
   files, 40
   styles, 227-228
   Word, 40, 206
Collate box, 79
Colors of desktop, 120
Combining paragraphs, 59-69
Converting mailing lists. *See* Mailing lists
Copies box, 79
Copying and pasting text, 68-75
   with Copy tool, 72
   with form letters, 178
   with Go To command, 73-74
   with Paste tool, 74-75
   styles, copying of, 225-226
Copy tool, 72
Create Directory dialog box, 29
Custom installation procedure, 235
Customizing. *See also* Text
   dictionary, 46
   moving Word to customized group window, 240-242
   return address, 137-143

243

D

Database Management tools, 161-165
Data entry table. *See* Mailing lists
Date, entry of, 14
Decimal tabs. *See* Tabs
Defaults
 margins, 7
 for return address, 136
 ribbon settings, 88
Deleting
 page breaks, 114
 Word group icon, 241-242
 words, 57-58
Dictionary. *See* Spelling and Grammar
  Checker
Directories. *See also* Searching for files
 checking new directories, 30
 creating directories, 28-29
 list of, 33-34
 naming directories, 29
 working directory statement, changes
  to, 30-32
Directory Tree search, 204
Diskcopy for work disks, 231
Documents. *See also* Editing; Form
  letters; Searching for files
 closing, 40
 naming, 33-35
 saving, 33-37, 39
 two sections, separating document
  into, 111-113
DOS mailing lists, conversion of, 187-190
Dot-matrix printers, envelopes with,
 133-135
Double-clicking, 4
Draft view, 124-125
 Normal view, return to, 125
Drag and drop moving, 63-65

E

Editing, 55-76. *See also* Page breaks
 adding letters and words, 55-57
 copying and pasting text, 68-75
 deleting words, 57-58
 drag and drop moving, 63-65
 mailing lists, 159-160, 195
 replace command, 62-63
 replacing words and paragraphs, 57-58
 saving edited files, 75-76
 soft return, insertion of, 60-61
 typing over highlighted text, 75-76
 undoing edit, 58-59
End mark, 11
Envelopes, 141-147. *See also* Mailing
  lists; Return address
 attached envelopes, 137-138
  closing without saving, 146-147
  letter, printing envelope without, 145
  printing letter and, 143-144
  without attached envelope,
   printing letter, 245-146
 closing without saving attached
  envelopes, 146-147
 with dot-matrix printers, 133-135
 with LaserJet Series II and III printers,
  131-133
 return address, printing of, 135-136
Envelope tool, 131
Exiting. *See* Closing

F

File dialog box
 opening of, 199
File Manager
 changing view of, 27

INDEX

closing, 30
maximizing File Manager, 27
opening of, 25-26
Files. *See* Documents
File Save tool, 33
Find command in Thesaurus, 51-52
First time, opening Word for, 3-6
Fonts. *See also* Point size
automatic page break and, 16
changing fonts, 8-9
in Draft view, 124
for return address, 139-142
size, changing of, 10-11
Wingdings, 18-24
Footers, creation of, 116-117
Formatting. *See* Styles
Form letters
attaching envelope to, 184
converted mailing lists, attaching of, 190-192
mailing lists, attaching of, 169-171
merge fields into address and salutation of, 171-175
personalized information
body of letter, insertion in, 175-176
header, inserting into, 177-178
printing of, 178-179
saving, 180-181

G

Glossaries, 207-213
creating Glossary item, 207-209
inserting Glossary item in new file, 209-211
saving Glossary item, 211-213
Go To command, 73-74
Grammar Checker. *See* Spelling and Grammar Checker

H

Hard returns, 60-61
Header record. *See* Mailing lists
Headers
creation of, 114-116
personalized information inserted into header of form letter, 177-178
with right-aligned tab, 97-99
style for heading, setting up, 216-217
Highlighted text, typing over, 75-76

I

Icons
clicking on, 4
deleting Word group icon, 241-242
Insertion point, 11
Installing Word, 232-239
backing up work disks, 231-232
Italicizing
in Draft view, 125
text, 85

K

Keyword, searching with, 202-203

L

LaserJet Series II and III printers, 131
Letterhead
creating letterheads, 11-12
margins for, 8
Letters. *See* Text

M

Mailing lists, 149-158
   adding fields to data file, 161-165
   cells, 154
   converted lists
      DOS-based list, conversion of, 187-190
      errors in, 192
      form letter, attaching converted list to, 190-192
      header record, adding of, 193-195
      header record added to, 193-195
      saving converted files, 189-190
   data entry table
      field names, entering of, 151-154
      names and addresses, entering of, 155-157
      setting up, 149-154
   DOS-based list, conversion of, 187-190
   editing of, 159-160, 195
   envelopes
      addressing of, 183-184
      attaching envelope to form letter, 184
      exiting without saving, 186
      merge printing of, 185
      saving envelopes, 186
   exiting without saving envelopes, 186
   field names, entering of, 151-154
   form letter, attaching list to, 169-171
   header record, 154
      checking of, 194-195
      converted list, adding to, 193-195
   letter, attaching list to, 159-160
   more data, entering of, 165-168
   names and addresses into data entry table, 155-157
   new document file, opening of, 149-150
   opening
      new document file, 148-150
      Print Merge Setup dialog box, 150
   saving, 158
      converted files, 189-190
      envelopes, 186
   updating of, 165-168
Margins
   automatic page break and, 16
   for letterhead stationery, 8
   Print Preview, display in, 122-123
   right margin, 15
   setting of, 7-8
   two sections, separating document into, 111-113
Maximize button
   clicking on, 5
   for File Manager, 27
Menu bar. *See also* Tabs
   left-aligned tabs set from, 99-101
   Normal view, return to, 125
   printing from, 78
Minimum installation option, 235
Moving Word to customized group window, 240-242

N

Naming
   directories, 29
   files, 33-35

O

Opening. *See also* Mailing lists
   File Manager, 25-26
   first time, opening Word for, 3-6
   saved files, 41-43
   tabs with new document, 104
Option button, 7

P

Page breaks
   automatic page break, 16
   changing position of, 67
   deleting, 114
   insertion of, 65-66
   two sections, separating document into, 111-113
Page Layout view, 119-121
   scrolling through pages in, 120-121
Page Setup for margins, 7
Paragraphs
   bulleted lists, 93-94
   combining, 59-69
   replacing, 57-58
   symbol, display of, 13
Paste tool, 74-75
Pasting text. *See* Copying and pasting text
Personalized information. *See* Form letters
Point size, 10-11. *See also* Fonts
   changes, 83-84
   in Draft view, 124
   for return address, 139-142
Printers for envelopes, 131
Printing, 77-80. *See also* Envelopes
   entire document, 80
   form letters, 178-179
   from menu bar, 78
   in Print Preview, 123-124
   with Print tool, 77-78
   selected pages, 79
Print Merge feature. *See* Mailing lists
Print Preview, 80, 121-124
   margins, display of, 122-123
   printing in, 123-124
   scrolling through pages in, 122
Print tool, 77-78
   with shaded text, 92

R

Reading the ribbon, 88-89
Replace command, 62-63
Replacing words and paragraphs in text, 57-58
Return address
   boldfacing first line of, 142-143
   customizing of, 137-143
   defaults for, 136
   fonts, changing of, 139-142
   omitting and restoring of, 137
   point size changes, 139-142
   printing of, 135-136
   Style dialog box for, 138-139
Returning to Word, 32
Returns, insertion of, 60-61
Ribbon, 6
   displaying, 6
   reading of, 88-89
Ruler, 6
   displaying, 6
   left-aligned tab set with ruler, 95-96

S

Salutations
   entering of, 14
   for form letter, 171-175
Saving. *See also* Mailing lists
   attached envelope, closing without saving, 146-147
   automatically, 37-38
   edited files, 75-76
   files, 33-37, 39
   form letters, 180-181
   Glossary item, 211-213
   mailing lists, 158

Saving (*continued*)
   opening saved files, 41-43
   styles, 224
   Summary Info, filling in, 35-37
Scissors symbol, 19-20
Screen savers, 231
Searching for files, 199-206
   current directory, finding file in, 200-201
   different directory, searching in, 201-205
   keyword, searching with, 202-203
   opening File dialog box, 199
Shading boxed text, 91-92
Show/Hide ¶ button, 13
   for bulleted lists, 94
Soft returns, 60-61
Source diskette, 232
Spaces symbol, display of, 13
Spelling and Grammar Checker, 45-46. *See also* Thesaurus
   adding word to dictionary, 46
   continuing check, 48-51
   ignoring suggested change, 46-47
   making corrections in letter, 47-48
Starting. *See* Opening
Status bar, 17
Styles, 215-228
   adding new style to style list, 217-219
   body text, setting up new style for, 219-222
   copying new styles to other document, 225-226
   creating new styles, 215-222
   different text, applying new style to, 223
   exiting Word, 227-228
   heading in document, setting up new style for, 216-217
   opening new document for, 215-216
   saving new styles, 224
   viewing style list, 222, 227
Summary Info, filling in, 35-37
Symbols, insertion of, 18-24
Synonyms. *See* Thesaurus

T

Tabs, 95-110
   applying tabs, 108-109
   center-aligned tabs set with mouse, 105-106
   clearing tabs, 102-103
   closing without saving, 110
   decimal tabs
      menu bar, setting from, 107-108
      mouse, setting with, 106-107
   leaders with right-aligned tab, 97-99
   left-aligned tab set with ruler, 95-96
   menu bar
      decimal tabs set from, 107-108
      left-aligned tab set from, 99-101
   mouse
      center-aligned tabs set with, 105-106
      decimal tab set with, 106-107
      right-aligned tabs set with, 104-105
   opening new document, 104
   symbol, display of, 13
Target diskette, 232
Text. *See also* Copying and pasting text; Editing documents
   body of letter, 15-18
   boldfacing text, 84
   borders, 89-90
   bulleted lists, 93-94
   centering text, 86-87
   entering text, 11-12
   highlighted text, typing over, 75-76
   italicizing text, 85
   shading boxed text, 91-92
   spelling corrections in, 47-48

Thesaurus, 51-53
    Find command in, 51-52
    replacing word with, 52-53
Times New Roman font, 8
Title bar, 5
Toolbar, 6
Two sections, separating document into, 111-113
Type size. *See* Point size

U

Undoing edit, 58-59

V

Views. *See also* Draft view; Page Layout view; Print Preview; Zoom view

clicking on, 6
Normal view, return to, 125
style list, 222, 227

W

Wingdings, 18-24
WordPerfect, 236
Working directory statement, changes to, 30-32
WYSIWYG in Draft view, 124

Z

Zoom view, 126-128
    magnifying the view, 126
    reducing the view, 127
    returning to Normal view, 128

Prima Computer Books

Available Now!

WINDOWS Magazine presents: Access from the Ground Up	$19.95
Advanced PageMaker 4.0 for Windows	$27.95
Desktop Publishing Sourcebook: Fonts and Clip Art (IBM-PC)	$24.95
Desktop Publishing Sourcebook: Fonts and Clip Art (Macintosh)	$24.95
DESQview: Everything You Need to Know	$22.95
DOS 5: Everything You Need to Know	$24.95
WINDOWS Magazine Presents: Encyclopedia for Windows	$29.95
Excel 4 for Windows: Everything You Need to Know	$24.95
Excel 4 for Windows: The Visual Learning Guide	$19.95
Harvard Graphics for Windows: The Art of Presentation	$27.95
LotusWorks 3: Everything You Need to Know	$24.95
Microsoft Works for Windows By Example	$24.95
NetWare 3.x: A Do-It-Yourself Guide	$24.95
Novell NetWare Lite: Simplified Network Solutions	$24.95
PageMaker 4.0 for Windows: Your Complete Guide	$19.95
PageMaker 4.2 for the Mac: Everything You Need to Know	$19.95
WINDOWS Magazine presents: The Power of Windows and DOS Together, Second Edition	$24.95
Quattro Pro 4: Everything You Need to Know	$19.95
Smalltalk Programming for Windows (with $3^1/_2$" disk)	$39.95
SuperPaint 3: Everything You Need to Know	$24.95
Windows 3.1: The Visual Learning Guide	$19.95
Word for Windows 2: The Visual Learning Guide	$19.95
Word for Windows 2 Desktop Publishing By Example	$24.95
WordPerfect 5.1 for Windows By Example	$24.95
WordPerfect 5.1 for Windows Desktop Publishing By Example	$24.95

Coming Soon!

DOS 6: Everything You Need to Know	$24.95
Freelance Graphics for Windows: The Art of Presentation	$27.95
PageMaker x for Windows: Everything You Need to Know	$19.95
Superbase Revealed	$29.95

To order by phone with Visa or MasterCard, call (916) 786-0426, Mon.–Fri., 9–4 Pacific Standard Time.

To order by mail fill out the information below and send with your remittance to: Prima Publishing, P.O. Box 1260, Rocklin, CA 95677-1260.

Quantity	Title	Unit Price	Total
_____	_____	_____	_____
_____	_____	_____	_____
_____	_____	_____	_____
_____	_____	_____	_____
_____	_____	_____	_____

                                                Subtotal _____

                         7.25% Sales Tax (CA only) _____

                                         Shipping* _____

                                                      Total _____

Name _____

Street Address _____

City _____ State_____ Zip _____

Visa/MC# _____ Exp. _____

Signature_____

* $4.00 shipping charge for the first book and $0.50 for each additional book.

If You Like This Book... You'll Love The Newsletter!

Be a POWER WINDOWS User!

Written in the same easy-to-understand style as this book, the **I DO WINDOWS Newsletter** is jammed full of *Hot Tips* guaranteed to be easy to follow and easy to use.

Get product reviews, step-by-step directions and answers to the most-asked questions.

◆ **Non-technical explanations**

◆ **All directions linked to graphic illustrations**

◆ **Easy-to-understand language**

◆ **Step-by-step directions detailing the easy way to do power functions**

Complete the form and return it for a free copy of I DO WINDOWS. And, if you choose to subscibe today, you'll get 50% off the subscription price!

6X per year / 8 pages per issue
3-hole punch paper

❏ I want to save 50% off the subscription rate of $59.95.

❏ My check for $30, payable to Waterside Productions, Inc., is enclosed.

❏ My Mastercard Number is: ❏ My Visa Number is:

#:_____ Exp. Date:_____

Signature:_____

❏ Send me a free copy of the I DO WINDOWS Newsletter.

NAME: _____

ADDRESS: _____

CITY, STATE, ZIP: _____

Mail to:
Waterside Productions, Inc.
2191 San Elijo Ave.
Cardiff-by-the-Sea,
CA 92007-1839

I Do Windows NEWSLETTER